GANGS OF RUSSIA

GANGS OF RUSSIA

From the Streets to the Corridors of Power

Svetlana Stephenson

CORNELL UNIVERSITY PRESS ITHACA AND LONDON

First published 2015 by Cornell University Press
First printing, Cornell Paperbacks, 2015

Printed in the United States of America

Library of Congress Cataloging-in-Publication Data

Stephenson, Svetlana, 1962– author.
Gangs of Russia : from the streets to the corridors of power / Svetlana Stephenson.
pages cm
Includes bibliographical references and index.
ISBN 978-0-8014-5387-8 (cloth : alk. paper) —
ISBN 978-1-5017-0024-8 (pbk. : alk. paper)
1. Gangs—Russia (Federation) 2. Organized crime—Russia (Federation) 3. Political corruption—Russia (Federation) 4. Russia (Federation)—Social conditions—1991– I. Title.
HV6439.R8S74 2015
364.106′60947—dc23 2015003676

Cornell University Press strives to use environmentally responsible suppliers and materials to the fullest extent possible in the publishing of its books. Such materials include vegetable-based, low-VOC inks and acid-free papers that are recycled, totally chlorine-free, or partly composed of nonwood fibers. For further information, visit our website at www.cornellpress.cornell.edu.

Cloth printing 10 9 8 7 6 5 4 3 2 1
Paperback printing 10 9 8 7 6 5 4 3 2 1

For Bob and Alexei

Contents

Acknowledgments ix

Introduction: In the Shadow of the State 1

1. Street Organizations and Gangs in Russia 16
2. The Transformation of Gangs in the 1990s 44
3. The Business of Bandit Gangs: From Predation to Assimilation 65
4. Gang Organization 92
5. Street Trajectories 127
6. The Gang in the Community 151
7. Life according to the Poniatiia: The Gang's Code 170
8. Navigating the World of Violence 189
9. Gang Culture and the Wider Russian Society 223

Conclusion: Out of the Shadows? 235

Appendix: Development of Tatarstan Gangs, Three Examples 239
Key to Interviewees 243
Methodological Note 245
Glossary 247
References 251
Index 269

Acknowledgments

There are many people whose support and friendship helped me to write this book. First and foremost I am grateful to the late Alexander Salagaev—whose energy, professionalism, erudition, and good humor made him a joy to work with—and his colleagues, Alexander Shashkin and Rustem Safin, who generously shared their expertise and knowledge at all stages of the study and organized the fieldwork in Kazan. I am also very grateful to Rustem Maksudov, who greatly helped with the fieldwork in Moscow and whose own experience of researching Kazan gangs at the end of the 1980s and beginning of the 1990s significantly enriched this book.

The Harry Frank Guggenheim Foundation provided the critical research funding, and I am very grateful to them for their support. I would also like to express my deep gratitude to all the research participants who were willing to share sensitive details about their lives and who, to protect their confidentiality, must stay anonymous.

Many friends and colleagues generously provided advice, support, and encouragement along the way. Special thanks go to Dave Brotherton, Dmitrii Gromov, Irina Kuznetsova-Morenko, John Lea, Alexei Levinson, Vincenzo Ruggiero, Daniel Silverstone, and Kevin Stenson. My dear friends Simon Hallsworth, Andrew Travers, and Elena Danilova read the manuscript and contributed thoughts and ideas throughout our ongoing conversations about Russia, its gangs, and the rest of the world's burning issues.

I would like to make a special mention of the University of Helsinki and the Aleksanteri Institute that provided me with the opportunity to spend a very fruitful two months in Helsinki as a visiting research fellow in 2013. I am also grateful to my colleagues at the University of Virginia, and especially Kate Makarova and Robert Geraci, for inviting me to present a paper at their workshop series and for their constructive comments on my work. My gratitude also goes to my colleagues at the Faculty of Humanities and Social Sciences at London Metropolitan University for all their support.

My sincere thanks also go to Roger Haydon, Ange Romeo-Hall, Katy Meigs, and their colleagues at Cornell University Press for all their encouragement, support, hard work, professionalism, and patience, and to their anonymous reviewers for their constructive and insightful comments.

Some of the ideas in chapters 1 and 8 were initially developed in my article "The Violent Practices of Youth Territorial Groups in Moscow," *Europe-Asia*

Studies 64, no. 1 (2012): 69–90 and in my chapter "'The Lad Is Always Right': Street Youth Groups in Russia as Local Elites," in *Subcultures, Popular Music, and Social Change,* ed. The Subcultures Network (Newcastle upon Tyne: Cambridge Scholars Publishing, 2014), 235–50. My analysis of Kazan gangs also draws on my article "The Kazan Leviathan: Russian Street Gangs as Agents of Social Order," *The Sociological Review* 59, no. 2 (2011): 324–47. Grateful acknowledgment is made to these publishers.

And finally, unreserved thanks go to my family, Bob and Alexei, for all their patience throughout the long process of writing, for listening to my ramblings, and for their enthusiasm and unwavering support.

Introduction

IN THE SHADOW OF THE STATE

As citizens of modern states, we often see the social world as the world of the state and its shadows. In these shadows we find corruption and predation, violence and crime, primitive brutality and self-serving parochial ties. Organizations that subvert the rule of law and order thrive in the shadows, making our lives unpredictable and unsafe. An organized "enemy" lurks there, and we fear that it can violently intrude into our world at any moment. We glimpse the shadow in films and books, in political rhetoric and in popular sentiment where it emerges in the form of street gangs and organized crime networks, often alongside the ethnic "other" and terrorist conspirators.

But the contrast between darkness and light, the shadow and the nonshadow worlds, is far less stark than it seems. Both are parts of the same social reality; they overlap and coalesce, taking a variety of different forms and configurations. Informal networks and ties extend from parochial systems into the mainstream institutional world, cutting across hierarchical divisions. They defy subsumption into the structures of economy and state. Complex relations of competition, cooperation, and mutual accommodation exist between the state and nonstate formations. State violence and nonstate violence are used simultaneously and often without a clear-cut distinction between public and private benefits. The same people can populate street organizations and criminal structures and aspire to making careers in mainstream society (with some achieving spectacular success). Individuals living in the shadows may have their own specific cultural traditions and beliefs while at the same time also holding deeply conventional, mainstream views. The "shadow" and the "mainstream" exist together, penetrating each other.

The gang is almost by definition an example of the shadow society. But far from being a group of isolated misfits and criminals, it responds to larger historical processes and can, in certain periods, move from the shadows onto the central stage. This is what happened in Russia during the period of radical market reforms in the 1990s. Street gangs sprang from the shadows and began to command allegiance, to claim resources and power in the street sphere and far beyond. Some went on to evolve into more sophisticated organized crime networks that competed or cooperated with the state as agents of regulation. The world of private individuals and groups, with their horizontal networks of solidarities and dangerous parochial loyalties, eclipsed the public state when the state's vertical structures were fatally weakened both by design and as a consequence of rapid societal change.

The gang as I conceive it in this book is a collective, predominantly male, violent endeavor, a militant alliance or clan that exists in the midst of modern society. In this social organization all forms of human existence are woven together. The gang is irreducible to its economic operations; it cannot be seen, as is now common in gang literature, solely through the lens of criminality and violence or rationalized as a substitute for the authority of the state. It is an elemental force—a form of tribal life with its struggles for survival and domination, its cunning plots and selfless sacrifice for the gang's warrior brotherhood, and its heroic history and foundational mythology. As the pioneer of gang research Frederic Thrasher (1963 [1927], 3) famously said, "The gang, in short, is *life*, often rough and untamed, yet rich in elemental social processes significant to the student of society and human nature."

In the uncharted waters of the Russian capitalist transformation, the gang warriors tried to find ways to stay afloat, to lay siege to, and to extract the wealth of the decaying state and the emerging entrepreneurs, who themselves were new to the capitalist territory and almost totally defenseless in the face of various predators. But for all their elemental qualities, the strategies developed by the gangs had many similarities with the strategies of others who were managing to find their way in the devastation brought by the collapse of the Soviet system. Many people tried to rise in society via cunning and violence, and relied on trust networks in their efforts to divide the spoils of the Soviet economy and gain access to a variety of rents. The new rules of the game that emerged after the collapse of the Soviet civilization brought new heroes and new strategies for success; and the gangs fought, competed, and cooperated with other networks that set out on similar paths.

As Russia embarked on its transition to capitalism, a whole set of economic, social, political, and ideological changes caused the rise of militant, networked, and acquisitive social formations and behaviors. Eventually, in the social settlement that followed the fierce struggles for accumulation in the 1990s, these formations became less prominent, and many of the participants found ways to join the legitimate structures of the state and economy. But these struggles left a lasting legacy—both in the continuing prominence of rent-seeking networks throughout Russian society and in the sphere of mass communication, which continues to be saturated with references to the gangs' codes of conduct—the street and criminal *poniatiia* (mutual "understandings")—and to their representatives, the lads (*patsany*, young men, a term commonly used from the late 1980s onward in Russia to describe street gang members) and bandits.

The analytical and conceptual framework of the book centers around the following main questions: What was the role of the street gang in the evolution of Russian organized crime? How do we analyze the gang as a form of society? How did the gangs' own structures and practices change in response to the historical transformation of Russia under late socialism and during the transition to capitalism? And what are the past and current modes of the gang's incorporation into the wider community?

Street Gangs and the Origins of Organized Crime Networks

The rise of gangs in the 1990s was a product of historically unique circumstances, when Russia, along with other post-Communist countries, embarked on a transition from state socialism to capitalism. This transition brought with it a rapid collapse of the whole social structure, a dismantling of the collectivist provisions of welfare and employment, radical privatization of state assets, and the emergence of private entrepreneurs who received almost no protection from the now debilitated legal and judicial apparatus. While nascent entrepreneurs set up their new businesses amid the ruins of the state socialist economy, masses of Soviet workers were trying to survive by clinging to their old enterprises (that had often stopped paying them a living wage), mining the depleting resources of their social networks, or developing subsistence farming at their dachas. But there was another strategy. It was developed by people who launched projects of economic accumulation and social mobility through violence. They appropriated state resources, exploited the new entrepreneurial class, and developed a variety of ventures in the overlapping domains of the criminal, shadow, and legal economies.

Among the new "successful" groups that gained wealth and power were the so-called *banditskie gruppirovki* (bandit gangs). The streets began to fill with grim-looking youths, dressed almost identically in cheap dark jackets and tracksuit pants. Their leaders, who were often not much older, flaunted their new wealth by wearing garish magenta blazers and heavy gold chains and driving around in foreign cars. Reports of gang-related assassination attempts and murders featured daily in the news. The bandit gangs often started out by racketeering local kiosks and street markets and then moved on to skimming the profits of small and medium-size companies. From here they progressed to establishing protection operations for large companies, with many of the gang leaders becoming company owners and shareholders themselves, and extending the gang's activities far beyond the local territory. Where did these bandits come from? Some scholars have traced them to an alliance between former Communist officials and the criminal underworld of *vory v zakone* ("thieves-in-law", professional criminals), built on Soviet-era black market collaborations (Handelman 1994; Finckenauer and Voronin 2001). Others see them as mostly novel groups of people whose mastery of violence gave them a particular advantage in the growing market for criminal protection. This advantage "could have been acquired either in specific social situations that cultivate physical fitness and fighting skills or in particular life circumstances that produced the psychological dispositions" (Volkov 2002, 6). The members of these new bandit groups (in contrast to more traditional *vory* societies) were former athletes, veterans of the Afghan war, and formerly and currently serving policemen (Varese 2001; Volkov 2002).

One social formation that played a major role in the rise of the bandit gangs has so far been largely absent from the analysis of the origins of Russian organized crime. This is the youth street gang. This omission is particularly striking because youth gangs were among the first organizations to move into the extortion and protection sphere in the post-Soviet period. But scholars of Russian organized crime, if they considered young people at all, regarded them mainly as bands of hoodlums who got together to make money via violent extortion or as fodder for the bosses of organized crime. Neighborhood social networks were largely neglected, while the category of "youth gang" did not play much of an explanatory role in this literature, in which gang activity seemed to fall along the same spectrum as forms of (adult) illegality.

The youth gangs were, however, central to the development of Russian organized crime. At the time when the Soviet system had collapsed and the new capitalist order was just taking hold, street gangs—alternative structures of youth life that were unrelated to the bureaucratic or professional structures of the Soviet state—survived, evolved, and prospered. These territorial bands of young people established their own local monopolies of force and achieved significant control over the street economy and small businesses in their areas. Their older members, who became widely known as "bandits," graduated to positions of authority in serious organized crime networks. The gangs came from a distinctive male street culture, with trust networks forged through street camaraderie and battles with local enemies. Male warrior brotherhoods rising from the world of the streets, together with other forms of solidarities (forged in communities of sportsmen or Afghan army veterans and also giving rise to bandit groups), created the social structures in which the illegal entrepreneurial activities of post-Soviet organized crime could develop.

Street Gangs as Warrior Alliances

Although they come to the fore in times of crisis of the social order, youth street associations have always been present in human society in one form or another. Groups in which boys have learned to be "real men" through collective violence have been a feature of social life from time immemorial. Countless generations of boys around the world grow up playing and fighting in the streets, in a space of freedom from adult control, where they can assert their masculinity, develop friendships, and protect their turf. From graffiti in ancient Pompeii that testified to victories of local street warriors over youths from neighboring settlements, who came to the city to watch theatrical performances or gladiator games but were really looking for a fight, to graffiti in modern cities marking the territory of various street fiefdoms, urban walls have witnessed and recorded many fights and confrontations. In these battles young men acquired skills and a mental outlook historically seen as crucial to societies in which frequent outbreaks of war demanded the cultivation of male violence, vigor, and honor.

These forms have lingered well beyond ancient times. Across the world, youths still form gangs united by the bonds of male kinship, collective violent experiences, and often promises of material spoils. The gang as a traditional social form embedded in the fabric of modern societies seduces its members with its claim of innate superiority to outsiders and by its members' apparent bravery and mastery of violence, freedom from the obligations and limitations enforced by adult society, and promises of fairness and mutual protection.

Modern gangs, as Randall Collins (2011) observed, have the same type of premodern authority as the warrior coalitions of Vikings, Germanic militant tribes, and ancient Greek colonists who formed their own settlements around the rim of the Mediterranean. Max Weber called such social forms "patrimonial alliances" (Weber 1978 [1922]). These bands of warriors that assembled for raiding and conquering shared tribal loyalties and pseudokinship obligations and developed mythologies about their fictive ancestors.[1] In modern cities, warrior forms, according to Collins, are reproduced by youths from working-class backgrounds who form their own small patrimonial tribes and rebel against the disciplinary power of schooling. While the modern bureaucratic state has tried to displace patrimonialism, the space of the street has remained resistant to state penetration, and here these forms still thrive.

Viewing the gang as a patrimonial warrior alliance allows us to see it in ways that are different from the traditional approaches of gang research, which tend to view gangs as vehicles of social and cultural resistance or as instrumental criminal enterprises. Although there are different types of gangs, they can all be described as multifunctional, largely male militant alliances held together by personal interdependencies and loyalties to the group and by the collective exercise of violence.

The archetypical figure of the warrior has a central place in the gang's own mythology and folklore. But while the archetype of a warrior possesses the imagination and informs the behavior of the gang, its appeal is much wider and cuts across social, ethnic, and class divisions. Whenever we talk about social constructions of masculinity, the figure of the warrior inevitably comes to the fore. In film, literature, and mass media, gang warriors, boardroom warriors, and police warriors provide templates for powerful masculinity. In societies organized in accordance with the patriarchal gender order, the idealized forms of masculinity involve qualities such as toughness, courage, aggression, adventurousness, success, loyalty, and dominance over women and weaker and homosexual men—all of which are concentrated in the persona of the warrior.[2] The warrior is not external to society as is, for example, the classical bandit as described by Eric Hobsbawm (1985), who attacks from outside, robbing the rich and powerful. He can be both outside and inside of society, subverting its rules but also asserting its deepest values.

The complex of values represented by the warrior is particularly prominent in certain cultural and class milieus, and among them is undeniably the culture of urban working-class youth. The association between urban working-class and low-class culture and street gangs has been the cornerstone of much gang research. Studies have shown that this culture accentuates the values of tough

1. Weber (1987 [1922]) developed the concept of "patrimonialism" as a tool to explore systems of political authority based on kinship ties, patron-client relations, and informal rules and regulations. In patrimonial systems power operates on the basis of arbitrary discretion, material dependence, and personal loyalty of members of the extended quasi-kinship network.

2. On patriarchy and the social construction of masculinity see, e.g., Connell 1987; and Messerschmidt 1993; 2000.

masculinity, reflecting class conditions in which a lack of opportunity to succeed makes personal bonds of peer-to-peer support, mastery over violence, personal bravery, and resistance to outside authority a source of masculine pride and status.[3] Lacking the opportunity for integration into mainstream society, young people can fall back on militant patrimonial forms as a source of identity and membership or as a vehicle for illegal economic success. Through violent street performances young men who otherwise possess very few resources can achieve situational dominance over more privileged members of society, "reverse" their structural disadvantage, and build their own street social capital.[4]

At the same time, it is important to note that gangs are not exclusively confined to working-class and low-class urban environments. Village fights between groups of young men learning to display their strength and manhood were a feature of most European peasant societies (Tilly 1974b). From Finland to France, group youth combats were still being fought at the end of the nineteenth century (Haavio-Mannila 1958; Ploux 2007). The same was true of Russia, and territorial fighting gangs (as well as entrepreneurial gangs) can still be found in rural areas. Apart from villages, gangs have also been present in socially mixed urban residential settlements. Multiethnic, socially diverse street groups of young people formed a core part of urban life in the Soviet Union. To this day, across Russia young men, united by allegiance to their turf and not by specific class origins, play out ancient scenarios of honor and territorial defense, with some drifting toward associations of a more criminal nature.

From Street Groups to Mafia Networks—and Back?

In modern society, youth street associations tend to be both endemic and short lived. Young people abandon their street groups when they move into the world of family and work. But during certain historical periods these short-lived tribes can become more permanent organizations. They can start to expand and colonize new territories and in some cases develop their own "extortionate platforms" (Hobbs 2013, 227) from which they launch protection operations and other acquisitive schemes.

---

3. The association between working-class and low-class culture, masculinity, group delinquency, and violence has been addressed in many classic sociological and criminological texts (see, e.g., Cohen 1955; Miller 1958; Wolfgang and Ferracuti 1967; Willis 1977).

4. On street violence and situational stratification see, for example, Collins (2004; 2008); on violence and street social capital, see Sandberg (2008) and Harding (2014).

When does this occur? Although historical research into the evolution of gangs has been scarce, Randall Collins (2011) has suggested that gangs can develop a long-term presence in the community if they get access to economic resources. If they find ways to penetrate the state itself, they can turn into another patrimonial form, a mafia. Eventually, the state finds ways to defeat the mafia, while the gang alliances continue to operate, albeit in constant confrontation with the state repressive apparatus. In the Soviet Union in the 1970s the gangs did indeed begin to gain access to economic resources during the period of the growth of the Soviet shadow economy, at which point some of them turned into stable neighborhood forms. With the collapse of the socialist state, many street gangs evolved into mafia-type organizations, penetrating economic and political structures of the state. All this took place in the condition of disassociation of youth from the structures of modern society and increasing influence of patrimonial structures that existed in the Soviet Union, including the associations of professional criminals, the vory v zakone.

In the late 1990s and early 2000s the Russian state became stronger, the capitalist economic order became more established, and the power of organized criminal groups began to wane. The vertical structures of mafia-type organizations were weakened, and the gangs began to revert to more disorganized forms. But, as the new power regime developed, it became apparent that the strengthening of the state did not lead to the triumph of law and order. The state does not function the same way in all countries, and in Russia the state and criminal networks are not involved in a zero-sum game but instead form complex relationships of competition and cooperation. Although they were weakened by gang trials and a reduction in racketeering opportunities, in many areas organized gangs did not disappear but became entrenched within well-established hierarchies of state power and local systems of violent regulation.

The Gang and Society

In the Soviet Union, those gang warriors whose key battles took place in the courtyards and on the streets of their neighborhoods and those who tried to lay their hands on the spoils of the country's shadow economy were not pirates or foreign invaders but residents of villages, working-class quarters, and socially mixed residential blocks. They lived in the community and led other lives when outside the space of the streets—as students in vocational colleges, factory workers, or young professionals (unless they found themselves in trouble with the law, which could lead them to the revolving doors of penal institutions). Apart from the dispositions acquired in the world of the streets—an aptitude for violence and loyalty to their comrades-in-arms—the members of street gangs might also share mainstream Soviet values. They believed that by fleecing dishonest and corrupt Soviet shop or restaurant managers they were upholding socialist justice. Similarly, when the new times came, they embraced capitalist ideology and began to see themselves as hard-working entrepreneurs.

Russian gangs are not alien to society; they are firmly embedded in it. They include both exclusively criminal operators and people who can be respectable and hold professional jobs. Their members have multiple connections stretching from their close neighbors and relatives to representatives of the Russian state. They are pragmatic and micropolitical in their social orientations, and they try to create a wide web of obligations and favors around themselves. Moreover, the organizational structure of the Russian gang fits with these orientations in that it is highly flexible and allows its members to maintain their multiple memberships and networks (themselves highly useful for gang business).

Throughout their history, Russian gangs have remained part of the community. In their glory days in the 1990s, their members rose above many of their neighbors and acquired significant power on the street, in the local economy, and further afield. But, as life stabilized and a new social settlement emerged in Russia at the beginning of the 2000s, gangs found other ways of incorporation into society. The days of their spectacular rise were over, but they found new niches in the shadow and criminal economy on and off the streets. Their violence has also remained a part of the wider field of private force that exists in the shadow of the state.

Although some have now become legitimate entrepreneurs, many bandit leaders remain well positioned in the web of official and unofficial power in their territorial communities, and they can still use the organizational and violent resource of street gangs if it is necessary for their business or political interests. Over time, the bandits' code of conduct has entered the wider sphere of cultural communication and become a constant referent when it comes to the unofficial rules of Russian politics and everyday life. New instabilities and new crises always risk bringing the figure of the bandit back to the foreground of social life.

"Abridged Maps"

Street groups in which boys grow to be "real men" are ubiquitous in Russia. There are various street peer groups (e.g., *dvorovye kompanii*—"courtyard groups"), territorial groups defending the local turf, and more organized entrepreneurial gangs. But research into the various Russian street organizations and gangs has been relatively scarce. To borrow Dick Hebdige's (1988) expression about youth subcultures, such organizations have been "hiding in the light."

In prerevolutionary Russia and the Soviet Union the imperatives of male street culture, the rituals of street life, and the various territorial practices of violence were off the radar of state officials, the police, and educators. In late imperial Russia and throughout the Soviet period the street life of boys and young men in its many manifestations—group recreation, fights, harassment of passers-by, or more criminal pursuits—was seen mainly through the lens of the catch-all category of "hooliganism," with working-class men being regarded as particularly prone to such disorderly behavior (Neuberger 1993; Tsipursky 2008; Fürst 2010; LaPierre 2012). From the early days of the Soviet regime the state viewed street hooligans as agents of resistance who corrupted young people and took them away from Communist organizations such as the Young Pioneers and Komsomol. This perspective continues to be shared by some academic authors who view street hooligans as agents of resistance to the Soviet state (Kozlov 1999; Gorsuch 2000). Whether or not they were deliberately resisting Soviet power in a political sense, the so-called street hooligans undoubtedly challenged state control by creating spaces of autonomy in the world of the streets. The state tried (largely unsuccessfully) to reclaim its youths, and its persistent failure to do so was blamed on the youths' poor upbringing (*vospitanie*) and on inadequate control of young people by parents, teachers, and employers (Connor 1972; LaPierre 2012).

Following James C. Scott's (1998, 3) argument about modern European states' visions of the social world, I would say that the Soviet state simplified social reality, working from "abridged maps" that represented only the slices of reality that were of interest to it. It was partially blind in its knowledge of collective street life, young people's territorial identities, and the actual meanings of the practices to which it applied its crude classifications. By projecting anxieties about the nonconformist, "unsocialist" behavior of citizens onto the figure of the hooligan and criminalizing routine misbehaviors, the Soviet regime created deviance on a massive scale (LaPierre 2006).

Social research into youth street organizations and gangs was virtually nonexistent, with the exception of research into the gangs of orphaned (*besprizornye*) and abandoned (*beznadzornye*) children in the Soviet Union of the 1920s and early 1930s (see, e.g., Fürst 2010). The first publications on street and criminal gangs appeared only toward the end of the 1980s, during Gorbachev's perestroika. Russian administrative criminologists—I refer to their work in chapter 1—analyzed group delinquency from a social-control perspective and used data collected in corrective institutions and detention centers. The notable exception was the work of the group of Kazan sociologists led by Alexander Salagaev, who studied violent gangs on the basis of interviews with gang members in the community, as well as interviews with law enforcement, businessmen, and local residents. More research about gangs in particular Russian regions appeared over the years, but these were relatively small-scale studies. I address them in chapters 1 and 2.

Street social organizations and the traditions of youth territorialism have also started to attract scholarly attention, mainly from Russian anthropologists (Kuleshov 2001; Shchepanskaia 2001; Golovin and Lurie 2008; and Gromov 2009 among others). But, generally, their practices are still poorly understood, and the members of street groups continue to be seen as low-class young men who are backward, ignorant, and dangerously prone to violence. In other words, they are still seen as hooligans, although the word itself has fallen out of favor, and now are widely known as *gopniks* (Pilkington 2002; Omel'chenko 2006).

The Setting and the Study

In order to trace the evolution of street organizations and gangs and follow the ways they integrated into the wider society and polity, we need historical and social research and data. Although the literature here is scant, there is one area in Russia where sources on juvenile street life and practices of violence can be found, starting with some famous literature that dates back to the nineteenth century. This is Tatarstan, a region on the Volga. In the late Soviet period, Tatarstan was the first place where the existence of violent street groups was officially recognized and where the first gang criminal trial (the trial of Tiap-Liap) took place. The gangs then became the subject of police research and journalistic investigations. In the 1990s, Tatarstan became renowned for its *banditskie gruppirovki*, which also expanded into other areas, including Moscow and Saint Petersburg, and then established their interests abroad. It became the region of Russia where the first trials of "organized criminal communities" (OPS) took place at the beginning of the 2000s. Tatarstan was also the place where the first major sociological project of research into gangs, directed by Alexander Salagaev, took place, beginning at the end of the 1980s and continuing well into the 2000s.

Tatarstan is the main case study for this book, and I was fortunate to work on this research with Alexander Salagaev and his colleagues Alexander Shashkin and Rustem Safin. In 2005 we conducted a study that involved interviews with gang members from gruppirovki across Kazan. The interviewees were all male, seventeen to thirty-five, of Russian and Tatar ethnicity—reflecting the social composition of their organizations. We also interviewed law enforcement officers, teachers, school psychologists, and local residents in communities affected by gangs. In 2011, I conducted additional research in Kazan. I have also drawn on analyses of the available sources on street organizations and gangs, past and present, in other areas of Russia and made use of the data from my study of youth street organizations in Moscow in 2006. I discuss the methodology in the Methodological Note at the end of this book.

While the book is mainly anchored in research and fieldwork in Kazan, a city notable for the advanced development and entrenchment of its gangs, wider research confirms that the results can be considered representative of Russia as a whole (although ethnic gangs still await their researchers). All gang research is highly contextual, as these organizations are rooted in local cultural traditions as well as in class configurations, residential histories, and patterns of settlement. But, for all that, Russian gangs share similar features that reflect the specific character of Soviet urbanism, whose legacy continues to this day. Here people have tended to live in socially and ethnically mixed settlements in relatively stable enterprise-based social systems, and, despite growing social and housing inequalities, in many areas across Russia these residential patterns are still in place. All over Russia, except in the hearts of major cities, young people grow up in *dvor* (courtyard) societies and participate in neighborhood social networks. A review of research on street social organizations across the former Soviet Union by Dmitrii Gromov (2009), with data covering the period from the mid-1950s to the present day, showed that these organizations have had similar codes of conduct based on requirements for members to demonstrate mastery of violence, loyalty to the group, authority, and integrity. They also set limits on violence in relation to noncombatants, young children, women, and the elderly. The considerable degree of ritualization of violence in these groups may reflect the late modernization of Russia and the cultural influence of village traditions of ritualized fights.[5]

Kazan's neighborhood street groups demonstrate all the characteristics identified by Gromov. More specific is the entrepreneurial gang or, to use the term that emerged in the 1990s, the bandit gang. This type of gang has particular organizational characteristics, such as age-based cohorts, a system of money collection for the *obshchak* (the gang's common fund), defined leadership roles, as well as strong connections with the world of organized crime that are absent in more disorganized street groups. But Kazan-type entrepreneurial gangs have been far from rare in the Russian underworld. By the mid-1980s, similar gangs emerged across the country (Pilkington 1994, 143–44), likewise developing serious organized criminal operations in the 1990s and showing signs of social entropy with the economic and political stabilization in the 2000s. I present available evidence of the existence and evolution of such gangs across Russia.

5. The groups are not all identical. While predominantly male, some admit girls, although they tend to stay at the periphery of group activity. These groups also differ in the strength of their organization, the degree of compulsion put on local young people to join, and the extent of violence and criminality.

What may be specific to Kazan is the extent of incorporation of the gang members into the larger society. With the exception of the more marginalized young men with low education and skills who come from highly disturbed family backgrounds, the participants in our project studied in high schools and universities, and many older members worked as builders, industrial workers, and even as junior managers, doctors, and lawyers. This quite extraordinary state of affairs (at least from the point of view of international gang literature) can be explained by the wide availability of legitimate employment, both in the state and service sectors but also in industry and the building trades. Here organized industrial labor is still an option for young people, although, as elsewhere in Russia, manual jobs are relatively low paid and no longer a source of collective pride and identity (Walker 2009). In Kazan, with its low rate of unemployment, we do not yet observe a fractious working-class and low-class culture in which young people, inhabiting the zones of postindustrial exclusion, may see the bottom rungs of the drug trade ladder as their only option (Hagedorn and Macon 1988; Taylor 1990; Padilla 1992). Moreover, perhaps paradoxically, the absence of concerted gang suppression policies and persistent criminalization of youth gangs (discussed in chapter 6) may prevent further disassociation and exclusion from society of those young people who do not commit serious crimes, and may leave them with the chance to build a different life.

To my knowledge, no other research has so far been conducted in Russia that addresses the issue of gang members' social incorporation into criminal or mainstream society (or, as often happens in Kazan, into both simultaneously). Having limited data makes it difficult to make assumptions about whether we can apply this "double helix" model of gang members' social memberships to other regions of Russia. As more research emerges it will become possible to fill in the details of gang life across the country.

Current study of the Russian gang and its evolution in the context of historical change under late socialism and during capitalist transformation is one part of my long-standing project, which aims to understand the social organization of Russian society "from below" at the time of transition to market capitalism. In the 1990s, I studied the societies of street children and youths, and adult homeless people (Stephenson 2001; 2006; 2008). In the course of that study I examined their social networks and their attempts to survive by finding ways to access the resources of the city. This book adds another dimension to this project. What I describe here is no longer the world of desperation and survival; this is the world of high stakes, the world of action, adventurousness, and a sense of possibility. I explore how gangs of young men attempted to take a shortcut to wealth and power through crime and violence, and what happened to them and to the country as a result.

Structure of the Book

In chapter 1 I look at traditional structures of youth violence and at the emergence of entrepreneurial gangs in the 1970s and 1980s. I suggest a typology of street organizations and gangs, dividing them into four types—street peer groups, territorial elites, entrepreneurial gangs, and autonomous ruling regimes—and trace the evolution of forms of youth collective violence in Kazan in response to the specific challenges and opportunities created by rapid urbanization, the proliferation of the shadow economy, and growing social differentiation.

In chapter 2 I examine the growth of violent street social organizations as a result of the crisis of the Soviet system and the emergence of new entrepreneurial opportunities amid the chaos of economic transition. I show how profound insecurity, associated with the collapse of livelihoods and the rise in crime, pushed young people to seek membership in various ground-level networks, including subcultural networks, organized prostitution, criminal networks, and gangs. I discuss the hopes and aspirations that young people associated with gang membership, which ranged from personal protection and subsistence to entrepreneurial success, and how they set about realizing these. I then examine the evolving composition of the Tatarstan gangs, their changing practices of violence, their territorial expansion over the course of the 1990s and how their development was paralleled elsewhere in Russia.

In chapter 3 I explore further how the gangs made their money. I discuss the historical context of the development of economic violence in post-Soviet Russia and then analyze the social relationship of protection and the predatory and clientilistic systems of power relations that the gangs established with businessmen and members of the public. I show examples of how they penetrated corporate and state-based networks and describe the social strategies their leaders developed to achieve legitimacy. I then address the changes in gang business as the state gained the upper hand and the gangs' retreat from large-scale protection rackets into more street-based operations and into control of markets for proscribed commodities (drugs, illegal gambling, prostitution, etc.).

In chapter 4 I analyze the organization of the gang, the devices it uses to ensure its social reproduction, and the challenges it faces in conditions of growing social and economic differentiation among its ranks. Although their leadership structures turned their attention to serious criminal business, I show that the gangs remained forms of weakly differentiated societies. Their egalitarian ethos and personal loyalties did not interfere with business but, on the contrary, proved to be highly useful, especially in conditions of constant instability and risk. It is the erosion of these bonds of solidarity as a result of social differentiation that weakens the gang.

In chapter 5 I consider the backgrounds of gang members, what attracts them to the gang, and their plans and aspirations for the future. I look at various biographical narratives and consider three types of transition to adulthood—criminal, working-class, and professional. I discuss a specific Russian "double helix" model of youth transitions, in which young people follow both criminal and mainstream careers. I show that gang members tend to see themselves as "normal" members of the community and that they actively invest in a variety of social ties and particularly value informal relations with the local police and other representatives of the Russian deep state.

In chapter 6 I look at the place of the gangs in the local communities and at their attempts to position themselves as agents of popular justice and popular violence who police the borders of belonging and punish transgressors of the local social order. I consider the opinions of local residents about the gangs and the ways in which the gangs fit into the interaction between power regimes in Tatarstan and elsewhere in Russia.

In chapter 7 I present my reconstruction of the gang code. I explain my methodological approach to the analysis of the code, set out the fundamental principles of the code, and address the similarities and differences between the moral rules of the bandits and those of the vory community. I finish by describing the evolution of both codes in the conditions of market capitalism.

In chapter 8 I address structures of feeling and behavior in the violent world of the streets and how they are produced through the membership of street organizations. I analyze violent rituals and trade-offs, conflicts, and how they are resolved by using the common understandings of right and wrong that exist in the shadow of the state.

In chapter 9 I address the wide dissemination of gang culture in post-Soviet Russia and how different sections of the population view the world of criminal organizations as either embodying values of heroic masculinity and brotherly bonds or as exemplifying the country's descent into primitive violence and parochial clans. I show how the gangs' code and vocabulary provide a new lingua franca that reflects the institutional conditions to be found at all levels of Russian society, from the streets to the corridors of power.

The conclusion to the book summarizes the trajectory of the street gang in the late Soviet period and during the time of transition, and addresses the ongoing penetration by gang members of formal structures and how they remain significantly incorporated in their communities. I end with an assessment of how gangs may change in response to new economic and social realities facing Russia.

1

STREET ORGANIZATIONS AND GANGS IN RUSSIA

The existence of violent youth gangs in Kazan was brought to the attention of the Soviet public in 1988 when *Literaturnaia Gazeta* published an article by Yuri Shchekochikhin called "Ekstremalnaia model'" (The extreme model). This included the first published mention of the "Kazan phenomenon." In this and further publications it emerged that this city had dozens of youth gangs involved in serious violence and crime. Similar gangs, many formed back in the 1970s, were "discovered" in Naberezhnye Chelny, Almetievsk, Nizhnekamsk, Buinsk, and other areas of Tatarstan, as well as in other parts of the Soviet Union.

Why did Kazan, Tatarstan, and the wider Soviet Union experience such a surge in gang violence in the 1970s and 1980s? To understand this we need to look at traditional structures of youth violence and at the specific challenges and opportunities created by rapid urbanization, growing social differentiation, and the proliferation of the shadow economy in the USSR.

Typology of Street Organizations and Gangs

Groups of adolescents seeking adventure, fighting for turf, developing their own small street ventures, and finding out in the company of peers what it means to be a man have been a long-standing feature of social life all over the world. Successive generations of young men have grown up on the streets before joining adult society and leaving their street adventures and misdemeanors behind them.

Commitment to their own societies and oppositional subcultures away from adult control generally begins to wane as young people move into adulthood, although some young men find ways to commodify their violence through various criminal collaborations (Willis 1977; Collins 2011; Hobbs 2013). The street world is usually a mix of various social forms, territorial and nonterritorial, criminalized and noncriminalized. Many different definitions and typologies of gangs have been offered by Western authors. Contemporary criminological classifications typically distinguish gangs by their illegal activities (Klein 1971; Miller 1982; Sánchez-Jankowski 1991; Spergel 1984). However, some criminologists (Hagedorn and Macon 1988; Venkatesh 2000; Moore 1991; Kontos, Brotheron, and Barrios 2003; Hallsworth and Young, 2005) take an alternative approach in which criminal involvement is seen as a relatively small element of what defines and distinguishes peer groups and gangs from one another, with social organization, and the meanings of their practices, playing more prominent roles. Taking the latter perspective, I look at gangs within a continuum of street organizations and divide them here into four types—*street peer groups*, *territorial elites*, *entrepreneurial gangs*, and *autonomous ruling regimes*. These types are differentiated by their structure, the type of violence they use, and the targets of their violent control.

The *street peer group* is perhaps the most common type of youth organization throughout the world (McGrellis 2005; Kintrea, Bannister, and Pickering 2011; McAlister, Scaranton, and Haydon 2011). While often lumped together with criminal gangs, street peer groups are characterized not by criminality, which, if it exists at all, can be opportunistic and episodic, or by some unconscious rebellion against dispossession but by their deep attachment to local places. The street peer group is held together by horizontal informal ties, and its violence tends to be spontaneous and situational.

In Russia such groups are ubiquitous. These are typically loose neighborhood networks without hierarchy or leadership. These street societies tend to comprise several friendship groups living in the same block of apartments, or apartment blocks from the same or neighboring streets. The core contingents of these groups are young men between thirteen and seventeen, although they can also involve girls. Small boys—and sometimes girls—from the age of seven or eight ("the little ones") often affiliate themselves to the network, although they are not usually considered real members. Young men leave the world of the streets when drafted into the army at eighteen or at the start of their working lives.[1] They hang out together on the streets in the warmer times of the year and in underground cellars and lofts during winter. They listen to music, go out

1. Pilkington (2002, 123) refers to these organizations as *dvor* groups, from the Russian word for the courtyard of a housing block.

in groups to soccer matches or the movies, and make trips to local parks and to the countryside to enjoy barbeques in the summer or to go skiing in winter. The traditional Russian urban residential pattern—several multistory buildings sharing a courtyard—provides a perfect setting for young men's societies.

Growing up in their street groups, young men develop particular character traits that can be linked to "hegemonic masculinity"—an ability to show toughness, bravery, and to inspire respect and fear (Connell and Messershmidt 2005). These masculine qualities are particularly valued in the volatile world of the streets. In his essay "Where the Action Is" Goffman (1967) showed that on the street, where many fateful situations with uncertain outcomes can occur, the most important qualities are being quick-witted, brave, able to react quickly to provocation and to show confidence, poise, and integrity. These skills are acquired by boys starting at a young age as they grow up playing and fighting outdoors and face the challenges and risks that life on the streets brings. The street requires an ability to take chances, to put oneself on the line, and the "capacity to receive and give injury of both a physical and a verbal kind" (211). These qualities, Goffman noted, are highly praised in the "Western cult of masculinity" (209), and they present a ceremonial backdrop to communal life.

In some ecologies we can observe the presence of territorial groups that take it on themselves to protect the local space against outsiders (mainly young people from other areas). Such groups exist all over Russia as *territorial elites.* These groups often have informal leaders, typically an older youth whose charismatic personality and physical force inspires fear and awe among local adolescents. They may have different age cohorts and "ranks" with their own "soldiers," "lieutenants," "generals," and so on. Despite this appearance of stratification, however, their world remains closer to the world of childhood play than to the world of modern organizations (Katz 1988).

Violence in these groups is ritualized and directed at categorically defined "enemy" groups (residents of neighboring areas and sometimes ethnic and racial "others"). Territorial elites are typically male structures in which young men construct themselves as elite fighters, masters of the local space, defending the territorial order of social relations (Suttles 1968). They develop defensive place-based concerns, which lead to fights with "outsiders" and harassment of "intruders" (Golovin and Lurie 2005; 2008).

Territorial elites tend to emerge in places where individuals have already established strong reputations in their community. Here, as Randall Collins (2008, 332) explained, the fighters use "social technologies of violence," specific forms of self-presentation and conversational devices, to assert their dominance without the need to resort to immediate physical confrontation. Where violence is used, this may take the form of a duel or arranged mass combat.

The emergence of entrenched territorial practices is more likely to occur—in Russia and in the West—in the urban periphery rather than in metropolitan centers (Thrasher 1963 [1927]; Hallsworth 2005; Golovin and Lurie 2008; Kintrea, Bannister, and Pickering 2011). In Russia these tend to be either peripheral areas of large urban settlements or whole territories of small and medium-sized towns. These practices are also present in rural areas.

Research by Russian anthropologists has shown that organized fights between groups of local boys formed a core part of village life at least until the 1960s. Groups of young boys and adolescents collectively defended their street or village against their peers from neighboring areas. Adults sometimes took part in these battles as well. In these territorial fights, participants followed particular rules, such as not to use weapons, not to hit an adversary when he is on the ground, and never to use violence against women, children, or old people. Ritually prescribed arranged fights were an important part of village festive life, often coinciding with weddings and other celebratory events. They were used to test the strength of adversaries and reinforce the solidarity of male peer groups (Kabanov 1928; Bernshtam 1988; Shchepanskaia 2001; Morozov and Sleptsova 2004). With the industrialization and urbanization of Russia at the end of the nineteenth century, mass staged combats between groups of young male workers began to take place in the working-class areas of the rapidly expanding cities. Neuberger (1993, 65) describes gang fights in the outskirts of Saint Petersburg around 1900 in which young men clashed over turf and local girls. They were reported to follow a strict honor code and fight one another only for specific, commonly agreed on reasons. While very little is known about urban gangs in late imperial Russia, in postrevolutionary Russia, gangs of orphaned and abandoned children, roaming the streets and riding trains from town to town in search of food, were more likely to be fighting for survival than engaging in the defense of turf.[2] But in the postwar Soviet Union, territorial fights between rival groups of youths became a common occurrence in industrial towns, where, as Juliane Fürst (2010, 185) explains, loyalty to one's factory or place of living "came to substitute family and village ties."

Even in the late Soviet period, arranged group fights were common in rural and peripheral urban areas, where the first and second generations of urban dwellers had come to live (Zabrianskii 1990, 129–30). Research conducted in many Russian cities and towns (Ul'ianovsk, Ulan-Ude, Murom, Tikhvin, Kirov, and others) reveals the continuing presence of youth territorial elites who

2. On abandoned children in Russia in the 1920s to 1930s and in the post–World War II period, see, e.g., Goldman (1993), Ball (1994), Kelly (2007), and Fürst (2008; 2010).

colonize local streets and engage in warfare with "outsiders" (Gromov 2009). In many urban areas, arranged combats are still a factor of collective street life. As in earlier times, these combats tend to take place on neutral territory—for example, on a bridge over a river separating two areas or, in winter, on the frozen river itself (Golovin and Lurie 2005; 2008). In my research in Moscow in 2006, I found that arranged combats were still fought in the outskirts of this now global city, with rituals resembling premodern village fights. In a typical scenario, street youths adopt formations with the strongest at the front and the back and the youngest in the middle. Someone has to start a fight, and often one of the youths will shout obscenities at the enemies to provoke them. Sometimes a fight is started by the group leader, challenging the enemy leader to a duel. If a group, or their leader in the event of a duel, is defeated, the reputation of the territory suffers. If the younger members of the group lose, older men may try to repair the territorial reputation and go into battle themselves. Alternatively, they may tell the younger members to arrange a revenge fight. This can lead to lengthy cycles of arranged fights in which neighborhood groups may build alliances to help each other out. The favors done by one group for another are returned, and it is not uncommon these days to offer some form of payment for extra fighters (usually a couple of crates of beer). The participants agree in advance on the approximate number of fighters and whether weapons such as chains, clubs, or brass knuckles—but never guns or knives—can be used. Arranged combats are used by territorial elites to test their strength, settle disputes, or confirm territorial boundaries. Friends of the fighters often record the fights on their mobile phones and then upload them to YouTube.

In certain historical periods, however, the street can produce new collective forms. Young people who are unable to grow up "properly" and move into adult society, which may have very little to offer them, stay in their street groups beyond the age at which their predecessors would have left to start jobs and families. From exploring the joys and dangers of street life, young men can move on to form *entrepreneurial gangs*. These groups often have a cohort structure and clear leadership. Using the resources and advantages at their disposal—deep links with the local territory, common identities and loyalties, and mastery of violence acquired in the space of the streets—they can build societies capable of developing serious criminal operations. Violence here becomes instrumental to economic gains.

In particular historical circumstances, typically those associated with the weakness of the state and the emergence of poorly regulated economic markets, the gangs can acquire economic and political control over their territories, with their leaders penetrating the structures of the state or competing with it as agents of social regulation. They can evolve into mafia-type organizations that can "claim to exercise a political dominion over their areas of settlement" (Paoli 2003, 142). I call these forms *autonomous ruling regimes* to avoid association with the Mafia as a specific Italian phenomenon. These groups develop stronger organization and try to establish violent control over markets and territories. But they almost never achieve supreme authority; they coexist with other power agencies and institutions, forming a part of the territorial kaleidoscope of power, a system of "fractured sovereignty" (Shearing 1992) at the local level. They can also become part of broader extraterritorial illicit networks.

Examples of the transformation of street organizations into entrepreneurial gangs and autonomous ruling regimes can be seen around the world. Under the influence of war, conflict, and economic devastation, brought on not least by neoliberal transformation, some street groups in Latin American countries have evolved from loose peer associations into organized entrepreneurial gangs, which run the drug economy and achieve a substantial degree of control over local neighborhoods and larger areas (Arias 2006a,b; Hagedorn 2008; Rodgers 2009). Similarly, studies conducted in the United States since the 1980s have shown that under conditions of deindustrialization and weak penetration of law-and-order institutions into low-income areas, street gangs can turn into illegal economic enterprises, with some acting as institutions of local power (Venkatesh 2000). Similar transformations took place in Russia, first on a small scale in the 1970s and 1980s, and then on a much larger scale in the 1990s in the historically unique circumstances of the crisis and collapse of state socialism. I will trace these processes in Kazan.

Kazan: Traditional Forms of Youth Violence

Kazan is the capital of the autonomous Republic of Tatarstan (a federal republic in the Soviet Union and federal subject of the Russian Federation). The city is situated on the Volga, about five hundred miles from Moscow. Modern Kazan has an ethnically diverse population, consisting of Slavs (mainly Russians) and non-Slavs (of whom the predominant ethnic groups are Tatars and Chuvash, members of the Turkish linguistic group). According to the latest census data, Russians make up 48.8 percent and Tartars 47.5 percent of Kazan's total population of 1,143,000 (Kazan government information portal 2011).

After 1552—when Kazan, then the capital of the Chingissid khanate, was conquered by Ivan the Terrible—the urban area and surrounding agricultural lands for a while formed part of the eastern frontier of the Russian empire. Further territorial expansion, however, meant that Kazan became a territory lying deep within Russia. For centuries, Russians and Tatars lived side by side relatively peacefully, partly a testimony to the success of the policy of religious and ethnic tolerance by the Russian imperial center. An abundance of agricultural land also helped to prevent intercommunal conflict in the rural areas. While the two groups historically formed separate communities, the industrialization of Kazan, which began in the middle of the nineteenth century, led to the gradual erosion of the ethnic borders of Tatar settlements. A process of ethnic mixing of the Kazan population started with the abolition of the separate Tatar city council in 1854, and Russians and Tatars began to mingle regularly, despite existing tensions along ethnic lines (Geraci 2001, 42). These tensions were often expressed and (at least partly) resolved through the practice of ritualized male fights.

Some famous literary accounts of organized fights in Kazan date back to the nineteenth century. Mass fights took place in the border areas between the Tatar settlements and the Russian part of the city. In winter, such fights, involving Russian and Tatar youths, took place on the frozen ice of Lake Kaban, which separated the Russian territory from the Tatar quarter. Accounts left by two Russian writers, Sergei Aksakov (1955, 167–68) and Feodor Shaliapin (1926, 19, 23–25, 69–72) about the fights they observed in their youth in Kazan are very similar despite the events they described being separated by eighty years, with Aksakov reporting the events of around 1806 and Shaliapin describing the fights he observed around 1886. The fights were carefully orchestrated. They were usually started by small boys and continued in a duel between famous fighters from both sides. The rest of the fighters would then engage in mass combat. Aksakov recounted how the victorious side often chased their adversaries home and how, when the Tatar men arrived on the Russian streets, Russian families—including women, children, and old people—sometimes joined in the fight. Shaliapin described waves of fighting within a single combat, in which different age cohorts—small boys, teenagers, young men, and adult men as old as forty—fought their peers from the other side. The rules of the fights included many limits to violence. The fighters could only use their fists and were not to beat those who were on the ground or crouching. They were not allowed to kick their opponents or to stuff weights into their mittens. Those who did hide a coin, a bullet, or a piece of metal in their hand would, if discovered, be beaten collectively by both Russians and Tatars.

Evolution of Street Organizations in Kazan

From the middle of the nineteenth century and throughout most of the twentieth century, the Kazan region developed from an imperial backwater into a major urban and industrial conglomeration. The Russian, and later Soviet, authorities were attracted by the territory's natural riches (oil and gas) and vast human resources that could be used for industrialization. (The region was still mainly rural at the end of the 1950s.) Its first-class educational centers such as Kazan University had many famous former students, including Tolstoy and Lenin. During the Great Patriotic War (1941–45) several major industrial and military plants were evacuated to the city, and by the end of the 1940s Kazan had significant machine-building and aviation industries. The industrialization of Kazan, and with it massive migration of the rural population to the city, intensified in the 1960s and 1970s. The population of Kazan exploded from 667,000 in 1959 to 1,094,400 in 1989 (RFE/RL 2005). A large population of new urban dwellers was created, comprising Russians, Tatars, and people of other ethnicities, all highly assimilated and forming ethnically mixed communities in the new working-class residential areas.

Young rural migrants to the cities left the older generation behind. The demographic composition of the urban population tended to be skewed toward younger age groups. According to one source, by the end of the 1980s, young people made up almost half of all urban dwellers of Tatarstan (Iskhakov 1998). Spending much of their time on the streets, without adult control, these youths formed peer groups and networks in which they played, fought, committed acts of delinquency and crime, and learned how to be "real men" through conflict. Frederic Thrasher (1963 [1927]) observed similar processes in a different context—the urbanization of the United States in the first decades of the twentieth century—and described the emergence of the gang as a product of social disorganization in the expanding city, where children of recent migrants were left without an effective community of adults to supervise them and formed their own tribes on the streets.

With new industrial developments and massive housing construction in Kazan, the processes of group formation intensified. According to a Kazan journalist who investigated the origins of organized Kazan gangs (Ageeva 1991), one area where street peer groups began to change from amorphous collectives engaging in episodic and festive fights into tightly organized gangs was Teplokontrol', a district built in Kazan around a large industrial factory. The cheaply constructed panel block apartment buildings—the so-called *khrushchevki* that were built in large numbers during and after the Khrushchev era of the late 1950s and early 1960s—housed the new migrant labor force. Another Tatarstan author (Safarov 2012, 8) described the area as "several *khrushchevki*, built for factory workers on the shore of Lake Srednii Kaban; the private houses of the Kalinovka settlement; and dozens of kilometers of industrial zone, where the different factory territories merge with one another. The streets are lit by the light coming from the houses; the roads are full of potholes." This was the grim background of young people's lives in these interstitial zones of Russian industrial areas.

One of the leaders of the future local gang called Tiap-Liap, Zavdad Khantimirov (Dzhavda), moved into such an area with his family when he was five. According to Ageeva (1991), soon after the Teplokontrol′ housing quarters were built, boys and young men from the adjacent villages began to make raids on their new young neighbors. Teplokontrol′ youths responded by developing at first defensive and then offensive territorial strategies. They created makeshift gyms in the basements of their apartment blocks, joined boxing clubs, made incursions into "enemy" territory, and eventually managed to overcome their adversaries by teaming up with young people from neighboring city areas. Khantimirov became the charismatic leader of this (still rather loose) peer group. The newly emerged power of the group was tested in the city's dance halls, over which his gang (the Khantimirovtsy) achieved undisputed control. In the period from 1972 to 1974 they managed to defeat their neighbors (the Kominovtsy) and made several raids into other territories to demonstrate their strength. The peer group was transformed into an elite territorial formation with an undisputed reputation as masters of their turf.

As with many street organizations that are not entrepreneurial but mainly social, membership in the gang started early and normally finished at eighteen, when young men were conscripted into the army. According to the Kazan researchers Gataullin and Maksudov (2002), fights were a part of the daily life of street groups, as they "structured" relationships between boys and young men. Fights served to consolidate a system of relations on the street and made it possible for young men to prove their bravery and toughness, to show that they were "real men." There were specific fighting rules with prohibitions on beating people when they are down or having an unequal distribution of forces. Fights were supposed to last till the first blood was spilled, and there was a ban on the use of weapons.

This transformation of a street peer group into a territorial elite was not, however, the end of the story of the gang. The late 1960s and early 1970s marked the appearance in the Soviet Union of *tsekhoviki*. These were managers of state companies who began to develop large-scale, off-the-books production and distribution of goods, expanding underground production that had emerged after Stalin's death in 1953 (Grossman 1977). There was also a black market involving *fartsovka* (the illegal purchase—often from overseas visitors—and sale of currency and prestigious foreign goods, such as American jeans or foreign-made tape recorders) and other consumer goods that were in perennial shortage. Undeclared incomes could be made through activities such as underground gambling and billiard players' rings, shadow antique businesses, illegal production of alcohol, taking bribes for allocation of plots at cemeteries, and off-the-books business in cafes, shops, and restaurants.

This unregulated economic sector started to attract the interest of professional criminals. The *vory v zakone* society emerged in Soviet prisons and labor camps, mostly during the Great Patriotic War, although it can be traced back to prerevolutionary communities of criminals and marginalized vagrants and beggars, and even farther back into Russian feudal history (Galeotti 2008; Siegel 2012). Together with corrupt Soviet officials, the vory v zakone began to offer "protection" to businesses in return for part of the profits (Gurov 1990; Salagaev 2001). Criminal groups provided shadow businessmen with investment capital, organized the transportation and sale of illicit goods, and conducted counterintelligence operations against competitors, while cooperating with corrupt Soviet bureaucrats (Sokolov 2004; Cheloukhine 2008). Youth street groups represented an important violent resource for the criminal entrepreneurs. The former also developed their own extortion operations independently of the vory, forcing people with illegal incomes to pay them tribute. They now turned into entrepreneurial gangs, commodifying their territorial dominance but not quite becoming professional criminals, as their members continued to go to schools and colleges and to work in a variety of legal occupations. Apart from racketeering, they were also involved in more conventional criminality such as burglary, car theft, and street robbery.

Despite great differences in context, we can find some similarities here with working-class groups in industrial Britain and the United States, some of which morphed from peer networks exploring the joys of violent street confrontations into more entrepreneurial structures engaging in protection rackets, extortion, black marketeering, and theft (Yablonsky 1962; Whyte 1993; McDonald 2000). As Hobbs (2013, 114) pointed out, describing the development of some of the famous organized crime clans in London such as the Kray brothers, the Richardsons, and others, "in working-class London, neighborhood based groups abounded, and territorial imperatives featuring individual local, and family reputations were forged in youthful combat that was ideal preparation for the world of acquisitive gangsterism." In Britain and the United States, he added, "countless working-class predators commodified their violent reputations to exploit opportunities offered by variations of extortion"(117).

In Kazan, Khantimirov's group and other local street gangs from Teplokontrol′ eventually coalesced into a larger street association called Tiap-Liap, which was headed by an ex-convict (but not a *vor*), Sergei Antipov. Antipov had grown up in Sukonnaia Sloboda —the same area that was described by Shaliapin in his account of fist fights in Kazan—and, like everybody else, participated in street collective life. He had also been involved in theft and burglary and had spent a short term in prison. On his release, Antipov set up a boxing club for Teplokontrol′ teenagers. In addition to teaching them fighting skills, Antipov also insisted that young people form cohesive and supportive teams, similar to prison families (*semeiki*) that were made up of those sharing the same cell or barrack. For example, Tiap-Liap bought a motorcycle for one of the young men who lived far away and was having trouble making it in time for the fighting class, and another young man, who had experienced a serious psychological trauma, received a paid vacation in a sanatorium (Salagaev 1999). Khantimirov became Antipov's deputy. Other deputies included Sergei Skriabin, a student from a teaching college (and former Young Pioneer organizer), and Mikhail Zakharovich, a child psychiatrist. This involvement of more educated people in gangs would also be a feature of post-Soviet developments, presenting a deviation from standard descriptions of gangs as collections of low-class delinquents.

At the beginning of the 1970s, Antipov's group counted about thirty to forty members (Beliaev and Sheptitskii 2012, 71). In implementing his strategy of developing serious criminal operations in the Teplokontrol' area, Antipov encountered resistance from another informal leader of the Teplokontrol' youth, Sergei Dan'shin. Dan'shin, who in his teenage years had also been a member of a local street group, was against involvement in criminal business. Antipov blamed Dan'shin's reluctance to turn to "serious business" on his having had no history of incarceration and thus being stuck in "Soviet" ways of thinking. Finally, Antipov wrote a letter to other members of the gang's leadership, accusing Dan'shin of reporting on him to the police. Teplokontrol' youth turned away from Dan'shin, who was then killed by Khantimirov's associates (Gataullin and Maksudov 2002). This was a taste of the violent fights within gang leadership that would become so prominent in the 1990s.

Under Antipov's leadership Tiap-Liap set out on a policy of aggressive territorial expansion, eventually covering the whole of the Privolzhskii District of Kazan (Beliaev and Sheptitskii 2012, 73). Existing street-fighting groups became Tiap-Liap's affiliates—either joining the gang peacefully or being annexed by it as a result of special "military" campaigns in which members of the local groups would be assaulted and told that they had to join Tiap-Liap if they wanted to avoid trouble. Many local peer groups retained their membership but were given new leaders appointed by Antipov. In many cases, the transformation of a fighting group into an entrepreneurial gang would happen in the space of two to three months.[3]

By the end of the 1970s, Tiap-Liap consisted of an alliance of different streets numbering about two hundred young men between fifteen and twenty-five years

3. Interview with K. N. Novikov, head of police investigations of Tatarstan, October 1986 (quoted in Salagaev 1999).

old. Similarly to prison groups, members now had their own *obshchaki* (common funds – the gangs' treasuries), into which they paid regular contributions. The gangs moved from fighting with belts, chains, and brass knuckles to firearms. The groups also developed their own style of clothing—dark padded jackets and winter hats with the flaps tied under the chin, a uniform that combines working-class and prison-inmates' styles of clothing. When other street groups adopted the same uniform, Tiap-Liap members started to wear Teplokontrol' badges. They developed a special symbol—a crown with the letters "TK" for Teplokontrol'.

Antipov presided over the transformation of the alliance of territorial groups into an entrepreneurial gang alliance operating mainly in the areas of extortion and protection of underground Soviet producers. Tiap-Liap's violent resource was now in demand, and it began to provide security for the transportation of illegal produce carried out by an auto transport company in the Teplokontrol' area (Salagaev 2005). At the same time, it extorted money from the so-called speculators, black marketeers, shop and restaurant workers, directors of state warehouses, and managers of cemeteries (a lucrative business both in Soviet and post-Soviet times). These were the representatives of the Soviet service sector who were massively involved in the networks of *blat* (informal exchange) and corruption (Ledeneva 1998). They were perfect targets for criminal extortion as they had substantial unaccounted-for incomes from black market activities and bribes, and so could be fleeced with impunity as they were unlikely to go to the police for help. The gang established a regime of racketeering of local restaurants, cafes, shops, and other service sector establishments. The gang also found ways to penetrate the networks of state power. Although never officially proven, there was evidence in the criminal case that the group was protected by the *militia* (police) (Ageeva 1991).[4] Fifty officers were fired from the police after the Tiap-Liap trial (Salagaev 1999).

Younger Tiap-Liap members were also involved in house burglaries and theft of cars, motor boats, and motorcycles, as well as (at the time) rare and expensive goods, such as tape recorders and foreign-made clothes. Some were involved in street extortion, attacking passers-by for money and valuables. But while engaging in antisocial and criminal behavior, Tiap-Liap members did not necessarily see themselves as agents of resistance to Soviet power. There is even evidence that they did not consider themselves to be criminals. As documented in the court proceedings, Tiap-Liap members saw themselves as morally upright citizens who, in line with Soviet ideology, were acting against the "unearned" incomes of

4. From February 1917 until March 1, 2011, the Russian police force was called the *militia*. They became known as the *politsiia* after that, but for simplicity's sake I will refer to them as "police" throughout the book.

black marketeers. The case files show that during pretrial investigation the gang members often refused to accept that they had committed any crimes. As Ageeva (1991) noted, expropriation of illegal incomes and expensive consumer goods was seen as a "fight for social justice."

As I will show in chapters 2 and 5, there are substantial similarities between Soviet and post-Soviet gangsters. Post-Soviet gang members shared the dominant ideology of capitalist entrepreneurialism, seeing themselves as the vanguard of hard-working "businessmen." They too were significantly incorporated into mainstream society, often studying in colleges and universities and keeping up legitimate jobs. And they, too, although on a significantly larger scale, developed various collaborations with the police and other representatives of state power.

Other Street Alliances

Other street groups in Kazan underwent similar transformations to Tiap-Liap. Some began to defend the interests of various business groups that Tiap-Liap threatened. Others retained the form of territorial fighting formations. However, keen not to be subsumed by Tiap-Liap, they built up their fighting prowess and sought recognition by engaging in fights with rivals at various local arenas. This process mirrors the history of US street gangs, in which some gangs did not emerge merely as spontaneous youth organizations but were also organized by adults—businessmen, racketeers, or politicians (Chesney-Lind and Hagedorn 1999; Adamson 2000; Wacquant 2006, 274; Hagedorn 2007, 16) or developed in order to protect their territory from new violent groups. As Ann Campbell pointed out, "where a powerful gang becomes a threat for nearby territories, new gangs arise for their defense" (1991, 236).

Street groups began to form alliances to defend themselves from Tiap-Liap. Two such examples, described in the Tiap-Liap criminal case, were the union of Novotatarskaia Sloboda, the old enemy of Teplokontrol′ youth, and the Manty group, which united the leaders of several groups "deposed" by Tiap-Liap. A war between Tiap-Liap and Novotatarskaia for the Kirovskii District ended in victory for Tiap-Liap, with Kirovskii declaring its neutrality and refusing to support Novotatarskaia (Gataullin and Maksudov 2002).

As the city's territory was being rapidly divided and redivided, the groups had to develop stronger organizations to defend their claims to a particular turf. They recruited new members, offering them not just protection against assault but also (just as with members of the vory community) material help in cases of illness or incarceration. Obshchaki were set up to cover unforeseen group expenses and also to pay for funerals (another practice that was similar to that of the vory). The gangs developed leadership structures, with war councils and systems of age-based cohorts. They expanded into schools, where members began to collect money for the obshchak. In each class there were several gang members, and most kids paid dues of two or three rubles a month to the gang. Many well-known Kazan gangs such as Boriskovo, Griaz', Zhilka, Kinoplionka, Kaluga, Pervaki, and Khadi Taktash were formed in those years on the basis of alliances of several street groups. According to police data, at the beginning of the 1980s there were ninety gangs in the city, some with three or four hundred members. Gangs also established a massive presence in other cities of Tatarstan, including Naberezhnye Chelny and Al'metievsk (Akbarov 1999, 27).

One of the leaders of Pervaki (from the Pervye Gorki area), Renat Shagvaliev (known as Skippy), described his gang history:

> My family moved into the Pervye Gorki microdistrict in 1973. At that time, I and my classmates came under attack by guys from the Starye Gorki microdistrict. They beat us, took away our bicycles, skates, hockey sticks, and so on. When we became older, about fifteen to seventeen, we decided that we needed to stand up for ourselves, unite and show resistance to Starye Gorki. From then on the guys were all united and named themselves Pervaki. Intensive training sessions in school gyms started, and prohibition on drinking and smoking was introduced. We followed the example of the OPG Teplokontrol' (Tiap-Liap), which, it seemed at that time, controlled the whole city. Every senior had two (younger) people whom he looked after. . . . In 1978 I first took all Pervaki to dances in Gorky Park to show my status. Fights with other Kazan gruppirovki also took place there. (Beliaev and Sheptitskii 2012, 207)

As we shall see, from these modest origins Pervaki eventually turned into an autonomous ruling regime in the area under its control. By the middle of the 1990s, Pervaki membership reached three hundred to four hundred people, with its youth controlling one of the city street markets, as well as cafes, illegal parking lots, and auto repair garages, and running extortion operations in their area and beyond (Nafikov 2012, 344–45; Safarov 2012, 363–66).

The Khadi Taktash gang was formed by young people living on Khadi Taktash Street (named after a famous Tatar poet) and Zhdanova Street in 1980. In 1982 it was among the first gangs in Kazan to be registered by the police. Its membership extended far beyond minors, with members whose ages ranged between twelve and thirty, and reached five hundred people in a short period of time (Beliaev and Sheptitskii 2012). In the 1990s, Khadi Taktash moved from participation in mass fights with other gangs into black market operations involving polyethylene from the neighboring Orgsintez plant, and eventually rose to become one of the most powerful gangs in Tatarstan (Safarov 2012, 73)

The process of gang formation in Kazan and wider Tatarstan speeded up rapidly, with groups organizing regular meetings, often in school courtyards, establishing obshchaki, organizing boxing or martial arts training for youngsters and developing various economic ventures (including street extortion and theft), sometimes simply to keep the obshchak coffers filled. Some of the territorial gangs turned to more serious criminal enterprises, organizing extortion and racketeering of the service sector and corrupt Soviet managers. Others continued to protect their pieces of turf, defend their group's honor, organize recreation, and support members who were ill or in prison for street crime (Ageeva 1991; Salagaev 2005).

At the time, the groups were called *motalki* (from *motatsia*—to wander), *kontory* (companies), or *firmy* (firms). The active members of the gangs, who called themselves *osnovnye* ("the main ones"), recognized different age strata: *shelukha* (nine and ten years old), *supera* (eleven to thirteen), *molodye* (fourteen to sixteen), and *starshye* (seventeen and above). Similar age stratification was developed by territorial gangs in many other areas of the Soviet Union (Pilkington 1994). The most active members of the groups were the *molodye*, who were the main "muscle" in battles with gangs from other areas. They often used metal sticks, bricks, and truncheons to injure their opponents. *Starshye* determined the "policy" of the group and spent much of their time in dance halls, where they provoked violent confrontations with other young men. On returning from the army, many young people did not cut their ties with peer groups as they would have before, and instead turned into *avtoritety* (informal leaders).

Like Tiap-Liap, the participants of these groups had their own insignia and marked the borders of their territories (Plaksii 1990). Territorial demarcation sometimes involved considerable ingenuity—for example, the gang called Chainiki (Teapots) suspended teapots from lampposts. Gang members, usually from the younger age groups, patrolled the borders of the territory and organized vigils at key points such as bus stops, parks, and playgrounds to look out for intruders from other areas. By the middle of the 1980s not a single street remained that did not belong to some gang (Safarov 2012, 19).

With the various neighborhood gangs now vying for power and control over territory, fighting practices also changed. From being "character building" experiences for young men and a traditional part of collective street life, fights now became a means to an end—a demonstration of force, intimidation, and territorial expansion. Previous fighting regulations were forgotten. Fights often took the form of wars and vendettas (Gataullin and Maksudov 2002). Gang members needed to be battle ready: young men had to be fit, and they were required to engage in sports and train regularly in gyms. Under threat of punishment, members were required to come to fights sober (Kashelkin 1990b).

Wars between gangs became routine—as a way to establish recognition and acquire territory and as a means of keeping the troops mobilized. When asked in a conversation with a journalist in 1989 (Smol'nikov 1989) why fights break out, a Kazan gang leader responded:

> No real reason. It's just a way of keeping the firm ready for battle—to maintain discipline and show respect to the elders. Any group will fall apart when there's nothing to do. So what we do is declare war on one region or another. Let the youngsters go batter each other. . . . Sometimes, while our forces are out fighting, the leader of the enemy firm and I just sit in a bar together.

With gangs vying for power and building their names through the use of force, the threat of violence became omnipresent for Kazan youths. A former gang member, forty-two-year-old Nikita, remembered how life was in Kazan before he went into the army in 1987 at the age of eighteen. The streets were arenas for gang fights. Not only that but boys from different gangs fought in school during classes. During a lesson a door could open and a gang member would call for his adversary to come out. Nikita, who practiced boxing, still felt he could not defend himself unless he joined a gang. He decided to join a gang from across the road. To hedge his bets he also stayed friends with his neighbors, who formed a different gang. Once, however, he crossed a young man who turned out to be one of the leaders of Tiap-Liap. The following day, youths from Tiap-Liap came to his apartment, dragged him out of the bath, got him onto a bus where about thirty other people were waiting for him, and took the bus to the cemetery. They started to dig a grave for him, but then his friends, alerted by a neighbor, arrived and saved him from what he felt certain was impending death.

The serious violence unleashed by Tiap-Liap went almost unhindered, as the Soviet authorities were terrified of acknowledging that a problem of organized violence and crime could exist in a socialist country. One episode in 1976, for example, in which members of Tiap-Liap started a shootout with members of other gangs, firing from their cars in the busiest part of the city, went unreported by the local police, who did not want to incur the wrath of Moscow (Safarov 2012, 10). Violence, unlimited by other power agents, was escalating in all directions. Tiap-Liap's quest for citywide recognition and the violent colonization of all "unregulated" spaces in Kazan was associated with harassment of unaffiliated young people and territorial groups that resisted its domination. The gang also used brutal force against Soviet black market *kommersanty* (businessmen) who refused to pay their "dues." Tiap-Liap's criminal case file contained evidence of beatings and killings of disobedient barmen and shop workers. In the community, much of the "action" took place around the dance halls, where Tiap-Liap members looked for fights with local youths. In one episode, recorded in the criminal case file, Tiap-Liap arrived in force at the popular Uritskogo club in specially rented buses and attacked everyone there (Ageeva 1991).

Tiap-Liap's undoing came in August 1978. The gang decided to make a spectacular show of strength against their old enemy, Novotatarskaia Sloboda. One day, forty to fifty masked men, armed with firearms and metal rods, arrived at Novotatarskaia. They spread out across both sides of the streets and started beating and randomly shooting at passers-by. As a result, a seventy-four-year-old male bystander, a war veteran, was killed, and ten people, including two policemen, were wounded. This raid could not be ignored by the Kazan police and Communist Party authorities.[5] The trial, which followed in 1978–80, led to death sentences for two gang leaders (including Khantimirov) and lengthy prison terms for twenty-eight other members. The Tiap-Liap case was the only legal case between the end of the 1950s and the mid-1980s in which a group of youths were sentenced for organizing an armed bandit group (Salagaev 1999). Even then, the authorities tried to present the case as an ordinary criminal case.

The conviction of Tiap-Liap members did not stop street violence for long. Starting around 1982, Kazan again became the stage for raging fights for *asfalt* ("asphalt"—territory). Young men fought street by street, quarter by quarter. They used sticks, bricks, and sometimes knives against their adversaries. Others in the city felt powerless in the face of the street gangs. The law enforcement agencies pursued the gangs vigorously, arresting and incarcerating their members, but that seemed only to serve to strengthen the gangs. Incarcerated leaders came back from prison even more skilled and determined. Gang recruitment intensified. The number of group crimes committed by minors exploded from 161 in 1984 to 454 in 1989 (Ageeva 1991, 181, 236, 246).

The gangs made raids into nearby cities, Naberezhnye Chelny, Chistopol′, Nizhnekamsk and other places, and even went on raiding expeditions to Moscow and Leningrad. Sometimes they simply roamed in the vicinity of the Kazan train station in Moscow or ventured to central areas of the capital. Young men, dressed in their Kazan street uniforms of dark padded jackets and felt boots, the latter known colloquially as "Good-bye, youth," frightened the local inhabitants with their aggressive demeanor and gloomy looks (Safarov 2012, 18–19). Sometimes

---

5. The first classified report about the presence of organized crime in the Soviet Union was written by Soviet criminologists from the All-Union Institute for the Study of the Causes of Crime and for the Elaboration of Measures for Crime Prevention in 1982. It was met with resistance from a range of opposing officials (Dolgova 2003, 419n1).

their visits were less touristy—they mugged local young people and committed thefts and burglaries. According to Ministry of the Interior (MVD) research, groups from the Volga area (Kazan, Naberezhnye Chelny, and Cheboksary) were responsible for half of all the crimes committed by nonresidents of the Moscow region, mainly street robbery and theft from local teenagers, as well as house burglaries. One of the objectives of these raids was to provide funding for the gang's obshchak at home. Vladimir Ovchinskii, who conducted research among offenders from Kazan gangs who had participated in the raids, noted that they did not admit that their behavior was criminal and explained it by the desire to have fashionable clothes and money. He reported that according to them "such behavior was common in the areas they come from." The interviewees had strong feelings of social deprivation and injustice (Ovchinskii 1990, 193).

Research conducted by Soviet police criminologists established that, by the end of the 1980s, every third young man between twelve and eighteen in Kazan was a member of a gang (Plaksii 1990, 90). Another study showed that up to 30 percent of adolescents who broke the law in Kazan were members of *motalki* (Ovchinskii 1990). Researchers pointed to the process of agglomeration of gangs at the beginning of the 1990s, when, according to police data, Kazan had sixty-eight gangs with 1,500 active members (Akbarov 1999, 97).

Although this data should be treated with caution (as the definitions of gangs used by researchers or their data collection methods were not presented in these publications) the problem of youth violence was obviously very serious. According to Kazan police statistics, eighty-seven mass fights took place in Kazan in 1988 alone. The Soviet criminologists noted an increase in violence and the use of weapons (metal sticks, spades, knives, homemade bombs). While women were not allowed to be gang members, sexual exploitation of girls by male gang members was widespread (Kashelkin 1990b).

Voices from the Past: Gang Members' Letters to the Press

The prosecution of Tiap-Liap members in 1979–80 was not reported in the press. Eventually, however, despite the reluctance of the Soviet authorities to admit the existence of organized youth crime and violence, this topic became a part of public discussion. In 1983 the first references to fights between street gangs appeared in local newspapers. They presented the views of gang members, nonaffiliated young men, and their parents and teachers.

Ageeva (1991, 49–55) cited several letters sent to the *Vecherniaia Kazan* newspaper, where she worked at the time when a moral panic about the gangs gripped the city. One young man recounted that he created his own gang because of fear of being assaulted:

> The most frightening thing for us was to come across guys who were two or three years older than us. We were beaten, mocked, humiliated, and robbed. I decided to resist them in any way I could. I went to a boxing school. . . . But if there were three or four of them, I'd get overpowered, and they would win. Then I decided to find a different way of resisting. I gathered my friends of the same age—mainly from my school and my courtyard—and said that we should fight against those guys together. This is how our gang was formed.

In what can be seen as an example of the use of rationalization or "neutralization techniques" (Sykes and Matza, 1957) to justify delinquent behavior, the letter goes on to show how this young man sought to provide moral justification for his gang membership:

> I understand that in *motanie* [gang lifestyle] there are more negatives than positives. But if you are being brought up in a gang in the spirit of camaraderie and mutual help, and not simply told to stay in the street between six and nine looking to attack "outsiders," then this is a normal group. Eight people from our group served in Afghanistan. One of them was killed and given a decoration posthumously—he saved the life of a young girl.

Again, we see here attempts to justify gang behavior by showing that many of the practices of the gang were normal for Soviet youth and that they shared the values of camaraderie and patriotism that were expected of Soviet citizens. Other letters sought to present a romanticized image of the gang as the local warrior elite. One young man wrote: "We will never make peace with one another, because if all the gangs in Kazan made peace, the teenagers would lose their drive. . . . And I want us to be kings, to be respected in the city." "Gang members are liked by girls; their peers respect them," said another letter writer. Several young people wrote a collective letter complaining that boys aged between ten and twelve were made to fight and to keep watch at bus stops to make sure that no stranger was let into the home territory. A fifteen-year-old boy wrote to say that out of nineteen boys in his class only seven were not members of a gang. One author complained, "We cannot venture farther than the courtyard of our block of apartments. Anywhere we go we can be stopped, beaten, and mugged. All the gangs in Kazan must come to a peace agreement!" (Ageeva 1991, 49–55).

An interview conducted in 1989 by a journalist presents a vivid picture of the dilemmas facing young men who had initially tried to stay away from the street groups. The interviewee, a leader of one of the gangs in his early twenties, joined his gang at the beginning of the 1980s when he was twelve years old:

> This was back in year 6 [7th grade]. I was already practicing self-defense back then—the old-fashioned kind. But I didn't hang out with gangs. I once went to see a film with a friend. One local firm had a place where they used to gather near the cinema. We didn't know that. So they tried to start something—thirty people or so. They surrounded us. They asked, "Where do you live? Who do you hang out with?" So we told them, "We're on our own. We don't have time to hang out on the streets." "Have you got cash?" [they asked].We had about eight rubles on us. They took them and beat us up for good measure. I was so upset I actually started sobbing. When they heard about it the guys from our local street group just laughed. "Well," they asked, "so you still don't want to join us? Then you can look forward to plenty more beatings like that!" A month later, the same thing happened. This time, another firm got me when I was walking a girl home. They got me so badly that I ended up in the hospital with a concussion. After that, I couldn't take it anymore and came to our street group. "I've had it," I said, "let me join you guys." (Smol'nikov 1989)

Youth Gangs in Other Regions of the USSR

Kazan was not an isolated case of the transformation of youth street peer groups into more organized territorial elites and entrepreneurial gangs. Research conducted by Soviet police criminologists (Prozumentov and Sheksler 1990, 225) showed that by the start of the 1990s "organized warring groups of adolescents created on territorial principles" were present in many areas of the country. Researchers pointed to the greater organization and increased levels of violence of these groups compared to the previous collectives of street delinquents.

Police criminologists who studied this problem noted the increasingly violent character of street fights and the use of weapons including knives and guns (Baal' 1990). According to police data, in 1988–89 there were thirty registered street violent groups in Gor'kovskaia Oblast' and twenty-two in the Chuvash Republic. In Volgograd, Izhevsk, Saransk, Yaroslavl, and Kaluga between ten and twenty groups were present in each city (Prozumentov and Sheksler 1990, 225). A survey of school and PTU (*professional'no-tekhnicheskie uchilishcha*—vocational school) students in Volgograd revealed that 32 percent of PTU students and 22.5 percent of school students were members of "informal street groups with a cult of force, protecting their territory" (Sibiriakov 1990, 170–71). In some of the cities, it was reported, the groups even attacked police officers. In all the areas where these groups were present, criminologists noted the practice of group fights, the presence of age-based strata, structures of leadership and internal discipline, collection of money into common funds, and various sporting activities, mostly boxing and martial arts clubs, that helped to build the youths' fighting prowess. The groups committed various types of street crime (extortion, assault, etc.). Most groups were male, although some had female members (Kashelkin 1990b; Prozumentov and Sheksler 1990; Sibiriakov 1990; Baal′ 1991).

It is difficult, however, to judge how organized and violent these groups really were. Most of the existing data were collected from criminal cases, in penitentiaries, and by the local commissions on minors that registered delinquent teenagers. There was no research into street groups in their own milieu. The specific street practices, the social organization of these groups, and the extent of their criminalization fell outside the researchers' interest.

One feature that later also became prominent in post-Soviet organized gangs was the presence of ex-convicts and sportsmen in leadership positions. Ex-convicts provided organizational expertise to the gang and transmitted the criminal norms (*poniatiia*) and rituals, while sportsmen were actively recruited because they possessed valued qualities such as self-discipline and physical prowess. In some cases sportsmen themselves, with or without criminal records, organized sports activities for young people in order to create their own gangs (Akbarov 1999).

Sergei Belanovsky (2009) documented these processes in the South-East Moscow working-class area of Zhdanovskaia, now Vykhino. In the 1970s, some of the youth peer groups in the area started to develop into entrepreneurial gangs. According to Belanovsky, the role of ex-convicts in this process was significant. By the middle of the 1980s, various street groups in the district had come together to form one larger gang called Zhdan′. The teams had their own leaders, who had typically served time, and they were stratified by age and had systems of internal discipline. Many members were actively engaged in sports. The members collected money for an obshchak. The gangs were involved in rackets and extortion as well as street crime. People who wandered into the territory risked being beaten and robbed of money and valuables. Mass fights were rare and involved the use of weapons such as chains, brass knuckles, and knives.

Similar processes of transformation of street youth groups into criminal organizations in the 1970s and 1980s were documented in the Russian Far East. Members of street peer groups established the borders of their territory in violent fights with other groups and moved into racketeering and other forms of crime. One of the leaders of such groups who later became a prominent organized crime boss, Anatolii Kovalev (Koval′), told a journalist in 1996 about those days:

> I am a native inhabitant of Vladivostok, born and raised in Morgorod, in a family without a father. My mother was often on business trips, and from early on in my youth I was on my own. Like a lot of my peers I went to the dances. Today one hardly remembers how popular the dances were back then. The youngsters met at the small House of Culture, further down at the restaurant Okean, in the big House of Culture, and in front of the submarine [monument]. We didn't drink and smoke back then. There were fights at every dance. Back then a strong division among city districts came into being. . . . During that time we were acquainted with and associated with everybody. We knew each other well and therefore could freely come to the other districts of town. . . . There weren't any criminal groups (*gruppirovki*) back then, just companions (*tovarishchi*) who were close to each other. I don't see anything bad in that. . . . Of course, during that time some connections started, but not in a criminal sense. It is true though, that when the street markets (*barakholki*) where the sailors sold imported jeans appeared, we collected the goods from them and gave them only the money they were worth. That means we didn't go into profiteering. (quoted in Holzlehner 2007, 57–58)

As Holzlehner suggests, Kovalev presented his story in such a way that it served to legitimate his behavior and identity. Kovalev talked about his past deeds as being nothing out of the ordinary, as part of the "normal" life of a young man at the time. However, we should not simply dismiss his account as pure falsification. His description of the origins of his group includes some essential features of the genesis of organized crime in Russia. Although it had many recruits from all walks of life, it was substantially socially and culturally grounded in street male peer networks.

As in Kazan, the development of gangs in the Far East was influenced by the organization, norms, and rituals of the vory v zakone society. When the leaders of the gangs were incarcerated, they learned the norms of the vory's social order and wider prison culture (Oleinik 2003). Coming back, they brought the knowledge of prison ritual practices and moral systems back to the community. In Primorskii Krai, one of the local avtoritety, Podatev (Pudel′), reported how, on his release, he saw complete chaos on the streets as violent groups fought with each other for control of the territory. He saw that the ideas of a vory brotherhood could be used to create similar rules for young "hooligans," as well as disparate criminal groups and individual criminals. The vory's obshchaki could be set up in the community as well. He started organizing these obshchaki all over the region (VCSOC 2004). At the end of the 1980s and beginning of the 1990s, the structures and norms of the vory v zakone and prison community exerted a significant cultural influence on the world of the streets.

Liubery

One famous place where street peer groups evolved into militant territorial elites was the Moscow suburb of Liubertsy. There are many parallels between Kazan and Liubertsy. Like Kazan, Liubertsy underwent rapid industrialization, accompanied by mass labor migration. In this area the age composition of the population was also skewed toward younger age groups (Belanovsky 1990). Liubertsy was built around a steam car factory at the end of the nineteenth century. Industrial construction continued steadily in the subsequent decades and intensified in the period following the end of the Great Patriotic War.

The town incorporated several nearby villages, and by the 1980s it had become one of the largest industrial areas near Moscow. It had around sixty large heavy industry enterprises. By the end of the 1980s, the population of the Liubertsy area was about four hundred thousand, mostly industrial workers. Liubertsy, like Kazan and many other urban areas, had numerous street peer groups. Intergroup violence was limited by a traditional masculine code, which forbade attacks on girls, young men accompanying girls, or small children. As elsewhere, group members were not supposed to use weapons in fights, and there were expectations of a relative parity of forces. After serving in the army, young people tended to leave the streets, with many of those who chose working-class professions going to work at defense companies (Belanovsky 1990).

At the beginning of the 1980s, Liubertsy youths went through a bodybuilding craze. Young people turned the basements of their apartment blocks into gyms and started pumping iron. While some young people, known colloquially as *sportsmeny* (athletes), were mostly interested in bodybuilding, others, known as *khuligany* (hooligans), were involved in street fighting and petty crime. Like their Kazan counterparts, once they established control over local turf, they started traveling to Moscow, which was very close. Sometimes groups of *liubery*, as they became known, only used the toilet at the train station and went back home, their adventure over (Gromov 2006). On other occasions, they attacked well-dressed Moscow youths, whom they called *mazhory*—"privileged ones"—in the slang of the time, members of youth subcultural groups (the so-called *neformaly*) such as hippies or punks, and representatives of street groups in the capital, with whom they were involved in long-running vendettas and wars. There were also reports of attacks against ethnic minorities. Younger boys, eleven to thirteen, especially liked to go to international exhibitions in Moscow where they would arrive in groups and hustle and steal foreign badges, pens, and colorful plastic carrier bags—all prestigious items at the time. Fights for these "trophies" would erupt between Moscow and Liubertsy kids at the exits from the exhibitions (Gromov 2006). Although much of the violence seems to have been expressive rather than instrumental, there were also reports that some of the leaders of liubery, those with criminal pasts, used their young followers to racketeer black market traders (Yakovlev 1987).

While no data exist on the social composition of liubery, who lived in the socially mixed areas that characterized Soviet urban settlements, in its essential features this was youth subculture heavily inflected by working-class male culture, with its stress on control over the body, physical strength, and masculine respect. Like other youth working-class subcultures (e.g., skinheads), liubery were socially conservative—but for them conservatism meant protecting the Soviet socialist order. These were suburban fighters for moral purity, standing against the "deviations" of degenerate city youth. They qualified trips to Moscow as campaigns for Soviet values and as attempts to preserve the decaying social order. For example, here's how a former *liuber* explained why he and his friends attacked soccer fans: "When they walked around, they vandalized newspaper kiosks and street stands. If we saw them, we fought with them. We were putting things in order" (Gromov 2006, 27).

Similarly to Kazan gangs, they were involved in wider networks that also included the Soviet authorities. But unlike the Kazan gangs, who formed corrupt relationships with the police, liubery were utilized by Soviet law enforcement as agents of social order from below. They saw members of this subculture as allies in the fight against westernized youth groups, as well as violent neofascists. For example, on Hitler's birthday in April 1982, a planned rally of neo-fascists was dispersed by liubery who were tipped off about the event by the police. Gromov quotes an interview with a former liuber:

> The idea was that there should be no pacifists or Nazis, nor anybody else. We thought, we are leading a healthy way of life; we pump iron, do sports—and somebody is walking around with metal chains shouting [political] slogans. We thought this was unnatural and also against what we were told by Komsomol and Young Pioneer organizations. We went to fight for an idea—not for money like those young people who later became bandits. (Gromov 2006, 128)

Liubery caused a moral panic in Russian society of the time (Pilkington 1994). The press saw them as young people from the urban periphery possessed of an irrational hatred toward their Muscovite peers. Many members of the intelligentsia suspected that the liubery were being organized by the authorities to fight the emerging *neformaly*, the representatives of youth subcultures who broke away from the mould of obedient and compliant Soviet youth. There were rumors that they walked around with badges bearing Lenin's image (a myth according to Gromov). Gromov (2006) noted that "ideological" motivations played a relatively minor role in the liubery subculture, and most of the boys and young men spent their time much like the rest of their generation, going to discos, parks, or cinemas, or having street altercations and fights. According to Gromov, the numbers of the liubery were also exaggerated. Most of the Liubertsy residents learned about the problem of liubery from the mass media. But, as with other moral panics, the public furor had the effect of drawing more young people toward this subculture—and not just in Liubertsy (cf. Cohen 1972). Young people from other areas also began to descend on Moscow to assault Moscow youth. The liubery subculture quickly extended to other peripheral Moscow areas (Kapotnia, Perovo, Tekstil'shchiki) and beyond. By the end of 1987, groups of people who identified themselves as liubery had appeared in various regions of the Soviet Union (Belanovsky 1990).

Toward the end of the 1980s, however, the liubery subculture was already in decline. Having initially looked on liubery favorably, the police started to persecute them as the authorities realized that these youth groups were hard to control. Even those liubery who sincerely believed that they were defending Soviet values soon turned away from politics. As perestroika progressed, the Soviet ideology rapidly disintegrated. The violence of the liubery found new application in the criminal economy that emerged around the new cooperatives and private enterprises. After 1988 there was a massive mobilization of liubery into racketeers, as their attention switched from the *neformaly* to members of the emerging cooperative and, later, private businesses (discussed in chapter 2).

Explaining the Transformation of Soviet Youth Street Organizations

The emergence of organized violent youth groups caught Soviet police criminologists by surprise. For many years, young people involved in street violence were seen as hooligans and petty criminals. The small amount of research on problem youth focused mainly on children in children's homes and special schools for young delinquents. Some publications touched on flawed socialization as a cause of delinquency, in particular the upbringing of children by single mothers or alcoholics. Delinquent behavior was either linked to individual psychopathology or to a specific stage in an adolescent's life when he is particularly vulnerable to harmful influences. Group violence and crime were rarely discussed, and Soviet experts were mostly preoccupied with finding ways in which various official organizations (Komsomol, schools, local authorities, etc.) could "improve" their work with young people (Connor 1972; Pilkington 1994; Stephenson 2001; LaPierre 2012).

At the same time, recorded youth crime rose sharply in the first half of the 1970s and continued to rise during the 1980s. This was not a matter of great concern for the authorities (McAuley 2009). But organized crime and violence were a different matter. After years of authorities trying to suppress any information about violent youth groups, after the trial of Tiap-Liap the genie was out of the bottle. The problem of "new forms of juvenile crime" such as racketeering, generation of "nonlabor income" through *fartsovka* and other black market trading, and the emergence of inter-regional criminal networks became a matter of public discussion. The explanations given by Soviet authors were still familiar ones: the absence of youth clubs and other youth facilities, weak control by the Komsomol, schools, and local authorities, and a general weakening of socialist morality among the young (Baal′ 1990; Ovchinskii 1990).

Some authors, though, pointed out the sense of relative deprivation experienced by young working-class people as the cause of gang affiliation. Criminologist Gennadii Zabrianskii explained that youths were not satisfied with their factory jobs and had a sense of being deprived of the opportunities enjoyed by their more educated peers (Zabrianskii 1990). Subsequent literature also pointed to the erosion of a sense of collective Soviet identity that had been forged through mobilization during the war and postwar reconstruction, which contributed to the demoralization of sections of working-class youth (Safarov 2012, 16). For large numbers of working-class boys and teenagers there was a withering of the dream of participating in the Soviet advances in science and technology that had been powerfully symbolized, for example, by Yuri Gagarin's flight into space. Mass participation in the after-school classes offered by schools and Young Pioneer houses, where children could learn, for example, airplane modeling or the history of space expeditions, was becoming disconnected from the actual prospects of working-class youth destined for the drudgery of factory work (Belanovsky 2009).

Indeed, the 1970s and 1980s was a period of growing social differentiation in the Soviet Union (Lane 1985).[6] Upward social mobility began to stall in the 1970s with the growing stagnation in the economy and a tightening grip by the party elite and well-positioned members of the intelligentsia on access to the best universities and jobs for their offspring. Research conducted among the cohort of young

6. Already in the 1960s, according to research by Shubkin (1965), there was a visible difference between the educational and professional aspirations of children of white-collar workers and manual workers.

people who started their working life in the 1980s similarly showed that rates of social mobility declined in comparison with previous generations (Filippov 1989).

For young people from less-educated backgrounds, a sense of being deprived of the chances available to their more privileged peers was exacerbated by a reduction in available opportunities to progress to university education. Facing a shortage of manual workers in inefficient labor-intensive industrial enterprises, the Soviet authorities wanted to strengthen vocational education and direct more people into factories rather than universities (Yagodkin 1981). Evidence from 1970s research suggests that in large industrial towns, recruits to vocational schools started to come almost exclusively from working-class families, with teachers encouraging students to go to trade schools rather than into higher education (Lane 1985, chap. 8). The 1977 Resolution of the CPSU Central Committee and the Council of Ministers of the USSR "On the further improvement of education, upbringing of the students of general secondary education and their preparation for labor" announced a policy of deliberate reduction of educational mobility. Schools significantly limited the numbers of students who could progress to the two final years, and underachievers were set on a path to vocational colleges. Many vocational colleges soon turned into "sin bins." In the 1980s, every year saw between 1.2 and 1.5 million juveniles passing through penitentiaries and corrective institutions (Ermakov 1990), and their transition to working life would commonly be through vocational schools or apprenticeships. In PTUs, young working-class school leavers encountered peers who had already spent time in special schools for juvenile delinquents or special penitentiaries; students who had received suspended criminal sentences; and students who had been expelled. According to Ermakov, these categories formed up to 20 to 40 percent of the students in PTUs and teenage apprentices in industrial enterprises. He observed that the period from 1985 to 1990 saw a significant increase in "asocial" groups formed by students from PTUs and working-class youth. As opportunities to better themselves seemed to diminish, the attraction and influence of criminal culture—always, as I will discuss in chapter 9, within reach in the Soviet high-incarceration society—became stronger.

At the same time, as we have seen, the growth of the Soviet shadow economy created new economic opportunities for street groups to exploit, and they appeared to offer status and prosperity (however illusory) that was otherwise denied to working-class young people in the wider society. While many traditional street peer collectives were still involved in group fights and petty delinquency, some now moved into extortion and rackets. All of this happened well before the collapse of the Soviet system and before the emergence of the cooperatives and private businesses that were to become the feeding grounds for post-Soviet organized crime.

Facing the Future

Youth street cultures and violent street organizations do not exist in isolation from wider local and national processes and conditions. From the masculinist imperatives produced by village and working-class cultures to the need to respond to social dislocation resulting from rapid urbanization or growing social differentiation, young people were affected by a variety of pressures. In the Soviet Union significant changes in the collective behavior of violent street groups emerged in response to high-speed industrialization, the emergence of a vast shadow market alongside the Soviet planned economy that offered young people opportunities other than the toil of factory work, and the increasing disaffection of working-class youth with the prospects the Soviet system had to offer.

As the Soviet Union was nearing its end, the troops that would march into the capitalist future, under new banners but retaining their fighting spirit, their organization, and their commitment to one another and their group "cause," were already in place. They were recruited, trained, battle tested, armed, and ready, and, together with fighters mobilized from other walks of life, these heroes of street warfare became bandits in post-Soviet organized criminal groups.

2

THE TRANSFORMATION OF GANGS IN THE 1990S

The 1990s witnessed the dissolution of the Soviet Union and the beginning of Russia's painful transition to market capitalism. This decade is commonly seen as a period of profound social crisis (Shevchenko 2009, 152–54). During these years the word *bespredel* (lawlessness), which originated in Soviet prison culture, entered common parlance to indicate the absence of any moral or legal order. People were at a loss as to how to navigate their way through a world whose normative map was torn apart and in which predators who had previously lurked at the margins now moved to center stage. Shady entrepreneurs, criminal groups, and youth gangs seemed to reflect a slide into the rule of unbridled greed and violence.

Academic commentators on the region often invoke the Durkheimian or Mertonian concept of anomie (normlessness) or the Hobbesian war of all against all when talking about the collapse of the previous social order and the profound disorientation of post-Communist citizens during the chaos of transition (Williams, Chuprov, and Zubok 2003; Kara-Murza 2013). But chaos does not mean the total collapse of social order. Nor does it entail people having to sink or swim on their own, as all structures of cooperation and trust are destroyed. As Dennis Wrong (1994, 243) argued:

> Societies never fell apart to the extent of literally lapsing into a war of all against all. Nation states may fragment dividing into two warring camps . . . or into several hostile groups controlling different localities.

> . . . But underneath these processes social order survives at least at a micro-sociological level—the level of families, small groups, and networks of interacting individuals cooperating in the pursuit of common goals.

As the country descended into seeming chaos, new pockets of order were created, and groups emerged to take advantage of the opportunities presented by market changes. The crisis of the Soviet megasystem gave rise to a myriad of small "systems," informal groups and networks in which people tried to find protection and build alternative careers. Some of these groups and networks managed to exploit the new reality to elevate themselves above the struggling post-Soviet citizenry. Networks organized by former members of the Communist Party, Komsomol, and Soviet local and regional authorities mobilized to capture economic opportunities during the privatization drive (Ledeneva 1998, 90; Humphrey 2002; Nazpary 2002). Criminal entrepreneurs also moved in to claim their slice of the pie in the deregulated and unprotected business sphere. A different configuration of order was rapidly emerging.

For those people now disconnected from the decaying carcass of the Soviet system of employment and welfare, the imperative was to join a structure of relations where one could find protection and economic opportunities. Anomie was not in evidence. Instead, Russian society showed a remarkable capacity for self-organization with a wide restructuring of social fields, a search for new allegiances and new courses of social action, and attempts to find coherence in life. For some young people, the street and its organizations became a place where new pockets of order could be constructed and larger ambitious projects could be launched.

The Growth of Violent Social Organizations

The decomposition of the key institutions of the Soviet state—the command economy, the state and legal apparatus, and the enterprise-based social welfare system—was accompanied by a violent redivision of assets and resources. As the Soviet Union imploded, state companies, now being privatized, began to operate in an unfamiliar market environment. Ordinary business functions such as raising capital, ensuring supplies, and making customers pay for goods and services could be extremely difficult to carry out and fraught with danger. Not only was the country in the grip of an economic crisis but the state legal apparatus was inefficient, and a functioning banking system was years away. In this chaotic environment both public and private companies became besieged by predators who were keen to access their assets and who used threats, bribes, and offers of "protection" to lay their hands on a company's money, products, and shares.

In Tatarstan, despite the economic crisis, many attractive assets remained. Although by the mid-1990s industrial output in the republic had decreased by 33.9 percent compared to the beginning of the decade, the economic crisis of the first half of the 1990s was less severe than in most Russian regions (Bushuev 2009, 27). Under Tatarstan's powerful president Mintimir Shaimiev, whose rule over the region began in the late Soviet period and ended in 2010, Tatarstan remained one of the few "donor" regions of the Russian Federation. Most major enterprises in the chemical, petrol, weapons-production, and food industries in Kazan still functioned, as did the big automobile factory KAMAZ in nearby Naberezhnye Chelny. The existence of a large economic base inherited from the Soviet times, together with the historical presence of gangs, helps to explain the particularly rapid development of organized crime in Tatarstan in the 1990s. Many of the major Soviet companies such as the packaging company Tatpak, Tasma (a producer of film and photographic materials), the Orgsintez chemical plant, the KAMAZ factory, the Kazan helicopter company, food processing and agricultural companies, as well as new private banks, hotels, and communication companies came under attack by predatory groups.

These newly privatizing companies were exposed to extortion from vory, bandit gangs, or indeed the state security services and police, which emerged as one of the key racketeering groups in post-Soviet Russia (Volkov 2002; Favarel-Garrigues and Le Huérou 2004; Gerber and Mendelson 2008; Taylor 2011). For example, talking about a large chemical plant in Kazan, M., a long-serving representative of the investigative department of one of Kazan's police districts, recounted that "at the time, Orgsintez fed so many lads from Zhilka [a local gang]. And so many cops fed off it!"

Alongside the ailing ex-Soviet companies there emerged a vast street-level economy and nascent small businesses. The private economic sphere was initially launched during perestroika when Gorbachev's 1987 Law on Cooperation allowed groups of citizens to establish cooperative businesses. These businesses immediately became targets for racketeers. The first case of racketeering in Kazan was registered in 1988, when the street group Dom Obuvi (literally "House of Shoes," a shoe store) attempted to extort protection money from a builders' cooperative (Safarov 2012, 46).

Although, in the beginning of the 1990s, most cooperatives disappeared under the pressures of state taxation and competition from new private companies, new small businesses soon began to emerge, mainly in the unregulated informal and semiformal service sector: outdoor markets, small stalls and kiosks, small currency-exchange businesses, and the like. With hardly any protection from the state, and lacking the means to protect itself, the sector was easy prey for a variety of predators. All over Russia, street neighborhood groups were at the forefront of the new processes of accumulation, although the specific dynamics of relationships between street groups and other violent actors still await investigation. We can say with certainty that in Kazan (and Tatarstan in general) the majority of organized crime groups rose out of street social organizations. Nafikov's (2012) study of the criminal cases of twenty-three organized criminal communities (OPS) active in Tatarstan between 1990 and 2012 showed that the vast majority of these organizations started out as youth territorial groups of "hooligans" with their own obshchaki. Contributions to these funds were systematically collected through extortion and other criminal means. Thirteen such groups started their criminal activities with the control of street markets, expanding later to exercise control over medium and large businesses (72–74, 334–55). In Kazan, according to Nafikov, at least 60 percent of all OPS, excluding specialized gangs such as drug gangs, emerged out of territorial youth groups. Currently all such communities have youth gangs as part of their structure (150–51). Many members of the youth street gangs of the 1980s graduated to positions of bandit avtoritety. Safarov, who worked as a criminal investigator—mainly on juvenile cases involving hooliganism—in one of Kazan's districts in 1984–87, noted in his 2012 book that "through my office . . . passed many of the future leaders of OPG [organized criminal groups, *organizivannaia prestupnaia gruppa*]" (17).

Some Kazan gangs, such as Zhilka and Boriskovo, also had vory v zakone at their helm, and some of the gang leaders—for example, in Tiap-Liap and Khadi Taktash—were men who had had experience of incarceration but were not themselves vory v zakone. But, unlike other areas of Russia (such as the Far East), the role of vory in Tatarstan gruppirovki was not substantial. In the late 1990s in Tatarstan there were only three "crowned" vory v zakone (the elite of the vor community). The last crowned vor died in 2002 (Sheptitskii 2009).

A new nomenclature was also emerging. Those groups encountered in the late Soviet period in the form of *kontory*, *firmy*, and *motalki* were now called "streets" (*ulitsy*—the smallest gang units, operating literally at the level of a street) and *gruppirovki* (groupings—larger criminal communities, often uniting several "streets" and expanding beyond the territorial level). The commonly employed generic, and indeed legal, term used to describe organized criminal groups is OPG (*organizivannaia prestupnaia gruppa*), which has also become a common self-identification for gang members. A larger criminal alliance is known as an OPS (*organizivannoe prestupnoe soobshchestvo*). Starting in the mid-1980s, the younger members of these groups came to be known as lads (*patsany*). They referred to themselves as *konkretnye* (solid), *pravilnye* (proper), or *realnye* (real) lads. Meanwhile, young male members of noncriminal place-based groups (courtyard peer groups or territorial fighting elites) by contrast called themselves *normalnye* (normal), *obychnye* (ordinary), or *mestnye* (local) lads.[1] To the outside world, however, both kinds were known pejoratively as *gopniki.* Older men (those around twenty-eight to thirty and older) who remained active gang members became known as *bandity* (bandits), although they too were also sometimes referred to collectively as "the lads."

Young People: From Displacement to Re-Placement

The massive movement of young men into racketeering in the late 1980s and early 1990s needs to be seen in the context of the wider processes of displacement suffered by Russian citizens as a result of the collapse of the Soviet social structure. Re-placement in the social structure and the re-creation of support systems became the order of the day for the whole population. In the process of rapid social change, millions of people were cast adrift from the stabilizing social structures of old. As the Soviet state disintegrated and radical market reforms destroyed millions of livelihoods while simultaneously undermining the collectivistic institutions of social protection, Russian society went though some of the most drastic poverty and welfare reversals in the world (UNDP 1998). GDP fell by over 40 percent, and industrial production more than halved in the five years of radical reform (Clarke 1999). Rapid inflation consumed people's life savings. As state companies made their workforces redundant, or kept them on the books while not paying wages for months on end, millions of people were plunged into poverty. Masses of the dispossessed clung on desperately to their employers in the hope that the economy would pick up. They also took on second jobs, developed various forms of self-employment, and cultivated their allotments for subsistence farming (Clarke 2002). In order to survive, people also developed reciprocal strategies of exchange with members of their social networks, neighbors, friends, and family, with personal relationships becoming a form of social security (Caldwell 2004, 6).

For people who became displaced from previously stable social affiliations, the imperative to find new connections and protective structures that could provide material opportunities was paramount. Even the most vulnerable people, such as child runaways, economic migrants and refugees, and adult homeless

---

1. But the distinctions are never clear, and members of criminal youth groups may also call themselves "normal lads" (Kosterina 2008). I do not identify *patsany* as members of a distinctive subculture. They lack pronounced class affiliations and share many of their practices with wider youth culture. As I explain in chapter 9, their beliefs and practices are also influenced by the criminal culture.

people, tried to find entry into informal systems of protection and subsistence to re-place themselves in society (Stephenson 2006; 2008). In the absence of any organized state support, and with an undeveloped civil society, finding protection and developing exchange through social networks became the main survival strategy of people at the margins.

My research in Moscow in the 1990s on the social strategies of runaway youth and homeless children showed that many young people tried to survive by joining social networks organized around various youth subcultures. At the beginning of the 1990s, youth subcultural groups including hippies, rockers, punks, bikers, Tolkienists (fans of the novels of J. R. R. Tolkien), and others—many of which had existed since the 1970s—turned from being vehicles for cultural expression into sources of material support that sometimes provided vitally important housing to child runaways and other young people who fell into dire straits (Stephenson 2001). Young migrants from other areas of Russia and the former Soviet Union tried to befriend the members of Moscow alternative subcultural networks, who, they hoped, could help them with food, work, and shelter. Some young people, escaping from domestic violence or traveling to Moscow in search of a better life, had little option but to join organized prostitution networks. In their accounts, they said these networks gave them some protection from violent predators and enabled them to avoid living on the streets. In one of my interviews with young sex workers in Moscow in 1997, seventeen-year-old Olesia described her reasons for deciding to join organized prostitution, "There is such a bespredel in life now. I do not know how some people survive in such a system. This is terribly depressing for a human being. Now all the professors who finished colleges, they are all trading in the market or work in business. Nobody pays wages anymore. And where would I live? Who would feed me?"

Olesia left home as her parental family disintegrated under the pressure of poverty with her parents, formerly respectable and relatively well-off skilled blue-collar workers, trying to coerce her into selling herself. She escaped onto the streets and ultimately ended up in organized prostitution. As another girl, Elena, explained, "We have our own system, similar, for example, to a system in prison or a system at the market, where there is a boss who comes and collects money. The same system exists here, you are protected for nobody to bother you, for you to stand quietly and work." These "systems," either created by young people themselves or provided by adults who exploited them, seemed preferable to the dangerous life outside any social structures (Sidorenko-Stephenson 2000, 121).

Some of the homeless young men I interviewed on the streets of Moscow dreamed of becoming vory or bandits. They were hoping to leave the world of the streets and join the support structures of the criminal community, which they thought would give them stability, protection, and income. Although this was very difficult for them as, living on the streets, they were not part of any recognized criminal networks, they made active attempts to achieve connections by sending food, cigarettes, or money to the inmates of prison colonies, by trying to get in touch with criminals in bars and cafes that they were known to frequent, and by building a "name," a criminal reputation for themselves (Stephenson 2008).

Although more research is needed here, there seems to be a gender element in people's forced choices at this time of mass dispossession. Nazpary (2002) documented how in Kazakhstan in the 1990s young women from poorer backgrounds found themselves vulnerable to sexual exploitation by their employers. Some of the women he interviewed had to exchange sexual services to find "sponsors." Getting a job in a private company could also depend on a woman's readiness to provide sex to the boss. At the same time, many young men faced the choice of becoming either victims or predators in violent street battles for respect and resources.

Vulnerability and displacement did not just affect homeless street children and young people from troubled families. Many "mainstream" young people faced a frightening world in which previous certainties had to be abandoned and the older generation was suddenly bankrupt. Their parents, who for the most part had held stable jobs in Soviet factories and state organizations, jobs that paid at least a living wage, were suddenly scraping for money to buy food or pay for housing and utilities. Decades of honest labor had led them nowhere, and the prospect of joining the struggling industrial companies or public sector institutions did not seem attractive to their offspring. At the same time, for those young people who were willing to take risks, there were new possibilities, new roads opening up amid the detritus of the Soviet system. What was necessary was to find a network, a group, a clan and try to navigate this new reality together and take advantage of the opportunities it offered.

Territorial groups and gangs were easily available structures with which many young people already had connections via neighborhood social networks. Street organizations were culturally familiar and accessible societies through which one could get money and find protection and companionship. They could also serve as platforms from which young men could collectively launch their quest for social and economic advancement in a society where everything seemed up for grabs. For young men who had nothing but wanted everything, the gang represented a community that they hoped would allow them to survive and "rise together" (*podniatsia vmeste*) in the dangerous and exciting world emerging from the ruins of state socialism.

Kazan Gangs in the 1990s: "With Whom to Be in Life?"

While some young men actively sought gang membership, others were pushed into it. The specter of bespredel, of a Hobbesian war of all against all, haunted Russian society. The streets became extremely dangerous, and young people were the prime victims—as well as perpetrators—of crime. Between 1985 and 1999 the rate of crimes committed by sixteen- to twenty-nine-year-olds in Tatarstan increased 1.7 times (Bushuev 2009, 41). Struggles for domination of public space, where success in appropriation of resources was often predicated on one's aptitude and skills in violence, forced many young men unaffiliated with gangs to reconsider their options in the face of increasing insecurity. Interviews with Kazan men who joined gangs at the beginning of the 1990s reveal the sense of an urgent need to join a group that would protect them from violence. Aidar, who eventually became one of the gang avtoritety, recounted the dangerous nature of the streets at the time when he was just finishing school. Prior to joining the gang he had limited experience of street life. Except for school breaks, he did not spend time on the street. Most of his time was taken up by education and various extracurricular activities, including sports.

> I came across the lads in 1990. Life then was very troubled. There were many fights in the streets. There were lots of hooligans and criminals around and, as they were then called, *gopniki.* In those days, just going to the store was pretty dangerous, because you could be severely beaten for the sake of a couple of rubles. The same situation existed in school. Therefore, there was a very serious question, with whom to be in life, and a lot of guys decided in favor of the lads. Most of my friends joined this or that street, and I did not want to be on my own and have no support.

Unable to find income elsewhere, many young people turned to the streets in hopes of making some subsistence money. M., who worked at the time as a police investigator in Kazan, recalled that "gruppirovki were created on the basis of economic interest. No one initially aimed to go out and smash people's faces. But the point was—where to get money for a living?"

Many gang members started from a very low economic base and then discovered that they could make serious money. M. explained:

> The lads wanted to have good clothes and shoes, to have money to take their girlfriends out. If they got an old car for five people to share, money was still needed for gas. They started making money and could buy a new car for their group. And now look how many houses they

> have built. For example, in Mirnyi village—on the right side, these are all gang members' cottages.

While some lads simply wanted to earn a bit of money to stay afloat, others aspired to become seriously rich and join the new moneyed class. At the time, people not much older than themselves were making their first steps toward becoming oligarchs. The lads did not want to be left behind. Forgotten now was the idea of "social justice" that had animated Kazan's Tiap-Liap in their assaults on Soviet restaurant managers or underground jewelers, or the *liubery* groups in their fights against better-off Moscow youths who could afford a pair of western jeans or a tape recorder. The cultural ideology of acquisitive individualism began to penetrate the streets along with the rest of Russian society.

This radical change in orientation can be compared to those in other countries undergoing neoliberal reforms. For example, writing about sub-Saharan Africa in the 1980s and 1990s, Bayart, Ellis, and Hibou (1999) noted that as members of state and business networks were becoming immensely rich on corrupt privatization of state assets and export of the country's natural resources, the ideological orientation of the young also changed. Material success began to be seen as the measure of all things, and following the general mood, young delinquents in these societies started to see their own criminal behavior as legitimate entrepreneurialism. A similar change of orientation among the young members of neighborhood networks took place in Nicaragua (Rodgers 2009).

The lads wanted to have spectacular success, to drive Mercedes and BMW cars, buy themselves big houses and possess the same status symbols (gold chains, colorful blazers, expensive shoes) that at the time were the basic requisites of a "New Russian". Moreover, they had the necessary resources to enable them to make money. These included social organization in the form of the street network or group, with its personal loyalties; the capacity to mobilize every member for the group's "cause"; and the group's collective mastery of violence, acquired in street battles and supported by centuries of cultural traditions. They also had deep links to the local territory, which many of them already "protected" from "intruders" by violent means, and which now became an arena for economic accumulation. Vigorous individualism combined with a strong solidaristic spirit created a powerful engine for the rise of the entrepreneurial gang that claimed territorial dominance.

Although many new groups emerged at the time, the informal social structure of relationships grounded in territorial networks was already in place, as was a presumption of the right to the territory. As M. put it:

> The principle of territorial division into neighborhoods, streets, and courtyards provokes the division into neighborhood groups, because

> they have all known one another for several years. They gather together. Somebody may have come out of prison, and they start to look around: "Here a cafe has opened in our territory, and what do we have from it? Nothing! Come on, let's sort this out." They go and extort money from the owner. Then they begin to monitor his affairs, forcing him to share his profits.

Existing territorial practices and the haughty "lordship" stance adopted by street lads who presumed a right to control the street space became the basis for their claims to economic appropriation.

Claiming the Turf

In the late 1980s and the early 1990s, young people embarked collectively on new projects of economic accumulation. For many groups of young people previously uninvolved in entrepreneurial violence, territorial control now meant not just enjoying safe passage along the streets of one's neighborhood or undisputed access to local dance halls and cinemas but having opportunities to make money.

As B., who at the time of our interview was an investigator with the Tatarstan Republican Prosecution Service (Prokuratura), said:

> Gruppirovki . . . began to emerge long ago, with Tiap-Liap in the 1970s. It used to be simple: a youth group from a courtyard goes to a disco and comes across another youth company. Words are exchanged, a fight starts, someone is beaten, then they come back to take revenge. The main cause of the gruppirovki then was the struggle for leadership among the youth; it was not connected with money. The emergence of big money in our country and the beginning of market reforms provided the impetus for the transformation of the youth street groups into groups that were engaged in all sorts of illegal activities to earn money.

What was important was to lay claim to turf. As Tadjik said, describing his gang's history, "our history is the same as anyone else's. There was a group of lads who were close friends. Other lads assembled around them. They sorted out the territorial borders and began to make money."

The main Kazan gruppirovki—Kvartala, Mirnyi, Shatura, 56th Kvartal, Sotsgorod, Telestudiia, Khadi Taktash, Zhilka, Nizy, Boriskovo, Pervaki, Tukaevo—sought to divide the city among them. In order to retain and expand their control over territory, they needed to mobilize significant forces. They put serious pressure on local young people to join their gangs. Although there were no physical tests for admission to the gang, the gangs particularly valued people involved in athletics because of their physical strength and self-discipline. Twenty-nine-year-old David, who was working as a pediatrician at the time of the interview, told us how he was forced to join a gang against his will:

> At that time, when I was pulled into the group, it was in the early '90s, and I just did not have time to spend on the street. Education and sports left little time. In the days when I joined, they usually recruited those people who lived in that street. Without false modesty I can say that I'm not stupid, and I'm physically strong, a former athlete. They invited me to join. I refused. I was warned that if I didn't change my mind, I'd be beaten up every day until I agreed. So it was like that—every day they waited for me near the entrance to my apartment block, and I had to fight. Finally my father got fed up with seeing his son with a battered face every day, and he turned to his friends from another street. They came round to our apartment and said to me, "If you want to live peacefully, join us; there is no other way for you." I had to follow their advice.

Thirty-five-year-old Il'nar also said of the same period: "It used to be like this here: you are either a member of a gang or you are constantly being chased, being harassed. . . . That is why there wasn't much choice."

As gangs were looking for new members to build their membership, they readily accepted people who lived beyond the neighborhood. For example, the Pervaki gang—whose operations were previously limited to the Pervaia Gorka area—began to recruit young people from all over Kazan for its burgeoning racketeering business. There are parallels here with some US entrepreneurial gangs (Sánchez-Jankowski 1991). Being territorial does not necessarily mean being confined to predefined boundaries in operations and membership.

Old groups were becoming larger, while new ones emerged alongside them. A major gang presence became a feature not just of Kazan but of most of Tatarstan, particularly in the industrial city of Naberezhnye Chelny and in small towns and rural settlements such as Nizhnekamsk, Vysokaia Gora, Buinsk, Zelenodol'sk, Kukmor, Nurlat, and Pestretsy among others.

The Changing Social Composition of the Gangs

The gangs expanded both in size and composition. Similarly to gangs in other areas of the world, late-Soviet violent street organizations were predominantly a working-class and urban phenomenon, although territorial elites involved in arranged fights with outsiders also existed in rural and suburban areas. While evidence of the social background of *gruppirovshchiki* (gang members) is patchy, the common opinion among police experts, academics, and local residents is that, prior to the 1990s, these groups were mostly made up of working-class lads living in peripheral, relatively poor areas and studying in vocational schools and colleges. According to Gataullin and Maksudov (2002), for example, at the end of the 1980s, Kazan gang membership was skewed toward working-class young people.

In the 1990s this began to change. Entrepreneurial gangs appeared in rural areas, where bands of local youths, often under the guidance of ex-prisoners, began to establish protection rackets covering local shops and kiosks, small businesses, and farms. And, with the massive collapse of livelihoods, these gangs began to draw their members from a wider range of social backgrounds, including young people from educated families. The sons of industrial workers were running around setting up protection rackets together with the sons of policemen, doctors, and engineers. Professional work was no longer protection against dispossession. Many older gang members in our interviews recalled how their parents (local council workers, engineers, and doctors, as well as industrial workers) either lost their jobs or struggled financially in the 1990s. The gangs also began to attract university students. In a 1995 survey, 7 percent of Tatarstan university students admitted that they were gang members, and a further 6 percent said that they were under pressure to join (Bushuev 2009, 44).

According to Kazan criminal investigator B.:

> In the past, up until about the end of the 1980s, the groups mostly consisted of street hooligans. Then representatives of different sections of the population began to join them. The reason for this was that, due to changes in the social and political life, no one was now immune from criminal assault; no one could guarantee their safety. In addition, there were economic interests. Therefore, new people got involved in these groups because they needed protection and needed to acquire financial means. An OPG provided all that, so there was a constant replenishment of its members.

Street gangs remained a youth phenomenon, but their membership was becoming older. As the limited quantitative data available suggest, toward the middle of the 1990s, a significant proportion of members were over twenty-five, and many were in legitimate employment. For example, in Naberezhnye Chelny in 1994, according to data cited by Nafikov, young people under twenty-five made up 76 percent of the membership of gruppirovki registered by the police. People between twenty-five and thirty made up 20 percent, with 4 percent over thirty. There were relatively high levels of employment among these registered gang members—70 percent were employed in private companies while 30 percent did not work. A substantial minority (30%) had criminal records. While 40 percent had not completed secondary education, 40 percent had, and 5 percent had gone on to complete higher education, with the remaining 15 percent having secondary vocational and incomplete secondary education. Nafikov (2012, 145–46) noted that many of the leaders and members of these groups were owners or managers of various commercial companies.

The ethnic backgrounds of gang members tended to be representative of the local population, although gangs formed by communities of migrants (Georgians, Azerbaijani, Chechens, Dagestani) also appeared across Russia. The Tatarstan gangs were ethnically mixed, uniting Russians and Tatars and any other ethnicities living in their neighborhoods. The multiethnic character of many organized crime groups in Russia has also been noted by Galeotti (2012), who described these associations as highly pragmatic, accepting people of all ethnicities into their ranks as long as they can make money for themselves and the gang.

The Rise in Violence

In the Wild West period of Russian capitalist development, with businessmen and companies powerless to withstand violent assaults and the police ineffective and corrupt, the first priority for the gangs was to capture territory and lay claim to its businesses. They then needed to delineate the borders of their influence, become recognized as a credible force, and establish internal cohesion and discipline. This was the case in Tatarstan and, as Volkov (2002) explains, also elsewhere in Russia. This was expressed very well by one of our interviewees, David, when he was asked what it takes to become a successful "street" (territorial gang): "A street should have several characteristics. It must have its own territory, have recognition, and live according to the code."

As the gangs tried to divide up the territory, they unleashed serious violence. This period of hyperviolence was often described by our Kazan interviewees as a time of bespredel. Wars between gangs for territory (so-called wars over asphalt) and violent intimidation of businessmen created a situation that everybody—local residents, the police, and the gang members themselves—recalled with horror. The whole city became a war zone. Street groups already located in a variety of city areas either had to assert their control over territory and try to expand outward or risk being swept aside. Brute force reigned supreme. Young men would arrive by public transport at the location of the next battle and assault anybody they believed to be a local gang member. In the years from 1986 to 1997 (the period of territorial appropriation by gangs), official data alone list fifty-one mass battles in Kazan, in which a total of nine hundred people took part (Safarov 2012, 18). This probably represents just the tip of the iceberg of the violence.

According to N., head of investigations at one of the Kazan district police precincts:

> During the bespredel organized by the OPGs, when everybody had to pay tribute, they recruited a lot of people who wanted to get rich quick without working, simply as a result of their membership in criminal organizations. At that time, organized crime groups actively fleeced different cooperatives and companies, which never contacted the police as they themselves did not always earn their money by legal means. Everybody paid somebody. These were very wild times. Almost all businesses were under protection rackets.

Il'nar described the period of struggles over territory in the late 1980s and early 1990s: "The fights were very dangerous. People were using metal rods to beat each other to death and using bricks to finish their enemies off. The score was not so much how many lads were beaten up on each side but how many were killed."

Firearms also appeared on the scene. For example, in a conflict between Pervaki and Khadi Taktash for control of the Privolzhskii street market, the gangs organized a *razborka* (arranged combat, a showdown) on the territory of the market with the use of machine guns. According to M., this *razborka* may have been provoked by the police, who wanted to weaken the two groups. Both suffered losses, but Pervaki, which by then had become the most powerful city gang after Tiap-Liap, was particularly seriously damaged.

When the borders between territories had not yet been drawn, several gangs could lay claim to the same business, which they thought belonged to their fiefdom. This often led to gang wars and to multiple victimization of businessmen. Local companies became arenas for battle between the warring gangs. Twenty-five-year-old Kirill recounted:

> Our senior members told us that back then there weren't just fights but also attacks on firms that were under the protection of enemy streets. For example, during the war with our neighbors, our gang organized an attack on their firms. Our lads came and broke into the building and began to beat up everybody inside, trashing equipment and computers. They assaulted one of the lads from that street who was in the office. Then they went to another firm and started doing the same there. On the same day, they went to four companies and raided all of them, ruining the credibility of our neighbors and showing that they couldn't provide a *krysha* [a roof—i.e., protection].

The gangs forced market traders, kiosk owners, and directors of newly privatized Soviet companies to pay them on the spot, without any guarantees that the next violent predators would not rob them as well. Businessmen who did not want to pay protection money were subjected to extreme violence. They were locked in cellars, tortured with soldering irons, handcuffed to radiators, or taken to forests and threatened with immediate death—sometimes being forced to dig their own graves—until they agreed to pay. Many were killed, either during attacks that went too far or as a warning to others. Intimidation of businessmen was seen as one of the key duties of the younger gang members, and some of our interviewees recalled how, after being forced to join the gang, they were then made to take part in the torture and even killing of disobedient businessmen.

By the middle of the 1990s, the Tatarstan gangs had established their fiefdoms, and large-scale intergang violence eventually began to subside, although conflicts continued to flare up from time to time.[2] Most disagreements between gangs were now settled at *strelki* (meetings to resolve conflicts). By the middle of the 1990s, the gangs' violent business had also become more ordered. While previously several gangs might have attempted to extort money from one local kiosk or market stall, now everyone knew their krysha. Having divided up their spheres of influence, the gangs became interested in ensuring the stability of their business. An idealistic understanding of the new order, unthreatened by new contenders, was expressed by David:

> Practically all the streets emerged in the same period, and consequently they have their own status and recognition at the city level. The whole city is divided into territories that belong to particular streets, and new ones can only emerge in new areas. Just imagine—a gang of young lads emerge and claim that they are also a street and that this territory belongs to them. Nobody would even talk to them. Because nobody knows them and nobody needs them—which means that they would simply be chased away.

Talking about the main events in his gang's history, Trofim spoke of "a gradual rejection of wars with the neighbors and a move toward a peaceful life, which started several years ago, when the lads were told at the *skhodniak* [general meeting] to stop provoking conflicts with neighboring streets." Whether such a key meeting actually happened or is merely part of gang mythology, it is clear that

2. In 2000, for example, one big *razborka* between Zhilka and Tatarskii Dvor lasted for two days. In the process, forty Zhilka members attacked a vehicle carrying the workers of the local Tatenergoremont company by mistake, thinking it belonged to their enemies. Many employees were burned and wounded (Safarov 2012, 83).

toward the end of the 1990s the street politics had changed. According to the Kazan gang folklore, in the mid-1990s the gangs came to a collective agreement known as "We won't divide up the asphalt" (i.e., we will no longer fight over territory) (Salagaev 2005). Mass fights between different gangs became much less frequent (Safarov 2012, 62).The gangs developed their own "patches," territorial areas and business spheres from which they drew more or less stable profits. The gangs acquired their own *tochki* (individual businesses) and their own *kommersy* (businessmen) who paid them "protection" money on a regular basis.

Similarly, across Russia, by the middle of the 1990s, the structures of organized crime became more institutionalized and, despite ongoing conflict and killings of rival avtoritety, the number of groups and their membership tended to stabilize (Volkov 2002; Dolgova 2003, 348). As Dolgova noted, in the middle of the 1990s, the processes of confrontation between various criminal organizations started to give way to consolidation and the building of alliances (346). The gangs now formed what I call "autonomous ruling regimes." They put other users of the street space, predominantly *kommersy* and *barygi* (businessmen and traders); the owners of local kiosks, market stalls, and small parking lots; street sex workers; and also some nongang young people into a variety of situations of dependency. Their leaders moved to control medium-sized and large businesses. As I describe in chapter 3—and in the brief histories of three of Tatarstan's most famous gangs (Zhilka, Khadi Taktash, and 29th Kompleks) in the appendix—in the 1990s and early 2000s Tatarstan gruppirovki developed from their rather modest street origins into large criminal empires. Like the Italian Mafia, these gruppirovki became power institutions that taxed the productive activities within their areas and conducted generalized extortion (Volkov 2002; Paoli 2004, 274).

Gang Alliances outside the Territory

From the beginning of the 1990s, the Tatarstan gangs started to expand into other areas. They formed alliances with other gruppirovki and attempted to move from periodic raids to establishing extortion and protection operations further afield, reaching as far as Moscow and Saint Petersburg. One such gang alliance, known as Sevastopol'skie, was formed in Moscow. It included bandits from several Tatarstan gangs (Nizy, Griaz', 56th Kvartal, Brigada Ilfateia, Chainiki, 29th Kompleks, Banda Tagirianova, and others). Another alliance of gangs from Kazan, formed around the Zhilka group, operated in Saint Petersburg. These and other such alliances outside Tatarstan were often seen by local residents and criminal groups as part of one gang, which they referred to as Kazanskie (Those from Kazan) or Tatary (Tatars), but it is important to note that the members of these gangs and alliances did not see themselves in this way and still identified with their original gangs in Tatarstan. No such separate entities as Kazanskie and Tatary ever actually existed.

Very often the pressure to move beyond the confines of Kazan came as a result of the expanding appetites of gruppirovki and their growing numbers or splits among avtoritety, some of whom had to escape from Kazan and settle elsewhere as a result of internal conflicts. As Valerii Karyshev, a self-styled "bandits' advocate" and a writer about organized crime, explains, groups from Kazan and other cities began to arrive in Moscow at the beginning of the 1990s. Initially, the influence of Kazan gangs in other areas was limited, as they simply tried to find compatriots who were engaged in business and offer them a krysha. However, their areas of interest gradually began to widen, and they started also to offer *kryshy* to Moscow businessmen. They also tried to take "tidbits" from the Moscow mobsters (Karyshev 1998, 47), which led to violent gang wars. In Saint Petersburg, Zhilka controlled the city port. In both Saint Petersburg and Moscow, the gangs controlled restaurants, security and insurance companies, auto repair shops, casinos, banks, and hotels. Eventually, though, control by Kazan gangs over other areas weakened under pressure from the local gruppirovki, whereas business in Tatarstan remained under their control.

Having accumulated substantial sums of money in Russia, the leaders of many Tatarstan gangs began to branch out internationally, developing significant foreign business interests. For example, several members of Griaz′ were arrested in France for brothel keeping, while in Austria, Boriskovo gangsters were reported to have defrauded their foreign partners out of a sum of around one million dollars. Part of the produce of Orgsintez was exported illegally to the Czech Republic, Poland, and Hungary, with the proceeds accumulating in the foreign bank accounts of Kazan avtoritety. In 2012, one of Zhilka's avtoritety, fifty-three-year-old Valerii Kirienko, was arrested for the murder of the owner of a car dealership in the Czech Republic (newsru.com 2012). Territorial expansion, movement into control over companies beyond the boundaries of the local turf, and development of sophisticated business operations by the leadership, all led to serious organizational changes in the gangs, which acquired a multicentered networked character. I consider this transformation further in chapter 4.

Gangs and Territoriality Elsewhere in Russia

The Tatarstan model of development of organized criminal gangs, which progressed from street neighborhood associations to territorial ruling regimes and created outposts farther afield, can be seen across Russia. In urban areas across the country, bandit gruppirovki fed, both in terms of their membership intake and in their economic base, off the local territory. While they may have supplied members for wider criminal networks (as, for example, alliances of several Tatarstan gruppirovki outside Kazan), the home territory remained their breeding ground and key base. Many of the Moscow bandit gruppirovki were formed on a territorial basis, including the most famous groups—the Solntsevskaia, Izmailovskaia, Liuberetskaia, Dolgoprudnenskaia, Orekhovskaia, and Medvedkovskaia (Karyshev 1998, 2005). The Izmailovskaia gruppirovka, for example, which is thought to be one of the oldest in Moscow, emerged out of the youth gangs that fought territorial battles with the liubery at the beginning of the 1980s. Like other bandit groups, they developed a variety of racketeering operations. These included taxing the Izmailovo outdoor clothes and arts markets, as well as providing protection for small businesses operating in train stations and bus terminals, parts of the large Izmailovo hotel, shops at the beginning of Leninskii Prospekt in Moscow, and many other businesses (Modestov 2001, 130–31). One of the most famous Moscow gangs, Orekhovskaia was formed on the basis of the neighborhood networks created by young men of seventeen to twenty-five who lived on Shipilovskaia Street. They were involved in territorial fights with other local groups until all were united into one racketeering gang by Sergei Timofeev (Silvestr), a criminal avtoritet (Karyshev 1998, 2005). The Solntsevskaia gruppirovka—which later developed a major national and international presence—also had territorial origins, as did many gangs in the city of Perm (Varese 2001).

A study in Ul'ianovsk by Elena Omel'chenko also revealed the strong presence of territorial gangs in the city, and a similar trajectory in their development to that of Kazan gruppirovki. At the beginning of the 1990s, Ul'ianovsk street gangs (also organized into age-based cohorts) were involved in territorial fighting and episodic extortion. However, by 1993 the gangs had moved on to control markets, parking lots, commercial stores, and restaurants. Their leaders were often older men who had served time in prison and were involved in wider entrepreneurial activities. According to Omel'chenko (1996), the leaders of youth street gangs were connected to organized crime bosses who were kept unknown to ordinary members.

Similarly, in the Russian Far East the development of many organized criminal groups proceeded along territorial lines. Many of Vladivostok's gruppirovki had at their core groups formed in the city districts. They started their activities with racketeering in the neighborhood, and, although the business interests of the criminal elite later expanded to control of specific industries (such as fishery or mining), local territorial affiliations did not disappear altogether.

One Vladivostok gang member explained how the branching out of the gangs into the larger economy did not obliterate their territorial roots:

> Before, during the time of violent confrontations [*razborki*], there was a strong division into different territories. For example, Petrorechenskii District is mine and Sovetskii District is yours, and if you come into my territory you will be beaten up. That doesn't exist anymore. Now the fight is about economic spheres, about influence in big business. Of course, the racket still exists, and territory is still important, but it takes on a different meaning nowadays. Of course, you don't want the others to operate on your territory, after all the chicken still feeds on its own seeds, but the influence of the economic sphere is now more important. (quoted in Holzlehner 2007, 66–67)

Some of the youth gangs, particularly those based in poor peripheral areas, retained their local character and did not evolve into serious organized crime structures. Breslavsky (2009) documented the practices of youth gangs in several Buriatiia villages. This very poor area in the Zaigraevskii District of Buriatiia has for decades been highly influenced by criminal culture, with many ex-convicts from nearby penal colonies coming to settle in the territory. In the 1990s, with the closure of local factories, these villages became dominated by youth gangs. The gang members paid into an obshchak, with the money used to provide help to offenders behind bars and their families. Similarly to Kazan gangs, regular meet-ups were organized where people discussed business, punished members for misbehavior, and collected money for the obshchak. The gangs had age cohorts, with a *smotriashchii* (overseer) heading each cohort. Members of the gangs harassed the children of more prosperous families for money and put pressure on teenagers to join them. In the absence of more lucrative opportunities for protection, the protection racket mostly affected shop owners. The gang leaders tried to establish their own businesses, but the gangs constantly lacked money, with those leaders who were not involved in commerce having to live off the obshchak, something that is typically prohibited in organized crime groups.

In the course of the 1990s, liubery groups also evolved from violent fighting organizations into entrepreneurial gangs. In the late 1980s and early 1990s some of their participants turned to extortion and formed local racketeering groups and some joined various criminal organizations in the greater Moscow area. A leading Liubertsy sportsman, Mansur, organized a group of local youths that started extorting money from the owners of street kiosks. Eventually, he formed an alliance with a vor v zakone, Leonid Zavadskii (whom he later killed), and established a krysha over TsSKA, a large outdoor market in Moscow. He developed a major racketeering business in Moscow but was killed in a police raid in 1994 (Karyshev 1998).

Epitaph for the 1990s

The crisis of the Soviet social system produced a resurgence of nonstate patrimonial social forms in many spheres of life. With the institutions of the modern economy and society in deep crisis, people began to look for affiliations in groups and networks that would give them access to resources and allow them to "rise" in society. Many young people, who would previously have left their street groups in their late teens to join the world of work, found it impossible or deeply unattractive to do so. Against this background, the gang presented itself as a structure that was available, familiar, and well adapted to developing new projects of accumulation. The lads created what Deleuze and Guattari in *A Thousand Plateaus* (2004) called a "war machine" and started making money by plunder. Soon, as we have seen, they began to collect payments systematically from the businessmen in their territories, and they expanded these activities into other areas. Their organizations became autonomous ruling regimes that put local businessmen into a variety of situations of dependency.

Thus the beginning of the capitalist era brought a regression from Soviet modernity to a patchwork of different private networks and power regimes. In the absence of a strong state, violent tribes and clans fought among themselves for power and wealth. For them, as it was for early medieval knights, "violence was the quickest way of becoming rich" (Martin 1977, 97).[3] Of course, unlike medieval warrior elites, the gangs did not have supreme power over the territory nor was their system of government legally enshrined. Rather, they coexisted with modern state bureaucratic institutions and developing capitalist forms.

"The emergence of big money in the country," as one of our Kazan interviewees put it, coinciding with a profound economic crisis, a weakening of state authority, and the erosion of the collective institutions of Soviet society, resulted in multiple struggles for appropriation and domination. New and old groups vied for money and influence, laid claim to resources, and eventually, to use Rousseau's formulation in his *Discourse on the Origin of Inequality*, "converted clever usurpation into inalienable right" (1993 [1754], 89).

Like any revolutionary period, the 1990s brought with them mass social upheaval but also a unique opportunity for those who were ready to use it. People

3. Several authors have explored the usefulness of the idiom of feudalism in relation to post-socialist transformation (Shlapentokh 1996; Verdery 1996; Humphrey 2002).

who were young, energetic, resourceful, and also—as often happens in life—in the right place at the right time could launch spectacular new careers. The generation that started their adult lives in the 1990s now occupies the top positions in the government, business, academia, and the media. Among the members of the State Duma, leaders of political movements, leading businessmen, and university rectors we can find many of those who rose from the streets or progressed in life via unsavory collaborations with bandits.

With opportunity came enormous risk, and no one was exposed to it more than the first generation of post-Soviet bandits. Scores of young people (and their leaders) fell victim to the violent fights and wars that accompanied redivision of assets and spheres of influence. Clusters of graves of gang members who perished in the 1990s figure prominently in many Russian cemeteries.[4] In Gromov's study of former liubery, conducted at the beginning of the 2000s, the interviewees reported that only between 25 to 75 percent of their friends, members of liubery groups of the 1980s, had survived. Gromov noted that their age cohort suffered a higher rate of losses during the social calamities of the 1990s than an army suffers on average in wartime activities, pointing out that in Afghanistan the Soviet Army lost no more than 2.4 percent of serving personnel. He suggested that "it is possible that with time the events of the 1990s will be regarded as a kind of civil war that accompanied the transition of the country to the new system of social-economic relations." As one of his interviewees proposed, "We could go to the Liubertsy cemetery at Novaia Riazanka and have a walk in the new part, closer to the road, and look at the graves and the dates of birth and death. But that would be a very sad story" (2006, 36).

There are no public monuments to heroes of the capitalist revolution in Russia. In their place we find tombstones with engraved photos of young men who once believed that the world belonged to them—the young, muscular, and brave—but who perished in violent battles to forge the new order.

---

4. For a discussion of the symbolic representations of mobsters in Moscow and Yekaterinburg cemeteries, see Matich (2006).

3

THE BUSINESS OF BANDIT GANGS

From Predation to Assimilation

The gangs began their economic activities at the end of the 1980s with extortion and protection operations, threatening businessmen with dire consequences if they did not pay up straight away and setting up kryshy for street kiosks, outdoor markets, small shops, and cafes. While youth territorial gangs were confined to the street economy, their leadership moved into operations off the streets, where they took control of medium-sized and large businesses and gradually (unless of course they were killed or incarcerated) managed to assimilate into legitimate business and political structures. The gangs also developed other forms of illegal and legal business, with protection becoming an increasingly small part of their overall operations.

In this chapter I address how the gangs' economic practices developed in the context of the historical transformation of Russia during the transition to capitalism; the social relationship between the gangs and the businesses and individuals under their protection; and how the gangs' business activities related to their members' attempts to gain entry into wider networks of power and influence.

The Historical Context: Economic Violence and Development of Capitalism

The rise in private economic violence in Russia occurred at a time when capitalism in the country was in a nascent state. Trust in institutions that could ensure sanctity of contracts was absent, and property rights could not be protected by the weak state justice system. So what was the relationship between the weakness of the market institutions and state regulation and the rise of private protection? Can the gangs that offered protection to businesses be seen as responding to the deficit of trust and justice, and ultimately performing a socially useful function? Were they providing a substitute, albeit in an unsavory, inconsistent, and often predatory way, for nonexistent state regulation? Or were they, as I argue, essentially taking advantage of the opportunity provided by the situation of general lawlessness to prey on businesses and members of the public?

Some authors view the role of agents of economic violence in the development of capitalism in Russia as following (albeit in a compressed way) the role of bandits, outlaws, or pirates in the development of market institutions and state formation in Europe and on the underdeveloped periphery of the modern world. Historical and anthropological research has shown that groups of armed predators and warlords played important roles in the rise of capitalist production and exchange across Europe, but also in India, Asia, Australia, and Latin America. A well-known example is the "men of respect" in Sicily and other areas of Italy, hired by landowners to protect their interests against peasants and anybody else who might threaten their property (Blok 1974; Schneider and Schneider 1976; Arlacchi 1983; Catanzaro 1992; Petrusewicz 1996). Bandits, brigands, buccaneers, and pirates—operating sometimes inside the law, sometimes outside it—protected property and trade routes and supported landowners in their struggle for power (Gallant 1999).

Starting from the 1990s, criminologists working from an institutionalist perspective focused on the role of mafias in compensating for the deficit of effective market regulation. Diego Gambetta (1993) saw significant similarities between Sicilian and post-Soviet mafia organizations, both of which he perceived as producers of the commodity of protection that they offered in response to a demand from businesses and the public. In both cases the state was unable to provide guarantees for business transactions, could not enforce laws, and was unable create an environment that fostered trust and cooperation between business organizations. Mafia groups responded to the institutional deficit by offering their protection services. This perspective was further developed by Federico Varese (2001; 2012), writing about Russian mafia groups during the time of transition to capitalism. He saw mafia both as a business of private protection and a form of extralegal governance. Describing the actual reality of criminal protection in the Russian city of Perm, Varese showed that mafiosi often behaved in a predatory way and in effect stymied the development of a competitive market and the rule of law. Nevertheless, in the absence of credible law enforcement by state authorities, they satisfied the existing demand for protection and provided real services to businesses and members of the public.[1]

In analyzing the rise of bandit groups and other violence-managing agencies ("violent entrepreneurs") and their role in the process of state building in Russia, Vadim Volkov (see, e.g., 2000; 2002; 2012) argued that they performed important functions that could not be performed by the debilitated state. In his opinion, the Russian society of the 1990s after the collapse of Soviet law and order was close to a Hobbesian state of nature. Emerging racketeering gangs employed brutal force, but they later moved toward greater institutionalization and relative pacification, which allowed them to draw more stable profits. According to Volkov (2000, 45–46), the "combination of high risks and the shortage of protection and justice created an institutional demand for enforcement partners, a kind of business mediator who could ensure the smooth functioning of private business." Criminal groups, together with private security companies and groups of policemen, FSB officers, and other state agents (acting in private capacities) created a system of economic and political constraints that underpinned fledgling economic exchange, a variety of regimes of "economic governance" (Volkov 2012, 325). Toward the end of the 1990s the state appeared to prevail over these private enforcers. In a process that, as Volkov explained, had significant similarities with the market building and centralization of the states in early capitalist Europe, the state managed to pacify the economic space, organize its own apparatus of power, and establish a fiscal monopoly.

Although the historical precedents of the development of markets and state centralization elsewhere in Europe provide analytically rich insights, it is important also to recognize the historically unique nature of the capitalist development that Russia (and other postsocialist countries) experienced at the end of the twentieth century and the beginning of the twenty-first century. Here capitalism was born out of the ruins of state socialism rather than developed from the feudal system. This period was also defined by neoliberal transformation, with its radical privatization of state assets and the rapid emergence of moneyed classes out of a society that hitherto had no private property and no serious private wealth.

No parallels are ever perfect, but I will risk offering my own here. The Russian transition to capitalism can be usefully compared not only to the development of capitalism in Europe but to neoliberal transformation in the capitalist periphery, from sub-Saharan Africa to Latin America. In these countries, inclusion into the global economy since the 1980s (mainly through export of natural resources) and rapid privatization of public assets in the course of structural adjustment programs also led to the rush for spoils by a variety of state-based and criminal clans.

1. For a review of the literature on mafia protection and extortion. see Varese (2014).

Thus, in Brazil, with the start of neoliberal transformation, various territorial networks of power formed what Arias and Goldstein (2010) called "violent pluralism" in which gangs and other agents of popular violence formed systems of predatory and clientelistic (that is, mutually beneficial but hierarchical and asymmetric) relations with members of the public, on the one hand, and representatives of state power, on the other.

Similarly, writing about sub-Saharan Africa, Jean-François Bayart (1999) noted that instead of helping to build democratic and law-governed societies with free market economies, neoliberal reforms further weakened the state structures and paved the way for the entrenchment of corrupt, factitious, and clientelistic systems of governance. Positions of power turned into positions of predation, both when it came to actors inside the state and criminal groups. In his words: "Insecurity, banditry and economic violence are particularly in evidence when the political situation is confused. . . . By heightening the general feeling of insecurity, violence intensifies the need to seek protection, even in privatized form, of those who wield economic and political power. In this way, it reinforces the tendency to clientilism, co-optation and collaboration" (111).

This description can be applied in equal measure to post-Soviet Russia. Although on some level it can be said that the bandit gangs provide necessary services that the state does not, the fundamental relationship between provider and receiver is asymmetric, clientelistic at best and predatory at worst. While the gangs' services can be very valuable to businesses, their use is not optional but imposed under threat of violence, with no clear rules to secure the client's rights or offer means of redress. This becomes more obvious when we consider the nature of these services in greater detail.

Protection as an Asymmetrical Power Relationship

The gangs built their power base and accumulated capital via protection operations. They progressed from pure extortion to establishing regular tributary relations with the companies and individual entrepreneurs in their territories and beyond, taxing them on a permanent basis. They also began to provide them with assistance in securing loans, avoiding taxes, and fighting off competitors. The gangs' avtoritety could help "their" businessmen to recover debts, usually in return for 20–50 percent of the recovered sum, or to collect information about prospective clients and partners (often with the help of corrupt policemen and bureaucrats). Sometimes the gangs would act as lending facilities for their businesses. If a businessman needed a loan and could not get it from a bank, he could ask his krysha for money. The gangs could help settle bureaucratic problems, using their contacts with the tax authorities, fire or sanitation inspectorate, or local councils. The gangs also took on a quasi-judicial role. They began to adjudicate disputes between businesses and helped businessmen resolve conflicts between themselves and with other gangs (or the police).

There is no doubt that in many cases the gang's protection was genuine and that a demand for protection did exist in situations where the state could not provide it. Nevertheless, criminal protection is essentially different from that provided in an ordinary service relationship. Rather than a simple exchange based on supply and demand, it is defined first and foremost by the aforementioned asymmetrical power relationship between the people who give it and those who receive it. The gangs' reproduction depended on taxing other people's productive activities, and they needed the businesses that they controlled to do well economically rather than go under. By extracting part of "their" companies' profits rather than indulging in wholesale plunder, and by offering to use their capabilities as violent enforcers and mediators, the gangs could ultimately receive more money from businesses under their krysha. This explains the episodes of apparently benevolent behavior, reported by businessmen under gang protection who sometimes praised their kryshy for giving them time to collect money owed or cancelling payments altogether in a period of economic difficulties. They also sometimes contrasted the gangs favorably with the police and FSB officers, who could be much more ruthless in their extortion and who often showed no care for whether the business would survive or not.

The gangs could also provide assistance in exchange for payment to other "clients" who were not already under their krysha. But even here we see the same motive. Unless these were one-off services to private individuals—or to powerful counterparts in public or private corporations—gang involvement led to further dependency on the part of those who might have turned to the gang simply to solve a particular problem. Provision of services needs therefore to be seen not as a business transaction, although gangs were paid for them, but a means of building a regime of dependency between businessmen and the gangs.

Seeking to apply the language of economic transactions to the world of gang and mafia power creates more problems than it solves, as we have to make too many additional provisos and classifications. The people who "purchase" these services typically do not ask for them, have very little say in what they receive, and cannot ask the providers to stop. As Gambetta acknowledged, protection is offered regardless of the demand for it, and "whether one wants it or not, one gets it and is required to pay for it" (1993, 31). At the same time, the protectors may refuse to provide it, require renegotiation of the terms, demand a stake in the business they are protecting, or even expropriate the business altogether. That is why, rather than seeing the activities of a bandit gang as a service that satisfies an existing demand for protection, I agree with those authors who argue that what organized criminal groups are primarily selling is first and foremost protection from themselves (Schelling 1971, 76; Humphrey 1999; Paoli 2003).

My research in Kazan showed that the relationship of protection rested not on service contracts but on vague "agreements" and "understandings" reached by gangs with businessmen and other civilians. The gangs claimed that they would provide a krysha and protect these people and their businesses from other predators in return for regular tribute. Although the offer implied defense from any other violent agents, mainly other gangs and unaffiliated criminals—the so-called *otmorozki* (the "thawed-outs") and in some cases the police—the immediate danger to businesses and individuals came from the "protectors" themselves, and this was the key element in the "understanding" between gruppirovshchiki and the subjects of their protection. Those gang members whom we interviewed in Kazan typically described their protection operations using the term *shchemit'* (to oppress). Oppression could extend to individuals, groups, and businesses. For example, the interviewees spoke of themselves as "oppressing" the Vietnamese market in Kazan and *azery* (ethnic traders) in other street markets. Gruppirovshchiki perceived this "oppression" as legitimate not because of any real services they provided but simply because of their presumed rights over the territory. One of our interviewees, Anvar, described the nature of the relationship between the gangs and the local businesses in the following way:

> We have our own territory, where you can't do business without the senior members' permission—no setting up stalls or parking lots or the like. Naturally, the construction of big shops like supermarkets happens regardless of the street, but all the small-time traders live under us. Anyone who wants to can walk around our territory, we don't charge tolls, but if someone wants to make dough, they've got to share because it's our territory.

The predatory nature of the gang's protection was obvious in the key method it used in commanding other people's resources: *zagruzka po poniatiiam* (literally, justifying one's actions on the basis of the gang code), or just *zagruzka*, which was followed by *razvod* (extortion). Rather than offering a specific contract for services, the gang presented claims. The claims rested on tradition ("It has always been like this"), territorial rights ("This is our territory, and everyone has to pay"), status (businessmen and nongang civilians are, according to the code, inferior to the lads and bandits), as well as the benefits of cooperation with these demands (avoidance of harm from the gang itself and protection from other predators).

After the gang presented a claim, a share of a person's or a company's money or assets was taken. This could be done with or without the use of physical force, depending on the victim's response. Alternatively, the victim was accused of having committed a *zikher* (a violation of the code), which he had most probably done inadvertently through incorrect answers or behavior. Because of this *zikher*, he now owed his money, property, or even his life to the gang overlords. While violence was not explicitly justified on the basis of universal abstract principles, it tended to be supported by one rule or the other from the gang's own arsenal of justifications.

The method of *zagruzit' po poniatiiam i razvesti na den'gi* (using the code to get people to part with their money) has a wider applicability in Russian society. In common parlance, *gruzit'* (literally, to weigh down) means to present one's agenda as an uninterruptible monologue with the aim of achieving some kind of advantage. Far from representing a provision of a service, this pattern of appealing to unopposable rules to justify the extortion of resources may be seen as an expression of power in its most instrumental and destructive form: power as violence. This form of power produces what Hannah Arendt called "unquestioning obedience" rather than consent (Arendt 1972, 140).

Actual violence or its implied threat was a necessary part of establishing "understanding" between the parties. When gang members offered protection, this, according to our interviewees, typically involved the following scenario. Gang members came to a kiosk owner, a trader at a market stall, or a company owner and enquired whether they had a krysha. If this was not the case, they offered protection in exchange for regular payments. If the owner refused, the kiosk, stall, or the company's office would catch fire, and then the offer would be quickly accepted. In other cases, the gangs would orchestrate the need for protection preemptively. This practice also came under the rubric of *razvod*. It typically proceeded in the following way. A group of lads damaged the property that the gang wanted to control—for example, they might trash a kiosk or a market stall. A second group would emerge to offer "help." Then a third would collect protection money. We were told that *razvod* operations at the territorial level were planned at gang meetings. Older and more experienced members, who knew the local economy well, suggested which businesses to approach. The cohort's *smotriashchii* then selected some younger lads who could be entrusted with running the protection operation itself. In another scenario, a group of lads who wanted to establish their own protection operation would come up with their own plan and then ask the *smotriashchii* to approve it. In all instances, a share of the takings was given to the *smotriashchii* for the gang's obshchak.

Like legitimate governments, the gangs used coercion and taxed the producers of wealth. But, as Tilly pointed out, "unlike most governments, however, the system has no accountability, no visibility, no means of representation for those under its control. . . . The murders, thefts and mutilations its operators use to maintain their control—'to make themselves respected'—are only the most lurid manifestations of its evil" (Tilly 1974a, xix–xx).

Generally, the gangs were under no obligation to provide any assistance to businesses under their protection. In our interviews it appeared that an owner of a business or a self-employed person was more likely to get support from the local gang if he was approached for payment by a rival gang or if there was a dispute with competitors. For example, R., a taxi driver I interviewed in 2011, told me that when he saw unknown drivers wanting to use the same taxi stop—and thereby threatening his business—he would call his krysha in expectation that the intruders would be asked to leave. If the intruders had their own protection, the two gangs would then meet to sort out territorial rights.

A key feature of any protection racket was that businessmen were unable to terminate relations with their "protectors" of their own accord, and the price they paid for the gang's assistance was that they now found themselves under the gang's control for as long as the gang chose. While businesses had to live up to their obligations unreservedly—by paying their krysha and obeying all the gang's commands—the gang itself was under no actual obligation to provide services. There are many accounts of the fickle and volatile nature of gang protection from different geographical areas. In Kazan the gang members typically gave the businessmen their cell phone numbers to call in case of trouble, but there was no guarantee that if the latter called them and asked for help anything would be done. If a business was subsequently attacked by hooligans, or something was stolen from the property, the krysha was unlikely to come to the owner's aid. Similarly, in Saint Petersburg, the bandits' kryshy did not provide any actual insurance against serious crime, such as robbery, assaults, car thefts, or burglaries (Konstantinov 2004). Protection of street businesses in Perm was likewise unreliable, and Varese (2001, 110–20) gave examples in which racketeers did not answer the phone when their clients called for help, refused to retrieve stolen goods, committed fraud against a kiosk owner who paid for protection, or switched to another "customer" and turned against the earlier customer with deadly consequences. For criminals living by the code, reneging on one's word, deceiving, and even robbing "their" businessmen was entirely legitimate. According to the code, bandits and vory only have moral obligations to one another and can *kidat' lokhov* (cheat outsiders) with impunity. At the same time, outsiders who had entered a position of dependency acquired iron-clad obligations toward the gangsters.

In some cases, people sought the gangs' protection when they came under threat from other organized groups or unorganized criminals (*otmorozki*) or could not recover their loans. Others turned to the gangs in disputes with former business partners. But turning to the gangs meant that from then on a relationship of dependency was established, one that clients could not terminate. For example, one businessman, K., whom I interviewed in 2011, ran a small office supplies company with a partner. The partner decided to start his own business and left with the complete client database. K. approached a bandit gang who found his ex-partner and "made him see the error of his ways." This however, meant that from then on K.'s business had to be under the gang's krysha, and he paid them 30 percent of the profits. The gang's accountant made regular visits to the company to keep an eye on its turnover and to ensure that the gang was paid its due. Fortunately for K., when the 2008 economic crisis struck and the company's profits dwindled, the gang's accountant told the businessman that the profits were now too small to make it worth their while to "cooperate" with his company, and after this they left him alone. Another businessman, L., the owner of a pharmaceutical company, recounted how his gang krysha helped him to avoid paying taxes and release company cash by setting up nonexistent contracts with companies created by the gang but later used the same companies to syphon money from his accounts.

Even in situations where the gang provides actual services for its "clients," the asymmetrical relationship of power between the "clients" and providers of services leads to the conclusion that these services are better described as favors that reproduce relationships of patron-client dependency between businesses and criminal organizations. When criminal patrons dominate particular areas and demand obedience through violence, their clients have no choice but to comply with the rules imposed on them without any negotiation. This does not mean, of course, that there was no demand for protection. Enormous uncertainty in public life and the removal of any guarantees that the state would protect its citizens from predators, taking place against a background of vigorous appropriation of public and private assets, created a situation especially conducive to the need to seek protection from powerful patrons.

When society is divided into systems of predatory and patron-client relations, businessmen may seek out better kryshy, with greater power and fewer propensities for brutal violence. Galeotti (2000, 36) reported a conversation with a young entrepreneur who told him in July 1998 that "choosing the right krysha is the single most important decision in setting up a new business in Russia." The krysha can be provided by organized crime, but also by the police, state security services, or private security companies. People may be in a position to make this choice, but they can never guarantee that their business will remain intact or that their krysha will provide reliable services.

Generally, the capacity of organized gangs to appropriate resources derives less from demand for their protection than from their ability to establish their own systems of domination. This is expressed in a phrase we heard from gruppirovshchiki, "*Glavnyi ne kto bashliaet, a kto stavit kryshu*" ("The one in charge is not the one who pays but the one who sets up the roof"). The gang's power, like any system of domination, is embedded in a structure of social interaction that creates asymmetric dependencies based on a lack of credible alternatives for those in subordinate positions (Martin 1977). This power is only limited by the existence of other power agents, such as rival gangs, other organized crime networks, and the police and other state bodies. But even they can collude, making their subjects' powerlessness virtually absolute. In chapter 6, I consider the case of the village of Kushchevskaia, where the local gang, state authorities, and the police established a regime of total power that crushed any resistance.

Fundamentally, we are not dealing with a dichotomy of malevolent criminal groups filling the gap left by a benevolent but temporarily absent state. As Bayart (2009, 76) explains, "positions of power can also be *positions of predation*. Holders of power use their monopoly of legitimate force to demand goods, cash and labour." Unequal predatory and patron-client relationships between the gangs and businesses are mirrored in similar practices used by Russian state authorities, confirming that it is often difficult to draw a line between the state and its shadow. In some cases, the state forces companies to pay extra "taxes" without any legal basis. For example, during President Mintimir Shaimiev's period in office (1991–2010), the Tatarstan authorities put pressure on businesses to fund various state projects, including the liquidation of dilapidated housing stock—a highly contentious program that has led to the destruction of many historic areas of Kazan. Shaimiev told those companies that did not want to pay their share to "get out of the Republic" (Murtazin 2007, 143). One Tatarstan author (Tabeev 2007, 96-97) described a practice of *dobrovol'no-prinuditel'nye* (voluntary-compulsory) agreements on cooperation between businessmen and local administrations, in which the former become obliged to make payments to various municipal funds and to sponsor organized events. Otherwise, they are likely to run into trouble from one or more of the forty-eight state structures capable of legally terminating their business. As Tabeev noted, the existence of an administrative krysha helps companies resolve many problems and can "promote their economic success." In their turn, businessmen use their financial resources and mobilize their employees to support the authorities during elections.

Street Kryshy

The bandit gang included different networks, street and nonstreet, and all were involved in setting up their own kryshy. While the older members protected businesses, the younger lads also developed their strategies for domination on the streets. Their power was limited to the street space, to harassing their non-gang peers and strangers walking through the gang's area, and their activities did not of course fall under the organized crime rubric. Nevertheless, the techniques of domination were in many ways similar. In fact, the younger lads, members of the lower-age cohorts of gruppirovki, talked about offering a krysha to non-affiliated young men who studied in the same schools or colleges or lived in the same neighborhoods. Although promises were made to protect these young men from unspecified assaults, in reality the lads only guaranteed protection from themselves. Setting up a personal krysha simply meant that members of a gang forced their victim to pay them money on a regular basis. If the victim refused to pay, the gang harassed him on the streets or in school until he started paying. Similarly to the protection offered to businessmen, the relationship of domination was continuous and based on implicit or verbal "understanding." Very often the same organizational devices of protection were used as those employed to set up a krysha for a business. A victim—who typically had no connections with gangs or relatives in the police or state authorities, and therefore was helpless in the face of assaults—received an "offer" from gang members, who promised to protect him from some unspecified aggressors. If he refused to pay, he was beaten. Alternatively, the need for protection was orchestrated in advance. Tadjik described an "action," organized by his *brigada* (team, the basic unit of an organized gang) when he was younger, which he characterized as *razvod*, a term also commonly used to describe the establishment of business protection:

> One of our lads found a *mazhor* and suggested that we *postavim ego na den'gi* ("put him on the money"—start regular extortion). The scheme was a standard one: he [the gang member] is a "good lad," willing to protect the *mazhor* from "bad lads," and we are "bad lads," who had been oppressing this *mazhor.* At first we caught him and forced him to give us money; the next time he did not have money and we beat him up a little. When the "good lad" came to him again with the protection offer, the *mazhor* was already prepared to discuss the financial side.

These "standard" schemes are very effective, but they are not always necessary. As Tadjik said, "I offer the *lokhi* [outsiders or "commoners," those who are not gang members] protection, and normally they can't refuse me."

When the victim pays up immediately after the offer is made or, failing that, after a violent attack, it is understood that he has entered into a continuous relationship of dependency with the gang. He is labeled a *terpila* (passive sufferer) or a *sladkii* (sweet one), and the convention is that he will have to pay for as long the gang thinks it is worth its while to collect the money from him.

By coming under the krysha, the victim does not acquire any firm obligations from gruppirovshchiki. This is how one gang member described the gang's treatment of *mazhory:*

> They are like dairy cows. The lads simply milk them for money, live at their expense. . . . I just tell him, like listen, pal, if you have any problems, just come to me, I'll help you. That's all. If he does come, I'll just brush him off, like I am busy, pal. "What's up," I'd say, "what happened?" He'd say this and that. I'd say, "Look, pal, you are in the wrong here, and you have to sort it out. I have my own problems now, my own business to take care of. I will not assist some *chert* [a person who has violated the code]." (Shashkin 2009, 172)

Like businessmen who do not trust the police to protect them and thus remain at the mercy of organized crime, young victims of extortion comply because they feel defenseless. Victims may of course go to the police or complain to their parents or teachers, but by doing this they risk looking even weaker in the eyes of their peers. As Salagaev and Shashkin (2005a) explain, if extortion happens at school, a victim who complains to adults risks being ostracized by the whole class.

Ultimately, gang members have no moral obligations toward the members of the public whom they "protect." After all, they construct themselves as a superior group who are above relationships of exchange with ordinary people. Similarly to businessmen (*kommersy* and *barygi*), members of the public can never be accepted by the lads as equals and can be deceived and tricked with impunity. The lads positively relish the stories of their successful *razvod* and *kidalovo* (deception) of nongang civilians.

The grammar of violent predation, as we can see, is the same for serious organized crime operations and for low-level street extortion.

Intersecting Power and Business Networks

While the gangs achieved significant power over the businesses under their control, they could not assume the monopoly of power in a territory. They coexisted with institutions of the modern economy and state, and the gangs' social and economic reproduction was dependent on deep penetration into these structures. The gangs' ability to expand into multiple spheres was facilitated by the mental orientations of their members, which were micropolitical, highly pragmatic and entrepreneurial, and adaptable to changes in the existing balance of power. The gangs went where money and influence were to be found, organizing terror campaigns against the weak, making deals with the strong, and trying to find the balance between necessary violence and the stable routines of business life.

The gangs tried to gain access to state-based and corporate agents and intimidate them, collude in money-laundering and tax-evading schemes, or co-opt them into their business. (The term "corruption," which typically implies the use of public office for private gain, does not adequately capture the complex system of cross-cutting economic and political interactions between criminal groups and state and corporate officials.) At the same time, members of the state and the corporate-based networks sought cooperation with bandits to use their criminal skills and their wide contacts transcending legal and illegal societies.

Sometimes the bandits were hired by public and private business corporations to facilitate various illegal schemes, which they did by using their now-expert knowledge and connections with state authorities. They could open up fictitious companies for money laundering or financial transactions that would go under the tax authorities' radar, or help with avoiding customs duties. For example, one of the companies controlled by the 29th Kompleks from Naberezhnye Chelny conducted financial operations in the electricity and gas spheres with support from top Russian government officials and legal banking organizations (Udovenko 2008). But things could go wrong, as the bandits never seemed to be able to control their violence successfully. One case illustrates this all too well. Eduard Tagirianov, the leader of Banda Tagirianova, another gruppirovka from Naberezhnye Chelny, was hired as a financial manager by the Russian state company Gazprom to "facilitate" their transactions (as an expert in various shady financial schemes). His career in Gazprom, however, ended when he killed one of his employees for allegedly channeling away money without Tagirianov's authorization (Nafikov 2012, 161–63).

His services to the administration of Lipetsk Oblast also resulted in extreme violence. The *Novaia Gazeta* journalist Igor' Domnikov was investigating administrative corruption in the region when the local top official, with whom Tagirianov had business connections, asked the latter to have Domnikov "warned" not to continue. Tagirianov's men hammered the journalist to death (Prusenkova 2013). The lengthy criminal investigation that followed culminated in the prosecution and conviction of the killers and arranger, including Tagirianov.

Representatives of law enforcement bodies were heavily implicated in gang activities. Salagaev, Shashkin, and Konnov (2006) made an in-depth analysis of the collusion between organized criminal groups and law enforcement bodies. These authors interviewed ninety-six people in various areas of Tatarstan, including representatives of law enforcement agencies, members of organized criminal groups, businessmen, and journalists. According to their research, some of the police officers and representatives of the office of the Prokuratura (State Prosecution Service) and the Department for the Struggle against Organized Crime (UBOP) received money or services for a range of illegal activities such as providing information about police operations, helping gang members avoid criminal prosecution or receive a reduced sentence, erasing data from police databases, and releasing gang members from police detention. They concealed information, tampered with evidence, or reclassified cases—for example, from murder to manslaughter or from grievous bodily harm to petty hooliganism. Officers helped to obtain forged passports or weapons. They provided information about competing gangs (and sometimes arrested their members "to order"), assisted with transportation of illegal goods, and helped to obtain permissions from the traffic police and other state agencies for establishing street parking lots. Officers assisted the gangs in securing trading places in the market for traders under their protection, helped to avoid administrative delays in setting up businesses, provided information about future partners, or helped to bring down competitors' businesses. Police officers often had side jobs as security guards in gang firms. They also helped gang avtoritety with obtaining contacts with state officials and even promoted their election to office by organizing dirty tricks against other candidates.

Two hierarchies, legal and illegal, intertwined, with junior officers communicating predominantly with ordinary gang members and senior officers dealing with leaders and avtoritety of the criminal community. But, while collusion with criminal groups affected almost all levels of the police, it was most prevalent at the top, among the heads of regional and municipal police departments and heads of divisions and their assistants (Salagaev, Shashkin, and Konnov 2006).

The personal and business contacts between the police and the gangs are also documented in the gangs' criminal cases. For example, the Zhilka case revealed a great deal about one Vladimir Baranov. Back in the Soviet days he had been a part of the famous group of police investigators working on the Tiap-Liap case. Then, in post-Soviet Tatarstan, he rose to the position of deputy head of Criminal Investigation in the Kazan Department of the Interior. But he also, it appeared, had many friends among the leaders of criminal gangs. After leaving the police, Baranov became the director of the Usadskii alcohol factory, which was controlled by Zhilka. In 1996 he was killed by a contract killer (as it later emerged, for the modest fee of one thousand dollars) on the orders of the leaders of Griaz′, who were competing with Zhilka (Safarov 2012, 310–11).

The gangs sometimes used former and current members of the police force as contract killers. For example, Tiap-Liap hired a former driver in the police Criminal Investigation Department, an ex-member of Spetsnaz (a special military unit), and a serving policeman to execute rivals and disobedient businessmen (Safarov 2012, 53). The Khadi Taktash gang had access to the police database of car owners and was able to target the cars of its enemies on the streets of Kazan. On the days of contract killings Radzha, the leader of the gang, would receive information about murders on his pager that told him to watch the evening news bulletin with reports from crime scenes (Salagaev and Shashkin 2005b).

One of the leaders of 29th Kompleks, Adygan Saliakhov (Alik), possessed a very useful document that certified that he was an officer of the Moscow UBOP. How he procured it is unknown, but this document, signed by the then Russian minister of the interior Anatolii Kulikov, helped Saliakhov at least once, when he was arrested in Naberezhnye Chelny after a drunken fight and brought to a police station. Despite hitting one of the officers in the face, he was released within the hour. Some of the gangs' fraudulent financial operations in the Udmurt Republic took place under the patronage of a deputy chair of the republic's council of ministers. The gang had associates who were ex-members of the Ministry of the Interior (MVD), Federal Security Service (FSB), and the Main Intelligence Directorate (GRU) of the General Staff of the Armed Forces. In Naberezhnye Chelny the gang established a foundation for the support of the city police through which the bandits supplied the police with cars—some were registered in the names of individual policemen—and paid bonuses to the most distinguished officers (Udovenko 2008).

The leaders of the gangs, the police, and local and republican authorities were often part of close-knit groups, fused together by personal and business ties. The case of the Kazan businessman Boris Bulatov (sentenced to a lengthy prison term for ordering the killing of his business partner) illustrates this quite well. Bulatov owned a company named Sandra, which distributed Coca-Cola. His father, Akhmetzian, was the regional Communist Party secretary in Soviet days and then moved on to work for the Tatarstan government, overseeing the food industry. His uncle, Aleksei, was the deputy head of criminal investigations of the Vakhitovskii District police and, simultaneously, a Sandra shareholder. The deputy head of Sandra's board of directors was one of the Khadi Taktash avtoritety, Nikolai Gusev, who also had shares in the company. Several other gang avtoritety worked in the company in an official capacity, and it may have also been the place where Khadi Taktash kept its obshchak (Beliaev and Sheptitskii 2012, 167–83; Safarov 2012, 200).

Relations between public officials and representatives of law enforcement bodies and the gangs often rested on primitive bribery, crass material interest, or outright intimidation of the state agents by the bandits. But they were also cemented by family ties, joint entrepreneurial activities, and employment opportunities provided for representatives of the state authorities in the gangs' structures and vice versa. Legal and illegal worlds merged with each other, creating stubborn local interest groups whose self-interest very effectively trumped considerations of law and order.

The personal networks were consolidated by constant communication, often involving rituals of joint drinking, feasting, or "baring it all" in the sauna. In an embarrassing episode in the history of Tatarstan law enforcement, Il'dus Nafikov, a former head of the Naberezhnye Chelny Prokuratura, was once photographed in a sauna with the aforementioned criminal leader Eduard Tagirianov. When this photograph resurfaced during Tagirianov's criminal trial, Nafikov explained that he was conducting an undercover investigation (Postnova 2006). Later he claimed that he met Tagirianov in the sauna by chance and had not known who he was (Murtazin 2013).

Gang leaders were involved in various charitable organizations and public associations. For example, 29th Kompleks organized concerts for Police Day for the Moscow region police. In return, one of the gang's leaders, Yuri Eremenko (Erema), received a certificate of honor signed by the head of the Moscow police department. The gangs' obshchaki were sometimes used to make donations to the district police departments, either through the accounts of their registered firms or in cash. The gang leaders also participated in local life—for example, sometimes avtoritety, especially those who were involved with the local administrations or wanted to make a political career, helped build churches, mosques, and sports centers. Similar practices existed in other Russian towns, where criminal avtoritety supported police departments as well as giving money to build sports facilities, children's homes, old people's homes, hospitals, and drug clinics (Dolgova 2004, 17–22). With the further incorporation of the leaders into the structures of legal business and legal authorities, these donations are now made in their capacity as respected businessmen and charitable benefactors.

The purpose of this involvement was not limited to instrumental money laundering and bribery. Through participation in various public events and ceremonies, the gang aristocracy was being assimilated into the legitimate networks of prestige and influence, into the proper elite. The new post-Soviet power class, whose various representatives were jointly involved in charity work and shared membership in prestigious nongovernmental organizations and foundations, as well as possessing intersecting business interests, created a fabric of personal relations in which state and nonstate, criminal and legal, orders were inseparable.

The Pursuit of Legitimacy

Using their illegally acquired capital, bribery, threats, and murder, and developing alliances and partnerships with representatives of the corporate world and state institutions, the gang avtoritety managed to make the transition from racketeering street kiosks and markets to becoming owners or shareholders of banks, soccer clubs, agricultural holdings, and large mineral resource companies. This shift took place during the unique window of opportunity that opened in the 1990s, when state companies were being rapidly privatized and the whole economy operated as a vast gray area. In some cases, property was captured through threats and violence; in other cases, companies and organized criminals formed alliances to develop various illicit schemes, commit fraud, and launder money together. In this respect it can be hard to draw lines between organized criminals and white-collar corporate crime—a phenomenon that has been particularly prominent in Russia but that can also be found in developed Western societies (Levi 1987; Ruggiero 1996).

From purely predatory operations, the bandits moved in the second half of the 1990s to appointing their own people to oversee corporate financial operations and to work in various management roles, with the primary purpose of making sure that the gang received its share of the company's profits. According to N., head of investigations of the Kazan district police: "Gruppirovshchiki have their own businesses, but protection still goes on. It's just not the protection that used to take place. Now the gang leader can get money purely for his authority; he can be listed as a company manager and get paid without doing anything."

The gangs forced companies they had put under the krysha to buy goods and services from firms controlled or owned by their members. As mentioned, some gangs started to assist companies under their control with resolving disputes, recovering loans, or providing protection through their official security companies. But pure exploitation also continued—not least through the gangs using the legitimate companies' accounts for their own illicit operations. As M., a Kazan police officer, explained:

> We can say that following the earlier primitive raids, groups are now not just involved in the provision of protection but also in consultancy, security, and mediation services. Take any branch of business today—beer, oil, tires, petrochemicals—and you'll find gangs there. But they are now acting in a more civilized manner from an economic point of view. Through these companies, they launder their money.

Eventually, more symbiotic relations with legal businesses began to develop. Many Tatarstan avtoritety, while starting from purely nominal employment in the companies under their protection, progressed to real management roles or created their own companies, predominantly in the restaurant business, security services, construction, and auto services. In doing this, they became even more enmeshed with the systems of legal authority. As N. told us, "in general, Kazan is a large village where everybody knows each other, and so those members of OPG who are engaged in business have to deal with different authorities, with the local authorities, with the police, and so on. Therefore, members of organized crime groups are trying to fit into this interaction as they open their own companies and start paying taxes."

By the end of the 1990s, most of the gang leaders and avtoritety who had managed to stay alive and avoid incarceration had finally consolidated their positions as respectable businessmen and politicians. Tatarstan's former gruppirovshchiki became heads of business holdings and large corporations, members of parliament, and state officials in the republic and beyond. Some became local council deputies. For example, the leader of Aidarovskie OPG, Aidar Israilov, was a deputy on the Elabuga District Council until he was killed in 1999 (Safarov 2012, 128). Others became oligarchs and parliamentarians. Among the most well-known examples in Tatarstan are two brothers, both former leaders of one of the Kazan gangs, who are now considered to be among the richest people in Russia (Biznesonline 2010). One owns a large network of supermarkets in Kazan. (His first company was registered in 1992 when he was a member of a street gang.) The other is a State Duma deputy and the owner of a major agricultural business holding in the Tatarstan Republic. In our interviews with police officers we were told that the brothers were among the first gang leaders in Kazan to have moved on to control large companies instead of simply racketeering street businesses. Other avtoritety also moved into the legal economic sphere. They own registered companies that pay their taxes but also, according to our police interviewees, give payments to corrupt state authorities, who in return provide "protection for them" and allow them to exist and grow.

Another famous Tatarstan personality, Sergei Shashurin, a leader of a Kazan street gang in the 1980s, eventually became a successful businessman and State Duma deputy. He became a friend of many members of the Russian political and cultural elite, including the movie director Sviatoslav Govorukhin, one of whose films he helped finance. His career was troubled by allegations of large-scale fraud, and in 2005 he was convicted of stealing 37 million rubles from the Tatarstan Bread Company (Konstantinov 2012, 373–75).All across Russia, former gang leaders were going legit. According to Vladimir Ovchinskii, a former head of the Russian branch of Interpol, when he was a police investigator at the end of the 1980s he came across one active member of a liubery group. The man, Vassilii Yakemenko, later became a leader of Putin's youth movement Nashi and head of the Federal Agency on Youth Affairs in the Russian government (Shevelev 2010).

Vladimir Podatev (Pudel′), mentioned in chapter 1 as one of the people who brought criminal organization to the disorganized street world of Khabarovsk in the 1980s, also had an illustrious later career. Having developed a substantial criminal business in Khabarovsk in the beginning of the 1990s, he made powerful enemies among other gang leaders and had to flee to Moscow. He then became a businessman, president of a human rights NGO (called Edinstvo, "Unity"), a member of the Presidential Committee on Human Rights, deputy supreme leader (ataman) of the Cossack associations in Russia and abroad, and a member of the presidium of the Central Committee of the Free Trade Unions of Russia (Dolgova 2003, 356–57).

These processes were not limited to the top echelons of the gangs. Bandits and lads of various ranks and ages, excluding only the youngest cohorts of street fighters, aspired to appropriate businesses and legalize their status. While the leaders and their associates became company directors and members of the management boards of various large business enterprises, local lads in their twenties were getting official positions as managers of legal gaming parlors, garages, construction companies, street markets, currency exchanges, and companies that produce and sell alcohol (Nafikov 2012). Some became owners of local shops and cafes. Others began to work as security guards, as, for example, the Nizy gang members who moved into security at Kazan's Moskovskii market, thereby quasi-legalizing the krysha (Safarov 2012, 313). Members of the *Kladbishchenskie* (cemetery) branch of Khadi Taktash, who used to racketeer cemetery personnel, legalized their business and now provide funeral services themselves. Unlike their former associates from other branches of Khadi Taktash, none of them was even investigated by the police for their past deeds (Beliaev and Sheptitskii 2012, 165).

Many bandits found jobs in private security companies or as security consultants. One street gang leader from Zelenodol′sk, Victor Kuritsin, was sentenced in 2005 to five years for possession of firearms. On release, Kuritsin moved to Samara where he found a position in a commercial company as a security consultant and started to develop contacts within the Samara city administration. His new career was cut short by a criminal investigation into his past and that of his associates (Safarov 2012).

A New Configuration of Power

Over the course of the 2000s, a new configuration of power began to solidify in Russia. Under Vladimir Putin, the coercive agencies of the state, the *silovye struktury*, grew in strength, expanded, and eventually managed to gain the upper hand in the system of violent regulation. Groups associated with state law enforcement institutions—the police, the FSB, the narcotics police, and the Prokuratura—became the main providers of protection. The legal private security industry also became a major provider of protection in the country, and businessmen preferred to buy its services rather than dealing with unpredictable and dangerous criminal groups (Taylor 2011; Volkov 2012). Criminal kryshy were still a factor, and, according to the Business Environment and Enterprise Performance Survey conducted by EBRD and the World Bank in 2005, in fourteen regions (regrettably Tatarstan was not included in the sample), 10 percent of Russian firms and 26 percent of foreign firms paid for private protection (Remington 2011, 160). But the krysha now tends to be provided by security services and the police. According to some estimates, while in the early 1990s, 70 percent of *kryshy* were provided by criminals, ten years later the police provided 70 percent of them and another 10 percent were provided by the FSB (Taylor 2011, 164). Security services and the police have also been working together with organized criminal groups in provision of "protection" and other illegal operations (Galeotti 2006). Although research in this area is understandably sparse, there is evidence that this was the case in Tatarstan (Salagaev, Shashkin, and Konnov 2006) as well as neighboring Bashkartostan, where top officials from the police provided kryshy to organized criminal groups or were themselves active members of these groups (Isangulov 2006).

From this we can see that the strengthening of the state did not lead to the emergence of a modern system of rational legal power or to the eradication of organized crime. As Brian Taylor has argued, in Russia the state bureaucracy and police are organized according to a Weberian patrimonial type of power structure, and their mission can be seen as predation and repression rather than protection of citizens (Taylor 2011). According to Alena Ledeneva (2013), in Russia under Putin a system of informal governance, which she calls the *Sistema*, substitutes for formal state bureaucracy. Within the *Sistema*, personal loyalties and interests, rather than formal rules, bind various power agents together.

Organized crime is part of the same regime. In over two decades of the new capitalist Russia, organized crime did not disappear but instead became more tightly incorporated into the state (Gilinsky 2006; Rawlinson 2010). Various state "rent seekers" (tax authorities, police, security services) and organized criminals often act together, plundering the country's resources and also becoming involved in fraud, money laundering, illegal gambling, machinations in the real estate market, drug trafficking, and other criminal activities.

One well-known example of cooperation between corrupt state officials and criminals is found in the Sergei Magnitsky case in which, according to the overwhelming evidence presented, representatives of Russian tax authorities and top officials from the Ministry of the Interior (MVD), Prokuratura, FSB, and civil courts, acting together with members of organized crime networks, defrauded the Russian state through the use of fictitious tax rebates totaling $230 million. Sergei Magnitsky, the lawyer for the US investment company Hermitage Fund whose investigation uncovered the scam, was arrested on false charges, tortured, and died in prison. Several of those involved in the tax fraud against the Russian state were from Tatarstan, including the judge of the Vakhitovskii District Court of Kazan, who authorized the illegal search of three law firms working for Hermitage in Kazan, and two judges from the Arbitration Court of the Republic of Tatarstan, who, in breach of proper legal procedures, first transferred the ownership of Hermitage subsidiaries to a company registered in the republic in the name of convicted criminal Victor Markelov and then fraudulently awarded a tax rebate to this company (OCCRP 2011).

These days, instead of providing a company with a krysha, other ways are found to appropriate business assets wholesale. This practice, also used in the Hermitage scam, is known as raiding, and it often involves corrupt police officers, tax officials, and judges. Results are achieved through putting pressure on minority shareholders; bribing managers and state officials; creating artificial debts; falsifying companies' charter documents, deeds, and titles; or breaking into and occupying company offices with the help of private security firms or bandits (Osipian 2012; Hanson 2014).

As the state strengthened its power vis-à-vis nonstate violent actors, some of the criminal avtoritety were incorporated into the system, while others were crushed in a concerted attack against the old-style criminal gruppirovki that had aspired to substantial autonomy from the state. In Tatarstan, although arrests and incarcerations had been a feature of gang life throughout their history, in the 2000s the authorities made a major effort to weaken large gruppirovki by arresting and incarcerating their leaders. By that time the republic had become one of Russia's major economic centers, and its leadership aimed to create better conditions for international and domestic business. The gangs were seriously damaging the city and region's reputation.

In 2001 Tatarstan's President Shaimiev, speaking at a meeting of the MVD's top brass, criticized the police for being too lenient and lacking the resolve to deal with organized criminal groups. As Safarov, who was the minister of the interior of Tatarstan at the time, recounts, Shaimiev's outburst was prompted by Safarov's report on the police's success in stopping an avtoritet from the Sevastopol'skie gang, Zafar Utiaganov, from being elected to the Duma. On hearing the name of another Sevastopol'skie gangster—Radik Yusupov (Drakon)—Shaimiev exploded: "Listen, who is this Drakon about whom you talk so much? Drakon, Drakon . . . a deputy? a state official? If he is indeed such a terrible criminal, put him in prison, prove his guilt. How long are we going to tolerate organized crime?

Enough! It's time to put an end to it. Set yourself a specific task and achieve it" (Safarov 2012, 103).

This was the start of a major campaign against the leadership of criminal gangs. Many of the leaders and avtoritety at the time were owners of legal businesses (restaurants, construction companies, banks, hotels, etc.) in Moscow, Kazan, and other places in Russia. But old cases were reopened, evidence collected, and law enforcement bodies succeeded in prosecuting many of the gang organizations.[2]

Changes in Gang Business

In addition to criminal prosecutions, the gangs were also weakened by the gradual modernization of the Russian economy. Toward the end of the 1990s, the shadow economic sphere contracted as networks of large supermarkets, banks, and car service companies replaced small shops, currency exchange kiosks, and street garages. The latter operated mainly in a cash economy and had been easy prey for gangs. At the same time, private security companies muscled in on the gang protection business. With large-scale racketeering opportunities contracting, the gangs retreated to the street economy and to traditional areas of organized crime activity (illegal gambling, fraud, prostitution rings, and, increasingly, the illegal drug trade).

For street gangs, street parking lots have become a prominent part of their business. Guarded parking lots are relatively new to Russia, as car owners have traditionally parked their vehicles for free on the side of the road. In the 2000s the gangs moved into this business en masse. Money from the parking lots helps to hold the streets together, as this business, being easy to organize and run, feeds the rank and file, giving an incentive to the younger members to stay in the gang. Setting up a parking "business" requires a campaign of primitive violence, conducted by younger lads, and organizational and legal work performed by older gang members and avtoritety, who use their connections with the traffic police to gain permissions to open up this business. Members of the middle-age cohorts collect the money, a share of which is paid into the gang's obshchak.

2. The gang-busting trials in Kazan involved prosecutions of the following gangs: Khadi Taktash (2002), Zhilka (2005), Banda Tagirianova (2007), Kvartala (2008), 56th Kvartal (2008), Banda Tashkenta (2010), Nizy (2010–11), Banda Khasainova (2010), Kinoplionka (2011), Banda Bazarovskie (2011), Sevastopolskie (2011), and Pervaki (2012). In Naberezhnye Chelny the prosecuted gangs were the 29th Kompleks (2006 and 2010), 48th Kompleks (2008), Kuritsinskie (2008), and Boksery (2012). Trials were also held over gangs from other areas of Tatarstan, such as Al' metievsk, Nizhnekamsk, Elabuga, Bugul' ma, Zelenodol' sk, and Nurlat (Nafikov 2012).

The campaign typically runs like this. In order to "persuade" the car owners that it is in their interests to put their vehicles into guarded parking lots, members of the younger-age cohorts create a crime wave on the streets: slashing tires, breaking windshields and lights, scratching paintwork, breaking into cars and ripping out music systems. As a result, car owners may decide that it is safer to put their cars into a guarded parking lot. In actuality, the real value of the gang protection is next to zero, and no compensation is paid to the owner if a car is damaged or stolen. In Kazan alone this industry creates a profit of three billion rubles a year. Together with the gaming machines, kiosks, and street markets, it constitutes the main "shadow" source of income of the criminal obshchak (Nafikov 2012, 124–25).

Despite the gradual reduction in racketeering by criminal gangs in Tatarstan that started toward the end of the 1990s, gang racketeering of commercial companies still takes place (Zagrebneva 2011).[3] Gangs attempt to establish control over some of the profitable spots for taxi business (airports, train stations, spaces near expensive restaurants and concert halls) and bus routes. In June 2012, police in Kazan arrested several members of the Kaspiiskie gang who were involved in extortion operations against local bus and taxi companies. The gangs had been demanding that companies pay them 20–30 percent of their profits and subjecting the drivers to violent intimidation, breaking windows and lights in their vehicles, and beating the drivers in full view of their passengers. Taxi drivers picking up passengers from the train station were also forced to pay dues (Biznesonline 2012). The gangs often operate in tandem with the police, who close their eyes to the gangs' extortionist activities.

In addition, the police often have their own predatory economy, using their power to extract money or labor from taxi drivers. For example, according to S., a Kazan taxi driver, the police make the drivers pay them a share of their profits, as well as using their services for free for periodic *subbotniks* (from the word "Saturday"; this was a term used to describe occasional unpaid weekend "voluntary" work expected from citizens under the Soviet regime).

Similarly to other organized crime groups around the world (Schelling 1971), the Kazan gangs increasingly seek to govern the underworld. With opportunities to racketeer legitimate businesses diminishing, illegal gambling, casinos, and legal bookmaking shops are now among the main areas for the gang protection business, although it is increasingly the case that avtoritety own these businesses outright. Although casinos are now prohibited in Russia (except in

3. The risk that a company would be appropriated by its krysha has been real, not just with the bandit gangs, but with police and FSB protection operations. See, e.g., the investigation by *Novaia Gazeta* (Kanev 2014).

six designated areas, none of which is in Tatarstan), Kazan has an abundance of gaming arcades (250 in 2010, with about 3,000 gaming machines in total). With each machine making a profit of about 3,000 rubles a day, this industry generates a substantial profit for the gangs that largely control it (Nafikov 2012, 122). The Tatarstan gangs also provide security during *strelki*, both locally and in other parts of the country, including Moscow (Safarov 2012, 123).

The Kazan gangs also control street prostitution in the city, with key "hubs" on Iuzhnaia Highway and Vosstaniia Street, and receive payment from sex workers who want to work in the gangs' territories. They also continue to be involved in other traditional forms of organized crime, such as illegal financial operations and smuggling of counterfeit goods; but unlike other organized criminal groups around the world, their involvement in illegal trade in weapons or trafficking of illegal migrants is negligible (Nafikov 2012, 120–25). Elsewhere in Russia, organized crime includes trafficking and the weapons trade, as well as money laundering and gambling, with operations extending beyond Russia's borders (Varese 2001; Cheloukhine and Haberfeld 2011; Varese 2011).

The drug market is a source of business for criminal gangs worldwide, and Russia today is no exception. Since the start of the market reforms Russia has become increasingly involved with and integrated into the international drug trade (Shelley 2006). The involvement of Kazan gangs in the illegal drug market has been expanding. This is a highly profitable business and one that neatly fits the gang structure, with leaders organizing wholesale operations and younger members working at the street end. In Tatarstan, although street gang members do not rely on drug dealing as their only (or even main) source of income, they do participate in the street level of the operation. According to Aidar's account of his gang: "Usually the senior members don't bother with the small stuff and deal with bulk sellers, but they might offer their juniors the chance to buy smaller volumes of drugs for further reselling: 'If you want it, here's the price; mark up and sell. Keep the profits. If not, that's fine. There are plenty of willing guys; we'll find someone else.'"

However, the heroin trade tends to be concentrated in specialized criminal operations organized primarily by ethnic gangs rather than neighborhood-based gangs. Nine specialized drug gangs were prosecuted in Tatarstan in recent years. One operation was organized in 2006–9 by an association of several Kazan criminal groups. They arranged the transportation of heroin from Tajikistan into Kazan, Moscow, and other Russian cities. The association distributed about thirty-two kilos of heroin, as well as other drugs, while sending money back to Tajikistan using local Russian banks. Most groups specializing in the drug trade (70%) were formed by ethnic migrants from Central Asia (Nafikov 2012, 171–72).

To members of organized crime networks, whether or not to get involved in the drug business is a common dilemma, particularly when they construct themselves as moral agents in the community. Paoli quoted an old Sicilian Mafia capo who said that "in my opinion, those harming others and especially those trafficking drugs are not Mafiosi; they are just simple delinquents. These substances are ruining the new generations. When I meet somebody who trades drugs, I immediately push him away from me because I have a loathing of him" (2003, 97). The same attitude was expressed by many of our interviewees. Both sale and consumption of drugs are prohibited by the vory and bandit codes. In the gang world, drug addicts are seen as subhuman; the gangs despise and openly harass them, and selling drugs to them can result in major reputational damage. Apart from cultural prohibitions on trading in drugs, for bandit gangs the heroin business is high risk, since it is eternally at the forefront of police attention and engaging in it can undermine the complex local social ecology in which the gangs rely on police cooperation (or at least turning a blind eye) to carry on with the rest of their business.

This explains why gang members often compromise by only dealing in marijuana. In those gangs in which drug dealing is still proscribed, the members tend to peddle marijuana independently, often in secret, without informing their comrades about their activities. The lads also try to bypass the gangs' prohibition by hiring drug dealers and paying them a salary rather than dealing themselves.

In a time-honored tradition of organized crime, the gangs also rob unaffiliated drug dealers, who are unlikely to seek legal redress (Jacobs 2000). The dealers may have a krysha (even one provided by the police), but this, like everything else in this outlaw business, does not give a foolproof guarantee of protection. Ansar described one of his gang's operations:

> These two weed dealers lived in our territory, but they weren't under our control; they had a police krysha. We couldn't attack them directly because the cops would arrest us for robbery straight away. That is why we sent the youngest members to keep an eye on the dealers, to see which cars they drive, when they come home, how many people there are with them. . . . We discovered that they had a day when they brought in the weed, because then they arrived with heavy bags. So we organized an ambush, beat up the dealers, confiscated the weed, and then gave it to our dealers to sell.

As in other organized crime structures, the gangs also give protection to common criminals, expropriating a proportion of their proceeds. Gruppirovshchiki can use their connections with the traffic police to facilitate the business of such criminals, for example by helping them to sell stolen cars. Some gangs (or businesses under their protection) sell stolen cell phones. The gang leaders use their connections with cell phone companies to organize the changing of phone numbers on these phones.

Another line of gang business is selling licenses to racketeer. A gang with an established reputation can allow an aspiring street gang to use its name in its operations in exchange for a proportion of the profits. This device is sometimes used by younger members who invite a group of local "wannabes" to form a "branch" and collect money for the gang's obshchak, with the promise of future membership. This is often a deliberate con. The "wannabes" rarely acquire any rights from the gang and eventually discover that they have been tricked out of their money. As Il'sur said, "Nobody is interested in feeding them and launching them into serious business."

Some gang members are also involved in opportunistic criminal acts such as robbery, burglary, or theft. These acts are seen as much riskier than typical gang activities and mostly involve less-educated members from troubled backgrounds with a history of criminality that predates their gang involvement. These activities are not considered by the gang to be proper gang business.

Blurring the Lines

As we have seen, the gang's economic power rested from the start on abuse and imposition rather than the provision of services. The gang used the strength of its organization, its "war machine," to force people to part with their money and resources. But its economy was not just based on the use of force. The gang exploited the lack of a clear border between the formal and informal economic spheres in Russian society. In the lawless climate of Russian transition, in which state organizations and private sector companies were engaged in massive money laundering, tax avoidance, and customs evasion, the gangs developed valuable expertise in setting up various illicit schemes both for those businesses that they protected or owned and for other public and private companies. The economic resources and social capital that the gang leadership accumulated by using this highly advantageous position in between different sectors allowed at least some of its representatives to make a transition into the country's elite and to become respected businessmen and politicians.

The gangs' economic activities had to change in response to the eventual strengthening of state power and the modernization of the Russian economy. By the mid-2000s some of the bandits had gone legitimate, while others increasingly moved from away from the protection racket and into provision of illicit goods and services, such as drugs and prostitution, and other illegal money-making activities.

But as Putin's regime has consolidated its power, the dividing line between "unlawful" and state-based networks has remained blurred. Russia has not managed to create the power structures of a modern state based on legal rationality, and the state continues to be mired in self-serving collaborations between state-based networks and, to use Girard's (2005, 170) expression, their "monstrous double," the criminal gangs.

4

GANG ORGANIZATION

The first generation of gang leaders, those at the helm of street gangs in the late 1980s and early 1990s, produced some of the richest people in Russia. But the rank and file of the gang, while serving as the source of this elite group (albeit in ever diminishing numbers) and providing muscle for the leaders' violent operations, lived their own lives, holding down the fort in their home territory and accumulating relatively modest resources. The leaders' own criminal networks and the street-based gangs became effectively separate entities, though interlinked and functionally interdependent and usually retaining the same name that they had originally derived from the city topography. While street-based teams or *brigady* and their alliances remained territorially bound, the groups run by gang leaders and their unpaid and paid associates were no longer attached to the specific turf but conducted protection operations within economic sectors in Russia and abroad and branched out into semi legal and legal economic spheres. The leaders' networks and the street-based gangs formed parts of the same alliance, bound together by ancestral origins that typically dated back to the glorious years from the 1970s to the 1990s, when their gang forefathers had established the original "street," and by rituals and quasi-familial commitments.

In this chapter I analyze the gang as a form of social organization, and discuss whether we should see it as a rational business corporation or as a traditional social form that is sustained by personal solidarities and bonds.

Patrimonial Organizations

If you are a young lad seeking to join a gang, the world of the streets may look to you like a place where you can develop a variety of money-making schemes. You need to be quick on your feet in looking for opportunities, and the gang will support you in your endeavors. United with other members by mutual interest rather than in service of some noble criminal cause, you will be able to pursue your own projects (*deliugi*) provided that you stay loyal to the organization, support other members, and pay into the obshchak. If necessary, you may be able to use the obshchak as a source of investment capital.

From this perspective, the gang could be seen as a business organization, a criminal corporation or firm dedicated to economic accumulation. The thesis of corporatization of gangs is common in modern Western gang literature (Hagedorn and Macon 1988; Vigil 1988; Moore 1991; Sánchez-Jankowski 1991; Venkatesh 2000; Densley 2013), in which the gang is seen as an economic enterprise, albeit operating in the shadow and criminal economy. There seems to be a "natural" process of transformation of juvenile fighting formations into entrepreneurial gangs. While members of juvenile gangs occupy themselves mainly with recreational violence, as they grow up, their concerns become more materialistic. The gang turns into a corporation dedicated exclusively to economic gain, and it acquires a structure that resembles a corporate one.

People who see gangs as mimicking business organizations can find many features of the gang's organization to confirm their view. The gang provides the disadvantaged residents of ghettoes and low-income areas with work—often extremely risky and not very well paid—while its leaders, like the heads of large corporations, can become spectacularly rich. It has its own structures of subordination as well as procedures of recruitment and advancement.

This seeming homology is, however, misleading. Coming back to our young lad who wants to make money on the streets, he will soon discover (unless he already knows this from his street upbringing) that to be in a gang he must "live with the lads." This means seeing them socially, spending as much leisure time as he can with them, helping them in their hour of need, attending regular meetings and ceremonial events, and embracing the moral code (*poniatiia*) and its discipline. From a self-interested pragmatic being, he will become a faithful member of a clan, a brotherhood, an extended family. He will join a patrimonial society that is not a replica of, but an alternative to, modern capitalist companies and corporations.

Material pragmatism coexists here with social solidarity. As Conquergood (1994, 24) commented in writing about US gangs, "although gangs span a remarkable range of organizational structures that vary in terms of complexity—from a neighborhood adolescent street corner society to a city-wide supergang that controls the urban drug market—in-group solidarity remains a defining characteristic." The gang combines a spirit of means-end rationality, orientation toward profit, self-reliance, and willingness to take risks—all the qualities that characterize the modern enterprising ethic (Du Gay 1996)—with a lifeworld of noninstrumental relationships based on feelings and personal obligations, propped up by constant informal sociability.

The Russian bandit gang is neither a purely social organization nor an illegal business corporation but a multifunctional clan. It is a form of social life in which quasi-kinship ties between members of the gang brotherhood become, to use the words of Deleuze and Guattari (1983, 147), "not a structure, but a practice, a praxis, a method, even a strategy." The gang's patrimonial organization is used to sustain social linkages, establish territorial alliances, and, in certain periods when social order weakens, to capture resources and even penetrate the state.

Gang Leadership

As heads of patrimonial clans, gang leaders are not elected or appointed but rise to power through a combination of ruthlessness and charisma. Such a leader retains his role until he is incarcerated or dies. The leaders of gruppirovki are powerful males who personify the qualities valued in premodern organic hierarchies of force. These tribal chieftains show strength, cunning, and a will to gain and exert power; they are ready to adopt the patriarchal role of the head of a family as a tough but fair leader who protects, directs, and disciplines his followers and negotiates with the outside world on their behalf. Our interviewees from the streets characterized their leaders in the following way. Petia expressed the view that "the leader must be a tough and confident person who loves power and is willing to fight for it by any means possible." Taking a similar view, Nafik said that "the leader should be determined, cunning, fair, and not afraid of anything." Il'sur suggested that "force is the main quality of a leader—force in everything, in health, in muscles, in intelligence, in connections."

In a gang, the leader has unquestionable familial authority and demands complete loyalty from the gang brotherhood (*bratva*). The realities of gang life, with the ruthless violence of gang leadership, frequent killings of leaders and their associates (avtoritety), and the ever-present danger for ordinary members of being accused of insubordination or treason, may be seen as contradicting the general ethos of kinship, but in fact they are typical of patrimonial forms of authority. Collins (2011, 18) commented on patrimonial power that it "involves personal loyalty, but it is also fraught with conflicts, betrayal, and treason—Shakespearean plots are virtual textbooks of patrimonial politics." Indeed, stories about members of the top echelons of bandit gangs are full of bloody conflict, betrayal, torture and assassination of gang leaders and avtoritety in disputes over power and spheres of control. In the 1990s, internal struggles and attempts to unseat the current leaders became an everyday reality for the gangs' top ranks. Many perished in intergang wars, often together with businessmen who were under their protection or police officers who "worked" with them. Leaders and avtoritety planned and often executed the killings of their enemies, or commissioned special brigades of killers, who were themselves highly likely to be killed afterward. These killers could be members of gruppirovki or invited from outside the gang. The relatively low sums paid for contract killings ($10,000 by 29th Kompleks in 2001, $8,000 by Zhilka in 2000) show how cheap life could be. In one-third of Tatarstan's criminal gangs the initial leadership changed as a result of assassinations or unexplained deaths, and the same happened in five of the seven largest gruppirovki (Nafikov 2012, 170–71). Murderers did not spare the children, girlfriends, or wives of their victims, or any other witnesses unfortunate enough to be present at the scene. Shootouts took place in crowded bars and cafes with no regard for the lives of innocent bystanders.

The leaders needed to demonstrate strength whatever it took. Displaying their authority; commanding fear through ruthlessness, unpredictability, and brutal force; and being constantly vigilant against potential threats, betrayals, or challenges from within one's own circle became part of a gang leader's treacherous existence. The former street hooligans who became leaders of large criminal clans needed to expertly perform power, and the previous tropes provided by street and *vor* cultures were not enough. Hollywood movies about the Mafia were studied for new clues on how to look and act like a criminal boss. The famous bandit Radik Galiakberov (Radzha)—the leader of the Khadi Taktash gruppirovka—modeled himself on Marlon Brando in *The Godfather*. Not only did he like to quote Don Corleone, he always wore a suit, a white shirt with a tie, and a long coat, and would even, like Brando, project his lower jaw forward (Beliaev and Sheptitskii 2012, 152). The leader of the 29th Kompleks, Adygan Saliakhov, made young members of the gang watch *Once upon a Time in America* and *The Godfather* as training videos. He honed his violent performance to create fear and awe among his gang. It was said that his favorite phrase was "Kill him!" The gang's folklore included an episode in which Saliakhov once reportedly ordered the killing of a young man who had been stupid enough to invite Saliakhov's girlfriend to dance. The young man only escaped because he was a good runner (Safarov 2012, 128).

In the beginning, the leaders' improvisations extended to attempts to establish heavily guarded "feudal" courts in the middle of run-down Soviet housing estates.

In the early 1990s Zhilka's leader Khaider built a restaurant in the courtyard of his apartment block, where he and his gang held regular meet-ups and drinking sessions. The courtyard was constantly guarded by members of the gang. Young lads even set up cordons on the roads leading into Zhilploshchadka territory and checked all incoming vehicles. Some of the roads in were blocked with concrete slabs. As a result of the gang's surveillance the police could not conduct any covert operations in the area. There were rumors that Khaider wanted to build an elevator connecting the balcony of his apartment (on the fourth floor of a modest Soviet building) to the restaurant below. However, before these grandiose plans could come to fruition, he decided to escape to Saint Petersburg with his close associates after being threatened by rival gangsters (Beliaev and Sheptitskii 2012, chap. 11).

After moving up from their territorial roots, many of the top brass have continued to be loosely involved with the street youth gangs, retaining their patrimonial roles as heads of their expansive gang tribes. Even those leaders who have branched into legal business, who have become company directors and in some cases also acquired political office (the two often going together), frequently retain their links to the territorial gangs, deciding the general direction of gang business (whether, for example, to get involved in the high-risk drug market), keeping an eye on the gang's affairs, and using their connections and authority to "solve problems" with the representatives of the antinarcotics service, the police, and other power structures at the ground level. The leaders and avtoritety thus act as a political force, creating political dependencies and alliances that make it possible for street business to function with as little hindrance as possible.

From time to time avtoritety (but not the leaders themselves) make ceremonial visits to the street gang's meet-ups, presenting themselves to the "next generation." They do it, as one of our gang interviewees, Il'nar, said "to remind them who's boss." Ultimately, the leaders want the street to continue existing as a united and cohesive force. In the words of Viktor, "Avtoritety make sure that we have strict discipline and that we remain a 'street' and not a mob." Of course, avtoritety have a pragmatic interest in the street's reproduction. However much they've moved toward legalization, the street gang remains an important resource in the event of conflicts with competitors (or for raiding somebody else's business), a force that keeps control over street territory and a violent instrument that can be useful in case of problems that might emerge in an *avtoritet*'s or leader's life. The street organizations can also be used for illegal business—for example, drug distribution.

In this system of authority, any weakening of the tribal leaders' positions inevitably results in disorientation and disintegration at the bottom. As in Homer's epics, "all focus is on the power-body of the chieftain. His men cluster around him. His individual destiny is bound with theirs and with the fate of the kingdom" (Nicolson 2014). Infighting between leaders or their murder, exile, or incarceration leads to a serious destabilization of the street gang, the contraction of its membership, and the migration of lads to other, more powerful gangs.

At the same time, while most street gang members we interviewed knew who the leader of the gang was, the vast majority had no clue what he looked like and had only vague ideas about the extent of his business interests. All contacts by leaders and avtoritety with the members of the street gang now take place via *smotriashchie* (the people responsible for overseeing each age cohort). The smotriashchie are entrusted with the day-to-day business of the gang. Among other things, they look for the most able and clever lads, who can be selected for involvement in serious assignments and eventually recruited into the top echelons. They also organize the "muscle" for the leaders' violent operations. But, although some lads do eventually progress to more senior ranks in the street gang, this does not gain them access to serious business opportunities. As M. put it, "ownership of a business and provision of a krysha to companies remains the prerogative of the senior members of an OPG, those who started the rackets at the beginning of the 1990s."

Networked Structures

Developing from street associations, the Kazan gangs turned into complex multicentered organizations. For example, according to Nafikov, one large Tatarstan criminal gruppirovka (29th Kompleks from Naberezhnye Chelny) had the following structure. At the top was the leader of the organization, who oversaw other leaders. (Nafikov does not distinguish between leaders and avtoritety, so the exact status of these associates is not clear.) Several people coordinated the gruppirovka's activities in Moscow, and they developed close contacts with state authorities, law enforcement agencies, and the judiciary. One leader oversaw all of 29th Kompleks's finances and economic activities. The gruppirovka also had teams responsible for group security, establishing contact with corrupt members of law enforcement agencies, conducting surveillance operations, and communications with lawyers and the mass media. There were special teams of killers. The gang also established its own private security company, named Bars, in Moscow, which gave 29th Kompleks legal access to weapons.

At the territorial level in Tatarstan, two 29th Kompleks leaders headed separate structures in the "base city," Naberezhnye Chelny. These territorial leaders controlled many businesses and individual entrepreneurs in the Prikamskii and Zakamskii regions of Tatarstan. Altogether they had about two hundred people under their command, including the members of youth gangs recruited from residents of the territories controlled by the gruppirovka. Each of these leaders coordinated five to six large teams (*brigady*) that controlled small and medium-sized businesses, the drug trade, prostitution, illegal parking lots, and the like (Nafikov 2012, 156).

The Khadi Taktash gruppirovka had a similar structure. Its leadership was mainly based in Moscow, and three teams operated at the ground level in Kazan. One, Kladbishchenskie, was a specialized gang that controlled most of Kazan's cemeteries. Another, Volochaevskie, was a street gang formed by young people who lived on Volochaevskaia Street. Among other businesses, Volochaevskie controlled the local auto service station. Finally, Radzhovskie was a youth street gang involved in the drug and weapons trades, street racketeering, prostitution networks, and fraud. Khadi Taktash exists to this day, despite a trial in 1999 that saw lengthy prison sentences given to its leaders and avtoritety. At the territorial level the gruppirovka currently consists of three *brigady* (Beliaev and Sheptitskii 2012, 140–66).

The clans have a common economy. As mentioned, all gruppirovki have common funds, obshchaki. The leadership's obshchak receives payment from the leader and avtoritety, who typically contribute up to 10 percent of their incomes from companies that they own or control. The "streets" have their own obshchaki, and they also send a proportion of their income to the leadership's obshchak. Nafikov's calculations, made on the basis of his research into Zhilka's criminal case, show the following distribution of a gruppirovka's expenditure. About 30 percent of the obshchak was spent on bribing officials and on "public relations." Thirty percent was spent on assistance to incarcerated members and payments to lawyers. Thirty percent was used to pay bodyguards, security guards working for avtoritety, drivers, and other trusted nongang members working for the leader; for payments for contract crimes; for single rewards to members of the gruppirovka; and for personal consumption by the leaders. The remaining 10 percent was spent on cars, phones, and weapons (Nafikov 2012, 161–63).

Various structures of the gruppirovka are united into one large "tribe" which often retains its original name (e.g., Pervaki, Zhilka, and Boriskovo in Kazan; Solntsevskaia and Orekhovskaia in Moscow). Despite the contrast between the stratospheric rise of many of the gang leaders—those who were not killed or incarcerated—and the relatively pedestrian existence of the street gang members, who are left to feed off the street economy, all of them identify with the same gruppirovka.

Research into large criminal associations elsewhere in Russia also points out the multicentered character of their organization. A study conducted by Varese (2001; 2013), based on the Italian police investigation into an outpost of the Solntsevskaia gruppirovka operating in Italy, showed that it had a flexible structure, where one umbrella organization coordinated a variety of autonomous crews working in different regions and even in different countries. The leaders of individual crews formed a "supreme council" whose members met regularly to discuss operational matters. Each crew sent money to a general obshchak for the organization, but a large portion of the finances circulated within the autonomous units. Similar conclusions about the flexible decentralized character of Russian organized crime groups were made by Galeotti (2000, 37). As he pointed out, the teams change depending on the nature of their operations and are driven by opportunity rather than long-term function.

The Structure of Territorial Gangs

Territorial gangs range from relatively small groups, uniting members living in one or two adjacent streets, to large associations (so-called families) numbering several hundred people. According to N., one of our police informants, in the mid-2000s one of the larger gangs, Pervaki, had fifty-four members in the older age cohort and two hundred in the middle age and younger cohorts. Another one hundred fifty to two hundred retained member status but no longer participated in the gang's activities.

Membership in the street starts at around sixteen to seventeen and lasts for life. However, after reaching twenty-five to thirty many members start moving away from gang activities, and their membership becomes largely nominal. They participate in the social life of the gang and use the gang's networks, but otherwise they move away from taking part in daily operations. As twenty-six-year-old Ispug explained:

> These days we only see other lads at meet-ups, because we can't spend time together as we used to anymore. Work, family—these things take up most of our time. It's quite rare for someone to suggest that we get together and make something happen. We don't do anything illegal—we're not looking for adventure. Many of us have our own businesses, and nearly everyone works somewhere. It's all above board. We come to meet-ups just to socialize.

The "above board" part of Ispug's account may have questionable veracity, but the fact that for many of the older gang members the street turns into a social rather than a business network was confirmed by gang participants and law enforcement experts alike.

Some members leave the gang officially, by paying a fine and returning any money they may have borrowed from the obshchak. A minority progress from lads to adult bandits by joining gruppirovki structures directly controlled by the leaders and avtoritety.

The street has three or four age cohorts. Typical names for the cohorts are *stariki* (elders), *starshie* (seniors in age), *supera* (superiors), and *pizdiuki* (kids). The oldest cohort is the *stariki*, people over thirty, gang veterans who often have income from local companies controlled by gruppirovki. Members of the middle cohorts, *starshie* and *supera,* are between twenty and thirty. Some of them have their own businesses, and they may also work for the *stariki*'s companies in various capacities. The largest cohort is the *pizdiuki*, young members who are going through their apprenticeship period and are often involved in violent enforcement activities, defending the turf, and collecting money from various street businesses.

The street gang is overseen by avtoritety, older members of the gruppirovka who have moved away from street activities to running off-the-street business operations. These figures, who can be seen as the clan elders, oversee the gang's activities without exercising day-to-day control. The avtoritety's concern is for the street to reproduce itself, remain a cohesive force, and not lose its territory. They help the street to resolve issues affecting its business, often using their contacts with local public officials; assist the younger gang members in dealings with the police; and get involved when wars with other gruppirovki break out.

Avtoritety appoint a general *smotriashchii* from the top cohort (the *stariki*). It is this general smotriashchii who exercises daily control over the gang and monitors all the cohorts. He attends all gang meet-ups and is expected to spend a lot of time keeping watch over the gang members. Each age cohort also elects a smotriashchii for the next cohort down from among themselves. Similarly to avtoritety, smotriashchie cannot be seen simply as business managers. While coordinating the members' business activities, they also act as ritual specialists. They conduct all the gang's rituals and ceremonies (introduction of new members, punishment, and ritual expulsion of wrong-doers, etc.). They also make sure that the gang keeps its cohesion, and members attend the necessary meetings and do not lose sight of one another. Among the qualities they are required to possess are fairness, intelligence, and "being able to speak properly," which means justifying their decisions and demands by reference to the code of poniatiia.

To protect their obshchaki, some gangs also have a *smotriashchii za obshchakom* ("common fund overseer") who keeps the cohort's money and makes sure that members make their regular contributions. The amount of money due depends on the member's age and income. All members contribute a weekly or monthly sum, plus up to two-thirds of any income gained from gang-related activities. The obshchak is used to provide assistance to the lads and their families (help to members who are placed in police detention or incarceration, payment for medical treatment, and money for funerals); legal protection (bribes to police officers and criminal investigators, payment to lawyers, and payment of various fines); and the business needs of the gang (loans for starting up a business, buying gasoline or hiring taxis for those occasions when the lads go to organized fights or formal meetings with rival gangs). Nobody can use the fund for any other purpose, and embezzlement from it is punished very severely and leads to expulsion from the group.

Members join the group during organized recruitment drives, held every two or three years, at which point a new cohort is formed. The recruitment process is the responsibility of the youngest cohort. The lads need to find candidates who will replace them as they progress into the next stratum. They ask their friends and neighbors if they know anybody who can be invited to join. Joining is a simple matter of consent. There are no elaborate ceremonies, kissing of the leader's ring, signing of oaths in blood, or any other spectacular rituals. Il'sur explained, "It's no different to how things work elsewhere. The younger lads bring their replacements, then grow into the next age category, and the ones they brought find themselves replacements a couple of years later. And so on. There's no initiation ritual for lads; it's all as mundane as starting a new job."

When recruitment is over, the new members are assembled at the regular meet-up and introduced to the rest of the gang. As Potap explained, "They are told: 'Lads, you are with us.' They learn when to come to meetings and how much money to give to the obshchak, and that's about it."

The reason for this rather mundane nature of transition into the gang is the significant overlap between street culture and gang culture (addressed in detail in chapter 8). By the time a street lad joins the gang he has already acquired many of the essential attitudes and skills it needs from him. He knows that he cannot lose face in any circumstances, and that even when dealing with overwhelming force he should try to talk his way out of the situation and never run away. He has mastered the art of projecting authority. He knows how to "speak properly." He has the skill of judging a person's position in the street hierarchy within the first few seconds of an encounter. He has learned that he needs to support his friends if they are in trouble and never abandon them. So all the gang has to do is check the candidate's street reputation to make sure that he has not done anything in the past that would disgrace him and, by association, the street. He should have no history of succumbing to extortion nor have worked for the police. Although a candidate does not have to be a good fighter, he should not be afraid to fight. Sometimes the candidates are tested—for example, if an older lad says something offensive to the candidate, he has to fight to defend his name, otherwise he will be rejected.

Ultimately, though, this relatively seamless entry is a consequence of the lack of a radical separation between the gang and wider society in Russia. This is very different from other national contexts. A young man who joins a Sicilian Mafia *cosca* has to "assume a permanent new identity—to become a 'man of honor'—and to subordinate all his previous allegiances to his mafia membership" (Paoli 2003, 17). Initiation rituals serve the purpose of symbolically removing all previous identities and asserting the new master one. This is not required in the Russian context because gang members retain membership in wide social networks alongside their gang affiliation (discussed in chapter 5). A radical separation from society is neither a required nor desired quality in the Russian gang world, where extensive social connections are highly valued.

Rising in the Gang

Having entered the gang, street lads are expected to obey the authority of their older comrades and follow the gang's discipline. They are forbidden to drink and are expected to do sports. In some gangs they do sports two or three times a day: running, weight lifting at a gym, and practicing martial arts. As twenty-four-old-year Risat said, "sports makes the younger lads stronger and distracts them from doing stupid things."

The younger lads also do all the routine work for the gruppirovka. The gang smotriashchie give them tasks they need to do for the benefit of the whole street—for example, to be on the lookout during *strelki*, to guard parking lots belonging to the gang, or to intimidate traders and force them under the gang's krysha. They protect the turf, fight with "enemies" during *razborki* (arranged gang fights) and wars, and generally do most of the gang's violent work. The young members are taught to see all this as their duty, and as long as they hope to progress in the gang and acquire better business opportunities, they have to put up with the inevitable risk involved in such assignments.

This was confirmed by B., one of our law enforcement experts:

> Older OPG members do not commit crimes themselves; they use youngsters for that, and they teach them accordingly. For example, they say, "When you came to our street, what did you say? You said that you wanted to stand up for our street. Well, the street needs your help. It has problems; go and do what you are told to do. Burn a kiosk. Break into a car. Hit somebody over the head with a metal rod." If they want to stay in the gang, it is impossible to refuse; they have to obey. Everybody in the younger age groups goes through this, and after a while, it's their turn to do the same to the next generation of youngsters.

This situation is somewhat similar to the Sicilian Cosa Nostra or the Calabrian 'Ndrangheta, where the lower-ranking members show their allegiance to the organization first and foremost through the use of violence, often in the direct service of the Mafia chiefs (Paoli 2003, 97). Other ecologies—for example, American ghetto areas—also produce organizations that seem to put a high value on a member's capacity for violence (Yablonsky 1962; Anderson 1999). However, in the Russian gang, the most dangerous operations are often subcontracted to outsiders. Thus, according to Aidar, "if there is a need to do something that may lead to a lad ending up in prison, members of the gang are rarely involved, as it is easier to use outsiders who would not necessarily know who contracted them. The gang code does not allow one member to force another to do something against their will." Gang avtoritety often recruit killers or killer teams from outside the gang if serious violence is to be committed,[1] or they organize special teams of experienced killers within the gang structure.

A capacity for violence is not a quality that the gangs value above all others. In fact, people who engage in gratuitous violence are expelled from the street. Violence and risk taking are seen as bad for group relations and for a person's future. Pavel stated: "You have to be careful in what you do, since you can easily end up in prison if you're arrogant enough to take every opportunity—especially the most dangerous ones."

The gang does have a number of *byki* (bulls), members who do violent work. Such work is seen as necessary but inferior and is generally reserved for younger members. Those lads who do not show entrepreneurial capacities continue to serve as "the muscle" of the gang beyond the initial stages of their gang careers.

Status within a gang is linked primarily with conformity to the group code and playing an active role in finding business opportunities for oneself and other gang members. Instead of talking about errands and commands, the older lads insisted on "mutual interests" that unite the members of different ages. This is how Aidar described his gang's involvement in the drug business: "[Nowadays], the most profitable business is drugs. The elders rarely sell them themselves, and deal with wholesale traders. The youngsters get offers to buy smaller quantities for resale. But there is no compulsion to do it, and usually there are enough volunteers. Everything works on the basis of mutual interest."

---

1. This, for example, was the practice in the violent Zhilka wars (Nasyrov 2008).

Time and commitment are rewarded by greater responsibility and better business opportunities. "Active lads" get more lucrative *deliugi* and can move to supervisor positions. As Viktor said, "The only people who can get ahead on the street are those who spend a lot of time on it, those who are constantly in touch with the senior lads, who do business, get involved in wars, and so on. An active lad has every opportunity to become a smotriashchii, and then a leader. Those who only attend meet-ups do not get such opportunities."

People who aspire to promotion in the gang need to be eloquent speakers and to know the ins and outs of the code and be able to use it skillfully to make people comply with the gang's demands. They also have to have good relations with the older lads and know how to find good money-making opportunities or, as Nafik put it, to "always have their ear to the ground."

Il'nar's description of what it takes to have authority on the streets emphasizes the following qualities of a street lad:

> You have to spend a lot of time working on yourself. First off, you have to overcome your fear. A lad shouldn't be scared of anyone—not cops, not prison, not enemies. After that, a lad's got to make sure he's always in touch with what's going on, that he's keeping his seniors informed and doesn't go too long without touching base with them. Then you've got to have a head on your shoulders so you can think and work things out for yourself. And, most important, you need your own patch to live off. That matters more than anything else.

In other words, the gang rewards people who are brave, loyal, smart, and entrepreneurial. Trofim, who at twenty-one felt that he had enjoyed a good career in the gang, expressed a firm belief that if a lad followed the rules and showed initiative, he could do well:

> In order to get ahead as one of us, you've got to behave like a proper lad. Then they gradually start trusting you with little things, then with bigger matters, and finally offer you a decent business. For example, I didn't do anything to begin with, just hung around as a brat whom the older lads were teaching how to live properly. I was offered my first business only two years later, when I entered the *supera* category. I became a parking lot smotriashchii, got 100 to 150 rubles a day. Then they gave it to one of the juniors and offered me control of a business where I could sell weed. So I started buying weed from older lads and turning it into cigarettes, which I sold through a certain shopkeeper. Now everyone respects me. I've got a car, money, and women. All of this is thanks to the street.

Egalitarian Structures

Although the group is hierarchically structured, it can still be seen as a fraternity, a closed male society with strong interpersonal bonds and essential equality of status. This is similar to the basic structure of Sicilian and Calabrian Mafia organizations (Paoli 2003).[2] In these clan-like societies stratification does exist, but it is either playful and ceremonial (in terms of relations between cohorts) or linked to patrimonial privilege (in the case of leaders and avtoritety).

How can the egalitarian ethos of a brotherhood coexist with the obvious inequalities in the gang? The gang has leaders with ultimate authority. It has its elite (avtoritety), supervisors (smotriashchie), and a hierarchical system of age cohorts. Members have unequal access to resources, with the younger lads usually getting pitiful amounts of money in return for their efforts to support the gang regime. At the same time, the younger they are, the more likely they are to be punished for various misdemeanors.

The presence of a structure, however, does not undermine the essential equality of statuses within the gang. The gang is not an arboreal society, like an army or a business corporation. It does not have a system of formal remuneration or functional roles apart from elected supervisors. Its smotriashchie and avtoritety are not just business managers but ritual specialists who make sure that the gang remains a cohesive moral unit. And, unlike modern businesses, the daily lives of the lads, although having elements of compulsion, undeniably have what Lacan (1998) called "jouissance," enjoyment typically denied to ordinary working drones in capitalist enterprises.

While there are considerable inequalities between an ordinary lad, who gets criminal rent from the owner of a street kiosk or a market stall or who peddles small quantities of drugs, and a gruppirovka leader, who owns a network of supermarkets or a huge agricultural holding, the nature of authority here is personal and familial rather than expressed through hierarchical control.

Both the gangs that evolve out of territorial fighting formations and those organized by their leader (or leaders) with the specific purpose of making money remain tight, highly ritualized, and weakly differentiated groups. Larger associations, which can number hundreds of members, still preserve the structure of small units—*brigady* or *semeiki*—as their basic forms. These units, while generally subordinated to the top echelons of the gang, have significant autonomy and develop their own independent business operations.

---

2. Writing about these Italian Mafia organizations, Paoli (2003, chap. 2) described them as fraternities, whose members, on joining the basic unit of the *cosca*, subscribe to what Weber (1978 [1922], 62) called a "fraternization contract" and begin to consider one another brothers.

Young Women in Gangs

Russian gangs tend to be male domains with women only allowed on the margins of the gang society, although girls sometimes also participate in separate female-only or mixed nonviolent street peer groups (Gromov and Stephenson 2008).[3] The subservient position of women in gangs results from the patrimonial nature of authority in these alliances, which are structured in accordance with traditional templates of male dominance. In most gang contexts, women, if they are accepted into a gang at all, tend to play only minor roles, and all-female gangs are a rare phenomenon. Some UK authors have argued that when women fight or commit other acts of violence in a street group context, this tends to be associated with a search for social acceptance and attempts at self-defense rather than instrumental crime and violence (Batchelor 2009; Young 2009). US gang literature sometimes points to deeper involvement in gang life by young women living in high poverty and crime areas, but even there they are typically not accepted as equals and tend to submit to the patriarchal gender expectations of male members, including sexual exploitation (Campbell 1991; Chesney-Lind and Hagedorn 1999; Miller 2000).

There is some evidence from Kazan and Ul'ianovsk of the periodic emergence of all-female street groups. However, these are usually short-lived associations that make no attempt to control territory. The popular myths and rumors of the longevity and violence of female groups do not stand up to closer inspection (Omel'chenko 1996; Salagaev and Shashkin 2002). In our interviews in 2005, long-serving representatives of law enforcement agencies in Kazan told us they had never come across durable female gangs. The only case of a violent female gang they recalled was an instance in 2003 in which several schoolgirls living in the Pervaia Gorka area briefly formed a group called PBK and committed a number of street assaults.

When it comes to female participation in Russian gangs, the limited data available show that, while women do sometimes participate in gang activities, they tend to play subsidiary roles. In Kazan the girlfriends and wives of gang members provide alibis or prepare food for gang celebrations, but they can never become recognized members of a gruppirovka. (This is explicitly prohibited by the gang code.) They cannot attend regular gang meetings, and those members who have girlfriends are expected always to put the interests of the gang first—for example, a date is never an accepted reason for missing a gang meeting. The lads cannot even stand up for their girlfriends if they are abused by other gang

3. On gender relations in traditional vory-v-zakone organizations, see Chalidze (1977), Modestov (2001), and Gilinsky (2007).

members. Exceptions are only made for wives, sisters, and mothers (Salagaev and Shashkin 2001).

Elena Omel'chenko's research in Ul'ianovsk in the beginning of the 1990s showed that women were not recognized as equal members there either. The girlfriends of the leaders did play a limited role in gang life. This included performing ceremonial functions, such as attending gang meetings and social gatherings, being at the side of their partners when business was being discussed (and trying to smooth out any disagreements), and providing entertainment for guests. In terms of wider "public relations" they also provided their partners with a certain respectability and supplied alibis for them to the police when required. Other young women, who typically had boyfriends in the gang, saw their role as looking after the "hardworking" men. They occasionally took part in fights and also fulfilled auxiliary roles such as preparing food for gang gatherings or acting as lookouts. The gangs also had "common girls," who were sexually exploited by gang members (Omel'chenko 1996).

In organized crime networks, although women may do paid work as accountants or legal specialists, they cannot become equal members of the bandits' brotherhoods. Only the women at the very top, the wives and girlfriends of the gang's avtoritety, are regarded as having relatively high status (although not equal to men) and may even be permitted to be involved in the gang's business in some way. In his analysis of the structure of the Solntsevaskaia gruppirovka—one of the largest and most powerful Moscow organized criminal groups—Varese had similar findings. He analyzed the transcripts of the telephone conversations of a group of Solntsevskaia avtoritety who attempted to set up a branch in Rome in the mid-1990s. Their telephone conversations were intercepted by the Italian police, which had been monitoring the group. It turned out that the wives of the top men in this outpost played an active role in the gang's business. They discussed sensitive operations, threatened other members on behalf of their husbands, and looked after the gang's obshchak (Varese 2001; 2013).

Ceremonies, Rituals, and Collective Events

The gang's society is strengthened by a range of collective events, ceremonies, and rituals, from periodic obligatory meetings to punishment of miscreants to gang wars (addressed in chapter 8). The gang typically has two meetings a week. One is mandatory, and the other is not. Both tend to happen in the evenings. The mandatory meetings usually take place on Sundays. The lads meet in a secluded area somewhere in a public park, suburban ski camp, or clearing in the forest.

According to our interviewees, these meetings are often very brief affairs lasting as little as twenty-five to thirty minutes, but attendance is obligatory, and if a lad misses one without a reason, he is punished. Other (nonmandatory) meetings are more social affairs and can last for two or three hours.

The lead at such meetings is taken by the gang's smotriashchii. He invites the lads to discuss what is going on with various gang activities and whether there are any problems with the businessmen "protected" by the gang or any incidents with other gangs. They talk about the state of the gang's businesses, such as gaming parlors or street parking lots. If someone brings the street an offer to do business, then the lads discuss it, see how it can be financed and whether there's enough money in the pot. Then they appoint people to oversee that business.

After that, the lads hand the smotriashchii money for the obshchak. It is then the turn of any lad who skipped earlier meet-ups or committed any other violations to be punished. The miscreant is marched through a row of older lads, each of whom strikes him with his fists on the upper body two or three times. Kicking is not allowed. Blows to the head are also forbidden. As Tadjik explained, "Normally, nobody hits people in the head—this is not the army." Sometimes the lad is fined instead of given a physical punishment.

After the business side of the meeting is over and the punishments have been meted out, the lads hang out with guys their own age. Then the members start drifting away. Some head back home and continue talking, standing at the entrance to their housing block or occupying the benches ordinarily claimed by local old women.

Crime and Punishment

Gang members' efforts to create a cohesive community can only succeed if certain behaviors are not only deemed unacceptable but also subject to public, and ritualized, condemnation. As Durkheim (1938, 67–75) explained, crime reaffirms collective conscience and serves to prevent anomie, a disappearance of morality and with it society itself. Identification of extreme cases that fall outside proper parameters serves to maintain ritualized reproduction of social order in the gang.

The gang makes the borders of collective morality clear through its punishment of those who violate its code. The most severe sanction is expulsion from the group, which is accompanied by extreme physical punishment. In some gangs, apart from physical punishment, the expelled member may also be required to pay a significant sum of money into the gang's obshchak. (This monetization of punishment is a relatively recent phenomenon, and some members consider this a lamentable break with the old ways.)

Snitching to the police or leaving other lads in danger leads to expulsion from the gang. The beating in these cases is so severe that it may result in death. One lad told us how, when his gang was attacked without warning, one member ran away under the pretext of calling for help but did not return and simply disappeared. At the gang's next meeting he was beaten to death.

Alcohol addiction and consumption of hard drugs can also lead to expulsion. An addict is not his own person and cannot be relied on. Risat was expelled from the group despite his highly successful business activities. He said, "I had one business after the other. I had a branch [another gang paid him to use his gang's name]; we protected prostitutes, and we had our own traders. Money just flowed, and I tried heroin for the first time. Eventually, I became a real addict. At some point our lads discovered this, came to me, punished me, and announced that from now on I was not with them."

Those lads who engage in open conflict and fights with fellow gang members can also be expelled from the gang. Expulsion also occurs when a lad is judged to behave like a *lokh*—for example, by falling victim to extortion. This is seen as compromising his reputation and the reputation of his street. Also, when somebody is expelled from the group, and is made to pay, he is inadvertently forced to act like a *lokh* for a second time. By agreeing to pay money under threat, he becomes the equivalent of a *lokh*, and this in turn severs any option for him to join another gang.

Smaller misdemeanors are punished by collective beatings. The lads are disciplined for offences such as missing the gang's obligatory meetings several times, owing money to the obshchak, being caught drunk by the elders, or failing to act on the smotriashchii's assignment. Lads who end up in the police station for being drunk or those caught fighting with each other or being rude to other lads also get beaten up.

If a person misses a payment to the obshchak, he may be verbally abused and shamed. In certain cases, the whole age cohort is punished for the bad behavior of one of its members.

If a lad has not committed a *zikher*, but the gang decides that he is not "fit for purpose"—for example, he is unable to do business and does not take easily to the street life—the gang can expel this person without any punishment. In rare cases a member can decide to leave the gang himself and not incur any punishment, but he will need a very good reason for this, such as an illness or moving to another place of residence.

Life in a *Brigada*

The *brigada* is the basic unit of a gang, although in some gangs the same unit is called a *semeika,* a little family—a term also used to describe groups of prisoners sharing a cell.[4] Its members usually live close to each other and are expected to spend leisure time together and do business together. The division of gangs into small close-knit units, seen by some authors as reflecting the need to maintain secrecy and thus likened to revolutionary or terrorist cells,[5] has in fact less to do with secrecy and more with the need to sustain the members' commitment to the common cause. The gang faces the constant danger that members may become unreliable, that they may stop actively participating in gang affairs as other obligations and interests take precedence. The forces of social entropy need to be counteracted, and what better way to hold the group together than to have constant informal communications. The need stay in touch and spend time together is seen as a family duty. As Tsigan put it, "We try to spend as much time as possible with each other. After all, we're not just *bratva* (bandit gruppirovka), we're *bratia* (brothers) too."

The lads hang out together on the streets where they have a very visible presence, often occupying benches at the entrances to housing blocks and withdrawing from public view when they need to talk about serious issues. They are also constantly on call by cell phone, in case the gang's business demands urgent action. Tuigun said:

> We have our own spot in the yard, an entrance to a block of apartments with a bench next to it. That's where we usually gather, chat, smoke, and maybe drink some beer. We normally hang out until ten or eleven in the evening and then split up. We don't talk about anything serious because it would be very easy for people to overhear. If there's something urgent, we have to go somewhere else. If a *strelka* with another gang is set up, for example, we usually get in touch via cell phones and head out together. If there are serious issues to discuss, we meet at someone's house while their parents are out or, failing that, in the yard as far away from other people as possible.

Those members who are engaged in full-time work or study still try to see their friends socially. In nineteen-year-old Tadjik's description of his typical day, we can see a constant involvement with gang life that coexists alongside his "other" life as a student:

---

4. On *semeiki* in the Tatary gang from Nizhnekamsk, see Safarov (2012, 202).

5. The cellular structure has been seen as being instrumental in hiding the identity of the leaders and protecting the profits of gangs and criminal groups (Lyman and Potter 2004, 52–53).

> A typical day: I get up in the morning, wash, have breakfast, then college. Then I do the next day's homework if I have any, and after that I'm free. I usually go to the lads in the courtyard and hang out with them until about eleven p.m. Sometimes I go away to take care of my own business, to meet people, or to meet-ups where certain issues might need resolving. Back when I was in year 11 [the last year of high school], I'd hang out at the lads' parking lot [controlled by the gang] until nighttime, where we chatted and guarded the cars at the same time. These days we leave the guarding to the juniors while we sit on benches and talk and have fun. Lately, lads we know have started to buy cars, so we spend a lot of time discussing car-related topics and listening to music from the car radio with the doors open.

Some members, usually the older ones, particularly those with full-time jobs, complained that they did not have sufficient time to spend with their pals from the *brigada.* Twenty-seven-year-old Nafik, for example, worked all day in his engineering job and could only participate in the mandatory meetings. "The rest of the time, I don't have a chance to see the lads, but if a free day does come up, I try to make the most of it."

The pastimes of the lads are typical of Russian urban dwellers—clubbing, weekend trips to the countryside, drinking sessions at home or in bars, and playing sports. When the lads get together, stories of various battles and wars are retold, and common narratives are created that also help cement the group. For example, Tadjik said, "In the summer, we go out to the countryside to relax. We pool money for food, head for Lebiazhie Lake, usually by car, and rest there. We play soccer, drink beer, and generally have a laid-back time. The lads tell each other stories about their own lives, like wars and how they were involved in them, what kind of *strely* there were, who they represented—basically fun things that you can pass time talking about."

Seventeen-year-old Viktor said: "I spend most of my time with my *brigada.* We normally hang out in our courtyard next to the apartment block entrance, chat up the girls, and drink out of sight of the [gang] elders. In the summer, we like to go fishing. Obviously, we go to meet-ups too, but this is how we spend the majority of our free time."

Local residents also reported seeing gang members happily spending time together. Fanil said: "If they have free time, then they will call each other up. They feel good only in their own company, because they understand one another. They stand around smoking, laughing, and joking with each other."

Many gang members said that they enjoyed being "in their own circle." Even lads from different streets, if their gangs were allies and not enemies, could have friendly relations and found it easier to understand each other than young people who were not involved with gangs.

These friendships last long after active gang membership ends. Unless a person leaves the gang formally or is expelled, he always remains a part of the street—even when he grows old, has a wife and children, and has long ceased doing "business" with the gang. Gang veterans stay in touch with one another. As they tend to continue living in the same area, it is easy for them to meet up and spend time together on weekends. They make trips to the countryside to drink vodka and have a barbecue, go bowling or play pool, or eat out from time to time. Gruppirovshchiki who fall on hard times may get some help from their old pals—perhaps a money handout or assistance with finding a new job.

Collective Mobilization

Because the gang members have many other interests and commitments outside the gang, the gang needs constant mobilization to keep the lads engaged, and economic activity is essential for the gang's social reproduction. It helps to direct the lads' energies toward the collective cause, turning it into more of a movement than a business entity. If that cause disappears, members' commitment slackens, and they can start to drift away. Kirill reported, for example: "When I was young and stupid, one of our elders explained to us: 'You are an organized criminal group with your own territory. You have to act as a group—be cohesive, organized, disciplined, and do business in your territory. Don't hang around aimlessly, but make money for yourself and for the street. Otherwise, you're not a street but just rabble."

It is this constant mobilization and the practices that support the group, extending far beyond pecuniary schemes into the heart of what it means to be social, that allows the gang to continuously renew itself. In Tatarstan, for example, major gangs such as Kvartala, Khadi Taktash, Pervaki, Zhilka, 29th Kompleks, and many others have existed for over forty years.

The gang combines a pragmatic ethos of material accumulation with affective and moral commitments. This is, of course, not peculiar to this type of organization. Profit under capitalism cannot be made without Durkheimian "precontractual" or moral solidarity, without pockets of trust that ensure that capitalist enterprise can function (Collins 1988). But a gang is perhaps one of the starkest illustrations of the continuing potency of premodern forms in modern societies. As with other traditional social forms, we can see here "a peculiar and distinct type of combination of instrumental and solidarity relationship, in which solidarity provides the basic framework; yet within this framework various instrumental considerations, albeit very diffusely defined, are of paramount importance" (Eisenstadt 1956, 91). It is this combination of instrumental aims and solidarity that makes the gang's business possible.

Kolia expressed the gang ethos very clearly when he defined the group's primary purpose as "to be stronger together, because no one listens to weak streets, and they don't have any money." Unlike members of juvenile peer groups, whose street existence is mostly spontaneous and concerned with leisure and dealing with everyday life challenges, gang members are expected to show what one of our interviewees, Kirill, called "purposefulness and concern for the common good." The members must look constantly for opportunities to make money for themselves and the street, while staying in touch with their comrades and being ready to help them in case of need. In Garik's words, "What I value about our lads is that they're always busy doing something, but they're still ready to support each other whenever necessary. They'll smash anyone if it's for my sake. I have absolute faith in them."

Il'sur said, answering the question about the main purpose of the gang, "There's this slogan: 'Together, we're strong!' It's a slogan about the lads, who are powerful when together but easy prey for cops when apart." Belonging to a powerful street means opportunities to get income, respect, and, for more senior members, good connections with state officials and the police. But in return, the members need to be ready for self-sacrifice. They must learn to ignore their own selfish desires and always have the group's interests in mind. This is particularly important for young members. In explaining why this is so, Zhenia, one of the gang's elders, used the example of Soviet youth labor mobilization. There is a mixture here of voluntary and compulsory elements (*dobrovolno-prinuditelnye*) that did indeed characterize the Soviet labor ethos:

> This is like the construction of the Baikal Amur railroad or the cultivation of the Virgin Lands [in the Soviet Union]. Not everybody wanted to go, but it was necessary, and people went as volunteers. Because they knew that if you're not with us, you're against us. We have very much the same thing. Sometimes the younger members do not like the regime or don't want to do certain tasks. But eventually they get used to them, because they know that everybody's been through the same thing and that eventually they will become *starshye* [seniors] too.

The differences between the Soviet young *entusiasty* (enthusiasts)—who were, in the words of one popular song of the time, "travelling for the fog and the smell of the taiga"—and gruppirovshchiki are, of course, quite stark. The latter want concrete material rewards in return for their sacrifice. But this comparison illustrates the importance of the principle of service for the gang, which is presented by Zhenia almost as a Communist enterprise rather than a capitalist firm.

The Brotherhood Ethos

Gang members see themselves as both businessmen and brothers. Talking about their friends, most of our interviewees seemed to exult in the strength of their friendships and presented a picture of relationships ruled by mutual respect, understanding, and fairness. This idealization of the group, especially as expressed to outsiders, needs to be looked at critically. Friction and violent conflict do exist. Members can be injured and even killed for the presumed violation of the gang's code, and the struggles for leadership also periodically claim their victims. In the 29th Kompleks, for example, no fewer than fifteen members have been killed in internal strife over the years (Safarov 2012, 128).

But everyday altercations and fights between members are almost invariably presented as deviant behavior that the gang tries to stamp out. What is important is the realization that conflict needs to be suppressed and interpreted as an exception to the norm. As Seva said, "Only youngsters quarrel with each other, and even then they're usually drunk." In Aidar's words, "Tensions do exist, but nobody would dare to demonstrate them openly, as this is a violation of discipline, and people are beaten for it."

However manipulative, callous, and profoundly antisocial the members of the bandit gangs may seem to us, they believe that they belong to a world that is morally superior to that of modern urban society. In their view, "civilians" live disorganized, meaningless lives and can easily descend into bespredel, a state of anarchy. Theirs, on the contrary, is a world of disciplined selves bound by a common cause and mutual responsibilities. The sense that the gang sees itself as a moral society was conveyed by many of our interviewees. Aidar, for example, when asked whether he liked Kazan and why, told us: "I like our city because we have many correct people here [a *pravil'*nyi *chelovek* or *pravil'nyi patsan*, a person or lad who lives by the code], compared with Moscow, where there are lots of people who live in bespredel, who do not give a damn. Many people here follow the code, and we do not have the same mess as other cities."

Such accounts can be easily seen as idealizations. The moral reasoning that gang members abundantly employ in explaining their behavior can be interpreted as justification for their brutality and greed. What is presented as the defense of group honor against a seeming provocation can be easily seen as a pretext for gratuitous violence. Claims to have rights to "tribute" from the local population can be used to justify primitive extortion. Tasking youngsters with acts of violence against businessmen who cannot or will not pay their dues seems like ruthless exploitation rather than necessary apprenticeship. But these beliefs in the existence a moral order in the gang are not just a cover for a variety of sins. They represent compelling ideas that constitute the members' social order.

The mental constructions of the gang as a perfect society, a "happy family," are important if we are to understand the members' moral universe. These are not just idealizations that mask a reality of purely instrumental and self-serving motives. These constructions can be seen as a Durkheimian social fact, as a set of rules that govern the lives of the gang members and that are unquestionably real for them. According to Durkheim (1938, 14–46), social facts can be seen as things, exerting genuine constraints on the actions of members of society. These constraints are also moral. Society is built on morals, and moral rules act both as a means of social control and as the glue that binds members together. Moral rules are particularly strict and uniform in close-knit societies, governed by what Durkheim called "mechanical solidarity" (Durkheim 1933 [1893], 111–99). This applies to gangs in full.

Weber also stressed the compelling nature of ideas. In *Economy and Society* he observed that social institutions and their rules possess a certain reality for individuals. Speaking about such social institutions as states, nations, corporations, families, or army corps, Weber argued that "these concepts of collective entities . . . have a meaning in the minds of individual persons, partly as of something actually existing, partly as something with normative authority. . . . Actors thus in part orient their action to them, and in this role such ideas have a powerful, often a decisive, causal influence on the course of action of real individuals. This is above else true where the ideas involve normative prescription or prohibition" (Weber 1978 [1922], 14).

In the members' accounts, the gang's brotherhood has an undeniable reality. The lads see themselves as being above instrumental and pragmatic considerations when it comes to their fellow gang members (but not the outside world, which is there to be taken advantage of). They rise above petty rivalries and squabbles, respect the elders, educate the youngsters, are loyal to their fellow lads, and suppress any negative feelings when they are directed against members of the gang. References to egalitarian spirit permeate discussions of the relations between age cohorts. When a youngster is rude to a senior or a senior is harassing a youngster unfairly, this is seen as a violation of the code. Ispug said: "We have excellent relations, like a big family. There's no hostility between the lads because we don't allow it to develop. If two lads are fighting, we tell them to make up. If you don't want to make up, you're no longer one of us." Nafik explained more fully:

> You can't even conceive of hostility or enmity on the street. All the lads are brothers. We are one brotherhood, and we live amicably. The only

> kind of conflict we have stems from misunderstandings, and those are resolved quickly because each person remembers that the guy in front of him is also a lad—albeit a kid—and his "brother." You have to respect your elders and instruct your juniors—show them how to live well. We have justice that is based on the lads' code according to which we all live.

The gang's collective conscience resembles the nostalgic imaginings of archaic "unspoiled" communities, which we find expressed in the German sociologist Ferdinand Tönnies's (1963 [1887]) concept of *Gemeinschaft*. Tönnies saw *Gemeinschaft* as a tightly knit traditional grouping where people lived in harmonic interaction with relations based on trust and mutual respect, underpinned by ritual and tradition. He contrasted *Gemeinschaft* with *Gesellschaft*, the modern society with its impersonal, instrumental, and exploitative relationships. Tönnies's *Gemeinschaft* was an idealistic construct that never existed in real life. It does not reflect the harsh and violent realities of gang life either. But the gang members themselves experience their *Gemeinschaft* with its community-based morality as real and superior to the modern world with its individualist ethos and formal rules.

Patrimonial Networks versus Modern Corporations

The gangs are often imagined and portrayed by law enforcement agents and the mass media, as well as academic commentators, as hierarchically organized corporations. They are represented as mirror images of modern institutions, such as armies or business companies (Hallsworth 2013). These representations often find their schematic expression in various charts depicting the gang structure as a hierarchy of generals, officers, soldiers, and "wannabes" or, alternatively, as a business corporation, complete with division managers and frontline staff. The problem with these representations is that, under close examination, they very rarely derive from firsthand investigation of gang organizations and tend to be based on interviews with "experts" (who may never have encountered an actual gang member), journalistic accounts, and even on movies and fiction. As the economic operation of the gang is dependent on its ability to create a local monopoly of force, one would perhaps naturally expect that it would operate as a highly coordinated unit and suppress any attempts by its members to develop autonomous operations or pursue other interests than the common interest of the gang. However, these representations are erroneous. Unlike a business corporation or an army regiment, the gang is a flexible networked organization.

To use the concepts of Deleuze and Guattari (2004), gangs are not tree-like arboreal structures with a clearly defined center, roots, and branches. They are more like rhizomatous structures, weeds, or animal packs. Rhizomes are horizontally inclined, flexible and dynamic, and they move wherever they can find opportunities to expand.[6]

The gangs' business operations do not show rigid coordination but rather have members working individually, in small teams, or in larger formations depending on particular jobs that can involve racketeering, illegal scams, or legal business. This allows the gangs to respond quickly to opportunities, to spread and retract wherever necessary, and to keep up the motivation and entrepreneurial drive of members.

The lads run their own operations, *deliugi*, acting on their own or teaming up with others members. If necessary, a gang can provide the initial capital to set up a business. For example, a lad can get money from the obshchak to set up a stall in the market. He would then hire a trader (as it is prohibited by the code for the lads to engage in trade) and give a share of the profits back to the obshchak. The gang also supplies information about business opportunities and arranges protection for the lads from the authorities or competing gangs and, providing they inform their smotriashchie about their activities and pay tax on their profits into the obshchak, they can be left to go about their business in any way they see fit.

Specific operations are designed by the members themselves or are suggested by their superiors. Those who have managed to demonstrate that they are smart entrepreneurs to their superiors get better business opportunities. Kolia said: "They can look at us, choose those who can do business, and give us a chance to prove ourselves. One of my friends, for example, got a list of game parlors. He was told to go there at the end of each working day, collect the proceeds, and solve any problems. That's what he is doing now, and he has his own share from it."

Members can move upward from supervising parking lots and game parlors to having control over market stalls and street kiosks; and eventually they can set up their own business.

The same ad hoc structure of operations continues through to the top levels of Russian organized crime (Galeotti 2000). Here teams are assembled to do specific jobs, which can include both small-scale scams and longer-lasting projects.

There are indeed some similarities between gangs and modern corporations, but not where some authors find them, not in the presence of a structure of subordination or a pragmatic business ethos. The key similarity is arguably with corporate "nonwork" social rituals—from team-building exercises, parties, and collective outings paid for from company accounts to the singing of corporate

6. See Hallsworth (2013) on the rhizomatous nature of gangs.

anthems and a "cult" of corporate forefathers. Unlike their Fordist predecessors with their sharp separation of work and nonwork, heads of modern corporations want the workers to engage in collective identity building to increase their economic productivity rather than simply relying on material and status incentives. Modern corporations also tend to have flatter hierarchies of regulation than Fordist enterprises, thus giving more initiative and self-management capacity to employees. The networked character of power within a modern enterprise, with economic activity built around specific business projects, resembles the decentralized organization of a gang's business activities (Castells 2001).

The way in which modern capitalist companies try to achieve better profitability and build a long-lasting business by developing tribal allegiances among their personnel can be illustrated by a master class on team building given by prominent Russian entrepreneur Vladimir Dovgan′. Here is some of his advice:

- If your company has a name, consider how it sounds. A name is important, sacred, cosmic.
- You need to have your own flag, your own badge. The army is a good example for imitation not in terms of subordination but in the importance of uniforms, signs, and symbols. . . . We all have herd instinct.
- Invent your own greeting. . . . When somebody calls or writes to us, we say: "Fortune and friendship is always with us; wealth and happiness are our destiny."
- A wise leader will always go beyond his professional functions. Organize the training process in such a way that people feel touched by something great, huge, fascinating—and they will acquire wings.
- An organization's foundation is based on its principles, idea, and mission.
- It is wrong to motivate your team just with earning money. A person's soul is greater than money, greater than their stomach. You need to inspire your team.
- Expectation of heroism from your people is one of the keys to success. This may only work for one in ten or in twenty, but it will help you to build your organization to last a thousand years. (Lubimtseva 2012)

This attempt to inject what Durkheim (1915) called "collective effervescence," emotional engagement, vivid collective representations, ritual, commitment, and informality into the alienating world of capitalist labor often does not produce the required result. Far from being invigorated and enthusiastic about giving more of themselves to the corporation and its wise quasi-patrimonial leaders, the workforce often remains bored and disillusioned (Cederstrom and Fleming 2012). The sense of a managed life that permeates modern corporations, and a lack of genuine identification of the worker with the company, undermines the attempts by heads of corporations to make the workers give up all of themselves, body and soul, to the cause of organizational profitability (Cremin 2011). The gang arguably does a much better job of creating emotional commitment by its members to their organization.

Growing Differentiation

At the beginning of the 1990s, the gang's brotherhood turned out to be highly suited to the regime of primitive accumulation of the new capitalist Russia. The bands of warriors that tried to capture the resources of the crumbling state economy and lay their hands on other people's incomes and property needed to be flexible polymorphous structures, with family-like loyalties and acquisitive drives bound together. Their members, beholden to the idea of essential equality within their street tribes, had to be answerable only to the gang's own code and to stand for the primacy of gang honor and obligation over individual selfish interests. But, as with many other organized criminal organizations around the world, the gangs' fraternities became destabilized by their exposure to the structures of modern capitalist economies (Paoli 2003). As the gang organization becomes more complex and more rational and its leadership progressively more involved in the structures of the capitalist economy, contradictions between the desires and aspirations of the younger lads and the pragmatic interests of the older members come to the fore. These contradictions become especially acute as avtoritety grow rich while rank-and-file members may, for all their efforts, have to rely on nongang jobs and help from their family for basic subsistence. This tension is obvious in Il'nar's explanation of how things work in his gang:

> The young ones need to catch the seniors' attention, so they try to build good relations with the older lads. Meanwhile, the adults want the youngsters to do the jobs they won't touch—rough up a shopkeeper, set a stall on fire, watch a business they control, and so on. That's why they give them jobs and say, "Take care of this, it'll earn you money." In reality, they get scraps, and the real money goes to the one who sets the job up. . . . The higher-ups won't do something that might run them afoul of the law—that's what the small fry are for.

Twenty-three-year-old Koshmar is disappointed in his gang and wants to leave it:

> I used to have the illusion that the group existed so that the members could solve their problems and protect their interests. But now I have come to the conclusion that this is all a deception, that the older members just use the

> youngsters for their own purposes—to collect money for their obshchak or to get money from tradesmen. They just use us as ordinary soldiers, as brute force. We are there to ensure the well-being of the leaders.

Their resentment stems from the fact that the leaders and their close associates by and large started their careers as members of street peer groups, but now there is very little that unites them and ordinary lads. The leaders are completely removed from the street gang. Avtoritety exercise a general oversight but entrust direct control over street gangs to the smotriashchie. They do not come to the regular meetings and do not personally take part in the violent aspects of the gang's everyday life, such as *strely* or *razborki.* Most of them have a hand in illegal businesses (drug trade, casinos, or prostitution), but very often they also work in top managerial positions in legal companies, own (or co-own) their business, or hold political office.[7] The movement of avtoritety into legal business, and increasing economic differentiation, inevitably corrupts the gang's communal spirit. Becoming increasingly detached from their territorial roots, avtoritety now do more business with nonaffiliates than with their gang "brothers." The younger members, who still hold on to their territorial roots and the gangs' cultural traditions, can feel that they are exploited or abandoned by the leadership. As a result, commitment to the organization slackens, and the gang starts losing its members.

While the leaders' business becomes increasingly integrated into the broader Russian and global economy, those members who are left to survive on the ground through street racketeering and various small-scale scams feel that they've missed the chance to "make it" that existed for the '90s generation. As Tsigan said, "Now everything that can be divided up has been divided up, and there are very few opportunities for us."

This tension comes to the fore when street business is not going well. With all the tribal commitments and loyalties that the gang tries to inculcate in its members, a weakened street economy leads to a dangerous destabilization and collapse of the gang's social order. Stagnation or recession in the street-level economy means that members can no longer rely on the gang for all or even part of their livelihoods, and younger members can become increasingly unwilling to invest their time and take personal risks for uncertain remuneration in the future. They may start leaving, with some turning to other, more successful gangs. In a worst-case scenario the street and its business can be taken over by competitors.

---

7. In media reports, leaders and avtoritety are often called *avtoritetnye bisnesmeny* (authoritative businessmen), which immediately indicates their origins in organized crime without directly accusing them of being criminals.

Complaints about lack of opportunities were frequently expressed by our interviewees. Twenty-three-year-old Banan, who was considering leaving his gang at a time of the interview, explained why:

> You can't really advance among us, even if you're the Second Coming of Christ. The reason is that there's nowhere to advance to—we have few opportunities to earn money, and the ones that exist are under the control of the over-thirties. That's why most of us do everything but earn money. As a result, no one wants to advance in this sort of situation, because why would you want to get promoted if all you get is more responsibility plus the same big fat nothing? We have high turnover in the street, so many leave without even telling their friends, just bow out quietly. If they get caught later, we explain to them that their behavior was impolite, and after this heart-to-heart they're left with traces of sorrow beneath their eyes, plus bruises all over their bodies. It's always the same reason: they don't like running around waving clubs in the cold when, in other streets, lads their age are showing off their cars. So many drop everything when they realize they have no prospects.

Staying with the lads becomes increasingly a matter of rational choice rather than normative commitments. According to Zhenia, "People leave for all sorts of reasons. Not everyone can work their way up through the group, and that kind of lad sees no reason to keep going. Some people want to stay but can't do so for mundane reasons. You have to get your priorities straight. What matters more—getting a higher education like normal people or staying on the street and hoping for something better?" The same process was confirmed by our experts. As M. said, "Young people don't want to work for nothing just to keep the gang going. If by the age of eighteen they don't see business opportunities and a chance to get a good income, they move away from the gangs and start working in legal jobs."

Disappointment in the lack of opportunities in the street economy is a common reason for leaving. But, unlike an ordinary workplace, the gang clan cannot simply let members leave for such prosaic reasons. Unless a credible reason is found, the gang has to punish those people who break ranks, if only symbolically. Trofim said:

> Here on the street, the guys who leave are usually those who couldn't find themselves. . . . In short, they are the guys who missed their moment. But since you can't give that as a reason for leaving, they have to come up with others—for example, family circumstances. Those who don't have a decent excuse just get themselves expelled. They say that they don't want to be from the street anymore. They get lightly beaten up and

> leave. Or, if they get expelled for becoming a drug addict or betraying other lads, then they get beaten long and hard.

Compared to the 1990s, it is now easier to leave the gang, or make one's membership nominal. Nafik told us:

> These days it is much easier to leave the street. Previously, they would beat you up or make you pay a fine, but now everything is much easier. You simply have to give a reason why you can't be with the lads anymore. And it is possible just to stay in the group formally. Then a person can simply stop participating in the group's affairs; he stops coming to meetings to fights and other fun activities, but he retains his status as a lad from the street and can introduce himself with the street's name if he comes into conflict with other gangs.

If a gang member wants to leave the street but has a business that he developed with the gang's help, he needs to give back a share of the business and repay the gang's investment and any debts to the obshchak.

A common issue for those members who go into the army or prison is that they find their business patches have been taken by others on their return. A lad's former friends may tell him that there is nothing for him to do, that everything has been divided up and the gang has no extra money to start new operations for his benefit. The lack of business opportunities means that those members returning from periods of incarceration can only rely on minimal assistance. As M. said:

> When he comes out of prison, this is what he sees: this guy's bought a car, that one has a kiosk, and he has nothing, even though he may have gone to prison for their sake. And he asks them to help him get involved in gang business, but they're not interested. He gets told: gather some youngsters yourself and do your own business. . . . It is difficult to come back to a gang after prison. Let's say a person has been locked up for five years. He comes back, but there are new people there; the youngsters have grown up, everything is divided up, everybody wants to eat. Of course, he will have authority because of the old days. Young people will treat him with respect, but he will not be given access to resources. If those people who knew him five years ago are still doing business, they can help him, give him some work, but in any case, life will be difficult for him.

At thirty-five Il'nar is one of the older gang members. At the beginning of the 1990s he received a five-year sentence in a penal colony for grievous bodily harm. He felt that he missed his chance to make big money as a result. All he can now do are odd jobs at construction sites. Despite being a gang veteran—he started his gang life at the beginning of the 1980s—these days he lives a very ordinary life. He is married and has a young daughter. Some of his old pals from the gang have drunk themselves to death. Others work in automobile service stations, and some have become businessmen. Despite his belonging to the oldest cohort, the leadership of the gang business belongs to even older men, those who are nearly fifty. Now his participation in the gang is purely social. He meets his pals once or twice a week to have a drink and a chat. He does not need to come to regular gang meetings anymore. He participates in all the communal events—weddings, funerals, birthdays, collective visits to the sauna. Although he does not do much in the gang, he is still a member and will remain one for the rest of his life. He continues paying money into the obshchak, although he can't afford to give much.

Il'nar is not happy about his life. He drinks and cannot seem to get over his prison experience. If he had not been locked up, he feels, his life would have been different. He would have had his business, but as it is, he has been sidelined, and people do not trust him with serious affairs, "and those who have authority—they are all busy. They have their own companies; they own cottages, drive jeeps. And the youngsters give them a lot of respect."

All he gets from his friends from the same age cohort is some money "for the family." He sees a lot of animosity and envy within the gang toward more successful members: "This is especially visible among people of my age. We all started equal. We had nothing, just our pricks and our souls, so to speak, and now some people direct whole companies and some are in dire straits. . . . Yes, I am from the street, and what do I have? Fuck-all."

The social order of the gang is decaying. The street brotherhood, morphing into the larger capitalist order, inevitably experiences increasing individualism and economic differentiation, which corrodes group solidarity and unity. As members no longer orient themselves to the presumed moral order, the gang as an organization becomes weaker.

The reduced street economy cannot feed every entrant, while most of the criminal opportunities have already been divided up. As Kazan police investigator N., told us:

> People who are engaged in criminal business don't need extra mouths in their gang at all. Right now, they've divided up everything that could be divided up. Everyone is looking for some way to get money, for something to do. Young people aren't going to work for an idea; they'll work for people who can point them to a lucrative business where you can earn money. That's why most youths lose interest in gangs after they

> reach eighteen: many are disenchanted, especially if they can't secure an income; many get jobs, families, and they leave.

Another police investigator, MT., explained:

> There are huge changes going on in Russia now, and for those young people who want to achieve something in life there are new opportunities for employment. This is why young people do not stay in OPGs for long. They join a gruppirovka, run around for a couple of years, and then they see that somebody else is making money while exploiting them ruthlessly. Nobody would want to be in that situation. So they leave the OPG, because [to reach success] you don't need to be in an OPG. In fact, it's best not to be an OPG member in order to earn money. Avtoritety and the leaders have good money, and those in the "middle" also do well, but they have no intention of sharing with the youngsters. Moreover, they are forced to give money to the obshchak, and those who do not work can only get this money through crime. For all these reasons, people only stay in the gruppirovki if they are engaged in some profitable business that requires gang membership.

In a downward spiral, with the street economy weakening and membership dwindling, it has become harder for gangs to recruit new members.

The scarcity of illegal resources means that the youth groups themselves are now involved in greater territorial violence, reverting in a sense to an earlier stage of gang development. As Banan said: "As there are no real opportunities for making money in our street, our relationships with the neighbors [youth groups from other streets] are bad, and our street has acquired a reputation for bespredel because we fight all the time. We do not have any other aims apart from having fun, because the street is very poor and all that is left for us is to have fun with empty pockets."

According to our police informants, some youth gangs not only dissolved themselves as a result of the lack of business opportunities and increased police pressure but also forbade ex-members to introduce themselves as "lads from the street." The avtoritety who rose from the streets, and who robbed, killed, bribed, and swindled their way to the top, now send their offspring to the best schools and universities and prohibit them from any contact with young gang members.

With the state's crackdown on organized crime and violence, and with greater stability and economic prosperity in the republic, the levels of registered crime have gone down. In 2010 there were 274 murders registered in Tatarstan, almost back to the level it had been in 1978 in the relatively "peaceful" days of late state socialism (Safarov 2012, 393).

Although the territorial structures of many gruppirovki have remained in place, their vertical links have been weakened, and the current members on the ground are much more cautious in their dealings with the outside world. As Safarov (2012, 394) observed, "the *gopniki* of today are not at all like the bandits of the 1990s. . . . Just nineteen years ago a member of a big OPG could open the door of any businessman with the words 'I am from such and such [gang],' and now a gruppirovshchik, from those who have remained, would never say such a thing publicly; he would be much more careful than that."

Nevertheless, the street gangs have not disappeared. Criminal prosecution (mainly of the gang leadership) has contributed to a small decline in the numbers of registered gang members, but it has not led to a serious decline in the number of known gangs that continue to be entrenched in local communities. According to the Tatarstan police, in January 2010, ninety "youth groups of an antisocial nature," comprising 1,802 teenagers, were being monitored by the police, sixty-three of them in Kazan. This can be compared with 2008, when ninety-eight such groups were being monitored, with a total membership of 2,075 (Muzychenko 2010). The division of city territory into patches of turf controlled by the local youth continues, and mass fights between different territorial elites in Kazan, and in the surrounding villages, remain a regular occurrence (Shtele 2012).

In some areas the gangs are creating new alliances or moving to occupy new territory abandoned by a weakened competitor. Describing the history of his gang, Kirill said that "the most significant event happened several years ago, when the majority of [a rival gang's] avtoritety were sent to the *zona* (prison or labor camp). Their street was significantly weakened and stopped being our enemy." His gang could now expand into the new territory.

Keeping the Spirit

The gang's use of nonrational foundations for the purposes of economic accumulation is arguably much more effective than that of a capitalist corporation. Its mobilization of ritual and its spirit of reciprocity and solidarity allow it to remain a coherent and integrated organization despite the many challenges the modern world throws at it. The gang's success is even more impressive if we remember that it includes people who may easily be seen as dangerous sociopaths, often coming from unstable, disturbed backgrounds. Both ordinary members and their ruthless and volatile leaders live in a world of violence, greed, and opportunistic predation.

Although some gangs do weaken and disintegrate under the pressures of internal contradictions, economic troubles, police repression, or the incarceration or death of their leaders, many manage to stay afloat and thrive for lengthy periods of time. This is achieved not as a result of some military-style discipline or cruel punishment for disobedience nor because of efficient rational organization. The gang is sustained by its collective ethos, cultivated and supported by leaders and ordinary members alike, who, despite a myriad selfish, pragmatic considerations, deadly disagreements, and petty squabbles, invest their identities and feelings into this organization. The gang can succeed where modern corporations fail.

But the gang's Achilles' heel is the social differentiation that arises in the process of capitalist accumulation. When organized crime moves away from its territorial roots, solidarity comes under serious strain. With the leaders increasingly seen as betraying the ideals of brotherhood and surrounding themselves with paid associates, their form of traditional patrimonial authority loses its legitimacy. As the economic activities of the gang's leaders progressively acquire the character of rational business, the practices and rituals that sustained collective identities lose their magic. Ordinary gang members can feel exploited and alienated. This is exacerbated by the fact that prospects for serious social mobility through the gang alone are long gone. Opportunities for lads to follow the gang's forefathers to the heights of social success are practically nonexistent, and street lads can no longer realistically expect to move from racketeering of local kiosks or running illegal parking lots to ownership of large companies.

In these conditions, street gangs risk becoming disorganized and "regressing" into more anomic violent groups or hyperviolent drug-distribution networks.[8] Once this happens, the spirit of gang brotherhood becomes impossible to sustain.

---

8. This is what Rodgers (2009) described in his research into the evolution of territorial gangs in Nicaragua.

5

STREET TRAJECTORIES

At this point it is apparent that the members of Russian gangs are substantially incorporated into the lives of their communities and into the larger society. The lads often live in socially mixed neighborhoods; many of them study and work, and their criminal and violent associations are typically only a part of their wider networks of social connections. Yet, from the very beginnings of sociological research into gangs, the members of these social organizations have almost invariably been seen as deprived and excluded social outcasts. Gang members across the world have been portrayed as coming from backgrounds of "multiple marginality" (Vigil 1988), exacerbated currently by deepening inequalities in the global economy (Hagedorn 2007; Pitts 2008). They suffer from low social support, have educational difficulties, and face a high risk of expulsion from schools. Unable to plan their lives, they develop fatalistic orientations about their future (Farrington 2000; Esbensen et al. 2009; Olate, Salas-Wright, and Vaughn 2012). Ultimately, the impoverished and disorganized urban ecologies, together with weakened social control by family and school, produce young men who are incapable of fitting into larger society.

In such accounts, typically based on the Chicago school's social disorganization theory (Thrasher 1963 [1927]) and variants of Merton's strain approach (Merton 1957; Cloward and Ohlin 1961), the young men who join gangs are largely defined by what they lack—educational opportunities, employable skills, and social capital beyond their immediate peer groups. At the same time, gang membership represents their main identity, their master status. Cut off from economic opportunity, they create their own illicit street economic operations or aspire to graduate into the structures of professional organized crime. According to Decker and Van Winkle (1996, 23–24), with regard to gangs in the United States, "as gang members are involved in violent events, both as perpetrators and as victims, members of the community attempt to distance themselves from relationships and contacts with gang members. Life in the gang is an existence characterized by estrangement from social institutions, many neighborhood groups, and, ultimately, conforming peers and adults."

From an institutionalist perspective, participation in organized crime groups also demands separation from the legitimate world, as this is the only way trust and common identity can be established. Applying Gambetta's (2009, 37) concept of signaling to the world of contemporary London gangs, Densley (2013, 130) argued that "gang members signal loyalty by 'burning bridges' back to mainstream civilian life. . . . Gang members may assault or insult old friends, quit their jobs, or fail to attend or even enroll in school examinations necessary to secure further education, employment, or training." None of this is common within Russian street gangs, although there are subsections of gang members whose lives take them toward greater separation from the mainstream.

The Tatarstan case presents a challenge to the prevailing orthodoxy and to its vision of the gang as a society radically separated from the rest as a result of a lack of economic opportunities, members' psychological propensities and values, or the imperatives of the criminal business.[1] The difference is particularly striking when we move from the troubled 1990s into the relatively prosperous 2000s. In the Kazan of the 2000s we see an urban society in which gangs existed in areas of high employment and wide educational opportunity, with not just universal secondary education but almost universal higher education. Tatarstan has relatively low levels of unemployment (less than 7% in 2005 and less than 4% in 2014). In 2003, 78 percent of high school graduates in Kazan went on to university (Mukhariamova et al. 2004, 68). Although our study did not attempt to construct a representative sample of gang members, most of our interviewees,

1. At the same time, some authors have presented an alternative perspective on gangs, showing that street gang members can straddle the worlds of legality and illegality. Fagan (1989) and Venkatesh (1997) have demonstrated that people move in and out of legitimate and illegitimate work and can be employed in both spheres concurrently. Legal and illegal work coexist, merge into each other, and involve the same individuals (Sullivan 1989; Taylor 1990; Padilla 1992). A street gang itself can help its members gain access to both legitimate and illegitimate work (Scott 2004). Members can perform different identities and have varying degrees of commitment to their gang (Vigil 1988; Garot 2010; Lauger 2012). Some gangs (e.g., the Almighty Latin Kings and Queens Nation) even develop collective strategies of emancipation, trying to help their deprived members gain a foothold in the world of legal employment (Kontos, Brotherton, and Barrios 2003; Brotherton and Barrios 2004).

the core members of various gangs, had finished secondary schools, and many were university students or graduates or held professional jobs.

In this chapter I will show that the social backgrounds of gang members in Kazan were very different from those of the "typical" gang membership described in international gang literature. Far from being excluded from the opportunities presented by mainstream society, they actively partook of them. As opposed to withdrawing into the world of violence and criminality, many pursued parallel careers in formal employment while at the same time remaining members of street gangs. In Russian society, where legality and illegality, and the formal and criminal economies, are closely intertwined, young people have invested in all possible avenues and in a multiplicity of social networks.

Gang Members' Backgrounds

Despite the absence of hard data on the backgrounds of gang members, according to local experts, police, teachers, and local residents, in the 1980s and the beginning of the 1990s gang members tended to be young men from working-class backgrounds, school dropouts, and delinquents. Throughout the 1990s, gang members were mostly recruited from poor backgrounds, although "poor" became an all-encompassing category incorporating state employees and workers who lost their livelihoods during the crisis. But, over the years, as gangs became institutionalized in the neighborhoods, they began to attract young men from well-off and educated families. This was similar to the changes in the social composition of Italian Mafia families from the 1950s to the 1970s, in which, as the Mafia developed a stable presence in communities, it acquired many middle-class members (Arlacchi 1986).

Generally, the gang is a territorial organization, and it attracts local youth, for whom the common denominator is their experience of spending time in street groups. Children from educated families are more likely to stay away from the streets and be more involved in schools and organized after-school activities, with working-class children and youth being more likely to join street organizations. But in the middle of the 2000s, gang membership in Kazan included people from educated backgrounds as well. To this day, gangs have many members who study at universities, and often in prestigious subjects such as law or medicine (ProKazan.ru 2012).

In our interviews, we asked gang members about their family backgrounds, including their parents' occupations, their own education and employment histories, and their plans and aspirations for the future, including whether they thought they were likely to remain connected to organized crime structures. The picture that emerged from these interviews was one of people who were mostly neither socially excluded nor drawn to criminal careers as the only possible social destination.

The common explanation for gang membership in Western literature is that the gang attracts boys without fathers; in this respect it acts as a substitute family. Members rarely marry or have stable relations with their girlfriends and mothers of their children.[2] This was far from the case in our Kazan study. Most of our interviewees had ongoing relations with their own families and did not come from broken homes;[3] instead, many had intact families where both parents were employed. Some of our older interviewees were married themselves or firmly expected to eventually marry and have a family. Some parents had no idea that their children were in gangs, while others were well aware. Twenty-year-old Farit, both of whose parents worked for the police, said that they were not at all happy that he was in a gang. He reported:

> Relations with my parents are tense because I'm from the street. They constantly try to control me. A typical punishment for me and my brother used to be not being let out onto the street, being grounded. When I'd just joined the street my father kept me under surveillance and tried not to let me go to meet-ups. At one later point, I wasn't even living at home, though our relations were restored later. These days, they know that I'm still from the street, but they see that I'm earning an income, and they don't particularly interfere.

Twenty-three-year-old Kolia was married with a child. The family lived with his mother. When he was a teenager, he had conflicts with his parents, who were not happy that he spent a lot of time on the streets. But even now he is careful when he comes home: "My mother doesn't normally know where I am when I'm out of the house, because I'm hard to control now—I'm my own master. But I don't come home late so as not to cause unnecessary trouble."

Some parents tolerated their children's gang affiliations, and some even gave the young men money to enable them to meet their obligatory contributions to the obshchak. This tended to be the case with younger members without any income of their own, who would otherwise have to get involved in street crime to pay money into the gang's fund.

---

2. Elijah Anderson, for example, found that the subjects of his research in ghetto areas of Philadelphia were involved in sexual contests but avoided marriage, which he believed testified to their inability to fulfill mainstream breadwinning roles (1999, chaps. 2–5).

3. This is similar to Martin Sanchez-Jankowski's findings in his study of entrepreneurial American gangs (1991, 39).

Those gang members who studied in schools and colleges were far from the stereotypical young delinquents. Although street life did interfere with school studies, most were concerned about their grades, and made efforts to improve them, particularly in high school. After finishing school, these lads typically moved on to university or to paid employment. Many also had jobs while at university. They had no desire to advertise their gang membership (one reason being that being in the police gang member database prevents employment in any government organization), and they never had gang-related tattoos. Only those people who "needed to know about us" were made aware of the identities of the neighborhood's gang members.

Street Backgrounds

Unlike the 1990s, when young people joined gangs driven by an urgent need to find some source of income or excited by the prospect of making serious money, in the 2000s people tended to drift into gangs in a kind of seamless progression of their membership in street peer groups. They had only vague expectations of what lay ahead, apart from opportunities to cement their street friendships, achieve greater street authority, earn money from small-scale pecuniary schemes, and acquire connections with the "right" people.

Most of our Kazan interviewees made smooth transitions from street groups into the gang. For example, seventeen-year-old Anvar had just finished school. He was looking for a job but had no definite plans for what to do next. In the meantime, he spent most of his time with the lads from his street:

> I joined the street very recently, no more than a year ago. I've been hanging out with the lads for a long time now, since I was fourteen, and I just didn't spend much time on the street before—I needed to keep my grades above a certain level. Then things got easier, and I could let myself skip classes, so I started spending most of my time with the lads and joined in 2004. I started to socialize more, to understand life and how things fit together. Nothing attracted me in particular; it's just that I was hanging out with them anyway and would have kept doing so. I just like that lifestyle.

Twenty-four-year-old Tsigan, a university graduate, explained how he joined the gang:

> As far back as I can remember I spent all my spare time on the street. We had our own group in the courtyard. In the summer, we played soccer, tag, and all sorts of sports-type games. In the winter, we had skiing,

> sledding, and snowball fights. [When I decided to join the gang], you could say I was just curious. I wouldn't say I had problems and needed protection. I just wanted to know what it was like to live as part of a brotherhood, and I wanted something new. So when they invited me to join the street, I agreed.

Like Tsigan, twenty-three-year-old Petia joined his gang at the beginning of the 2000s. At the time of our interview he was employed as a factory worker. Having spent a lot of time on the streets in his childhood and youth, he saw joining the local gang when he reached the proper age as a natural progression: "I followed my friends into the street. That was the time when being a street lad was fashionable—it was the cool thing to do. That was when a whole load of people joined [gangs] without giving much thought to the future."

Twenty-four-year-old law graduate Risat followed a similar trajectory. He said, "When I was a child, there wasn't much by way of entertainment, so when I wasn't studying I either read or wandered around the street. And then I followed the crowd. There came a time when many of the guys I hung out with drifted toward the street. I wasn't going to be the odd one out."

Other young men followed their older brothers or fathers into local gangs. The brother of twenty-year-old aviation student Tuigun used to be a member of a large local *gruppirovka*: "He [my brother] was my role model in every way, so I followed him. I just thought it made sense to be where your brother was." His father was an old member of a different gang. Needless to say, all Tuigun's friends were gang affiliated as well.

Kolia, who spent a lot of time on the streets in his childhood and youth, also followed his brother's example: "I asked him about the street, found out what they did, and it seemed interesting. When they were recruiting in the junior age groups, my brother suggested me to the lads and said that I was a proper lad and worthy of belonging to the street. They agreed and took me in."

Eighteen-year-old Radik's father was a gang member himself. Radik studied tax accounting in a university and combined his studies with gang membership relatively easily. He explained:

> While I was in school, I first joined up with S. gang, just out of curiosity—many of my friends were with them, and then my father, who's an old hand from G. gang, joined that street. Back then, I was attracted by the possibility of doing business, being under protection, somehow feeling more confident on the street. Plus my father later arranged it so I didn't have to attend meet-ups, except for mandatory ones; but I still had protection. So I didn't lose anything and didn't have to sacrifice my studies but was still from the street.

Twenty-five-year-old car mechanic Kirill found out about the street from his cousin, who joined first and then suggested Kirill do the same: "As for the reason, I was just curious about the street and wanted to try living with the lads." Young men who migrated to Kazan from other areas where they had been members of local street organizations explained how on coming to the city they actively tried to join the local gangs. Nineteen-year-old university student Tadjik had come to Kazan from the nearby town of Buinsk:

> When I was living in Buinsk, I was always with the local lads. You could say I grew up in that environment. Then I came to Kazan. There I started out just hanging out with my classmates, but through them, my social circle expanded and I became closer to the lads. I joined the street at sixteen when I was in year 10 in 2002. This was nothing unusual for me; I knew the lads, and everything carried on like before, except that I had more confidence. I was attracted by the opportunity to be surrounded by like-minded people and to have protection in a new city.

For twenty-three-year-old physics graduate Banan, the gang was more about "becoming a man." While at school, he did not have much street experience, being a diligent pupil, and felt that he had somehow "missed out":

> I only spent time on the streets in the summer. The rest of the year, I studied dutifully. After all, I graduated from a mathematical school. It's funny to think now that once my friends and I used to often sit around and solve various equations. These days, I sometimes think about how I joined the street, and I realize that it was all childishness, just some stupid curiosity or something. I just wanted to try street life because I was fed up with being classified as a physics faculty nerd. So I joined at the first offer, without even taking the time to work out which street I was joining.

Membership in a gang is not predicated on an emotional commitment to a particular "tribe." Instead, young people see the gang as a natural form of male collective life. The choice of a particular gang is often a matter of circumstance. Twenty-five-year-old Nemets reported: "I actually used to belong to two streets. I joined the first when I was just a little brat and stayed there for three years. I joined together with a classmate who knew some lads there. Three years later, I left and spent a couple of years on my own. Then some friends from another street invited me in, to go straight into the third age group, which is what I basically did. I was just fed up of being on my own."

Attractions of Gang Membership

From its origin as a street peer group, the gang does not transform into a purely economic enterprise, a violent criminal corporation, but remains a multifunctional organization. Those teenagers who, at the age of seventeen or eighteen, were making the transition into an organized gang did so for a variety of reasons. Some wanted to use the gang's opportunities to make money. Others were mainly interested in protection and companionship. The most frequent answer given when we asked these young men why they joined the gang was "to live with the lads." They wanted to be a part of a quasi-kinship group, a society of equals bound together in one collective life. For them the gang was more than a business enterprise and certainly not a criminal entity. Ultimately, it was seen as an ideal society where one learned "how to live properly." It also helped them to earn money along the way. As Tuigun put it: "The group is a framework for living, like a university where you learn how to live properly. . . . The point of the group is to be safe together, to live like a family so that everyone benefits. That's exactly why we need the street. . . . The street gives you a chance to make something of yourself, to earn some money, to learn how to live."

Many were attracted by the ritualistic side of gang life and the world of ceremonies, codes, and mythologies that often constitute street "nations" (Katz 1988, 188). Garik, a twenty-four-year-old engineering student, described what brought him to the gang:

> My perspective on this changes with every year. When I was young, everyone thought that if you weren't from the street, you were nobody, even if you happened to be God himself. So you joined the street just to be on the same level as everyone else, didn't set any particular goals, and didn't think about it too much. Over time, I saw better opportunities to make money, to develop useful contacts. Just don't assume that the street is merely a way to earn easy money. It's a way of life, so to speak, big politics on a small level, with career growth, statuses, and all the other paraphernalia.

According to twenty-three-year-old Potap, the gang attracts "young people who want some street romanticism and to live the high life." This "street romanticism" was often invoked by our other interviewees, and by experts, when they talked about the lure of the street. The idealistic vision of street brotherhood, and the life of exciting adventure its members supposedly lead, still draws young people toward gangs despite the serious reduction in money-making opportunities.

Learning "how to live" in the gang context was another recurring motive in the interviews. For many, growing up as part of a brotherhood rather than subjecting oneself fully to the rules of modern society's impersonal institutions seemed deeply attractive. Twenty-four-year-old Zhenia, who spent much of his time on the streets in his school years, explains how he saw the gang as a natural environment for a person like himself, an informal leader in his school: "I joined when I was still at school. I always carried myself confidently and acted fairly. I was respected and feared, and I had a lot of authority within the school. Then, when a friend who was already in the street told me they were recruiting, and that he'd nominated me and got approved, I agreed straight away."

For others, particularly those who had not been members of street peer groups in their teenage years, the gang's main attraction tended to be the opportunity to make money. Twenty-one-year-old Trofim, a technology student who also worked as a low-paid assembly worker in a computer company, joined the street after the end of school at the suggestion of some close friends: "In my school years, while I didn't stay at home all the time, I didn't spend days and nights on the street either. [When I decided to join the gang] I wasn't interested in support from the lads, since no one threatened me in any case, but in the fact that these lads started to run their own businesses and went pretty big with it. I wanted to have money of my own, and ideally a fair bit of it."

Farit joined his street quite late and did not have much prior experience of street life. For him, the gang primarily offered material opportunities that he could seize while he was still young, and not in some distant future. Farit studied physics but also worked in the street economy, providing "security" to gaming parlors. He also owned several food stalls in the local street market:

> I was interested in the street because there is no other way for young people to live well. There's practically no decent work available, but you need to live, and you want to have not just decent clothes but a car and the ability to bring your girlfriend to a restaurant rather than a bar. So I decided that, if I was with the lads, I would get all these things, whereas if I worked like everyone else, I would only get rich by the time I no longer needed any of it. That's what brought me to the street.

Some members were invited to join. At the time of our interview, twenty-six-year-old Il'sur, a former athlete, was a qualified lawyer working in a security company. He was also a member of the local gang, which he joined seven years earlier: "An acquaintance who said they needed sensible people brought me in. I came because I was curious and wanted opportunities to do business and earn money."

Nemets, who worked as a manager in an oil company, did not see the gang as an important source of immediate income, saying that he was in the gang because "being with the lads is no trouble, and everyone needs connections in life."

Tadjik captured the common opinion about the benefits of gang membership well: "First off, my friends are normal lads who don't just know how to wag their tongues but also how to make money. It's easy for me to find a common language with them; I know that I can rely on them and that they'll help me out when I need it. Second, you have to stick with the lads, and then everything in your life will be okay."

Criminal Transitions

Members of street gangs are not a unified group of marginalized delinquents. They are making highly diverse transitions to adulthood.[4] Some of them were profoundly disassociated from mainstream society and saw a life of crime as the only available option for them. These youths tended to be from poor families, where one or both parents were unemployed. Some grew up in single-parent families, with their fathers either living apart or serving time in prison. These young people spent much of their lives on the street. They typically had histories of petty delinquency and crime (joyriding, theft of cell phones and bicycles, and burglary). Their employment history was patchy or nonexistent.

Twenty-three-year-old Bogdan came from a very poor family. His father was an unemployed alcoholic, and his mother only had an intermittent income. He'd finished school but had never had a permanent job. His main income came from odd jobs and theft, as well as small-scale drug peddling via a *baryga.* He grew up on the streets and wanted to be in a gang from early on. He described his persistent efforts to join a gang:

> Fundamentally, I knew since I was little that there were streets, that lads gathered together, and that they had their own activities. I was curious about it all, and I remember that at twelve or thirteen I already wanted to join the street. But while I was little, they wouldn't let me in, and when I grew up, at about sixteen, I went to some lads I knew and told them I wanted to be one of them. They said that you could only join when they were recruiting for the younger age group, and that they'd bring me in then. When recruitment started, I went in with them.

Bogdan did not believe he would ever have a proper job. He wanted, while remaining in his gang, to join the vory society as well, and eventually to become a criminal avtoritet or a *vor.*

---

4. Youth transitions can be defined as "the pathways that young people make as they leave school and encounter different labour market, housing and family-related experiences as they progress towards adulthood" (MacDonald and Marsh 2005, 31).

> I recently started attending vory meetings, because I myself live by theft and I was invited to do business with vory. The vory law is not the same as the lads' code, and it used to be very severe. The vory did not have families or jobs, and they were required to have served time. Now the vory law has changed, so it is possible to have a family, a house, and it is not necessary to have served time, but it is desirable not to have a job.

Potap's story was similar. Both of his parents were unemployed alcoholics. His father had no income, while his mother did odd jobs in the market, worked as a cleaner, and stole from time to time. He had a little brother and sister, and the family led a very precarious material existence. From the age of eleven Potap spent most of his time on the streets. He dropped out of school at fifteen and earned money by theft and street robbery. He hated well-off kids "who have everything without having done anything for themselves" and migrants from the Caucasus: "black asses . . . [who] . . . behave like they own our city." As for the future, he had only vague ideas: "I'd like to have a business that brings in a lot of money." In any case, he saw his future inevitably linked to the world of crime: "That's how I've lived my entire life." He claimed he liked the life he led: "It's all good, except that I could do with more dough." For him, the gang offered a way to make a day-to-day living. This is how he described how he spends his time:

> I have a lot of free time, so I often meet up with the lads. Usually I sleep till the afternoon, and in the evenings, if there are no meet-ups, I just go with the lads to have fun. If we have money, we can have a drink. Sometimes we travel together to do *gop-stop* [street mugging and extortion]. We quickly scan the streets, find someone we can nail down and force money out of, and hurry back home so as not to get arrested. Then for a few days I avoid public places.

Working-Class Transitions

Other gang members took traditional routes into manual jobs, often following their fathers into the same factories, car service stations, or construction companies. But these jobs paid very low wages, and the young people tried to supplement them with other income, including from gang activities. Some also considered higher education as a way out of manual labor and pursued other avenues, trying a variety of non-manual jobs.

Twenty-one-year-old Maksim finished vocational college and worked as a driver at a construction company. His father, who worked there too, got him the job. The wages were poor, but Maksim hoped eventually, together with his pals, to be able to start their own construction business. He also wanted to go to university, feeling that this would give him better chances in life.

Kolia worked as a loader in a construction team. He got this job through an older lad from his gang. He came from a family of modest means and was brought up by his mother, who worked in a kindergarten. He had an older brother who was also a gang member. The brother now owned a shop. Kolia also aspired to have his own business, such as a stall or a small shop, and he was not sure if he would stay in the criminal world or not: "It's too early to say; time will tell." For the time being, Kolia and his family lived with his mother, and his dream was to buy his own house.

Kirill got his job as an auto mechanic through a friend. This provided his main source of income, but before that he used to do a lot of street crime. His mother was retired; his father, who had worked as a security guard, was killed in a drunken brawl. Back in the Soviet days his father had served time for theft. Before Kirill found his job, he and his mother often had no money for food. Now he mostly saw the lads at mandatory meet-ups, as most of the time was taken up by his work. He said that he would happily remain an auto mechanic, but he was not planning to leave the gang, and saw his gang associates as lifelong friends.

Twenty-three-year-old Grisha worked in a factory where he got a job thanks to his father, who had also worked at this factory as a supervisor. He complemented his wages with street racketeering. He was happy to continue doing this for now but intended to look for a better-paying job when he got married. He thought that he would probably leave the gang in a year or two.

Those lads who did not have stable jobs led a relatively precarious existence, with their main income coming from low-skilled part-time work or odd jobs. Many worked as loaders at the market or as laborers in construction. Gang business supplemented this income, but it was not enough to solve their material problems. A good job (or even better, their own business) was a dream for many young men. As eighteen-year-old Pavel said, "I think I like my life, though there are a lot of downsides too—for example, the lack of a regular income." Many gang members were getting material help from their mothers and fathers, and some led a real hand-to-mouth existence, in constant fear of becoming destitute or homeless.

Professional Transitions

Many of the lads were from families where both parents had a university education and professional jobs. Their parents were doctors, lawyers, businessmen, and, as we saw, even police officers. One such example was the family of twenty-seven-year-old Nafik. His father was an employee of the local district council, and his mother was a schoolteacher. Nafik himself had graduated from vocational college and worked as a service engineer for office equipment. He was married and lived with his wife in a rented apartment. Nafik's dreams were conventional: to buy the latest model Lada car to replace his cheap Oka and in five years or so to start a family. He was happy with his job and yet saw himself continuing with his gang affiliation. Although he only saw the lads at the mandatory meet-ups, he saw no reason ever to leave the gang.

Tsigan had a law degree but did not enjoy the field and was not planning to look for a job in law. Both his parents had higher education. His father worked as a factory engineer, while his mother was retired. He had his own team of construction workers. When asked if his future was going to be linked to the world of organized crime, he replied: "It's the only way."

Trofim came from a family of doctors. For him, his low-paid work in a computer assembly company was a first step in his formal career, giving him valuable work experience while he was also studying. The gang business provided him with additional income for the time being: "The business helps me live rather than just exist."

Nemets also came from a professional family. His father was an engineer and his mother a German teacher. He graduated from the university and had a job at a chemical company, which he liked and which paid quite well. As for other sources of income, he said: "I try to earn my daily bread honestly, but sometimes it doesn't hurt to get a bit on the side. When I have financial troubles, I can turn to my parents, or I can turn to my lads." In the future he would like to do "profitable work of some sort." He suspected this would require keeping his contacts with the gang world.

Twenty-nine-year-old David was a pediatric surgeon (a highly qualified but relatively low-paid position in Russia). His father, formerly an engineer, had opened up his own business. His mother worked as a police doctor. David had had several unspecified "businesses" apart from his doctor job. He wanted to move into the banking sector and said this meant that he would need to maintain his contact with the world of organized crime.

Banan also came from a relatively well-off family. His father was a factory engineer and his mother a dentist. Although his father went through a period of unemployment in the 1990s, things later got better and he found a permanent job. Banan himself tried many jobs while he was a student and after graduation. He worked as a laborer at construction sites and as a security guard. As for his gang, he wanted to leave it:

> I'm looking for work now. Just the other day, I got a job offer as a manager at one company, but I'm still considering it. I like using my head,

> and I'd like to pursue some sort of well-paid intellectual activity. . . . I don't really feel a serious need for the street now, especially after getting to know it better. It's just that circumstances right now don't permit me to leave without difficulties, so I'm waiting for the right opportunity.

"Double Helix" Model of Transition to Adulthood

As we have seen, for young people in Kazan the decision to join a gang did not mean dedicating oneself to a life of crime. The majority of our interviewees studied or worked, and very often they did both. Some had manual jobs—at parking lots, garages, or construction sites. Some were employed in security companies, while others had professional occupations, working in the public or private sectors (as doctors, lawyers, engineers, etc).

The world of the gang coexisted relatively easily with those of the family, school, and employment. This meant that joining a gang was not a radical break from the rest of society but simply one piece of a patchwork of memberships and roles.

The vast majority of our interviewees did not follow a single "criminal" version of transition to adulthood. Gang business did not bring huge dividends and mostly supplemented other sources of income or occasional handouts from parents. It was universally accepted that the time when a lad could rise from street racketeer to oligarch was long gone. Such fantastic careers, made by those gruppirovshchiki who were lucky enough to survive the gang wars and not end up in prison, were no longer possible, although for some the dream of "making it" was still alive. As Tsigan said, "Every soldier aspires to be a general." Careers in the legal sector seemed to be more reliable. Most of our interviewees wanted to work in the formal economy, including government, which could now be more lucrative than organized crime. Their family and educational backgrounds influenced their opportunities and aspirations in the world of work, and their life chances were highly stratified. But regardless of their backgrounds, most members believed that being part of gang society was far from a hindrance and, in fact, could benefit them throughout their lives. Through their gang activities, the lads believed they were expanding their opportunities and creating a good foundation for their future. They hoped the gang would give them the contacts, material resources, and entrepreneurial skills necessary to succeed in life.

Some thought that the gang would help them to open their own businesses and become legal entrepreneurs—while guaranteeing the security of the business. Others were looking at careers in the public sector, often with the tax authorities, or in law or medicine, and were hoping that their contacts in the gangs would be helpful in gaining access to business opportunities, opening their own practices or companies, dealing with the state authorities and the police, and guaranteeing security. Some members from poorer working-class backgrounds simply expected their friends from the gang to be able to help them find jobs, commonly in construction or service stations, and help them out in case of trouble.

Twenty-three-year-old Koshmar joined the street while at law school but without any plan to make a career in the gang structures. He was from a notorious gang area. His father was a retired police colonel who now worked as a defense lawyer, and his mother was a company lawyer. He had never had any trouble with the law nor had he been registered by the police as a delinquent or a gang member. He made a brief foray into gang life at eighteen. Before that he was part of a street peer group and was involved in all the usual leisure pursuits—soccer and barbecues in the summer and video arcades in winter. His first attempt at gang life did not last long. His father was very angry when he learned about it and went to talk to the avtoritety, whom he knew from his policing days. As a result, Koshmar was allowed to leave the gang without any punishment or having to pay a fine. But in three years he went back and joined the older cohort straight away. Now he wanted to step away from the gang business again because he did not see many prospects for himself with all the good businesses already divided up among the gang's avtoritety. He had graduated from law school but did not want to practice law. Instead, he wanted to be a professional musician. He composed music and had his own band that performed in local clubs. Koshmar had no plans to try to move up in the gang and intended to stop actively participating in its affairs, but he did not intend to leave the gang formally; he wanted to continue belonging to the street in order "to solve the problems of security for my music business."

The members of Kazan gangs in the 2000s had access to both legitimate and illegitimate opportunities in their communities. Unlike professional criminals, the vory v zakone, they were not fully subscribed members of the criminal subculture, nor did they universally aspire to achieve their goals only via legitimate means. For many of the Kazan gang members we interviewed, a career in a gang, so often regarded as being at odds with conventional youth transitions, was simply one of a number of parallel life strategies. A conventional strategy, associated with education and employment, coexisted with an alternative strategy through membership in a criminal organization. The lads realized very well that these apparently parallel lines in fact intersected, as indeed had been postulated by their famous Kazan compatriot, the mathematician Nikolai Lobachevskii, one of the founders of non-Euclidian geometry. Our interviewees understood this nonlinear reality very well. Gang members tried to inscribe themselves both within their own "alternative" order and the larger social order in a way that made it possible for them to successfully navigate both worlds.

These multiple career strategies had serious implications for the everyday behavior and identities of gang members. They did not want to have problems with school or university authorities or with the police. Unlike members of the vory v zakone community, a truly clandestine organization that defined itself through opposition to mainstream society, the lads saw no value whatsoever in acquiring a name and reputation via being incarcerated. As Garik explained, he did not want to find himself behind bars, "not because I'm scared but because it would take away so much time." For this reason the lads tried, as much as possible, to avoid trouble with the law. Il'sur said that he wanted to stay out of illegal business: "Everything I do in outside work is legal. I don't need money. If I have to borrow, I prefer bank loans."

Despite their relatively young age some lads had already explored a vast variety of different avenues, including a career in politics. Twenty-year-old Vlad, who had graduated from a vocational college, came from a working-class family. His father was a *shabashnik* (day laborer), and his mother worked as a manual worker at a large pharmaceutical company. At one time, Vlad joined the youth wing of the Russian Party of Life, which for a while seemed to have good electoral prospects: "I was a member of the Russian Party of Life's youth wing and joined it during the last elections. I liked this party's ideas, the fact that they are pro-youth, and then I wanted to develop connections within party circles, so I even attended party conferences and spoke with the leaders."

When he realized that this party did not have an electoral future he decided to try real estate. When we interviewed him he was working as an intermediary in construction, finding teams for building and decorating work. He found out about this job from a friend who was in the same business. He was not sure if his future would involve the world of crime. At the time of the interview he was planning to try to enroll in a law school.

Vlad was not alone in his political ambitions. Radik told us about his friend, also a young gang member, who used to go to meetings of the regional branch of the country's ruling party, United Russia: "This lad cannot string two words together properly. I asked him, 'Why do you need all this?' and he explained that he's developing useful connections." Twenty-nine-year-old Aidar also said, "I don't like any of the parties but would personally go for United Russia, if they had a decent position available, as it's a strong party with a promising future."

Many of the lads were optimistic about their prospects and downplayed the risks inherent in their criminal activities, even though in some of the gangs up to a third of the members were at the time incarcerated for a variety of offences, mostly drug related but also hooliganism and burglary. They had high expectations for their futures, which they associated both with legal employment and with organized crime. Twenty-one-year-old Arkadii was a part-time student of management. He graduated from a vocational legal studies college. In his early youth, he spent time in a prison colony for underage criminals. His father also had experience of incarceration. But now his parents had opened up their own business, where Arkadii also worked. He had a variety of sources of income, but mostly, he claimed, "these days I earn money through honest labor and by using my own head." As for the future, he had not decided what he wanted to do yet but thought it would involve "some form of manufacturing." He would like to achieve "great influence" and was confident that his contacts with bandits would turn out very useful.

Being "Normal"

Although the gang is a closed society that puts its own interests and the interests of its members above everything else, this does not mean that young people are separated from the life that goes on outside their street or district that is not connected with their group interests. While seeking domination in the street economy, in their broader lives they play the conventional roles of children, students, or employees. Members of the Kazan gangs try not to attract unnecessary attention to themselves at schools and colleges and try to play by the rules set by the teachers. This seems to be in sharp contrast with young gang members in some US schools, who consistently challenge school authorities (Garot 2010), or with the rebellious and negativistic subculture of English working-class youth described by Paul Willis (1977) or David Downes (1966). The Kazan lads do not systematically play truant and try not to let the teachers know what they do outside school, although their classmates know about their gang membership, and the teachers claim that they can identify a gang member by their manner, walk, body language, etc. As I have mentioned, tattoos are rarely used by gang members, who try not to advertise their gang membership to the world at large.

The lads' typical behavior in schools was described by O., a Kazan high school teacher, in the following way:

> I'll tell you that a real gang member, someone who has a place in the gang's structure, is never rude [to teachers]. He is politeness itself. He will always say "Hello," for example, or help you carry heavy things. Although it's all obviously a performance, he will attend all the classes, so that de jure he will not break the rules. You try to prove that he is doing something wrong outside school. . . . If you challenge him, he looks you openly in the eye and says, "Prove it." And you ask the whole class, and they will all confirm that he never does anything wrong.

Seeing themselves as a part of a social and moral majority, gang members share many prejudices afflicting Russian society as a whole, particularly when it comes to "deviants" and "outsiders." They are generally tolerant of local ethnic minorities, but at the same time they share widespread animosity toward migrants who come to Kazan from other areas, blaming the latter for all that is wrong in the city, including crime. Petia told us, "I do not like migrants from the Caucasus and Central Asia. It's thanks to bad people like them that we have problems with crime and drugs. They bring drugs to our country and turn our youth into addicts. They traffic our girls to their own countries and force them into prostitution. The fewer of them that come here, the better."

Gruppirovshchiki also expressed their pride in being Russian citizens and were hostile toward Russia's perceived enemies. Aidar said, "I don't like those nationalities that oppose our country. I am a patriot, and so if these people do not respect my country, they will not get my respect. I do not respect people from the Baltics, Americans, Chechens, and the rest."

The nationalities mentioned here are the subjects of widely held negative attitudes, whether as a result of endemic xenophobia or anti-Western propaganda by the Russian mass media (Levinson 2009). These attitudes can be seen in the results of public opinion polls conducted around the time of our research in Kazan in 2005. In a representative survey of the Russian population conducted by the Russian polling organization the Levada Center in 2004, 46 percent of respondents wanted to impose limits on residence in Russia for people from the Caucasus, and 31 percent for people from Central Asia (Levinson 2005). In 2006 a survey by the same organization found that 74 percent of respondents agreed with the statement "The US is using Russia's present weakness to transform it into a minor country, a raw material appendage of the West" (Levinson 2006). The United States and the Baltic states regularly appear as the key "enemies" of Russia in public opinion polls (Delphi 2011).

When it comes to Kazan, the gang members generally saw it as a good place. In their understanding, a good place meant a place with low levels of social disorder. "I generally like our city," said Il'nar. "What I don't like is that there is a lot of bespredel—druggies and *otmorozki*."

The gangs share common apprehensions and prejudices about those who are seen as deviants and outsiders. As well as drug addicts, the members also disliked homeless people, refugees, and beggars. They were seen as unwilling to work and as sponging off hard-working Kazan citizens. Garik said, "So-called refugees, who beg for money at crossroads and in public places, piss me off. They've got arms and legs, and judging by the number of kids, their genitals are fine as well. But no, they don't feel like working. Why break your back in a factory for five to six thousand rubles a month if you can earn them in just a week? Their kind deserves to be beaten."

While seeing themselves as hard-working entrepreneurs, gang members expressed contempt for people who were not productive, who, in their opinion, did nothing to help themselves. They categorically rejected any suggestions that the rank-and-file of the gangs, or the more prosperous avtoritety, might help the poor in their area, although they were quite willing to give money to churches, mosques, or local sports facilities. As Potap commented: "No one helps the poor. They have to fix their own problems."

Most of our interviewees showed little concern for wider Russian politics, not seeing how it influenced their own life and business, although, as mentioned, some young people tried to launch their own political careers or at least establish useful contacts in the political parties. Viktor's views were typical: "Overall, I don't like any of the politicians. Not one of them would do anything for me." But some of the more educated members voted in elections. They valued parties and politicians who were seen as pragmatic and strong, with the pro-Putin United Russia being their favorite.

The Gang and the "Russian Dream"

The massive movement of young people in Kazan into the control of street businesses took place at a time of crisis in the Soviet planned economy and the beginning of market reforms. The reformers hoped to transform the Russian populace into active and enterprising economic agents. While a significant proportion of the population disappointed the reformers, clinging to their old workplaces (even though the latter stopped paying them a living wage) and supplementing their income with subsistence farming on their dachas instead of becoming new capitalist entrepreneurs, the gang members enthusiastically followed the call of money. In this sense they were faithful adepts of the new spirit of capitalism and hardly marginal or deviant in the new social order, at least in their aspirations. Just as their Soviet predecessors believed that by robbing shadow speculators and dishonest shop workers they were in some way restoring socialist "social justice," the new generation of gang members tended to think of themselves as capitalist entrepreneurs. They wanted to achieve financial success and believed that the way to do it was to develop innovative money-making schemes.

Interviews reflect the sense that gang members wanted to reach the new Russian dream and to join, in the terminology of the times, the ranks of the New Russians. As opinion polls conducted among Russian youth showed, the lads were far from alone in their aspirations of achieving material success; acquiring wealth was widely cited as their number one ambition (Chernysh 2003).

Although gangs (and the world of organized crime in general) are typically seen by international academics and media commentators as a site of resistance and subversion of mainstream values, our interviewees always emphasized their entrepreneurial aims rather than their criminal means. They saw themselves as industrious and hard-working people on the make. Risat characterized his and his pals' key objective in the following way: "Since we won our place under the sun, we've had just one aim: to work and to keep on working." Illicit economic activities were universally perceived as work rather than crime. A common aspiration was to earn enough money to retire from business. As Aidar declared, his dream was "to secure my financial situation to the point where I don't have to work at all." This is very different from the ethos of the vory who belonged to their closed society till their dying day.[5]

The Gang in the Russian Deep State

The gang members do not regard the world as a hostile place where it is a case of every man for himself. On the contrary, they believe that only those people who are able to establish wide-ranging social bonds can get access to better opportunities in life. Positive personal relationships can and should be built—with teachers and university lecturers, neighbors, and even policemen. This orientation makes the borders between the official and unofficial worlds very permeable.

Networks of favor and exchange have always played a key role in Soviet society, and despite growing individualism, they continue to be highly important for post-Soviet citizens (Kryshtanovskaya and White 2011; Ledeneva 2013). As Leo McCann (2005, 70) has shown, in Tatarstan "informal networks are extended across all sectors of economic life, participated in by elites, small- and medium-sized business actors." People at all levels are involved in an informal and personalized system of relations, in a dense system of patron-client and peer-to-peer ties. This informal web of connections and ties extends, as we have seen, to people who pursue strategies that put them on the brink of, or beyond, legality.

Most of our gang interviewees considered it a matter of priority that they establish a broad range of personal ties straddling formal and informal worlds.

---

5. Writing about American entrepreneurial gangs, Sánchez-Jankowski (1991) showed that the gang members, while being ruthless in the pursuit of criminal profit, wanted what everybody else in America wanted—namely, material success. The gang reflected a wider individualistic culture in America, which values competitiveness in achievement of personal goals. Other authors have shown that marginalized young people living in deprived deindustrialized areas in the United States and the United Kingdom are at once profoundly conventional and antisocial. Seduced by the rampant consumerism of late modern society, they also attempt to use illicit and criminal activities as vehicles of success (Hall, Winlow, and Ancrum 2008; Nightingale 2008; Young 1999, 2007).

Particularly striking was their attitude toward police officers. While informing the police of the gang's activities or assisting with their investigations is strictly prohibited, having personal contacts with representatives of law enforcement, or even having family relations in the police or Prokuratura, was considered a major benefit. Even being on friendly terms with officers was seen as a good thing. Thirty-five-year-old Il'nar told us that he always said hello to local policemen and was on good terms with his neighbor who worked in the transport police. He said he had "normal" relations with police officers, especially with the older men who "do not need to flaunt their importance and needlessly humiliate gruppirovshchiki."

Il'sur knew policemen through his work in a private security firm. He proudly reported that he had received many favors from them:

> Because I work in the security services industry, I have to work closely with members of the Ministry of the Interior, and I have excellent relations with many of them. Thanks to that, I've frequently gotten out of unpleasant situations. I can get away with having zero tint [completely darkened] car windows, and the road cops are patient with my Formula 1–style driving. Before, when I didn't have connections, I had to put up with their rudeness.

In a society where informal relations rule, connections with the police are a highly valuable resource. This is very different from the traditions of the vory v zakone or the Italian Mafia. For example, according to Paoli (2003, 125), in both Calabrian and Sicilian Mafia consortia, "law enforcement officials and their sons are absolutely prohibited from becoming members." In the Russian case, far from being regarded as a stain on a member's reputation, such close connections are seen as positive. If there is a "beef" with a rival gang, the help of an uncle or a brother who serves in OMON (the special police commando unit) can be invaluable. Our gang informants had mothers, fathers, uncles, and other relatives working for the police, and this could be of great practical assistance.

Gang members, police representatives, and a variety of other actors coexist and exchange favors and services that bridge the gap between official and nonofficial, familial and nonfamilial. It is in these local systems of tightly interconnected reputations, networks, and social ties that life unfolds, and it is here that the formal law is subverted on a daily basis.

As Salagaev, Shashkin, and Konnov (2006) pointed out in analyzing the ties between police representatives and the gangs, "The ties that we have studied are deeply embedded in social networks and the creation of social capital, and thus are not limited to financial benefits or struggle for political power. In other words, it is a mode of existence based on mutual trust, exchange of gifts, traditional personal relations in which kinship and friendship are valued higher than professional duties." Relations between police officers and gang members often begin in their childhood or are formed on the basis of neighborhood ties or family relations. As these authors also note, people continue networking and exchanging favors as they rise in a hierarchy, either in a gang or in the police. Relationships are maintained through periodic meetings, which tend to take place either at dachas in the countryside, where the participants enjoy "drinking alcohol, having a bath together, calling for prostitutes, and other entertainments." Exchange of favors can involve free car parking for police officers—this is where gang-controlled parking lots become useful, supply of building materials, apartment repairs, or invitations to pleasure trips. Criminal avtoritety can smooth the careers of their friends in the police using their vast contacts at the regional level and help with finding jobs after discharge or retirement from service.

The Russian deep state, informal networks of public officials, is involved in a dense web of relations with members of illegal organizations. Economic, personal, and familial ties stretch from elite groups to the level of the street. Young people who, by virtue of their gang affiliations, become immersed in these networks from early on in their lives do not see any benefit in breaking with their contacts as they grow older. For them, to succeed in Russian society requires being loyal to members of their own close circle but also building wider connections, playing by the rules of school and work but also developing money-making schemes of different degrees of legality. Seeing others around them employ these same strategies in their lives, it is no wonder that they regard themselves as perfectly normal.

The Best of Both Worlds

The Russian territorial gang is very different from the assemblages of deprived individuals eking out their survival in city ghettos in the developed world or those forming states within states in fractured cities in the global periphery. It is, with the exception of some ethnic or migrant gangs, a part of the local community. In this sense, it is closer to the territorially and culturally embedded Sicilian or Calabrian Mafia than to the violent street groups described by many scholars of contemporary North and South American gangs (Bourgois 1995; Anderson 1999; Bourgois 2004; McIlwaine and Moser 2006; Hagedorn 2008). Generally, the common denominator for membership in a Kazan gang is not the class origins of its members but juvenile experiences of participation in street culture in socially mixed areas. When it comes to the destinations of gang members, criminal transitions do not preclude more conventional ones. Young people can partake in criminal opportunities provided by the gang without abandoning legitimate opportunity structures accessed through education and work. Their street organizations do not demand full commitment, and it is relatively easy to leave the organization or turn involvement into a more or less nominal one. Unlike the 1990s, when young people were drafted into the local gang and could not leave it without very serious sanctions, young people in the 2000s could drift in and out of gangs. Although many of them violate the law on a daily basis, they can also play by the rules of mainstream institutions of education and work, attempt to join political parties, and try to follow the extant rules of Russian social life to extract maximum benefit for themselves.

Wide educational and employment opportunities available for young people in Tatarstan mean that those involved with the gangs do not necessarily feel resigned to the world of criminality. Moreover, opportunities accumulated in the gang (material capital, social connections, access to agents of organized violence) are seen as potentially beneficial for mainstream careers. The lads have diverse business portfolios that include both legal and illegal sources of income. In this they are very similar to other members of Russian organized crime networks (Galeotti 2012).

In the Kazan gangs, which are well established in the community, young people have access to what Cloward and Ohlin (1961), following Merton (1957), called illegitimate means of achieving success, such as the knowledge, skills, and contacts provided by older criminals. But these authors, who studied poor American communities, did not consider the possibility of the dual-opportunity structure that we find in modern Russia, in which illegitimate opportunities coexist with legitimate ones in the systems of education and employment.

Gang members see themselves as members of the normative majority and express the same prejudices in relation to outsiders and deviants and the same orientation toward material success as their nongang compatriots. Instead of using the neutralization techniques applied by their Soviet predecessors in trying to justify their violence and crime, the lads living in capitalist Russia believed that what they were doing was simply good business and that any means was acceptable for making money and moving upward in society.

The sharp dichotomies posited in criminological literature between the "outside" and the "inside," gangs and law-abiding communities, the world of illegal enterprise and the legal economy, simply do not exist in Russia. People live in a messy reality, not in some clandestine world beyond the looking glass. Instead of committing themselves to one interpretation of reality and one possible future, in which the only world available to them is the world of violence and criminality, gang members weigh their options, hedge their bets, and exploit all possible avenues of success. The membership itself is highly diverse. It includes students who have a bit of gang business on the side and people with criminal records who resign themselves to always living on the wrong side of the law. There are working-class young men dreaming about buying a new model Lada and a cottage in the suburbs and ambitious professionals aspiring to buy a Lexus and a villa in Cyprus. For some, the gang provides economic opportunities; for others, it becomes more of a social club. Gang membership does not erase one's social and economic advantages and disadvantages. Young people coming from troubled and deprived backgrounds are more likely to become immersed in street criminality, while members from educated professional families are likely to be on their way to leaving street crime behind. But in all cases the connections acquired through the gang, and the violent resource the gang provides, are seen as useful in furthering every type of career. And the "school of life" provided by the gang is considered to prepare its young graduates well for what awaits them beyond the street corner in the wider Russian society with its own clans, networks, and "gangs."

6

THE GANG IN THE COMMUNITY

In a book published pseudonymously but widely attributed to Vladislav Surkov, once a powerful gray cardinal of Putin's administration and currently an adviser to the Russian president, one of the characters says, "Sad though it may be to admit, corruption and organized crime are foundations of social order in the same way as schools, the police, or morality. Remove them, and chaos will ensue" (Dubovitskii 2009, 80). Indeed, in Russia, corruption and organized crime, from being disturbing but perhaps inevitable features of transition to the market economy, have become essential building blocks of social order. An interwoven system of the personalized power of state agents and criminal bosses has formed the underlying structure of social life. Corrupt bureaucrats, the ever-more-powerful *siloviki* (state security or military services personnel), and members of organized crime networks have created an unsavory but functioning regime of power. The interactions of the various violent actors brought about a system that somewhat limited and regulated their activities, thus creating relative order (Volkov 2002, 21).

In areas with entrenched gang presence, the gang became part of the system of local violent regulation, and in this chapter I explore the uses that Kazan residents were able to make of gang violence, the instrumental use of gang power by the police and the police's own attempts to subject gang members to the force of community control. I then address the different configurations of gang and state power in other regions of Russia.

Violent Regulators

The starting point in the analysis of the role of the gang in the local social order is that in its quest to develop a permanent presence in the community the gang has to obtain a degree of popular acceptance and be seen as performing some socially useful and culturally accepted functions. In this the gang follows the rich legacy of nonstate social regulation in Russia. The country has a long historical tradition of popular violence that developed as a result of the weakness of the state or deliberate delegation by the state of some of its justice functions. But Russia is far from unique. All over the world structures of popular justice and popular violence can be found in prisons, in vigilante groups, street violent networks and mafias, in associations where, as Jonathan Spencer pointed out, there is also "a structure of feeling which combines issues of justice, violence, democracy, sovereignty, and possibly masculinity too" (Spencer 2008, xii).

The traditional peasant community (*obshchina*) was not only responsible for joint management of communal land and its members' welfare but also provided basic policing (including registration), judicial, and fiscal functions (Shanin 1986, chap. 1). As Galeotti (2008, 90) pointed out, at the end of the nineteenth century, "to a large extent, a community was left (or even required) to police itself, with the tsarist state only intervening in the most serious cases, and then using extreme violence in a bid to deter future criminals." Brutal forms of social control, such as vigilante justice (*samosud*), protected the community against local miscreants and outsiders (horse thieves, arsonists, etc.). From the 1930s, the Soviet regime actively used neighborhood communities and workplace collectives as the interface between the state and society (Kotkin 1995; Kharkhordin 1999). The role of informal agent of justice was given to "communal courts"—organizations of residents or co-workers who had considerable power to discipline local deviants, "parasites," alcoholics, and troublesome neighbors—that often resulted in expulsion and subsequent homelessness of those who did not fit in (Stephenson 2006).

In prisons and labor camps, informal social control was executed by the vory v zakone society.[1] Beyond the prison walls, vory had their own "courts" where they judged transgressors according to their code. In the 1990s vory became active in informal policing and delivery of justice in those areas where their outlaw community had a strong presence. In the Russian Far East, for example, vory took it on themselves to punish not only criminals unaffiliated with their organizations but also those members of their own society who committed acts of bespredel, extreme violence that was forbidden under the code—for example,

1. On the development and main features of prison culture, see Oleinik (2003).

brutally attacking or killing a woman or a child. The famous vor v zakone Evgenii Vasin (Dzhem) and his fellow vory, who formerly had significant influence in Komsomolsk-na-Amure, established a "zone of informal order, partially replacing the judicial authority of the state" (Holzlehner 2007, 76). Dzhem had his own office where he received complaints and delivered verdicts.

Although research into the role of members of the criminal community as regulators of violence is very scarce, there are many indications that vory saw themselves as agents of informal authority across Russia and in other post-Soviet states as well. For example, while researching street violent youth networks in the peripheral areas of Moscow in 2006, I found that in some areas "retired" members of the vory society acted as local experts on violence. They provided advice and guidance to young people involved in territorial battles, sometimes organizing additional fighters for arranged combats. They could also help find redress if a crime was committed against a local resident (Stephenson 2012). Similar neighborhood structures of informal criminal authority have existed in Yerevan and Tbilisi (Koehler 1999; Zakharova 2010; Ponomareva 2014).

In the 1990s some of the bandit gangs turned effectively into agents of patrimonial power, acting as a structure of quasi-familial welfare and violent regulation in their neighborhoods. For example, Zhilka established its own fiefdom in its local area (Zhilploshchadka). The poor residents were given financial support from the obshchak. In 1993–95 Khaider gave struggling pensioners and families free potatoes and cabbages (taken from vegetable warehouses controlled by the gang). He also tried to ensure that the local apartment blocks were secure and installed metal doors in the entrances. Children's play areas were set up in the courtyards. Zhilka almost managed to put a stop to street crime in its area, and the police asked the gang to investigate the most prominent cases of theft. The gang returned stolen goods to the owners but stopped short of informing on the perpetrators. Khaider was known to call police officers and wish them a happy birthday. The gang's penetration into the community created huge difficulties when the authorities opened up an investigation into Zhilka's activities, as none of the local residents were willing to cooperate with the police. At the gang's trial in 1999–2002, local witnesses only agreed to give evidence after being guaranteed witness protection. They gave evidence via video link; their voices were changed, and many wore wigs, false moustaches, and beards in order to change their appearance. With a perhaps unintended comic effect, one witness was made up by a local theater makeup artist to look like the Russian writer Nikolai Gogol (Beliaev and Sheptitskii 2012, 225–26; Safarov 2012, 79–80).[2]

2. Post-Soviet organized crime in the 1990s was not dissimilar to criminal organizations in other countries that meted out punishment for crimes committed against local residents, provided

Although, by the middle of the 2000s, attempts to establish regulated gang enclaves in the local territories had largely stopped, the gangs still regard themselves as bastions of order and morality in the community. According to the lads, they have their rules—the code—while people around them have no strong moral compass and are always prone to descending into normlessness (bespredel). The lads assume the right to sanction people they regard as local deviants and outsiders—drug addicts, criminals not affiliated with gangs, and other people with no fixed place in the local social architecture. The case of drug addicts is paradoxical, because many of the members consume drugs themselves (or even deal in them). Nevertheless, in many gangs this activity still tends to be clandestine, as it is prohibited by the code. Drug addicts are construed as the abject "other," polluters of the local territory. Similarly to city authorities who conduct periodic *zachistki* (cleanups) to purge the territory of homeless people, beggars, or people with criminal records, usually undertaken in the run-up to important celebrations such as the 1,000th anniversary of Kazan in 2005 or the World University Summer Games in 2013, the gang also periodically cleans up the territory. For example, Aidar reported that "we do not like druggies, and at regular intervals we arrange cleanups in our territory to get rid of as many as possible."

The Kazan gangs also conduct operations against drug dealers who want to operate within the gang's territory. Garik said, "We started getting a lot of drug addicts in our territory, so naturally the cops began cracking down more often. We started by finding out exactly where the druggies got their poison. Then we just hit those locations, fucked over the dealers, and took the goods. Then we got the druggies and fucked them over so they never wanted to turn up in our area again."

Criminals coming from outside to commit theft or burglary in the local territory are also punished, although the gang is permissive toward similar crimes committed by their own members—"the lads need to feed themselves," in the words of one of our interviewees. Crime committed by outsiders is seen as bespredel because the territory "belongs" to the gang. As always with the gang, moral reasoning goes hand in hand with pragmatic considerations. The members admitted that the gang fights bespredel largely because it does not want additional police

---

mediation in disputes, and generally substituted for slow or nonexistent legal justice. This was a feature of the Sicilian Mafia (Blok 1974; Arlacchi 1988; Catanzaro 1992; Hess 1998; Paoli 2003; Wilson 2009) and the Cosa Nostra in America (Abadinsky 1994). In some poor ghetto areas in US cities, organized agents of informal violence often become a substitute for, or an addition to, state regulation (Venkatesh 2000). Research in Latin America shows that gangs, while being themselves a major source of violence in the community, can provide residents with personal protection from outside thieves and gangs and effectively build links with segments of state and society to gain a degree of localized power (Winton 2005; Arias 2006a,b; Rodgers 2006).

attention in its territory. As Zhenia said, "we act against bespredel actions on our territory because they can harm us—for example, when somebody not from our gang commits street crime on our territory and it sets the police against us."

Kazan Gangs and Social Order: Some Local Opinions

The gang presence in the neighborhoods creates a sense of fear and insecurity, and people in Kazan invariably stressed that life became much better once the days of the 1990s gang violence were over. Nevertheless, some people living in areas with a high gang presence thought that in a situation where the state was inaccessible and corrupt, the gangs could be a "necessary evil," acting in certain circumstances against the total chaos of bespredel. For example, Airat, an eighteen-year-old local resident and not a gang member, told us: "I would say that the gangs do not like bespredel. If the gangs did not exist, there would be more violence and bespredel. If there were no organized criminal groups, people would still do what these groups do. But the gang members at least control the situation somewhat and do not let others commit certain acts—for example, mugging pensioners."

Some of those people who became objects of the gangs' "taxation" believed that as long as this enforced payment was predictable and not excessive it was preferable to being under the constant threat of sporadic and violent extortion by a variety of predators. In a world where the rule of law in its modern sense was absent, they gained a semblance of stability. Taxi drivers, for example, talked about having "peace of mind" thanks to having a krysha. This did not mean that they firmly believed that the krysha would provide them with security against all eventualities. Rather, having a krysha was a necessary condition for being able to work in the local economy. They were inscribed in the territorial order, and as long as relationships between various power agents above them remained in balance, their economic activities could continue. As in any relatively stable system of social relations, this state of affairs was naturalized. People could not imagine a different way of living. They said: "That is how it is," "Everybody pays," "If we did not pay Zhilka, others would come and demand payment." Despite many examples to the contrary, people seemed to have latent hope that their krysha would help them in a crisis and protect them from violence or unfair competition. However nebulous the protection provided by the gangs was, to some at least the gangs were preferable to corrupt policemen, who were believed to be simply taking people's money without making any commitments to provide protection, even unreliable ones.

Similar sentiments have been found in other areas of Russia where organized criminal groups were present—for example in Saratov (Ries 2002, 284, 305). Research conducted in 1999 in Komsomolsk-na-Amure and other Russian Far East urban areas showed that residents and businessmen saw criminal kryshy as a necessary institution that helped solve their personal and business problems (Bliakher 2012).

In Kazan we heard the opinion that gruppirovki were preferable to other violent youth groups such as skinheads. For example, Fanil said, "Organized criminal groups and skinheads have a lot in common. Skinheads are just another gang, only more brutal. A gang member can adapt himself to society, but I doubt a skinhead could manage to."

The mixed attitudes toward violent social regulators coexist with a lack of trust in effective state protection. Many surveys have shown that Russian members of the public distrust the police and the judicial system. For example, in a public opinion survey conducted in Tatarstan in 2004, when asked where they would go to defend their interests, only 22 percent of respondents said that they would go to the police, and only 18 percent said that they would ask the state authorities for help. Thirty percent answered that they would go to court. At the same time, 16 percent said they did not know what to do, while 21 percent said that they "would do nothing" (Tabeev 2007, 107).

A victim survey conducted in several Russian regions at the end of the 1990s showed that people most often went to law enforcement bodies in cases of car theft (about 80%), other types of theft (40% of cases), and destruction of property (30%). In cases of bodily harm or fraud, only 25 percent of victims applied to law enforcement bodies, with about 20 percent doing so in cases of serious threat, including threats of murder. For victims of extortion and hooliganism, the proportions seeking support from law enforcement agencies was even lower (around 10% and 15%, respectively) (Dolgova 2003, 388n1).

The distrust of institutions of law and order can explain why people may decide to turn to the local strongmen for assistance instead. People who hesitate to go to the police (who are likely to be very slow in their investigation or to do nothing at all) may find it easier to ask gang members for help, if they know somebody personally or are able to make contact through friends or neighbors. A person can ask a local gang for assistance from assaults from other gangs or for help finding stolen property. The gang's capacity for violence becomes part of the ongoing exchange of favors, provided free to relatives and other members of one's social circle. Potap said, "I know one guy—he was not an avtoritet, just a lad from the street. People from his apartment block came to his father to ask his son to help with the repairs of the building. They wanted him to grab the block's manager by the throat and force him to get the repairs done. I think that's how they sorted it out in the end."

Similarly, Kirill reported: "My father often makes use of my position. There was this thing the other day: I'm on my way home from work, and my father calls me and says, 'I need some lads this evening.' Apparently, someone was rude to him, and he wants to punish him. In short, Dad's started to feel like some sort of Don Corleone."

The gang becomes a part of a parochial, deeply personalized system of relations, in which violence can be used to resolve everyday personal conflicts and problems. Being on good terms with the local gruppirovshchiki can make life much easier for residents, while being excluded from these networks of favor and exchange can have dire consequences.

At the same time, in contrast to honor-based groups like the Sicilian Mafia (Catanzaro 1992, 92), or even the Russian vory, the bandit gang does not aspire to a monopoly of honor in the territory under its control and does not attempt to supplant the official powers in the administration of justice. Although, as we have seen, some of the gangs did attempt to achieve significant social control in their areas in the 1990s, now they typically look for an immediate utilitarian benefit from their transactions and only offer free help to members of their own social network. Grisha said:

> You can't come to the lads just like that—they're not members of parliament; they don't have visiting hours. If someone contacts them, it's because they've got concrete business. On the street, the rule is "give and take," so if someone does come to them, it's only with something that's in both theirs and the lads' interests. For example, if a trader asks for protection, he pays, and he gets protection. Whereas, if someone comes to beg for money, even as a loan, this isn't a bank; no one's handing out credit.

In a situation in which the rule of law is absent, acceptance of the power of the strong is reinforced by the pragmatic uses that "civilians" themselves can make of this power. After all, corruption and predation are not just the domain of powerful groups; they are found across society. Gang illegality and popular illegality, criminal and private violence, are closely interwoven. Taxi drivers, for example, recounted how they chased away competitors who attempted to collect passengers from "their" turf. A word with the local strongmen (or the mere threat of such) was enough to resolve the issue. We heard stories of businessmen who used gangs against former partners or employees who wanted to poach clients for their own businesses.

Gangs and Law Enforcement Agencies

Back in the 1990s, when the state law enforcers were relatively weak, their representatives could themselves become victims of gang intimidation and be forced to enter negotiations with the gangs. For example, police officer M. recounted the following episode:

> I used to have my own company [he had a private business on the side], and four people came to my office and started saying that they lived there, that this was their territory and that I should pay them. I told them, "If you can protect me from the largest gangs in Kazan—Khadi Taktash, Kvartala, Tsentralnye—then come to me, and I will pay you. But I have a different proposition. You can ask me for help when you are incarcerated, and I can help you to get your sentences reduced." One of them was from my area. He recognized me, and they just got up and went, and I saw no more of them.

By the mid 2000s gang power had diminished, and yet gangs were still recognized as agents of local informal authority and had a certain institutional accommodation with the police. While the gangs were interested in stable conditions for business, the police saw them, at least partly, as an instrument for maintaining order in the territory.

Salagaev, Shashkin, and Konnov (2006) quoted from their interview with R., a former law enforcement officer from Kazan: "Every organized criminal group has its territory. When a crime is committed, the gang that controls this territory is contacted first of all."

Our interviews similarly showed that police officers had contacts with the top ranks of the gangs (the avtoritety and smotriashchie) and used them to monitor the gangs' activities and control crime. These contacts cannot be simply dismissed as corruption. Many officers took their job of fighting crime extremely seriously and used their contacts pragmatically in order to reduce crime and violence. The head of the investigative department of a police precinct, A., explained:

> Youths in the gangs often commit burglaries, but not because it's a way of earning money to survive—rather, this is done for thrills because they think that they're gang members and they can do anything. That's why they also attack their peers. For example, there was a case recently when they came up to some kid at the market, demanded money, and when he didn't give them any they beat him and took his cell phone. Sometimes they raid shops to demonstrate their courage. We let the elders know about all this, and they literally force their juniors to stick to legal business because if it's their territory, they shouldn't pollute it. The other

> common kind of crime is fighting, when they go to rough someone up. But on the whole, they try to settle all disagreements peacefully, because the alternative benefits no one. They understand very well that if something happens they'll have big problems—they might get arrested or have their property taken away. That's why gunfire and violence happen only as a last resort.

Another interviewee, M., from a different police district, reported:

> In the gang structure, all contact between the youths and the seniors happens through smotriashchie. We use the same idea ourselves, so that, for example, when the juniors start to play around and create problems and misunderstandings, I just call the smotriashchii and say: "You've got this, that, and the other thing going on. Deal with the problem!" If that doesn't work, we call an even more senior smotriashchii and tell him about it. Usually, that's enough.

A police investigator from Kazan, N., explained:

> We know them, and they know us, and if something happens then the older members of the gang are sitting in my office, and I tell them firmly: "Listen, lads, you must solve the problem. If you don't solve it, I will solve it myself. But then I will not look at which of you is right and which is wrong. I will close your shops, tow your cars away, and then you'll be trying to get hold of me for years." This normally works, and they say of their own accord: "Fine, we will solve the problem. Everything will be all right."

The police's use of their contacts with avtoritety and smotriashchie to manage the low-level criminality and violence of younger gang members became an important tool of crime control. Moreover, while the representatives of law and order were hardly loved by gang members, they were considered to be a part of the wider social order and as such accepted as legitimate and necessary. As Tsigan said: "Although they have a bad reputation, the police are doing their work too. If they did not exist, there would be complete bespredel."

Policing the Street Gang

Instead of adopting an American-style "war on gangs," Russian law enforcement agencies have used a diverse range of approaches to street organizations. The everyday work of the police in relation to street gangs represents a combination of criminal investigation for more serious crimes, attempts at surveillance of gang membership through registration and monitoring, and investigation and assessment of individual cases to see if a gang member can be "normalized" and returned into the community. Other methods deployed by the police include "disassociation"—attempting to undermine gang solidarity—and isolation of the leaders. Police officers talk to young people and their parents and try to dissuade the youths from associating with other gang members. Sometimes they spread rumors designed to sow discord in the gang.

When the Tatarstan MVD decided to intensify its efforts to keep the gangs under control, three major approaches were adopted. The first was to introduce better coordination between the various law enforcement bodies; the second was to create a joint database on all criminals, including members of all gangs; and the third was to implement measures designed to assert control through a demonstrative display of state power. This last approach involved a series of special operations in which the police received information about preparations for serious crimes or *razborki* in which weapons would be used. Mass searches and detentions, cleanups (*zachistki*) in the places where gruppirovshchiki met, and car checks by road patrols followed. A spectacular show of strength by the police could involve the police ordering half a dozen or more gruppirovshchiki to lie on the floor in full sight of decent customers in cafes and restaurants (Safarov 2012, 49).

In these and more routine operations, the police conduct special raids on places where gang members congregate and register any arrested gang members. Such raids are sometimes organized in response to the concerns of local residents, who may phone to report a mass gathering of young people in their courtyard. Police patrols travel to the site, seal off the surrounding area, and arrest any gang members who have not managed to flee. Those who are caught are charged with "minor hooliganism" or violation of public order. Anyone under fourteen is taken to the police division for minors, and older gang members are processed by the police criminal investigation divisions, which have special gang task forces.

Registration is a key instrument for the police in monitoring and controlling the gang situation. Since Soviet times, registration has been, and remains, the main regulatory device in Russia (Holquist 1997, 2000), and it is believed by the police to have both preventative and corrective power. As A., from a Kazan regional police department, told us, "the very act of arresting and registering a young person is intended to have a certain reforming effect." Representatives of the law enforcement bodies we talked to believed in the preventative power of registration. B., from the Tatarstan Republican Prosecution Service, said, "The preventative element works as follows: the details of a gang member who is caught are put into a registration file, and a so-called operative case is opened. [In cases involving serious crimes] this is "realized"—that is, transformed into a criminal case and then dragged through court. There are no other means of battling criminal groups, either here or in the rest of the world. These are the most effective measures."

Gang members are registered for six months, and, if at the end of that time they have not been arrested again and have a positive report from their official workplace or place of study, they are removed from the register. The police also visit neighbors and ask them for references for the young person in question in order to decide whether to remove him from the database. If there is no evidence of improvement of behavior, the registration is extended. Once registered, underage gang members are sent to the special police divisions for minors for "re-education," which typically involves a talk from one of the inspectors. Police also inform their schools and parents. Gruppirovshchiki can also be invited to a meeting of the Inter-Agency Working Group on Minors under the regional Prokuratura. This is attended by representatives from the Prokuratura, the chairman of the Commission on Minors of the district administration, representatives of the military commissariat, and the district Department of Education. Juvenile gang members attend with their parents. These efforts are aimed at making gruppirovshiki even more subject to community control. In gruppirovshchiki accounts, these routine measures are not particularly effective. Vlad told us, "I've faced the cops when they were taking us from our yard—several times—and eventually they filed me as a member of the K. gang. They acted the same as usual—they weren't gentle, but they didn't beat us either. They just wanted to carry out their plan for tackling gangs. They talked to us, took fingerprints, took photos, and then let us go. I've never been brought in for anything serious."

The talks conducted by overworked police inspectors were regarded by many gang members as merely bureaucratic exercises. Nevertheless, the system seemed to be working to a degree. Our gang interviewees were well aware that being on the police gang register could have an adverse effect on their lives, mainly preventing them from applying for a range of coveted jobs in the public sector. The threat of registration seemed, at least partly, to put a brake on excessive violence, as gang members preferred do their business in the shadows without attracting unnecessary police attention. Parents, informed about their offsprings' registration as gang members and perhaps unaware that their sons were in gangs, could also put pressure on them to leave.

Street gang members tend to be prosecuted for minor offences such as violation of public order and minor hooliganism, which normally means fighting or swearing in public places, as well as burglaries and drug-related offenses. Although organization of, or participation in, an organized criminal group (OPG) or community (OPS) are criminal offenses according to articles 209 and 210 of the Russian Criminal Code, Russian gang-associated youths are not routinely prosecuted and incarcerated just for being part of the local gang—for example, for associating with gang members or wearing gang colors rather than for committing concrete crimes. Russia does not have the arsenal of gang-busting measures, such as gang-related antisocial behavior orders (ASBOs) and gang injunctions that are used in the United Kingdom, or restraining orders used in the United States and similar measures in Europe, to deal with the gang threat (Hallsworth 2011).

The Russian light-touch system of rehabilitation and community control, however, is undermined and discredited by the predatory behavior of some police officers. The Kazan police are notorious for using brutal methods. A 2012 case in which a male suspect was raped with a champagne bottle in the Dalnii police station in Kazan and subsequently died received major national publicity. According to gang members with personal experience of arrest and detention, violence (or its threat) and extortion were routine in Kazan police stations. Violence was especially common when police were looking for evidence of a crime having been committed. Gang members described a range of their and their associates' experiences in police stations. Koshmar said, "The police behave the same as usual. You don't feel any particular love from them; they rarely beat you. More often they threaten to beat you. If they're taking one guy in rather than a group, for hooliganism, drunkenness, or excessive swearing, they usually extort money and threaten violence." Nafik concurred, "I've often been picked up, usually from a meet-up or for drunkenness. The police take fingerprints, take photos for the database, and take your money. For drunkenness, they hold you all night and let you go in the morning. The cops are pretty rough—I've never met a gentle one." Tadjik elaborated on similar experiences:

> They often pick you up when it's your first time, and they just fingerprint you. They photograph you for the database so that afterward they can identify who you are and where you're from. I've never been arrested for anything serious, and I'm not on the register. I just got brought in on suspicion of committing crimes—namely robbery. They hold you for a couple of hours and then let you go. Lads from our street were taken during meet-ups and then given the full treatment. They don't normally beat people. They just shout at the lads and humiliate them. They beat you when they want you proven guilty of something. Then they use sticks and go for the kidneys.

Aidar remembered his days as a young lad and how police treatment varied depending on the nature of the crime and the attitude of individual policemen:

> The greater part of my experience with the cops took place when I was first getting used to the street, but back then the police were very weak,

> and so there was a lot more breathing room and attending gatherings was a lot easier. They were always hostile toward us, but they understood as well as we did that giving us records as members of organized criminal groups wouldn't solve anything, so they didn't come down particularly hard on gatherings. The ones who really got hit were the ones who'd clearly broken the law—they could get locked up for a long time while the police put their case together. But I never experienced this myself and only know about it from friends who got caught. Besides, cops aren't all cut from the same cloth—sometimes you get ones who are prepared to work with the lads rather than bullying them.

The reluctance to see youth group violence and crime through the prism of the "gang" that we saw in the Soviet period persists. For example, in Ul'ianovsk, capital of an oblast that borders Tatarstan, where organized street gangs have again established a visible presence, law enforcement agencies for a long time denied that youth organized crime had been on the rise. A mass fight in March 2006 between two large gangs, Kisinskie and Tsentr Kamaz, in which three people died and fifteen were injured, was qualified by the regional police chief Valerii Lukin as an "ordinary fight." According to one press report, "only at the very end of 2006 did the authorities of Ul'ianovsk recognize that there was reason for concern. Police finally voiced a fact known to every schoolboy—'There are nine youth gangs in the city'—but then they said that 'there is no reason to call them criminals.' The operation [against gangs] was called Avalanche. The [police] report indicates that they detained about seven thousand people. In fact, the operation involved randomly grabbing anyone they could get their hands on" (Iurieva and Iliukhina 2007).

The seemingly half-hearted attempts to address youth gang participation may be accounted for by the weakness and inefficiency of the state. But there are cultural explanations here as well that have to do with the sense that collective street life is a "natural" element of a young person's upbringing and that ultimately young people will grow up, get jobs and start families, and abandon street groups. This expectation of traditional transitions to adulthood can also be explained by the relatively low rates of unemployment and the continuing availability of industrial jobs in the 2000s.

Russian policies toward youth street organizations have more in common with twentieth-century systems of punishment in advanced industrial countries, which combined the apparatus of control with welfare ideology and the "hidden discipline" of community control (Garland 1985) rather than with the punitive methods of the late-capitalist security state (Hallsworth and Lea 2011). For the most part, there is no presumed association of youth street organizations with the dangerous ethnic and racial "other" (although this is increasingly seen in perceptions of ethnic migrants). Attitudes toward young people who spend their time in street groups seem still to be informed by a paternalistic vision of childhood, in which children and adolescents are seen as innocents who may be seduced into bad ways by the mass media, the Internet, and the street because of a lack of parental or school control. As for gang organization, a street gang is often seen not an alien body that tries to subvert urban civilization but as a form of adolescent collective life, an extension of a street play group, and a "natural" form of social life generally. When I organized a workshop on youth gangs in Moscow in 2006, one invited representative of the Moscow police youth division said: "Youth gangs? How's that a problem? We all live in gangs." This phrase can be read as a sign of a strangely blasé attitude toward gangs or as an expression of a deep sociological understanding of Russian society. The officer believed that young people might commit crimes for a variety of reasons, such as bad parenting, lack of control by educators, or the pernicious influence of television and the Internet, but gangs themselves were a natural fact of life, unwelcome but also unavoidable, like the long Russian winter.

Although they have come down hard on "hooliganism" and other typical forms of street crime, the Russian authorities have yet to develop a discourse on street gangs as groups of dangerous outsiders that we see elsewhere in the world. By and large, the youth gang still remains part of the community and is treated as such. But this situation may change. If Russia, like other advanced capitalist societies, moves toward greater economic inequality and social exclusion, toward the emergence of spatially and socially segregated ghetto areas, this will undoubtedly have consequences for gang life. Russian youth gangs would then be likely to follow the international trend of increasing involvement in heroin and other illegal drug trafficking (Venkatesh 2006; Hagedorn 2008; Rodgers 2009). This would almost certainly lead to more persistent and explosive violence, endemic in the drug trade (Goldstein 1985), and consequently to the disassociation of the gang from the wider community and to much more punitive attitudes and policies toward it.

Gangs in Other Russian Regions

In its heyday in the Kazan of the 1990s and early to mid-2000s, the gang was, on the one hand, deeply embedded in the local community where it enjoyed significant influence. But, on the other hand, it was limited in its power by state agents and the institutions of modern society. In this large urban conglomeration, with its variety of autonomous forces and interest groups, neither one specific gang nor state-related violent agencies could monopolize power. In various social ecologies (for example, in small towns and villages) the gang can subsume all other wielders of force to become the sovereign power. This is what happened in the large village of Kushchevskaia in Krasnodar Krai in the south of Russia, where the local gang, which emerged at the beginning of the 1990s and was supported by elements of the police and the judiciary, turned into a despotic ruler. The gang expropriated land from farmers, racketeered businesses, had their representatives on the local council, and enjoyed complete immunity from prosecution (including for their systematic rape of young women). It actively recruited local youth, particularly boys from a children's home and vocational schools, who had to go through gang apprenticeships to be able to join it. In this relatively small settlement, whose population numbered around 28,000 in 2010, the gang built a system of almost totalitarian control. A criminal investigation only took place in 2010, when the killing of eleven local residents, including small children, coincided with the presence of a film crew from Moscow that brought the story to millions of viewers. This resulted in the eventual prosecution of key gang members. At the time, the governor of Krasnodar Krai, Aleksander Tkachev, admitted that similar gangs existed in every area of the region (Lenta.ru).

The Kushchevskaia village gang regime provides a striking example of the coalescence of power structures, as the criminal gang's leadership became fully integrated into the local elite not just on the official but also on a personal level. The head of the gang, Aleksander Tsapok, was a close friend of the head of the local police Department for the Struggle against Organized Crime (UBOP), who became a godfather to one of Tsapok's children. Tsapok was also a deputy on the local council and even participated, as part of the regional delegation, in the inauguration of President Medvedev in Moscow. The girlfriend of the other gang leader, Nikolai Tsapok, was a judge. The gang used its almost limitless power to establish economic control over the area, forcing the majority of businesses to pay protection money and expropriating the land of many of the local farmers, which it then incorporated into its own legal agricultural holding. Local residents were afraid to speak out against them, and attempts by some of the victims to complain to the police fell on deaf ears. Some who complained were brutally punished by the gang. Even teachers from high schools and local colleges seemed powerless to defend their students from gang members coming into classes to take teenage girls away for sex or assaulting their victims in their dormitories. When one college director complained to Moscow about these assaults, a commission that was sent to investigate not only found no wrongdoing but instead discovered irregularities in the college's financial accounts. As a consequence, the director was imprisoned and later committed to a psychiatric hospital. It appears that the gang only exceeded the bounds of its power once, when, together with the head of the UBOP, they started to siphon oil from the pipeline on the border of Krasnodar Krai and Rostov Oblast. When this was discovered by the owners, the Transneft' corporation, the gang—and the Kushchevskaia police who provided security for the operation—had to terminate their lucrative new business. They were told that "the oil level is too much for you." The Rostov Oblast FSB even started an investigation, which was short-lived and did not lead to any prosecutions.

A similar attitude to the one we saw in gang-affected areas of Kazan, a sense of the inevitability of living one's life under the yoke of predators and a preference for at least a semblance of stability rather than a war of all against all, also existed among Kushchevskaia residents. A *Novaia Gazeta* journalist (Kostiuchenko 2010) quoted a local resident whom she interviewed soon after the arrests of the key members of the Tsapki gang:

> You ask us how we used to live? We lived normally. Because we knew the rules of the game: "If you revolt against a *tsapok* [member of the Tsapki gang], we'll crush you." They preyed on us, but they also kept other predators out. Everybody was afraid to stick their head out, but it was possible to live quietly. . . . And now we are going to have a redivision of power, redivision of the land belonging to the *tsapki* and those under their krysha. Blood will be spilled—and new [rulers] will arrive. People are already waiting for them. This is not a question of the power of one OPG. This is a question of mentality. People are used to living like this here. And they will continue living like this. With *tsapki* or without them.

The Kushchevskaia scandal brought public attention to other instances of unchallenged gang rule across Russia. In 2010 a group of citizens of Gus'-Khrustalnyi, a town in Vladimir Oblast, sent a letter to Putin in which they complained that mafia occupied the key positions in the town and that the streets had again—just like in the 1990s—become a space of criminal bespredel. The explosion of criminal violence started after the election of a new mayor, who brought people with criminal pasts into the local administration. They promptly set their sights on the city budget and private businesses. People who refused to pay the new krysha were harassed and beaten; their shops and businesses were set on fire. According to the authors of the letter, the police closed their eyes to all this or even colluded with the bandits, who were acting together with the city administration. The bandits even offered a krysha to the local state electricity company, which had never happened before, even in the 1990s.

In Novosibirsk the vice-mayor and his father, the regional governor's adviser, were accused of being part of a criminal gang that had been terrorizing the city's businesses for twenty years. More evidence emerged of bandit gangs operating with impunity in small towns and villages in Perm Krai and Sverdlovsk Oblast (Fedorenko and Sleptsov 2010).

Evidence suggests that although many of the larger bandit gangs that once commanded unquestionable power over whole sectors of the economy and formed autonomous ruling regimes in the community are becoming a thing of the past, entrepreneurial gangs of varying levels of organizational sophistication continue to thrive in many areas of Russia. According to Galeotti (2012), there are currently twelve to fourteen major criminal networks in Russia, including the Solntsevskaia Bratva (Moscow) and the Tambov Gang (Saint Petersburg).

Territorial criminal networks are still present, particularly in the peripheral areas. For example, according to an FSB report, Moscow Oblast is still divided between "red" areas (controlled by the police) and "blue" areas (controlled by criminal associations). Unlike in the 1990s, the gang smotriashchie no longer attend *strelki* proudly wearing thick gold chains around their necks. They have become deputies in elected assemblies, businessmen, and charity benefactors. Nevertheless, they still control their territories, and it is impossible to start a business or build a house without their agreement (Kanev 2012).

A report from a criminal trial in Chuvash Republic showed that a large gang Gruppirovka Fina (named after its leader, Andrei Finogenov) that was formed in 2002 operated until 2012 in a vast area embracing five administrative districts and also "controlled" two of the largest cities in the republic, Cheboksary and Novocheboksarsk. It united nine separate gangs. The gang had links to the criminal leaders of other gangs across Russia. It had a common obshchak, and its main business was racketeering of local companies and private individuals, and the organization of illegal gambling establishments. In a trial in 2013–14, ten members of this organized criminal community were prosecuted together with two former police officers who assisted the gang (Eruslanov 2014). In Mordovia Republic, the large Mordva gruppirovka, formed at the end of the 1980s, was also engaged in the protection racket, again with assistance from the corrupt police. The trial took place in 2011–14 (Vikulova 2014). Gangs in Orel, a relatively poor town in Central Russia, like their predecessors in the early 1990s, were predominantly racketeering street markets, where their members worked in an official capacity as security guards, fleecing small shops and businesses, and committing theft and robbery (Vardanian 2010). In Cheliabinsk in 2011, bandit *brigady* (and small independent street groups) were, in the style of medieval highwaymen, robbing long-distance truck drivers on the city roads. Paying the gangs protection money did not guarantee safety, as the gangs did not respect one another's rights of taxation. Drivers could, however, pay a private company whose representative then accompanied them as they drove through the city (Antipin 2011). Members of the two main Ekaterinburg gangs of the 1990s, Uralmash and Tsentrovaia, which, according to the police, were officially "dispersed" in the middle of 2000s, continued to be involved in illegal operations and, in particular, moved en masse into the street parking business (Antipin, Diatlikovich, and Gladkii 2010).

According to Breslavsky (2009), the gangs in Zaigraievskii District of Buriatiia lasted well into the 2000s. By the mid-2000s the gang regime had settled into a relatively stable social form, with some smotriashchie setting up shops, bus companies, and auto repair garages. The gang turned into an established neighborhood institution. All businesses in the villages had to pay protection money (unless they belonged to gang members). Even the teachers seemed powerless to defend their students. Breslavsky (2009, 92) quoted a seventeen-year-old school pupil as saying, "The gang smotriashchii comes to our school. He challenges teachers on behalf of his own people. No one objects because they are too frightened. Everyone knows him, and he knows everyone. If something [happens], he can come to your house or catch you on the streets."

After a lull in the early 2000s, when "everything that could be divided up had been divided up," Ul'ianovsk began experiencing a resurgence of gang violence. Experts speak about the emergence of new generations of young people who aspire to their share of street incomes and who are trying to redivide the territory. There were sixteen organized territorial gangs in the city in 2012 (Filin 2012). The main source of gang revenue is illegal parking lots. Most of the city's overnight parking is controlled by youth gangs, who force car owners to pay protection money. The youths who collect the money, armed with a bat and a cell phone on which they can call for backup, get about 150 rubles (5 dollars) a night. The rest of the money goes into the gang's obshchak. Other members resell stolen cell phones. The gangs actively recruit new members, terrorize nongang teenagers, and fight each other in violent "wars over asphalt." Members have their own style of clothes resembling those of the working-class gang warriors of the 1980s and 1990s—tracksuit pants, heavy boots, dark jackets, and black woolen hats. The structure of the groups has not changed since the early 1990s. Young people form stratified age cohorts, with younger lads forming the violent "troops" and older members eventually progressing to positions of authority.

Most of these teenagers come from poor families, but, as sociologist Irina Kosterina suggested in her newspaper interview with Iurieva and Iliukhina (2007), they are drawn to the gangs not only by the money but the way of life offered by the street brotherhood. "We asked, why are your peers in the group? Here are the answers: 'They're afraid of nothing', 'Together they're strong.' Many recalled the image of the 'good' on-screen bandit Sasha Belyi.[3] Groups provide not just safety, but also male fraternity." She also observed that the other options—unemployment or work in badly paid industrial jobs—do not present an attractive alternative.

Part of the Community

We have seen that the Russian bandit gang seeks to find a place in the local system of social relations, and it often manages to establish some degree of popular acceptance. The gang can be seen as an adaptable and dynamic structure, which in some situations fills the crevices of society, and in some periods starts to dominate the whole social ecosystem. In the 1990s it achieved substantial influence in Russia, and from the 2000s, under pressure from the state and following the contraction of the unregulated economic sphere, it withdrew into a much reduced role, while the leaders tried to legalize themselves. But the gangs are a form of collective life that, in various forms and guises, are ever present and never confined to the past. They also need to be seen not as elemental and pathological forces of destruction, the "malicious other" (Rawlinson 2009), but as conscious and context-sensitive agents. Their actions, just like the actions of the Sicilian Mafiosi, "depend on a peculiar set of economic and political arrangements" (Tilly 1974a, xiv). In the 1990s the gang acquired substantial power vis-à-vis a seriously weakened Russian state. When a new configuration of power emerged in Russia in the 2000s, the territorial gang generally adapted to a more limited role, although pockets of considerable gang power remained in some areas where the territorial state authorities were weak or particularly corrupt.

The astonishing, truly meteoric rise of organized bandit gangs in Russia in the 1990s; their rapid expansion from local groups that racketeered kiosks and street markets to criminal networks controlling—and owning—businesses in the major cities of Russia and beyond, and the subsequent gradual diminishment of their power as their leaders decided (or were forced) to play by the rules set by the state, can serve to obscure the ongoing existence and tenacity of localized territorial, communal structures of violence. Here, in the Russian "deep state," there is no firm border between formal and informal networks of power, between public and private violence.

---

3. The popular television series *Brigada* (2002) presented a highly sympathetic portrayal of a bandit gang. Its leader, Sasha Belyi, is a decent and fair man and a Russian patriot (for example, he refuses to sell weapons to the Chechens), while the gang itself is shown as the epitome of strong male friendship.

7

LIFE ACCORDING TO THE PONIATIIA

The Gang's Code

Similarly to other street organizations, vigilante groups, mafias, prison communities, college fraternities, or military recruits, the Russian gang has its own collective code of conduct. In it, like in all these other societies that exist on the borders of the modern state, social life is organized not on the basis of the universal law but on the basis of informal conventions and rules. In the gang this code of conduct is known as poniatiia. The code has a central place in the lads' mental and moral universe. Whatever they do—fight, play, do business, or even, as I will explain below, have sex—everything must be conducted and justified on the basis of this gang code. We have already encountered the poniatiia, but in this chapter I address more closely the nature of this code, its evolution, and its relationship to another code of conduct that we find in the shadow of the state, that of the vory.

The Moral Reasoning of the Gang

The moral rules of street organizations and gangs began to attract the attention of anthropologists and criminologists around the world following the publication of Elijah Anderson's *Code of the Streets* (1999). Studying the interpersonal violence on the streets of Philadelphia's black ghettoes, Anderson came to the conclusion that it was governed by a set of rules that he called the code of the streets. These rules "regulate the use of violence and so supply a rationale allowing those who are inclined to aggression to precipitate violent encounters in an approved way" (33). The basic requirement of the code is that a person displays a certain predisposition to violence—a particular facial expression, a way of talking, the right look. In an ecology in which violence is an omnipresent threat, he needs to show that he is not a person to be messed with and to show strength and nerve "by taking another person's possessions, messing with someone's woman, throwing the first punch, 'getting in someone's face,' or pulling a trigger" (92). "Street" individuals who follow the code do this for fear of death and invest their whole identity in it, to the extent that they find it very difficult to function in conventional society, although some can, as Anderson explained, "code-switch" and adapt to different rules in different environments.

This view of the code as a set of definitive prescriptions that precede behavior contrasts with the ethnomethodological approach to the status of rules in everyday life. According to ethnomethodologists, moral rules are collectively produced fundamental principles of seeing and acting in the world that underlie a group's social order. These rules are not definitive. Instead, they are indexical, meaning that their specific meanings and semantic expressions are imprecise and vary with the context (Garfinkel 1967, 4–7). The moral code is "a schema which produces reality," not a detailed list of what one can or cannot do (Wieder 1974, 198). It is created as members of society conduct their everyday lives, as they give meanings to their actions via observed behaviors and conversation.[1]

The ethnomethodologist D. Lawrence Wieder, in his famous 1974 ethnographic study of the "convict code" in a halfway house for ex-prisoners, discovered that the residents were routinely involved in violation of institutional rules, segmented themselves from the staff, showed disinterest and disrespect, lied, and made demands of the staff. Wieder concluded that, although this behavior seemed to be totally counterproductive to their interests as they were sabotaging their release from the institution, it displayed strong moral patterns and created a cultural unity among inmates. It was organized around a number of fundamental principles (showing distrust of staff, being loyal to inmates, etc.) The residents learned the code of behavior in the course of their daily lives, observing the behaviors of people around

1. Jimerson and Oware (2006) suggested a compromise between Anderson's ethnographic approach and ethnomethodological approaches to the code of the street in their study of black male basketball players. The code, in their view, can be seen both as a cognitive map and a set of conversational tools.

them and collectively interpreting their experiences. The convict code was never explicitly formulated, and its fundamental principles had to be deduced by the researcher.

Of these two models, the ethnomethodological approach fits best with the data on the Russian lads' moral reasoning. Poniatiia are flexible and can be applied differently to different situations. While expressing a multitude of specific regulations, they are based on a structure of fundamental principles that reflect profound beliefs about the world and the place of the gang in it. This Weltanschauung, the gang's worldview, is not passed on to the members as a set of prescriptions but is produced in the context of life in a gang.[2] In contrast to Anderson's conclusions, the code builds the social order of the gang but does not inherently inhibit members from adapting easily to the normative expectations of the wider society.

When talking about the code, the lads always stressed that there were many more poniatiia than were being recounted at the time. None of our interviewees would even attempt to recite the code in its totality. One member, Tsigan, when asked to describe the gang's code, said:

> It is impossible to describe in a nutshell what you learn over the years. I can say that the poniatiia do not exist in some pure form. There is the life of a lad, about which you learn by being in this environment. You learn how to behave in specific situations and what you must never do. You can't learn it the same way as we learn things at school. You have to go through it yourself and understand it from within. That is why I can't simply say to you, this is this and this is that. . . . I started understanding the code in my school years, coming across different situations. Some things I understood myself, others I learned from my friends who were more experienced.

As Zhenia said, "I could try to sort everything out, what the lads' poniatiia are . . . but I'm afraid this is simply impossible. In my case it took me many years to understand it all, and in order to do this, one must lead the same way of life as we do."

---

2. By contrast, in Volkov's (2002, 2012) analysis of the normative order of the bandits, poniatiia are seen as an elementary legal system. They enable these groups to create and protect a part of an illegal marketplace and support their regime of economic governance. They secure cooperation within the bandits' organizations, help them resolve conflict situations, and are used to justify their violence in relation to businessmen.

The lads learn the code through experiencing life in a gang and through hearing the descriptions of particular behaviors as being in accordance with the code or in violation of it. Zhenia described the following example:

> There was an incident that went like this. We were still little brats, and we went out to get revenge. We came up against a crowd and started fighting. Right when we were retreating to our cars, we forgot one wounded lad and left without him. Of course, he was really lucky, as he didn't get taken prisoner, but we really got torn apart by the seniors! "You should always look out for each other—if someone gets taken down, you bring him to a car straight away! Always watch each other's backs!" They were shouting this stuff at us, and I've remembered it for the rest of my life.

The gang does not have a compendium of specific rules designed for every concrete situation. The members artfully use the cultural resources of the gang, applying them to the situation at hand. In Tadjik's words: "There are no rules of fairness as such; everybody can defend their point of view if they know how to talk and justify their opinion based on the code."

The code was not set in stone, and the lads were aware of the flexible nature of their moral rules. Il'nar said, "Of course, the code is always changing; there are always new additions. Life moves on, so if you don't update the code, you'll soon become completely isolated from the real world; it'll be as if you were still in the Dark Ages."

The Fundamental Principles of the Gang's Social Order

Although the code is flexible and constantly evolving, it remains based on a strong framework of basic principles. In describing the code gang members themselves tend to invoke it as a set of specific instructions (poniatiia) and rarely reflect on the reasons for particular prohibitions or injunctions. The underlying principles of these "taken for granted" rules are never fully explained, and it falls, as Wieder suggested, to social researchers to deduce their organizing principles. Indeed, without understanding what lies behind concrete injunctions, some of the rules that the lads quoted could be quite opaque and open to a multitude of interpretations. How do we explain, for example, the prohibition against the lads working as ticket collectors on public transport or selling their old clothes? Is it because they cannot work in poorly paid occupations or admit material need? Why does one need to fight if called a trader (*baryga*)? Is it because the lads follow the traditional norms of the society of vory, who see trade as a disreputable profession? How can we explain the requirement that the lad be physically strong and the prohibition on consumption of drugs? Is this because of the instrumental needs of criminal business, which require that the gang build an effective force to protect its share of the market? From analysis of gang members' descriptions of poniatiia, it became clear to me that in fact other principles underlay these injunctions. The prohibitions on working as ticket collectors or selling old clothes, and the need to protect one's name if called a trader, derive from the fundamental principle of being a member of the elite and being nonequivalent to "commoners," whose status is inferior to that of the gang members and who are fodder for them to live on. The need to be physically fit and avoid consumption of drugs relates to the principle of control and integrity of elite male warriors.

I have set out below my own reconstruction of the gang code, made on the basis of conversations with gang members and their descriptions of poniatiia. I list these poniatiia under each principle. I see the code as resting on the following principles: behaving as a representative of the elite and never being equated with "commoners," showing control and integrity, and being loyal to the gang. The code also includes principles of democracy and procedural equality and fairness; the subordinate position of women; and, finally, autonomy outside the organization.

Behaving as a Representative of the Elite and Never Being Equated with "Commoners"

A lad should always introduce himself by his nickname and gang name. If asked "Where are you from?" he should never reply "Nowhere." He should name his gang. (This relates to encounters with street populations and to the gang's business activities but not to interactions outside the gang's spheres of interest, such as with teachers or employers.)

A lad should not do anything that brings down the reputation of the street. He cannot lose face publicly. He should never compromise his superior status—everything he does has consequences for the gang as a whole. For example, if he runs away from his attackers, and thus loses face, he discredits the whole street and can expect to receive severe punishment and most likely be expelled.

The lads act as the superior force in the territory. In the local social structure they are the elite group, elevated above ordinary civilians, the *lokhi*. The code dictates that a lad should avoid doing anything that could put him on the other side of the classificatory divide and thereby equate him with the *lokhi*. He should not be afraid to fight. He should not give in to extortion, suffer humiliation without retaliation, or go to the police for help. He should never betray weakness. The lad must fight if he is called a *lokh* and retaliate if somebody expresses doubt that he is a real lad. Similarly, if somebody tries to extort money from him, he should attack; otherwise he would accept an inferior status. The same radical divide applies to the distinction between the lad and *komersy* or *barygi*. To be called a *komers* or a *baryga* is a mortal offence for a lad, and gang members would go a long way to show that they cannot be equated with people in such occupations. This extends to prohibitions on trading, which lead to complex arrangements to avoid being seen as a tradesman even if one has a retail business (for example, by acting via intermediaries). A gang member cannot personally sell anything, including drugs (although he can control those dealers who do sell drugs in the gang's territory), or trade in a street market or in a shop. Service occupations are proscribed. As mentioned, a lad cannot work as a ticket collector—this is considered to be demeaning. He cannot sell his own clothes or personal belongings even if in need (although he can sell the proceeds of theft or extortion).

In terms of status, the lads only accept parity of status with members of other gangs (or vory groups). All lads, irrespective of the street to which they belong, are equals.

The sovereign role of the lad is encapsulated in the *poniatie* (rule) "The lad is always right." This imperative implies that the lad's power cannot be challenged. A lad is a source of law, and he must develop communicative skills that make it possible for him to perform his dominant role in day-to-day interaction with the subdued population and members of other gangs ("be able to speak properly"). A lad should always be able to justify his position or opinion on the basis of the code.

Control and Integrity

The lad should keep his cool and behave with dignity. He cannot consume drugs or be addicted to alcohol. (Younger lads are expected not to smoke either). He should show control over his body and appearance. A lad's clothes should be practical and comfortable and not too flashy. The lad should be clean and tidy. (Some gangs even punish youngsters who do not clean their shoes.) The lad needs to "watch his words" (*sledit' za bazarom*). He should not make empty threats or accusations. One of the rules is "What the lad says, the lad does" (*patsan skazal, patsan sdelal*), meaning that intentions, claims, and promises should have direct and immediate consequences. Lads are not allowed to make frivolous displays of weapons; if they produce a knife or a gun, they should be prepared to use it. If asked a question, a gang member should answer straight away and not respond with a question.

Loyalty to the Gang

The lad's main loyalty is to the gang. He should always support other members, both from his age cohort and from his gang as a whole. He should not "eat as if alone" (*ne iest' v odno litso*, i.e., spend all his money on himself). He should never expose his friends to danger or betray them to the police. He must strive to prevent any personal conflict, resolve disagreements, and abstain from fighting with other members of the same gang. He should not deceive or steal from other gang members.

Subordinate Position of Women

Women are fundamentally unequal to men. They cannot be members of the gangs. No girl gangs should be present in the territory controlled by a male gang. Members' girlfriends are not allowed to attend the gang's meetings. Gang business always takes priority over a member's relationships with women. Members should not get into conflict with other members because of women (except for defending close relatives, such as a mother, sister, or wife). If a lad flirts with one's girlfriend, one can only ask him to stop but should not fight over it. A lad should control his girlfriend and never allow her to show disrespect to his friends. A gang member is not allowed to perform oral sex on his girlfriend—this would seriously undermine his status as a lad, and, if any of the other gang members learn about it, he can be expelled from the group.

This principle, like all other principles, is applied flexibly. In Russian gangs, particularly in their higher echelons, women can work as hired accountants or lawyers, while the wives of avtoritety can play more serious roles in running the business of the gang—especially if their husbands are away or incarcerated. But this does not negate the fundamentally male character of these violent fraternities and the profound machismo of their members.

In addition to these substantive prescriptions, there are also procedural norms and norms of fairness, which can be seen as relating to the gang structure and organization. These norms, however, were also recounted as part of the code and thus also have the status of agreed-on moral rules.

Democracy and Procedural Fairness

The lad must obey the rules of internal discipline. He must show respect to older lads and obey the commands given by the group smotriashchii or avtoritet. He must be present at obligatory meetings when decisions are made regarding the gang. He must pay money (up to two- thirds of his income) to the obshchak. Situations that call for moral adjudication need to be resolved democratically—by the street at a meet-up or by a smotriashchii. If the smotriashchii cannot decide, the dispute is resolved by avtoritety. Lads expect fair treatment from their superiors. Aidar said, "It is considered bespredel if a lad who behaves in line with the code is punished simply because a smotriashchii doesn't like the way he looks." Anvar reported how a smotriashchii asked a gang member to repay a debt owed by his friend, who had by then left the gang. However, the lad argued successfully that the case should be decided at the general meeting: "To ask a person to return money he did not owe was against the code, and the smotriashchii had to agree." The older lads are not supposed to humiliate the younger ones or treat them unfairly. They are also not allowed to use money from the obshchak of the younger lads.

The code prohibits more than one punishment for one *zikher* (transgression). This means, for example, that it is improper to impose both physical punishment and a financial fine for a single *zikher.*

Social and Ethnic Inclusivity of the Gang

The gang should accept all young men who want to join it if they subscribe to the code. Discrimination in recruitment on the grounds of social background or ethnicity is prohibited. In Tatarstan gangs, the majority of members are ethnic Russians and Tatars, but there are also members from other ethnic groups—for example, Armenians, Bashkirs, or Georgians. As Tsigan put it, "I guess it's only the representatives of African nations that can't join us, and even then not because of their race but because they would stand out too much, and we don't need that."

Members can have personal prejudices, but the code prohibits the use of these in decisions involving the gang. Violent skinheads who attack members of other ethnic and racial groups are seen as being involved in bespredel: being violent for violence's sake. Kirill, for example, said, "I haven't seen any skinheads in Kazan. Maybe they're around, but they're not active, since we don't like *bespredelshchiki* around here."[3] This principle of inclusivity, obviously, does not apply to the ethnic Roma, Georgian, Assyrian, Chechen, Ingush, Dagestani, Azerbaijani, and other such criminal gangs that also exist in Russia (Anzhirov 2010) and whose social organization and moral codes have not yet been researched.

Autonomy outside the Organization

The lad can and should have wide social connections outside the gang and use them to the benefit of the organization. The lad has a right to a private life; he can have a family and property and spend his free time as he wants to. He can work wherever he wants to (with the exception of working for the police and in proscribed service and trade occupations) and socialize with anybody outside the gang, including members of other gangs, unless their gang is the enemy of his group. The lad is also free to earn money by committing crime that is unrelated to the gang's business. Thus, if necessary, he can steal and rob—as Tadjik put it, "because a lad needs a means of subsistence."

---

3. An interesting parallel can be drawn here with the society of high sea pirates of the eighteenth century, which had many similar organizing principles, such as parity of status, democratic governance, and procedural fairness. Many of the pirates were former black slaves, and at least some were given equal rights with the white pirates, including voting rights and equal shares of plunder. As Peter Leeson (2009, 175) noted, the treatment of blacks on pirate ships was often much more racially progressive than could be expected given the predominant racial views at the time.

The Quasi-Tribal Moral System

The code of poniatiia supports the social order of the gang, and at this point we can return to the nature of this social order. I have already mentioned in the introduction Randall Collins's (2011) characterization of the gang as a Weberian patrimonial alliance, a quasi tribe, a type of social organization found in the raiding bands of ancient Greek warriors seeking to colonize the Mediterranean rim, or the Viking conquerors. Analyzing poniatiia as a whole, it is possible to see that the gang's moral code does indeed support this type of organization. Like ancient and early medieval warrior coalitions, the gang is a male militant tribal alliance that is cemented by quasi-kinship obligations and loyalties. Its warriors are required to display control and integrity, and its internal order rests on primitive democracy and on the essential parity of statuses within the gang fraternity. Class or ethnic distinctions have no place in this fraternity, but women cannot be accepted as equal members. In relation to the populations they seek to subdue and exploit, *lokhi* and *barygi*, the gang members adopt an elite warrior pose and seek to impose their will by might and right. But unlike their historical predecessors, the gang quasi tribes we are looking at here are situated in the midst of a modern society, and they need to find ways to either subvert its institutions or fit into them. That is why the members are orientated toward wide social memberships and affiliations.

But the code of poniatiia itself is not a universal moral system. The world of the gang is indeed tribal. In the context of gang life, while in-group behavior is tightly regulated, behavior toward outsiders is not: the lad can commit acquisitive crime, cheat, steal, and rob for his own benefit in addition to any illegal acts committed in the group context. Only extreme or gratuitous violence toward civilians—particularly old people, women, and children—gets condemned by the gang as bespredel. Beating up a "little one," an old man, or hitting a girl or a woman is seen as dishonorable, although to beat one's own girlfriend or wife, over whom the man has "special" rights, is perfectly fine. The lads, who see themselves as an elite group elevated above the "commoners" and as a source of law in their territories, also regard extreme violence toward dominated categories, *lokhi* and *barygi*, as morally reprehensible.

Nevertheless, these limitations on violence are easily overcome. The "adrenaline rush" to which the lads made constant reference explains many misdemeanors, while people who end up on the receiving end can always be seen as blameworthy in one way or another. Ultimately, constraints on violence are set by the gang itself; they are not part of a wider social compact or a formal legal system, and therefore they can be stretched and interpreted with considerable freedom. Il'nar said:

> To beat up anybody you want would be bespredel. If you are not an *otmorozok* you would at least draw the line at beating children and women, although women behave in such a way that from time to time you have to hit them. Violence changes a person's behavior, making him think about what he's doing. Unless you give them a good beating, people have little sense. I often beat up people, and I do not care about others' opinions; I beat whoever I want.

The code creates cultural unity, bonds, and obligations for the group members, but it does not extend them to the larger society. In encounters with the outside world, the members' constructions of right and wrong have to work in their own favor. Within the context of gang life, the lads, just like warriors in the Homerian epics or the heroes of ancient Greek tragedy, are not supposed to feel guilty about what they do to outsiders. As the Russian philologist Viktor Jarcho (1972) argued in his essay "Did Ancient Greeks Have a Moral Conscience?" only dishonor and public shame could cause the hero moral suffering. The same is true of gang warriors. When it comes to the gang's life and the gang's business, members can lie to outsiders, cheat, abuse, and, if necessary, kill them, with very few self-imposed limitations defined as bespredel. But the obligations to their own society are next to absolute.

Transmission of Vory Cultural Practices

The gang members' worldview has many similarities and overlaps with the mental orientations of the members of the other Russian organized crime community, that of the "thieves in law," the vory. Many of the gang's poniatiia are interchangeable with the laws of the vory, who have many similar beliefs and speak largely the same language.[4]

Gruppirovshchiki themselves had various mundane theories of where their code came from. Many reflected on their experiences of street life before they joined the gangs and on how they learned how to live like a lad in their peer groups. But the main source was thought to be the code of the Russian vory.

4. Dmitrii Likhachev (1935), in his account of the unwritten law of the vory written on the basis of his observations during his own incarceration in Solovki labor camp, described it as both a belief system and a system of norms that regulated their lives down to the minutest detail.

Some thought that the bandit code had been deliberately created by their "founding fathers" on the basis of the vory's poniatiia. Il'sur said, "The code of the lads emerged out of the vory's code. But it doesn't duplicate the vory's law. It simplifies the vory's laws as the base for the code of the lads. It is impossible to apply the vory's law [formed in prisons] to life in the city, so our seniors gathered and decided what the code of the lads should be."

The code is presented here as a sort of tablet of Moses, in which the tribal ancestors wrote a new law that fitted with the reality of urban gang life, life outside of the confines of prison.

Garik, on the contrary, thought that the code, while influenced by prison experiences, emerged in the context of the lads' everyday life, as they came out of incarceration and adapted their behavior to a new reality. He explained, "The code of the lads is not the *zona* code [prisoners' code], but much is taken from it. This code appeared after the gangs began to emerge, and some of those lads ended up behind bars. Having returned from the *zona*, they began following the same code, only adapting it for their current life. The *zona* laws were at the root for sure."

Of course, the bandit code was not created deliberately; nor does it represent an "advanced" or, conversely, "corrupted" version of the vory rules. In its totality it is a separate moral system that organizes the social order of these entrepreneurial gangs. But its semantic expressions are often derived from the vory culture (e.g., *sledit' za bazarom*, to watch one's words, or *razvesti lokha*, to cheat a victim), as is its nomenclature of key concepts (obshchak, smotriashchii, *semeika*, or avtoritet). The word *patsan* (lad) in prison jargon means a young candidate who is not yet a vor but aspires to become one.

This culture was transmitted by gang members coming back from incarceration, but it was also widely accessible in Soviet, and then post-Soviet, society, and one did not have to have spent time in prison to learn its basic vocabulary.

Prison has always had a major place in Russian culture and the Russian psyche (Oleinik 2003; Piacentini 2004; Pallot, Piacentini, and Moran 2012), and Soviet street youth culture in particular was profoundly influenced by the criminal tradition. The Gulag culture, consolidated in the Soviet penal system during the long years of Stalin's rule, began to be transmitted to the "civilian" population by returnees released from the camps after Stalin's death in 1953. According to Miriam Dobson (2009), prison culture received a particularly enthusiastic response from young people, some of whom began to emulate criminals by learning their slang, songs, and poems. There was also evidence of young people joining criminal gangs organized by recidivists.

In the "delinquency areas" (Shaw and Mackay 1942) of the Soviet urban landscape, where young people lived in poor housing in low-income zones, street culture and criminal culture overlapped considerably. In these settlements, particularly in those areas where there was a substantial presence of former criminals, young people spoke the criminal argot, knew the folklore and songs, and in some cases also had personal and familial links with ex-convicts. Those youths who had been incarcerated enjoyed higher status among their peers, with those who had been inside more than once being held in particularly high esteem. Some groups collected money, food, and clothes to help those in the *zona*, and people tried to get to know them because of the particular respect they enjoyed in their milieu (Kozlov 1998; Raleigh 2006, 224–25; Tsipursky 2009; Karbainov 2009, 135). The romantic images of criminal outlaws with their opposition to the state, their strong unflinching masculinity, and the perceived wisdom of the criminal *avtoritety* all held an undeniable appeal for young people.

There is evidence that the youngsters sometimes created secret societies and clubs in imitation of vory organizations. Gleb Tsipursky (2009) described one such group in Rostov, consisting of school children and workers of the Rostselmash plant, which was "uncovered" by local police in the mid-1950s. The group's participants held regular meetings in the heavily guarded basement of a house in the Rostselmash settlement, where they "played cards and learned vory's jargon and methods" (83). Members of the group were arrested for a variety of crimes. Tsipursky noted that "the source that fed the internal culture of this group is more or less clear—these were the young people's perceptions of the world of the vory" (83). For some young people, the criminal culture, associated with the romantic brotherhood of outlaws, held a greater attraction than the pastimes that the Soviet system offered—young paratroopers' clubs, parachute classes, aircraft modeling, and theater studios (Smol'nikov 1989). Vory poniatiia became a part of the local street knowledge and, together with the more recent bandit poniatiia, are to this day widely used by members of street groups.[5]

There is also some evidence that the criminal fraternity made deliberate attempts to exert influence on young people living in their community and to educate them in the vory law. Razinkin quotes a letter that one criminal avtoritet wrote from prison to his fellows: "Educate the youngsters; they do not know how to behave. They have their own laws, and this should not be the case. They live in our house, and here there is only one law" (Razinkin 1995, 35).

The peak of the influence of the vory v zakone on the juvenile gangs' and adult bandits' cultural repertoires came at the end of the 1980s and the beginning of the 1990s, when the street violent elites were becoming racketeering gangs en masse. Ex-criminals supplied a ready-made (if not carved in stone) set of ritual

5. On the intersection between noncriminal and criminal street identities, see Kosterina (2008).

practices and semantic expressions. But the bandits quickly emerged from under the influence of the vory, and their code started to reflect the realities of violent accumulation and inclusion of the gang into multiple networks in a modern urban society.

The Differences between Vory Codes and Bandit Codes

The clandestine society of the vory, the exotic, tattoo-covered aborigines of the Russian criminal underworld, who are thought to have penetrated the depth and breadth of Russian society and established their outposts in the West, have fascinated many Hollywood filmmakers, writers of crime fiction, and politicians. But this society, born in Soviet prisons, did not fare too well in capitalist Russia, and while some of its representatives did prosper, they were largely displaced by more entrepreneurial and flexible bandits (Volkov 2002). The social orders of these societies are very different, and so are their codes of conduct. While the law of the vory reflects the almost continuous imprisonment of its members, with its hierarchically organized prison groups, the bandits' code is mainly organized around illicit entrepreneurial activities in modern society.

The vory v zakone, who formed a tight and closed society of professional criminals in the Soviet Union, spent most of their lives behind bars. Outside of the confines of penal institutions, they lived in secretive groups and strictly maintained a radical separation between themselves and the rest of the Soviet citizenry. As Galeotti (2008, 104) pointed out, "Whereas originally the *vorovskoi mir* [the community of the thieves] was simply a culture which arose amongst outsiders excluded by poverty and ill fortune, there increasingly emerged a strand within it that did not just accept but embraced and exalted this exclusion, actively turning its back on the mainstream."

The vory had to dedicate themselves wholly to the *vorovskoi mir.* They had to make their living solely by crime. They were not allowed to accumulate individual wealth and property. Criminal incomes had to be put into a common fund, also (like the bandits' fund) called the obshchak. Members of the vory society could not marry, and although they could have relations with women, the latter were generally held in contempt. A mother was the only female figure that was accorded respect and love (Chalidze 1977).

Vory could not cooperate with the state. They were not allowed to serve in the army or join Soviet youth organizations such as the Komsomol. They were not allowed to work, even in prison, which set them against the prison administrations, sometimes with very harsh consequences (Chalidze 1977; Gurov 1990;

Oleinik 2003). Those who crossed the line and formed any relations with official authorities were expelled from the community and severely punished or even killed. The separation of the vory from mainstream society, and their core identities as professional criminals (and prison elite), were expressed in an elaborate code of tattoos, which inscribed a person's status, penal history, and position in the vory hierarchy directly onto the body.[6] These tattoos immediately announced the status of the criminal to the rest of the world and could be easily read by the police if a vor was apprehended.

Very little of this applies to bandit gangs. Their membership is significantly incorporated into the larger society. They can be members of various youth organizations and serve in the army. They can accumulate money and property, have jobs, be members of political parties, and even have relatives in law enforcement agencies. Although they have to give a part of their incomes to the obshchak, these common funds can be used for individual business investment. Criminal tattoos, a symbol of separation and exclusive identity, are not commonly used by gang members. Contacts with the police (as long as they are not used to inform on one's associates) are not only allowed but encouraged by the gang.

Like the bandits, the vory distinguish themselves from outsiders to their society, whom they call *fraiery* or *lokhi* (peasants or commoners) (Chalidze 1977). The latter are figures of contempt and seen as fair game. In the *zona*, vory also see themselves as the master caste, dominating other prisoners—which is similar to the bandits' presumption of their elite status. But an important distinction exists between the remits of the vory and bandits' power. As one commentator put it, "a central concept in the thieves' philosophy is the sense of their own exclusive right to be considered human" (Glazov 1976, 147). In other words, the rest of society is so alien to the members of the vory brotherhood that they could well be members of a different species. This is definitely not the case with the bandits, who, while having a sense of innate superiority over most nongang people, are still involved in a variety of social networks and can, as we have seen, successfully adapt to the expectations of college or a workplace.

From Vory to Bandits

In the 1990s the vory society continued to have significant influence in many Russian territories, particularly in the Far East, Siberia, and in the region of the Ural Mountains, as well as Pskov, Omsk, Smolensk, Buriatiia, Krasnodar, Rostov,

---

6. On the symbolism of the Russian criminal tattoos, see Baldaev and Plutser-Sarno (2003).

and other areas (Serio and Razinkin 1995). They still commanded respect among members of youth gangs, and to this day young lads see vory as a source of moral authority and ritual expertise. If a vor dies, bandits are expected to attend his funeral. In 1997, for example, 102 young Kazan gang members attended the funeral of a Kazan vor, Rustem Nazarov (Krest), killed in Perm (Beliaev and Sheptitskii 2012, 96). Vory have also retained a lasting influence in prisons. A survey of Tatarstan penal colonies conducted in the beginning of the 2000s showed that most of the convicts were following the prison code and that in the event of problems they would turn to incarcerated avtoritety rather than to the colonies' administrations (Solopov 2013).

But the real influence has moved to bandits. In capitalist Russia, not only vory v zakone but all people with criminal convictions have become marginalized in the communities where previously they had wide social and cultural influence. Prison is now seen as a repository for losers, petty hooligans, and people who were not smart enough to find ways to avoid incarceration. As M., a police officer, said:

> People with criminal records do live in our area, and there are quite a lot of them. But they do not enjoy any prestige now. It's not the 1950s, when half the country went through the camps. Now life is very different, and, accordingly, the attitude toward those who serve time is quite different, more negative. It doesn't matter now whether you were in jail or not—it only affects the fact that you won't be given certain types of work—for example, in law enforcement agencies. Besides, the smart ones don't end up in jail. Mainly people get there for minor crimes, for smashing someone's face in and things like that. Those who made millions are all free or in hiding. Gusinskii, Berezovskii [Russian oligarchs] and others—they robbed the people, and now they're rich.

Even if members of the bandit gangs end up in prison, they are not interested in investing in prison status and generally see no benefit in incarceration. Nafik told us:

> Among the lads, you don't have a higher status because you've been in prison. On the contrary, it's more important for people to be "clean" in the eyes of the law, because if everyone's locked up, who's going to look after the street? Just like in the army, it used to be that not serving was beyond the pale, not in terms of the code, of course, but not having served was considered a failure. These days it's the other way round—the guys who get out of serving are the ones who get praised.

Generally, the vory v zakone society, with its historical prohibition on contacts with the outside world (particularly agents of the state), found it difficult to adjust to a new reality. Capitalist accumulation demanded deep penetration into the corporate and state structures, and the new bandits, whose code, as we have seen, allowed and even encouraged wide social connections of their members, had a great advantage over the rigid and closed society of the vory. As Karyshev (1998, 245) explained, "Vory v zakone, especially the younger generation, try to establish and maintain connections with the criminal world. That is, vory usually live according to the principle 'deal with the people you know, the ones with whom you were in prison.' [Bandit] avtoritety have a different principle: to live as far as possible without violating the law, to have connections among politicians and government officials, bankers and businessmen, top law enforcement officers and representatives of power." Gruppirovshchiki readily reflected on the differences between their code and that of the vory. Ansar said, "The code of the lads does not duplicate the vory code, though they have much in common. In general, it is forbidden to inform, to steal from other lads—one must answer for everything one says. The rest is different."

In the lads' descriptions, their code is constantly evolving, unlike the immovable, highly prescriptive law of the vory. Fundamentally unchangeable traditional authority is not for them. Instead, they are flexible, pragmatic, and open to new challenges. The following fragments from interviews illustrate the differences between the rules of the vory (and their subset, the prison law that regulates informal relationships within the penal system) and the gangs' moral outlook. In answer to the question "What is the difference between prison law and the bandits' codes?" Kirill replied:

> We can deal with this question using the following example. One of the prison laws states: "Don't trust, don't fear, don't beg." That means you trust no one; you fear nothing; and god help you, if you ask anyone for help. If you apply this to lads' relations, then everything falls apart. You live with the street, and you have to fully trust every one of your lads and be certain that he won't abandon or betray you. Relations with the elders are built not only on respect but on the fear of punishment. If this fear disappears, so will the respect. As for the third point of the law, that's just complete nonsense. The very reason the street exists is to solve your problems. It's always ready to help you, no matter what mess you've ended up in. Based on this, we can see that the prison code and the lads' code are different things, though they share certain fundamentals. As for changes, at every stage of street evolution, life makes its own corrections, and I think that's how it should be. We mustn't stand still, and the code should not limit growth, though the fundamentals will always be immutable.

In response to the same question, Il'nar said:

> The code of the lads copies the prison code, but it is not a carbon copy. It's more free than that. Out in the *zona*, everything is very harsh. You're constantly watching your words and actions. In the street, it's the same, but it's a lot softer because you're living among your own lads. In the *zona*, you have your own *semeika*, but even they can't always be trusted. In the street, we don't live by the prison code, and that's how it should be, since everything is different when you're free.

According to some of the lads, the vory have not managed to adapt quickly to changing reality, or if they did, their order was simply corrupted by money. And that is why their power is rapidly disappearing. Tadjik said:

> Their order is similar to ours. There are certainly some differences—for example, the vory cannot have work or family, but the lads can. It's just the lads who are strong these days. In real life, it's the lads who have power, and I don't think there'll be many real vory left soon enough. After all, many of them pay money to get crowned. I've got nothing against them—vory are basically old-school lads, and their era is coming to an end.

Indeed, the vory society has also undergone significant changes. They now invest obshchak money in commercial enterprises; the obligation to spend a significant amount of one's life in prison has been removed; and younger vory can now buy "crowns" (Volkov 2002, 61–63; Siegel 2012, 35). Nevertheless, the bandit society has turned out to be more flexible and better adapted to the realities of capitalist Russia. Unlike the vory organization, which emerged under conditions of Soviet oppression, its social order is less hierarchical and prescriptive. It is more orientated toward the pragmatic rationality of the modern world and complex systems of mutual interdependencies and diverse interests.

Ultimately, while supplying some key cultural repertoires and modes of organization, the vory could not impose their order on the emerging groups of bandits and their street troops, entrepreneurial youth gangs. Their code and principles of social organization no longer corresponded to the changing realities of Russia. They had developed in response to conditions of almost permanent incarceration and belonged to the social order of a traditional, closed society with highly restricted communication with the outside world. Outside the prison boundaries, even though attempts by the vory to become involved in the Soviet underground economy set them on the path of change, they gradually lost their cultural influence in the new Russia, and their code became increasingly outdated.

By contrast, the bandit groups, while in many ways reproducing traditional authority, became highly incorporated into mainstream society. Their groups were not closed to the outside world. Prohibitions on working, marrying, and accumulating property no longer existed. Today's criminal organizations do not see themselves as being at war with the state. Instead, they penetrate and subvert it.

Evolution of the Bandits' Code

Unlike the vory, whose society was formed under the repressive Soviet regime, the bandits organized themselves to take advantage of opportunities in the emerging Russian capitalist economy. The bandit gang became well-integrated into the new economic regime, and its code allowed members significant autonomy, including making careers in mainstream society. The code permitted and facilitated individual accumulation. For a long time bandit gangs seemed to avoid the cultural stasis that befell the vory and made them largely a spent force.

But eventually the underlying structure of the bandits' order itself began to come into contradiction with a new reality. As more and more members moved into business, the fundamental opposition between the lads and traders became increasingly redundant. With the leadership enjoying the fruits of capitalist accumulation and basking in conspicuous consumption, and increasingly surrounding themselves with paid associates rather than members of the brotherhood, the rank and file started to feel left behind. This has been accompanied by a contraction of economic opportunities in the informal sector, particularly at the street level. As a result, some of the gangs have relaxed many of their prohibitions. Il'sur explained:

> They say that now some streets have their own code. But even in such streets they comply with the basic things such as not behaving like a *lokh*, not allowing people to get one over on you, not informing on one's friends. The code has changed lately, and it's even possible to assume that it will change further in terms of different businesses. The lads are not allowed to trade in the market, but not everyone can now have their own trader, because there is great competition in the markets; it is very expensive to start up, and the situation for business is not favorable—it is much too dangerous to get engaged in it; the market is all divided up. Therefore, I assume that soon the prohibition on trade will disappear, and it will be even honorable to engage in it. Speaking for myself, I have never stood and sold stuff in the market, but I have no animosity toward traders.

The growth of an organized drug economy also presents a big challenge to the world of the gang. Ispug commented, "The lads' code is changing; many streets are now creating their own rules, making lawful what used to be unlawful. This especially concerns drugs. Previously, drugs were forbidden. Then weed appeared, then selling drugs through dealers, then the lads themselves started selling on the quiet. Now many are almost bragging about this; they will soon start paying into the obshchak in kind, with drugs."

Many other former prohibitions no longer apply, and the members expressed a sense that the code was being eroded. Potap said, "It used to be forbidden to kick a street lad, even if he was from an enemy street. Now nobody cares. Or, it used to be that if you were walking with a girl, nobody could touch you. Now nobody cares."

Local Kazan residents who were not gang members also commented on the weakening of the gang ethos. Interviewed in 2011, seventeen-year-old Alik said, "While it used to be prestigious for a girl to be with a gruppirovshchik, as they did not drink or take drugs and did a lot of sports, now they are known to be drinkers and drug addicts, and this is what they are thought to do at their meet-ups instead of discussing business."

The Kazan bandit gangs risk moving toward anomie, the removal of binding moral regulations. If the illegal drug economy does take a firm hold in their business, then they will almost certainly become volatile, hyperviolent, and much more individualistic criminal societies.

8

NAVIGATING THE WORLD OF VIOLENCE

The gang operates in the world of private violence that exists where the modern legal apparatus does not reach or where it is deliberately circumvented or privatized. This is a world in which reputations for the use of force are forged, where groups of local strongmen make alliances and launch wars against each other, where the rules of violent conduct are agreed on or contested, and where violence is exchanged for money and favor. So far, however, this complex violent world that exists in the shadow of the state has remained poorly understood. Scholars have tended to study economic violence (particularly when it comes to organized criminal groups and mafias), popular vigilantism, the rules of behavior of violent street gangs, or the seemingly disorderly world of the so-called hooligans. The local architectures of violence, the social systems in which street groups, gangs, and other organized criminal groups operate in cooperation and competition with one another and with agents of the state violence have received relatively limited attention.[1]

Gang violence can only be understood as a part of the larger system of local social relations. While gang members do engage in spontaneous acts of aggression that give them pleasure and help affirm personal status on the streets (Anderson

1. But see Lea (2001) and Stenson (2005) on the informal governance of crime in Britain and Arias (2006a,b) and Venkatesh (2000, 2006) for analysis of the alliances between nonstate and state enforcers in low-income areas of Brazil and the United States.

1999; Collins 2008; Katz 1988), by and large their strategies of violence are orientated toward the reproduction of the gang's place in the local system of private power. To participate in this system, the Russian lads develop a particular warrior persona that helps them overcome their adversaries (and achieve domination over ordinary nongang civilians). But they also need to deal with challenges from the police and security services (acting in a private or public capacity), from other gangs, from violent "civilians" (so-called *otmorozki*, hooligans, and drunks), and others. In this risky and unpredictable world of action, clouded by what Clausewitz (2005 [1873]) called "the fog of war," we can begin to identify the strategies that gang members use to gain power, to settle scores—or just to stay safe. As many authors have shown, sheer physical force (or a reputation for it) plays a large role in gang life,[2] but gangs' violent strategies, as I will demonstrate, are also often symbolic and linked with linguistic practices, with the artful use of the gangs' code. The physical control of violence, the skills of symbolic domination, ritualization, negotiation, violent trade-offs—all these dispositions and devices, learned in the context of collective life on the streets, assist the gangs' adventures in violence and help members become expert practitioners of violence without necessarily making them safe in the long run.

Violence: Learning the Game

To be able to operate in the volatile and treacherous world of nonstate violence, people have to develop a certain persona, a certain way of being in the world. Starting from their childhoods, young men who grow up on the streets develop certain qualities that help them sustain confident violent performances. They acquire a feeling of social competence, an easy ability to improvise, and an instinctive knowledge of what to say and what to do in a violent encounter. Violence becomes their second nature, which Bourdieu has seen as the practical accomplishment of successful interaction (Jenkins 2002, 72). This second nature, which can be also called a violent sense, is a result of a learning process in an environment where violence constantly circulates—the world of the streets—and it is acquired in the context of collective practice, observation of other people's reactions, and joint elaboration of meanings.

People become artful players in the game of violence by developing a set of dispositions, a manner and style in which they carry themselves, and generative

2. For a helpful overview of the literature on the role of violence in gangs and organized crime groups, see Wright (2006, 41–47).

classificatory schemes, ways of seeing in the world. To show how this mastery of violence is acquired in street life, I will use both interview data from Kazan and the data from my focus groups with young members of territorial groups in the peripheral areas of Moscow. Aged between thirteen and seventeen, the Moscow lads were younger than their Kazan counterparts—whose ages ranged from seventeen to thirty-five—and called themselves normal lads (*normalnye patsany*) as opposed to Kazan's real lads (*realnye patsany*). Their groups were involved in episodic street crime but not in entrepreneurial violence. Some of them admitted making deliberate attempts to enter the criminal community by trying to get to know the "right people" in their neighborhoods and building criminal reputations for themselves. They are known in the street world as *tseleviki* (the purposeful ones).[3] Most, however, expected to leave their groups behind as soon as they started working or joined the army. Although they did not belong to entrepreneurial gangs, the street culture in which they grew up was very similar to the one that produced the Kazan lads, as were their collective practices of violence.

While violence can be used as an individual resource, its mastery, as the interviews show, is learned in the group context. Growing up on the streets, young people learn many skills from their peers—to stand up for themselves and to show toughness, bravery, quick wit, and the ability to overcome fear. Young people valued these skills and saw them as essential both for their present life and for their future as adult men. Here is a fragment from a focus group in Moscow:

> VADIM (THIRTEEN): The [street] group prepares you for the future. It means you're not a mama's boy and you know when and how to respond. If somebody challenges you, you know how to behave. But if you sit at home all day playing on the computer, then when you're thirty and you have a family and somebody asks you for money, you'll just have to give it to them. You won't even know what to say to them.
>
> MARAT (FIFTEEN): And you'll be dishonored. Let's say some teenagers come to you when you are thirty. Even if you're stronger than them, they'll still get what they want.

People significantly immersed in street culture and street networks acquire a "feel for the game" (Bourdieu and Wacquant 1992, 223), an embodied knowledge that is unreflexive and preconscious, almost instinctive, giving them easy orientation in various practical situations where violence may be encountered. This

3. A similar category of young men who try to establish links with organized criminals exists in street societies in Tbilisi (Zakharova 2010).

violent sense, an automatic understanding of how to project threat and react to provocation, when to attack and when to wait and buy time, and how to suppress fear, gives the street lads a great situational advantage.

One of the striking features of our discussions with young people both in Moscow and Kazan was their strong emotional reaction to any conversation about violence. Usually quite reticent, the young men would get extremely animated when remembering various threatening situations, altercations, and fights. They gave very detailed accounts of conflicts, how they developed and how they were resolved. Once the subject of violence was raised in interviews and focus groups, stories poured out of young people, who then found it difficult to move on to any other topic of discussion. When it came to violence, broad and often sketchy accounts of their lives suddenly changed to close-up shots, where every detail, every scene, every emotion would be captured and amplified.

Violence obviously had deep affective meanings for these young people. It was something they celebrated and feared. Some of this fascination with violence may, as cultural criminologists explain, be associated with its transcendent properties, with the possibility it offers to many young people, particularly those from low-class backgrounds, to overcome the mundane and oppressive reality of their lives and even provide enjoyment and fun (Katz 1988; Ferrell and Sanders 1995; Presdee 2000; Hayward 2004). But, although violence can indeed be exciting on an individual level (for the perpetrator, not for the victim) it is also frightening and dangerous, and individuals learn to experience it as relatively safe, and even to enjoy it, in a collective context.

A young person learns to neutralize his fear of violence in a group. Violence is seen as rarely leading to serious injuries or death, and in any case, your pals will be there to defend you. As a seventeen-year-old Moscow lad Dmitrii told us: "You're not afraid of a fight because you know that your pals are with you, that they won't leave you if you get into trouble. Even if you know that you will all take a beating, and a heavy beating at that, you still know that together you will fight back."

A theme frequently raised in interviews and focus groups with the young Moscow lads was that the practical skills of exercising control over one's emotions and body in the face of violence can only be acquired on the streets, through living the life of a lad. Fifteen-year-old Andrei said: "A lad should know how to fight. He shouldn't be afraid to have a dirty or bruised face. Let's say there are people who go to school. People who are mostly involved in 'useful activities.' They study, go to after-school classes. For them what matters most is that they have no scratches, no cuts on the face. You have to not care about all this."

In a focus group with sixteen- and seventeen-year-old lads, Alexei (sixteen) said: "We are safer than the rest who are afraid to fight. The most important thing is to hit first."

In our discussions, lads emphasized the "biological" drive to fight. Violence was often presented in terms of irrational or compulsive acts ("We felt like a fight and went to the neighboring district") or as behavior aimed at achieving a desired physiological response ("We like the adrenaline rush we get from fights"). But these representations are produced in the group context. By observing the reactions of other people around them, lads learn ways of experiencing their feelings during fights as joyful and seeing violent altercations as celebratory events. This is illustrated by the following fragment from the same focus group when the interviewer asked "Why is it that some guys like to fight and others don't?"

> Mikhail (seventeen): It depends on their upbringing.
>
> Alexei: And on their group. Let's take our group. Let's say we have one guy who doesn't like to fight. We tell him, come on, let's go together, everything will be fine. He tries it for the first time and sees that we are stronger. We told him that he'd get an adrenaline rush. He's happy that we've won. And then he starts fighting automatically.
>
> Mikhail: I remember how my brother came back home after a fight. I was a little boy then. He came home, all covered in blood, with a stick in his hands. He looked very happy, covered in blood, with no teeth.

In the course of their group experiences, through learning and observing the behavior of their pals, street youths develop specific gestures and ways of walking, looking, and speaking. They often have a particular "swinging" walk, as if they are wading through oil, abetted by exaggerated shoulder movements. This "*gopnik*'s walk" dramatizes the presence of the lads on the streets as they create a menace of violence and demonstrate their readiness to take on any challenge. It seems very similar to the American ghetto "cool walk" and "barrio stroll," which, as Katz (1988, 88) observed, transform "walking from a utilitarian convention into a deviant esthetic statement." This walk also involves seemingly accidental or intentional "bumps" against other people. Recurring references are made in stories about street life to "brushing shoulders" with other people. This practice is used as a device of provocation, challenging those on the receiving end either to start a fight or show deference.

Both Moscow street youths and Kazan gang members made constant reference to "bumps." As Tadjik from Kazan succinctly explained: "I have brushed my shoulders against other people on the streets many times. I simply walk with my shoulder forward, not in order to create conflict but because I am not going to walk like a *chushpan* [a nonstreet young man]."

Street Hierarchies

For street youths the world is divided into "us" (members of a group) and "them" (nonstreet young men, weaklings and losers, underdogs). Their mental schemas become the dominant classifications in the street social order. They express the lads' symbolic power, "the power to constitute the given by stating it, to create appearances and belief, to confirm or transform the vision of the world and thereby action in the world and therefore the world itself" (Bourdieu 1977, 117).

In the accounts of our interviewees in Moscow and Kazan, both the "ordinary" (nongang) and the "real" (gang) lads contrasted their own manly order with the disorganized and senseless world of nonstreet young men, who in various geographical contexts are given the pejorative names of *baklany*, *chushpany*, *chukhany*, *botaniki*, or *cherti* (broadly analogous to "geeks," "nerds," or "punks"). These are young men who back down from fights and other collective street activities and live by the rules set by school and family. Lacking street competence, they are easily victimized—humiliated, harassed, robbed, or forced to pay protection money.[4] They are boring, unmanly, and timid, figures of ridicule. They try to escape from tests of their masculinity and the dramas of collective existence into the world of school and family. But that is a world where adults rule, and that is why they are not their own men. The lads, much like the "lads" in a classic study of working-class youth subculture by British sociologist Paul Willis (1977), deny manhood to these cultural cousins of Willis's "ear'oles," young men who comply with the adults' requirements.

In the lads' narratives, a *botanist*, *lokh*, or *chushpan* is an a priori inferior human being. His lack of willingness to fight for his reputation, for male honor, makes him unable to participate in the lads' brotherhood. In street interactions, these young men become what Goffman (1953) called "faulty persons." Such a faulty person, Goffman explained, lacks the linguistic skills necessary for communication, has the wrong appearance, and lacks command over his body. Clothes, manners, demeanor, walk—everything about the public behavior of such people is seen as unacceptable.

---

4. These young men can also be seen as having subordinate, as opposed to dominant, masculinity (Connell 2005).

Here are some fragments from a focus group conducted in Moscow with members of street groups aged between fourteen and sixteen in which the participants were asked to define *botanists*:

"They're not like normal people, not like the rest of us. They're disliked because they're a minority."
"You can't talk to a *botanist* about anything. He can only talk about his studies."
"These are people who do their homework and study hard. They don't go out. They stay at home all the time at the computer doing homework."
"They say, 'My mama doesn't let me go out. My mama told me to be home at nine o'clock. My mama told me not to smoke.'"
"They all wear round glasses."
"They have schoolbags, you know, like kids from primary school. They put on straight pants and a homemade sweater and walk with a book in their hands."

These caricature-like images (round glasses, homemade sweaters, unfashionable schoolbags) in reality have nothing to do with how most teenagers dress these days. But these descriptions highlight the fact that, for a street lad, the *botanist*'s inferiority is manifested in his body presentation. A *botanist* is humble, unconfident, and unable to talk back. He shows fear and submits to demands. His reactions to provocation are slow. Instead of responding quickly and clearly, he betrays his insecurity. He is afraid of confrontation, and he does not look you in the eye. It soon becomes apparent that you can take anything you want from him. When asked in a Moscow focus group, "What does one have to do in order not to be a *botanist*?" Mikhail responded: "In order not to be a *botanist*, you have to lead a normal way of life. Not be a loser. Someone spits at him, and he has no idea what to do. He ought to do something, to spit or hit back. Not to be afraid."

In a different Moscow focus group, one sixteen-year-old explained how he could tell if a person was a *botanist*:

Boris: You come to him and ask "Do you have the time?" and you have a watch on your arm or a cell phone. And he says that he doesn't know and keeps going.
SS (Author): Instead of saying, "Look at your own watch?"
Boris: Yes. Some guys answer like this. But a *botanist* . . . you can see him immediately. You ask him something, and he says like a little kid, "What? Where?" He should respond straight away; he should not be slow. Then you'd understand that you won't get anything from him just like that. If a guy starts mumbling, you understand that you can do what you like.

Distancing themselves from the world of their street peers, once outside the doors of their homes, *botanists* find themselves in an alien environment. They do not understand how to behave in this complex and treacherous space. They do not know how to respond to provocation and are not ready to give an immediate rebuke or to name allies and friends. *Botanists* are easily deprived of their watches, money, or cell phones, and they do not know whom to ask for help. By turning to their parents or to the police, they distance themselves even further from the world where their peers exercise their own justice.

Ritualized Practices of Violence

On encountering their nonstreet peers, street lads, especially in a group, never miss an opportunity to show them who is boss. These nonstreet youths are despised because they are not their own persons. They are seen as unwilling to risk injury or even death by confronting the enemy, choosing instead submission and humiliation.

Openly mocking their victims and often making them part with their possessions—the whole game is intended to confirm the lads' picture of the world, in which they are the lords and their counterparts are incompetent "commoners" who deserve to suffer.

Interaction almost always has a scripted, ritualized character. These violent rituals confirm the lads' dominant position in the street order and naturalize their schemes of classification. As the anthropologist Catherine Bell explained, "ritualization, the production of ritualized acts, can be described . . . as the strategic production of expedient schemes that structure an environment in such a way that the environment appears to be the source of the schemes and their values. Ritualizing schemes invoke a series of privileged oppositions that, when acted in space and time through a series of movements, gestures, and sounds, effectively structure and nuance an environment" (Bell 1992, 140).

Let us look at how these violent rituals proceed. Lads use a limited number of openings to start a conversation with a victim. These openings commonly appear quite innocent—the victim can be asked to lend the lad his cell phone for an urgent phone call—but everybody understands that the request cannot be refused. This is how the participants of a Moscow focus group with sixteen- to seventeen-year-old street youths described their encounters with their victims:

> IVAN (SIXTEEN): I'd say, "Come on, give me your cell phone. I'll get it back to you in an hour." He doesn't know what to do, and I draw a line—"That's it. I need it now." And he gives me his cell phone. I take it and walk away with it.

KONSTANTIN (SEVENTEEN): I tell him, "Give me the money. I'll give it back to you tomorrow." He gives me the money, and tomorrow I'll tell him to get lost. He'll become a *terpila* ["sufferer," someone who has accepted their victimization] forever.

Very similar practices of victimization of nonstreet young people exist in Kazan. In a typical interaction between gang lads and nonstreet youths, two or three (sometimes more) lads approach a young man and start a conversation. Common opening lines include: "Where are you from?"; "Have you got a cell phone? I need to call my pal"; or "Our pal is in prison, can you help? We need to send him some money." The victim, disorientated and confused by the lads' confident performance, typically starts to play by the lads' script and "willingly" parts with his money or cell phone. If he shows any signs of resistance he will be beaten. Once somebody becomes a victim and accepts it without fighting back, further victimization may ensue. The victim is forced to accept his new position as a *terpila*.

Through a ritualized conversation, the victims are construed as inferior human beings who lack the moral qualities that lads possess (self-determination, strength, control, etc.) and who have to accept their place in the lads' order. By accepting it, they further confirm their designation. If they challenge the lads' power in any way, by refusing to pay or not showing enough deference, they are punished.

In other words, quite apart from physical victimization, the lads engage in acts of symbolic power, as they make the dominated groups accept their place in their own classificatory schemas. Every act of the victim can be constructed as a *zikher* (a violation of the code) and thereby deserving of punishment. Twenty-five-year-old Kazan lad Kirill said, "I prefer to resolve issues peacefully, without bloodshed, even though we can come and grind them into dust at any time. You have to know how to find the right solution, make mutual concessions. But even more I prefer to put people into situations where they are wrong according to the code."

Alexander Shashkin (2009, 174) quotes a Kazan gang member's reconstruction of a typical interaction between a lad (P.) and someone who was not a street youth (Zh.):

P.: Hey listen, where are you from?

ZH.: I am not from the street.

P.: Have you got any money?

ZH.: No. (This is the first *zikher*—he responds to a request for money.)

P.: Turn out your pockets!

ZH. turns out his pockets. (This is the second *zikher*—he is now definitely a *lokh*.)

> P.: Do you know that only *cherti* [slang term for a person who violates the code] turn out their pockets? And who are you after that? Right, tomorrow after three be here with fifty rubles. If you go to the cops, I do not envy you.

Fluency in the language of the gang's moral code enables gruppirovshchiki to construct themselves as moral arbiters of other people's behavior and to present acts of violence as punishment for transgression. One of the Kazan gang members we interviewed, Nemets, said: "If you dig deep enough in anyone, you'll find some kind of flaw. And when you've found it, you can beat them up for it."

Anything—being weak or, on the contrary, showing resistance by looking a guy straight in the eye or, conversely, averting one's gaze—can be seen as a violation of the implicit order. The self-proclaimed guardians of the order, the lads, will be only too happy to punish an offender if they feel like it.

A gang member's claim to the right to punish people for violation of moral norms is based on a general understanding of how street social order operates. Apart from that, morality is always contingent, circumstantial, and is artfully constructed by the lads in specific encounters. This point was also illustrated by Bogdan: "To say definitively who you can or cannot beat up is impossible. Everything depends on the situation. I've used violence against those older than me, and those younger, but there was always something to punish them for, so I don't consider myself an *otmorozok* [a hooligan] for doing it."

By humiliating their victims and showing them that, to use the criminal slang, "they are nobodies, and they have no names worth saying," the lads are confirmed as the source of classificatory and normative power and therefore as agents of authority. As the gang rubs their faces in their inferiority, nongang young people experience classificatory terror, disorientation, detachment, and dislocation. One of our interviewees, twenty-three-year-old Rustem, who did not belong to a gang, described how encounters with gang members felt: "When talking to people, the gang members try to show that they are 'from the street,' that they have support, that they are the kings, and that you are just a *lokh*, and your life is theirs to do with as they will." Another Kazan interviewee, twenty-four-year-old Fanil (also not a gang member), explained: "What's crucial is that they always think of themselves as being right and will always make you wrong. If they want to, gruppirovshchiki can always find a pretext to punish you."

Even without actual violence, people are left with a sense of anxiety, entrapment, isolation, and humiliation as inferior beings. Potential victims understand perfectly well that they are powerless, that it is almost impossible for them to win against the lads. One conversation thread on a Kazan web forum illustrates the "choices" nonstreet young people face when they come across street lads, whom they called *gopniki* (Gainullin 2013). The thread contained the following advice on how to behave:

Take out a cell phone and pretend to be calling your gang friends, saying something like "Hey lads, where are you? I am waiting for you."

Try talking to them competently, using the code (though the common consensus is that this is unlikely to work if the *gopniki* are determined to have their own way).

Try to seize the initiative in the conversation and answer a question with a question ("Why are you asking?"). But this may be seen as rudeness and lead to an attack.

The common opinion was that the best way to stay safe was to avoid any communication or to try to disrupt the *gopniks*' violent scenarios:

If you come across a crowd of *gopniki*, try to walk past them without looking in their direction.

Try to behave in an unpredictable way or act outright crazy—shout loudly, start to sing or dance, or pretend to faint or have a fit. This will disturb the *gopniks*' plan of action, as they expect you to passively follow their lead.

One forum participant recounted how he came across *gopniki* in a city park after dark:

> Two lads came up to me, allegedly looking for the person who'd hurt a girl here. They said they suspected me. I understood that this was a ploy. We talked for about an hour and a half. I had to improvise. When they asked if I was going to boxing classes, I said, "No, I am only doing karate." They asked me who I knew from my district, and I named whoever I could. This worked. The *gopniki* calmed down and went away. But generally, it's best to avoid such conversations, and it's not cowardice simply to run away.

This was the most common advice, as all other methods were deemed ultimately unreliable: if you sense danger, it is never shameful to cross the road and go the other way or simply run. The conversation was later joined by people who obviously belonged to the hated *gopniki*, and who, in no uncertain terms, using swear words and street slang, expressed their disdain at the unmanliness and cowardice of the forum's nonstreet participants and concluded that with such attitudes they deserved all they got.

One local resident, eighteen-year-old Nikolai, interviewed in 2011, explained that he often came across gruppirovshchiki in his area (the Kirovskii District of Kazan):

> I try to avoid them. It is very difficult to deal with them. They harass younger kids, ask for money or cell phones. Several of my friends have been beaten up. They always walk in groups looking for trouble, and they solve all issues through violence. But they have their hierarchies, and it is good to know somebody who they respect if you want to stay out of trouble. I've never been beaten up. They once asked me to give money to help their pals in the *zona*, but I replied that it was their own business to help their pals. It is important for them to always be in the right, to use the code. When talking to them one should reply politely and calmly, with dignity. There is always a point after which the conversation turns into violence. One must be careful not to reach it. Also, one has to be careful not to bump into a gruppirovshchik by mistake or say anything that they could see as offensive.

The gruppirovshchiki construct a terrifying presence, which rests on the implied threat of violence and is supported by a haughty personal stance and cultural ideology of dominance that makes resistance almost impossible. The only way to counteract a threat is to demonstrate that one has their own violent resource—knowledge of the right people, boxing skills, and so on—or an ability to construct a confident performance. But the lads may still decide to take offense at one thing or other and assault a person anyway.

Conversational Practices versus Physical Violence

We have seen that far from lashing out with violence, the lads often engage their victims in lengthy conversations before extorting money, watches, or mobile phones. (In one example, quoted in the above-mentioned forum discussion, a young man talked to *gopniki* for an hour and a half.) What we found in Moscow and Kazan was far from unique in Russia. According to Breslavsky (2009), gang members in the Buriatiia villages where he conducted his research were also proud of being able to make their victims part with money or valuables without having to resort to physical violence. Similar practices were reported in other urban areas of Russia and the former Soviet republics of Armenia and Georgia (Koehler 1999; Kosterina 2008; Zakharova 2010; Ponomareva 2014).

The wide presence of nonphysical strategies of domination contrasts with the ubiquity of physical violence in other street cultures—for example, in some American barrios and ghettoes or in the multiply deprived areas of Britain where hyperviolent street gang culture has taken hold (Katz 1988; Anderson 1990; Bourgois 1995; Anderson 1999; Hallsworth and Silverstone 2009). Here guns and knives are used in minor provocations, and lethal violence is frequently unleashed against members of other gangs, nongang victims, or bystanders. Success in violent physical confrontations (physical capital) formed the basis of what Thomas Sauvadet (2005; 2006), is his study of the gangs in French banlieus, called "warrior capital."[5] In the Russian streets, though the threat of violence is always present, lurking behind the demands of street youths and unleashed if the victim does not "understand" the meaning of the situation, the object of specific pride is the ability to get the upper hand without using physical force.

Why do the Russian lads not also use their abundant violent resource to get what they want simply by assaulting their victims—something they say that they enjoy—without engaging in sometimes lengthy conversations? The answer is that being able to force the victim to recognize their superiority by complying with their demands confirms their elite status in the local social structure. Resorting to violence every time they want something would not only compromise their status but would also expose them potentially to more serious criminal charges. For these reasons, gruppirovshchiki often try to avoid the use of physical force (unless they are in danger of losing face). Instead, they use conversational devices of violence, using their system of symbolic production of difference as encapsulated in the code and relying on their counterparts to be able to read the script and demonstrate obedience.

In addition, creating situations where the victim is manipulated into a powerless position has its own emotional thrills. The victim, feeling that he is weak, that his manliness is judged as wanting, gets extremely uncomfortable, while gruppirovshchiki get high on the feeling of absolute power. "Conversation" in which the lads take a leading role leads the victim further and further into a trap, in which he feels he is at a mercy of his attackers. A trap constitutes a site of maximum power, depriving the victim not just of capacity but often of any inclination

5. The French gangs also valued verbal and social skills, as well as moral discipline, but physical capital, according to Sauvadet, mattered most.

to resist. Unlike pure force, which is purposive, direct, and immediate, a trap creates a space where power can be exercised at leisure. In *Crowds and Power* (1973, 327) Canetti argued that, unlike pure force, power can also be ceremonious and slow. He used the example of the cat and the mouse to illustrate his point. Playing with the mouse, the cat does not use immediate force.

> It lets it go, allows it to run about a little and even turns its back; and, during this time, the mouse is no longer subjected to force. But it is still within the power of the cat and can be caught again. . . . The space which the cat dominates, the moment of hope it allows the mouse, while continuing however to watch it closely all the time and never relaxing its interest and intention to destroy it—all this together, space, hope, watchfulness and destructive intent, can be called the actual body of power, or more simply, power itself.

When gruppirovshchiki entrap a victim in a conversation, they create a space where the victim suddenly finds himself at the mercy of those who set the trap and who now control the situation, possessing the victim's time, establishing the limits to his mobility, and effectively manipulating his emotional state. Entrapment is much broader than simple situational manipulation. The lads design scenarios that are meant to ensure their victims lose their capacity for purposeful action, thus becoming powerless. They establish the script, and their victims do not know what it is. Walking into a trap means finding oneself in a place where the stakes are set against you.

There is another, more pragmatic explanation for the delay in using violence. The victim, powerless at the given moment, may have access to private redress later. While reading the person's status from his body language, manners, and style of clothes can help establish whether or not he is a warrior or a nonstreet "commoner," the lads cannot be sure whether or not the potential victim has "some force behind him." He may happen to have relatives or neighbors working in the police, FSB, or Prokuratura; have friends in other gangs; or have connections to vory or with other powerful people. That is why extortion is sometimes preceded by an interrogation to establish the person's position in the local violent system. The proximity and denseness of social relations in the Russian urban areas, where people from various social groups often live side by side, unlike in the multiple deprived and ghetto areas of modern Western cities, creates situations in which perpetrators cannot assume that the victim has no access to alternative sources of power.

The ultimate aim, of course, is for the situation to be resolved to the lads' advantage. They are manipulators who have mastered the art of using social norms and violent rituals to get what they want.

Reputation for Violence

Even in high crime, high violence areas the gang usually cannot become the only source of power. It must compete with other gangs and groups with violent resources—the police, the security services, and professional criminals. This creates an environment that is volatile but where nevertheless strategies of action do exist, where reputations circulate and violent resource is used and exchanged.

Out on the streets gruppirovshchiki face constant status challenges from members of other gangs. These challenges are both individual and collective in nature. The lad has to defend his reputation and fight for respect, but he also has to defend the reputation of his group. The lads represent their gangs, and if they lose face, this can threaten the whole local architecture of violence. The gang's "name" becomes tarnished, and this can lead to militant incursions into the gang's territory by other local warriors and even to economic weakening if rivals decide to try to appropriate the gang's business "patches." That is why the gang demands that the lads respond violently to any provocation from enemy gangs. Kazan gang member Banan said: "When you're from the street, even if you have an opportunity not to start a conflict, you have to remember that you can then get called up for it at a meet-up. They'll say you screwed up when someone offended you. For example, they barged into you with their shoulder, and you didn't respond. So it's best to challenge someone like that and punish him if necessary."

An imperative to be seen as a part of the warrior elite makes it difficult to back down in confrontations with other local warriors even if a gruppirovshchik would prefer a peaceful resolution. One of the commonly quoted rules is "The lad is always right." This means that the authority of a member of a gang cannot be challenged and that he has to be seen to prevail in every confrontation. As Nemets said, "Just as we had it drilled into us by the seniors, we now drill it into the kids: a lad is always right and must always insist on it. This means that it is often difficult to avoid a conflict."

For a gruppirovshchik, backing off may constitute a violation of the gang's code. As Garik summed it up, "Everyone who deserves it must be punished. I won't break the code and put up with insults from anyone." The lads, particularly from the younger age cohorts, are constantly fighting with young men from other gangs on the streets, in crowded bars, and night clubs. Fights often start with "bumping." In certain situations bumps can be ignored, but bumping seen as deliberate requires a violent response. Trofim said, "If you're walking down the street and brush up against someone by accident, that's one thing. You can get away with just an apology. But if you're walking around and someone's rude to you, then that calls for use of force."

Vlad confirmed:

> There are always fights in night clubs. Recently we went to the Paradiz club, and it was full of members of the Kvartala gang. We bumped into them several times—you don't really notice when you're dancing. They got on to us, took us to the toilet to talk, and the fight started. There were three of us and five of them, so the fight did not go in our favor. They did not beat us too severely, but it wasn't nice. Then of course there was an *otvetka* [revenge fight], and we beat them up.

But the lads cannot accept challenges from everybody. Their aristocratic warrior status means that they cannot have a group fight with members of a street peer group that is not a gang. They can only fight with equals. Nafik said, "With some of the lads we are friends, and with some we are enemies. . . . The lads make war and peace, but in any case, they are lads, and you can only deal with them."

If the lads come across a group of ordinary young men, they usually prefer to pick on a couple of guys and beat them up as an example to others. Kolia recounted a situation when the gang's honor was slighted by a young man they believed was spreading a rumor that their street was full of drug addicts. When the lads summoned him to a *strelka*, he unexpectedly brought his friends with him. Kolia's friends were startled that they were being collectively challenged by these "commoners":

> "Who are you?"
> "We're just his friends, and there will be a fight."
> "Go fuck yourselves; nobody will fight with you."
> In the end, they picked out one guy, beat him up, and left. But I remembered this case—some people have brave friends!

A gruppirovshchik can never apologize to a nonstreet young man without risk of losing face. Trofim said: "When I'm in the wrong, I'm ready to apologize to a lad. But if it's not a lad, then I won't apologize. I'll just leave."

The trickiest situations arise in cases of mistaken identity, when a seemingly defenseless "commoner" turns out to be a fellow warrior, a street lad, or has protection from another gang, and to assault him may lead to serious escalation of intergang violence. In these cases, gruppirovshchiki can resolve the situation peacefully—as long as they do not lose face. Seventeen-year-old Anvar said:

> Fundamentally, any situation can end peacefully or with a fight. For example, suppose you want to extort cash from someone, but he turns out to be a street lad. In that case, if he has not done anything to offend you (for example, not called you names, not insulted your street), then

> you can smooth things over, just say "Sorry pal, I made a mistake." You can even have a nice chat with him. Or if you go for a *lokh*, but he turns out to be under someone's protection—if his krysha talks to you quite normally at a meeting, doesn't throw words around, then there's still no reason for a fight. It all depends on your behavior as well as that of the person you've encountered.

Sometimes the lads mistakenly challenge young people who belong to friendly gangs. But this does not have to lead to a conflict. As most fights are preceded by an investigation of the counterpart's position in the local violent arena ("Where are you from"? "Who do you know?") the misunderstanding can be quickly resolved. Kolia concluded: "If the lads are from allied streets, this will end in apologies, and that is it. People will go on their way peacefully. But if there's no alliance between the streets, there will be a conflict."

Revenge Attacks and Wars

The world of nonstate violence is a world where the rule of law does not apply. It is a complex social arena where one's status—and ultimately one's life—depends on one's reputation for violence.[6] Constant vigilance about one's standing among other combatants, the need to retaliate immediately if one's status is challenged, the imperative to acquire a reputation for violence that would keep other people from challenging you, and ultimately the prospect of mutual self-destruction—all this we find in the violent world of the streets and in the top structures of *bandit* hierarchies. The same imperatives exist in other ecologies where state penetration is low. Here individuals immersed in the world and codes of the streets feel compelled to campaign for "respect" by using violence or its threat (Katz 1988; Bourgois 1995; Anderson 1999; Barker 2005; Lauger 2012). Associating status with "manhood," they get involved in destructive cycles of violence to protect it. As Anderson pointed out in his *Code of the Streets* (1999, 91), "If others have little regard for a person's manhood, his very life and the lives of his loved ones could be in jeopardy. But . . . one's physical safety is more likely to be jeopardized in public *because* manhood is associated with respect." Both in the streets

6. In his analysis of contemporary London gangs, Simon Harding (2014) extends Bourdieu's concept of field to the social world of urban street gangs. He suggests that "the urban street gang represents its own social field—a structured space with actors (gang-affiliated young people) competing to accumulate scarce resources, namely money, respect, reputation and status" (55). This approach emphasizes individual rather than collective accumulation of resources by gang members, who compete with each other for precious social goods.

of Philadelphia ghettoes described by Anderson and in areas of Russia where we find high gang presence, we come across constant status challenges.

These challenges, however, are not just individual but collective in nature. The gang tries to establish a collective violent regime in the territory, and if one gang member publicly loses face, this can affect the gang's reputation. Between gangs, the smallest provocations and slights can lead to group warfare. When a lad is insulted or attacked by a member of another gang, the rules on violence are very clear. This calls for an *otvetka.* Younger lads, who cause most of the street violence, need to be defended by the whole group, however stupid and unnecessary their behavior is deemed by the elders, because otherwise the reputation of the whole gang can be affected.

If confrontation between gangs involves bespredel (for example, if a lad was beaten up for no apparent reason, in violation of the code) this can lead to a war. The war is a highly important event in the life of the gang. Although these days the wars are not as deadly as they used to be in the 1990s, and people rarely get killed, it remains a central ritual form for gang society. The war creates unity among members of the group, while confirming the division between "us" and "them."

Seva described war preparations that turned out to be unnecessary on that occasion because the challenge turned out to be false:

> There I am, sitting at home. Out of the blue I get a call from our smotriashchii. "Get your younger lads together," he says, "we have an emergency meet-up." So I get two age groups together, and mine comes as well, and we stand around wondering what's going on. Then the seniors and the avtoritety turn up—sixty people altogether. I thought, "Oh, screw it, another war." Then they tell us that one of our lads got a call, got told to go somewhere that evening and that if he doesn't turn up the other guy will kill his family. And he didn't even give his name, so we don't know if it's lads or not. To cut a long story short, we get in cars, and 100 to 120 of us go to the meeting place. There are three people there—two brats and a girl—and we start pouring out of our cars like a tidal wave. Those three are standing there pissing themselves, unable to say a word. In the end, it turns out that our lad goes to the same college as the girl and that he was rude to her that morning. She told her boyfriend that our guy had been harassing her, so he decided to sort it out. Apparently, he'd just recently joined the street and was feeling on top of the world. Well, we didn't give them a hard time, but we did give them an educational thwack, told them to fuck off, and warned the guy that next time he makes a threat like that, we'll cut off his tongue and shove it up his ass.

While a single *otvetka* is usually over in a day, wars can last for several days. The war campaign is carefully prepared. Operations are planned, surveillance is used to identify the addresses of the enemy gruppirovshchiki, traps are set, unexpected ambushes are unleashed, and prisoners are captured and interrogated. The street comes out in force during wars, and everybody apart from the older cohorts has to take part. The street has to be mobile and have access to suitable vehicles to be able to get from place to place in time or to make a quick getaway if necessary. Very few military actions happen without the lads using their vehicles, and like any other business expenses, the cost of gasoline is compensated from the obshchak. Victory in the war belongs to the gang that manages to inflict the most damage on the opposing side by beating up its troops, wrecking or appropriating their cars, and taking prisoners. The war ends when the defeated side asks for peace or the winning gang decides that the war has been won to its satisfaction. Then a meeting takes place between several representatives of both sides. If they cannot negotiate peace, the war may continue.

Unlike the 1990s, "wars over asphalt" or division of business opportunities are now extremely rare. Koshmar commented, "We don't come out in force to take over businesses. Everything's long since been divided up. Taking a sizeable chunk from our "neighbors" would mean we had to start a serious war, not our usual little ones that last for a couple of days."

According to Ispug, "Obviously, we don't start wars unless matters get really serious. But there hasn't been a serious war like that for a very long time."

The situation had been very different in the 1990s. The history of the Kazan gangs at that time is full of examples of extreme violence. For example, in a conflict between Khadi Taktash and Pervaki (started over 200 grams of cocaine that one of the Pervaki leaders took from Khadi Taktash without payment), the leader of Pervaki was killed. In retaliation, Pervaki killed a member of Khadi Taktash. Radzha, the leader of Khadi Taktash, declared war on Pervaki. He promised to pay five thousand dollars for the murder of an ordinary gang member and fifty thousand dollars for the murder of the gang's leader. Lists of enemies with their addresses and car numbers were photocopied and passed to all Khadi Taktash members. Seven members of Pervaki were killed. No Khadi Taktash members were killed, but after this Radzha began to wear an armored vest (Safarov 2012).

These days the nature of the wars tends to be different. Guns or knives are rarely used. The lads' aim is to settle scores and demonstrate the gang's strength, not to kill or seriously injure their adversaries, although, of course, once violence breaks out people can get carried away and the outcome becomes unpredictable.

Ansar described one such short war that, the clear danger the lads faced notwithstanding, seems closer to a children's fight than to a mafia war:

> I can recall one relevant incident. I call a girlfriend of mine, tell her that I'll be there soon, and ask her to heat up some soup and some other stuff. But right when I am ready to go, I get a call from the smotriashchii: "Everyone assemble, a war's broken out." I went to the gathering, and while I was on my way I saw a bunch of lads with clubs. They surrounded me in a flash, and one of them recognized me. I got bashed on the head and put in a car. Two stayed to guard me while the rest charged ahead to tear up our guys before they finished gathering. In short, they took me prisoner, held me for three days in a senior's flat, beat me, and burned the palm of my hand with a lighter. They tortured me to try and get our lads' addresses out of me. But I didn't give them away. The war ended three days later, and I was returned. I had to go to the doctor's straight away, but apparently, no harm was done. So I only saw my girlfriend a few days later. She was in shock, of course. There was a row, but later everything cooled down. I didn't tell her where I'd been. It's not something a woman needs to know.

Similarly, Seva's account can be seen as presenting a war as a kind of game in which people try to increase their team's score (although the implications for one's health and survival can be extremely real):

> There's a war on, and we're sitting around and wondering what to do. We're winning 5–1, so the seniors tell us to keep our heads down and wait for our rivals to sue for peace. Well, we wanted to increase our score further by taking a few more guys down. The five of us got in a car and went to the addresses we knew. But we were careless—in one house entrance we came up against twenty enemies or so and were brutally beaten. On top of everything else they took our car. In the end, it was our street that had to sue for peace, and our seniors tore us to shreds.

The outcomes of the wars, although not as important as they were in the 1990s when the wars were led for territorial expansion and capture of economic resources, still matter. A war confirms the division of territory and can even improve the standing of a particular street. Zhenia said:

> When we were fighting a fairly large and powerful street, we had to show that they needed to pay attention to us. So we decided to take them using audacity and surprise. This group's territory is very large and takes up around half the district, so here's what we did. Four groups of twenty people headed to the center of their territory. Each group was backed

> up by several cars so they could move fast or even escape if necessary. So these four groups, with car backup, started quickly moving out from the center to the periphery. On the way, we stopped every young lad, and if he turned out to be local, we took him down on the spot. We beat them on the street, in house entrances, and in public transport. And in twenty minutes we took down a huge number of people and safely made our escape. The next day, we offered to negotiate, and that was the end of it.

There are some limits on violence during a war—for example it is considered bespredel to deliberately maim a prisoner or to humiliate a member of a different gang by pissing on him when he is down. Although the wars are rarely meant to be lethal, serious conflicts can involve the use of weapons, and this can result in grave injuries and even killings.

Resolving the Conflict When Overpowered

What happens outside ritualized encounters and wars? What if the gang members unexpectedly come across people who can trump their violent cards, if they encounter overwhelming force? In these cases their artful mastery of the code can sometimes help them wriggle out of seemingly desperate situations. When finding themselves overmatched, members of Russian gangs try to appeal to the shared understanding of fairness in street and criminal culture, to the system of unspoken rules that structures informal violent interactions.

We asked our interviewees to recall any potentially threatening episodes from which they and their associates had managed to emerge unscathed. Some stories stemmed from personal experience; others were part of the gang's heroic folklore. The general principle in encounters with stronger force was to "use one's mouth" to try to end up on top. Appeals to shared understandings of right and wrong could sometimes turn a desperate situation into one in which the weaker party could walk away with life and dignity intact. In the following description of one such situation, twenty-four-year-old Tsigan displayed his and his pals' mastery of the art of verbal acrobatics when finding themselves in a tight spot:

> In any situation, you've got to try to resolve the conflict peacefully, though without making too many concessions. There was this one incident where the three of us bluffed a crowd of forty people who'd come to give us a seriously bad day. We were in the wrong, of course, but we managed the conversation correctly and got out of trouble without losing face. We all parted ways without any complaints. Here's how it went. We were on our way to my house in the country. My friends and I were going to celebrate my birthday—ten of us, but only two from my street. We go

> to the house, and then we hear these shouts, "We've caught a thief!" So we go look, and we see that the local guys have caught two little kids, thirteen and fourteen years old, who'd broken into someone's house and stolen some cereal and some other random junk. So my friends and I came over, started sorting stuff out, and took away the stolen goods. While we talked, one of the young kids started shouting, giving us lip, claiming that my pal had punched him in the mouth. The issue was resolved, and we were pretty satisfied. We decided to get moving, especially since some women came to pick the kids up and started shouting that they were coming after us that evening, and should get ready. And, indeed, that evening forty lads or so, all fourteen to seventeen years old, came for us, all with crowbars, clubs, brass knuckles, and bricks.
>
> Finally, the three of us (everyone else arrived much later) found ourselves in the middle of a crowd. We started talking. I asked where they hailed from, introduced myself, and asked the seniors to leave the crowd and talk to us separately. Five older guys, seventeen years old, came out. We went to the side. Then I said, "Lads, we're talking to you unarmed, and you've got bricks and sticks." So the seniors told the younger guys to drop their weapons, and before you could blink, there was a small mountain on the ground. Then we started talking, and I asked what the problem was. They explained that their brat got hurt here, and with bespredel, too, 'cause you can't ban stealing. I told them that it wasn't bespredel because he'd earned it—not by stealing but by being rude, which called for punishment. The seniors said that the brat hadn't been rude (which was true). But I said, "What're you listening to him for? Listen to what people are telling you. Your brat's compromising your street. He's lied his head off, and now you're putting yourselves on the line for him. He's a liability to the street." The seniors asked what we had in mind. I told them, "Your guy's stolen from us. He's given back the goods, and he's paid for his rudeness. If you have no further complaints, let's shake hands and go our separate ways in peace." The victim was asked whether he had any complaints. He did, and wanted to go one-on-one with the guy who'd hurt him. But my pal was three heads taller and refused, justifying it by saying that he'd bury the guy waist deep in the ground with a couple of hits and didn't want to become a child killer. His refusal was accepted, and there was nothing left to resolve. So we all went home.

Like Odysseus, who was "all navigation, subtlety, invention, dodging the rocks, story-telling, cheating and survival" (Nicolson 2014), the gang warriors escaped from retribution at the hands of almighty adversaries by using cunning and quick wit. By first appealing to the principle of fairness (parity of forces), then accusing the adversary of further transgression of the code (being rude to a lad), then arguing that they were unwilling to fight with a person who was weaker, they escaped unscathed and with their honor intact.

In another episode, Seva remembers how he and his associates, while expecting to deal with defenseless *lokhi*, were suddenly confronted by ex-prisoners (who claimed to be vory v zakone):

> One day me and my pals were sent to collect a debt from one *chushpan*. He'd had a month to collect the sum, and on the appointed day we turned up at his place. When he opened the door we saw two men, forty-five or fifty years old, covered in tattoos. So one of them shouts a load of rubbish: "Are you retarded, extorting money from my nephew?" "I am," he says, "a vor v zakone. Now we're going to kill you." Well, I wasn't thrown by that. I said "I don't give a shit who you are. Your nephew committed a *zikher*, and for that he owes us money. He agreed to give it back." In other words I'm bullshitting him according to the code. It turns out that the nephew hadn't told his uncle anything about it and presented it to him as if someone was simply demanding money. The criminal promised to punish his nephew, and he even asked for an extra week for his nephew to collect the money and promised to check that he'd returned it. We in our turn promised to leave the guy alone, then shook hands and went on our way.

Sometimes one must rely on bluffing and pretending to have greater power than one actually has. David said:

> There was one period when I kissed my wife goodbye each morning without knowing whether it was the last time. One time we took a really big risk. Somebody started harassing a firm under our krysha; nobody knew who they were, and they didn't know about us. And, as luck would have it, just then our leader went to a different town, together with many of the avtoritety and some of the fighters, but the *strelka* was agreed for the next day. We decided to do it all ourselves and pretend to be tough avtoritety. I was to play the leader. We came up with the script in advance and rehearsed it several times. First of all, we chose the coolest cars and fancy clothes. The lads collected the most massive golden chains and rings for me. We decided what everyone should say and do. We go to the *strelka*. Twenty people are waiting there, and many of them have weapons. And here's what they see. Ten cars drive in, all foreign made, and in front is a huge SUV with toned windows. Guards in leather coats with Kalashnikovs get out. One of them opens the door and helps me get out. I come out, all in gold, with a hat and in an expensive coat. The *bratva*, all huge guys and

> all armed, follow me. I make several steps toward the enemy; one of the guards produces a chair, the other takes an expensive cigar out of a holder and lights it with a golden lighter. Everything was thought through to the last detail—servile guards, a chair, a cigar. We see they have gone quiet; their bravado has evaporated. I say in a relaxed tone, without raising my voice: "Well, who's come out here to take on my lads?" Immediately they started to assure us that nobody wanted to quarrel, that this was all a silly mistake. And only in the evening, sitting in a cafe, we laughed with relief at how we managed to pull the wool over their eyes. Although if these lads had been a bit more smart things might not have ended so smoothly.

Many stories like this read like Hollywood scripts and may, of course, have similar relationships with the truth. Nevertheless, it is apparent that the use of deceit and cunning in this way is a necessary survival tactic in potentially life-threatening situations. It is a world in which people need to be able to perform with confidence and authority, making use of whatever props are available or their imaginations can provide.

Uses of Violence

Gang violence is not only used instrumentally for economic gain or in order to fight for "respect" in street battles. Where trust in the police and courts is low, and people take the law in their own hands, mastery of violence (both physical and linguistic) can protect one from assault, help one to prevail in conflict situations, or be used as currency in the local system of violent barter between the gangs and other agents of formal and informal power.

From the stories told to us by Kazan gang members, it was obvious that nobody felt safe. Relatively protected in their own territory, gruppirovshchiki faced threats of violence in other areas of the city or when they left it to go to the countryside. A persistent theme in our interviews was the threat faced by Kazan gang members when visiting their dachas outside the city. The villages may well have their own gangs, and Kazan gruppirovshchiki, seen as outsiders by the locals, may find themselves the targets of crime, theft, burglary, or extortion. Radik told of such a situation in which a gang member had to call in forces from Kazan:

> I'll tell you about a guy I know who happens to be a senior in one of our city's streets. He had a dacha in Mari El [a neighboring autonomous republic], and youths from a nearby village got into the habit of sneaking into it. He got fed up with it, so one time he surprised

> them—prepared an ambush and caught the thieves. Naturally, they were worked over and kicked out. But the guys turned out to be from a village gang and threatened to burn his house down. Then my friend called a meet-up with them. At the appointed time, he comes in with his friends, just four people whom he'd invited down from Kazan, in their old Ladas. And there's a crowd there: forty to fifty people, all with clubs, pitchforks, a few with hammers and axes. The Kazan people came out and the crowd starts to surround them, clearly planning to bury the lot. So our guys come out, calmly open the trunk, where there are several machine guns, and my friend takes one and lets loose a few rounds into the sky. The villagers stopped straight away. My friend told them to get on their knees, and they got on their knees. Then he explained to them that stealing from his house was bad, as was threatening his neighbors' houses. At the end, he finishes with this line: "In case anyone still doesn't get it, next time we'll come and . . . well, you've got such a big forest, plenty of room there for everyone. We'll bury you there and give you a common grave."

In another situation, a similar response was needed when a gang member became a victim of extortion. Farit reported:

> There's an incident I remember really well when we went out to help a senior. He'd bought a plot of land outside the city, started to build, and there was this situation: two retards from the village come up to him and say, "Do you live here?" So he says "Yes." They say, "See, this is our land; you're going to pay us tribute." So our senior says, "How about I show you the paperwork proving this is my land?" They say, "You can wipe your ass with your paperwork. Bring the money tomorrow, or it's curtains for you," and they tell him where to bring the money. So the senior calls for help, and we decide to go there as a big crowd with several age groups, just for fun. The next day, the local gruppirovshchiki are waiting there, with five more people with axes, pitchforks, and clubs. And ten cars drive up, surround them, and our lads come out, many with guns, and the senior says, "So, guys, how much do you want?" They're speechless. The senior tells them, "I'm building a house here, and I need laborers. How much for you to build me a house?" He says this while toying with a pistol, randomly pointing it at them and lowering it. They realized that they weren't getting away scot free and promised to build him his house for nothing, just as good neighbors. And they did, you know.

In another situation recounted by Farit, a gang member was threatened with extortion by students in his university:

> We had an interesting situation with one of our younger lads who was a student in KFEI [the Kazan Institute of Economics and Finance]. There was a small gang in his year, three to four people, who were extorting money and things from various *mazhory.* They decided that he was a dumb *mazhor,* that he had lots of money and they could demand it from him. They came to him after classes, began to pressure him, and told him to bring lots of money next day. He asked, "How much do you want?" "That much." "OK." He promised to bring it. Then he told this to the seniors and proposed a way to punish them. The next day two of them turn up, expecting sacks with money. Then a car drives up and a guy with a shotgun gets out and says: "Get into the trunk." They take them into the forest and give them shovels: "Dig a hole!" They dig it. Then they're told, "You see, here is a hole. We won't put you in, but just be aware that this hole is here, and next time we'll simply have to throw you in and bury you.

The violent skills and resources that the gang members possess—confidence, poise, knowledge of how to make credible threats, and connections with the local strongmen—help them to prevail in situations in which ordinary people would be totally powerless. In the following episode, Il'sur makes a variety of threats that persuade the gang that controls an illegal parking lot (not his own gang) to pay him damages—something that for a "civilian" car owner would be little short of a miracle:

> I always prefer to resolve a conflict through words instead of violence. And I practically always manage to persuade the other person that I'm right. Once, when we moved to a new apartment, I left my car at an overnight parking lot. When I come out in the morning the side of the car is damaged. I come up to the guards and explain the situation, ask them to pay for the damage. The guards—young lads—refuse, saying that it happened after their shift was over. I say, "OK, so who did it?" They look coy and say nothing. I say, "Right, lads, we can do this another way. I have connections at the police station. I can arrange it so that your parking lot gets closed. Or I'll come at night with a shotgun, fire buckshot across half your parking lot and leave it to you to mop up"—and so on in this spirit. The lads sensed that they were getting into trouble and said that a lad from the middle age [cohort] was driving in his car and

> bumped into me because of inexperience. I asked them to tell him that I wanted to meet him. We met, discussed the issue; it turned out that we had common acquaintances, and he paid me for the repair without further ado.

A whole gamut of credible threats is used when a reasonable request for damages fails, and, as this example illustrates, these threats can be highly effective when used by highly skilled violent practitioners such as Il′sur.

The gang's violent resource can be lent to other violent agents (for example, the police). Salagaev, Shashkin, and Konnov (2006) described the following episode told to them by a twenty-two-year-old gang member. A police officer's brother got in trouble with gang members at his school. Instead of the officer going to school to investigate for himself (something that would be counterproductive for his brother's reputation), the officer asked his acquaintances from another gang for help. Gruppirovshchiki came to the school and settled the problem. The young man's status in school, instead of being negatively affected, went up as a result of such "mafia" intervention.

Navigating the City

By showing a readiness to fight at the slightest provocation in some situations, while displaying the utmost caution and readiness to compromise in others, the lads skillfully navigate the complex reality of the modern city. They show striking pragmatism when faced with overwhelming force and try to avoid conflict or resolve it peacefully. As local resident and school psychologist, MK., said: "If the situation can turn out against the gang members he will avoid using violence. If a gruppirovshchik comes across a person who turns out to be the son of a policeman, he will not be violent to him and will try to resolve everything peacefully."

Gang members can never take their superiority for granted. Il′sur described a situation in which gang members, hoping to set up a trap for a *lokh*, ended up in a trap themselves.

> Two young ones from our gang were pestering one young man for money. He did not give them money and told them that he does not "claim" anyone [does not belong to a gang]. They had a talk, and this ended up in the guy setting up a *strelka* with our lads. The young ones came back all happy; they were retelling the situation with glee and shouted that they will do *razvod* to this guy in the evening and will get

> his money. Because there was no danger, only five or six people went to the *strelka* from their age, with their smotriashchii, my pal. They came to our usual spot for *strelki*, in a rather secluded place, and this guy and his pal were already there. Our lads set on them, and started shouting that they will not get back alive, that they will bury them right there. The guys are strangely calm; they do not react. And then suddenly some huge guys emerge from both sides, in blue camouflage, in masks, "Everybody freeze!" Those who tried to run were almost trodden into the ground. They threw everybody into a bus and took them to the district police station. The guy with whom they had sat up the *strelka* turned out to be the son of a police boss, and he had decided to have some fun, to see how "bandits" were ambushed. That is why he did all this and did not say straight away who he was, because in that case he would have been left alone immediately.

As we have seen, careful navigation of the local system of power relations is evident in the practice of *strelki*, meetings with potential victims or with members of different gangs where gruppirovshchiki would first investigate whether a person or a group has any violent resource—who they know, what is the potential threat they can represent—and only then decide whether to resolve the conflict peacefully or start a fight.

Nevertheless, gruppirovshchiki can be their own worst enemies when, under the influence of alcohol or a burning sense of having been disrespected, they decide to go ahead and challenge other local agents of force. One such episode led to the undoing of the leadership of a once powerful Kazan gruppirovka, 56th Kvartal. This gang, which traced its history back to the 1970s, collapsed because of one relatively "minor" episode. In 2005 three members of SOBR (police special commando unit), all veterans of the Chechen wars, were sunbathing at the Volga River beach in Kazan and stood up for a girl who was being pestered by drunken 56th Kvartal youths. After a fight, the gang youngsters, who were beaten by the policemen, complained to their seniors, who reported the incident to the gang's leader, a famously volatile alcoholic and drug addict, Oleg Grinin (Grinia). Grinia ordered the punishment of the cops. Twenty youngsters were dispatched to the beach and beat the three policemen to a pulp. This challenge to the police's authority could not go unpunished. As a result, in a few months' time, after sufficient evidence had been collected, mass arrests of the gang members began. In 2007 eleven people, including the main leaders and avtoritety, were prosecuted, and Grinin received a twenty-four-year prison term for his past crimes (Beliaev and Sheptitskii 2012, 255–56).

Everyday Violence

Street violence is only a part of a much larger field of social violence. Some anthropologists use the concept of "everyday violence," suggested by Scheper-Hughes (1992) in her work on violence in Brazil. This concept focuses on "individual lived experience that normalizes petty brutalities and terror at the community level and creates a common sense or ethos of violence" (Bourgois 2004, 426).[7] Our interviews with both gruppirovshchiki and ordinary "civilians" in high-crime areas revealed high levels of anticipation of violence in the community. People on both sides of the divide had a sense of profound insecurity. As local resident Airat said, "everything can happen; nobody can guarantee anything. Only God knows what will happen, where violence will come from: from the *gopniki* or from the cops." The same feeling of living in the shadow of violence was displayed by gruppirovshchiki.

The accounts of our gang interviewees were full of references to domestic violence, sexual violence, and street violence inspired by alcohol—where they and their relatives and friends were on the receiving end. Safarov noted that at the peak of gang crime and violence in Tatarstan in the mid-1990s, there were also extraordinary rates of crimes committed under the influence of alcohol, often in the course of disputes and conflicts between family members, neighbors, and friends. Safarov pointed out that in 1996 Tatarstan police recorded between fifty and sixty murders a month committed by family members and acquaintances of victims. He chronicled bizarre and macabre killings of wives by husbands, children by fathers, even a murder of a grandson (a violent alcoholic) by his grandmother. Unmotivated drunken violence during public festivals and drinking sessions added to the picture (Safarov 2012, 42). Although Tatarstan in the 2000s saw less serious criminal violence than in the 1990s (see table 1), for the young men we interviewed, who lived predominantly in the peripheral areas of Kazan, the threat of violence still felt omnipresent. Membership in organized violent groups provided some protection against violence, but it could not prevent it and often, as we saw earlier, exposed them even more to violent situations. The very existence of violent gangs in the community may have exerted its own pernicious influence on social life, promoting expectations of violent solutions to individual and business conflicts and thus raising the overall levels of violence.[8]

---

7. Everyday violence includes domestic, interpersonal, and delinquent violence (Scheper-Hughes and Bourgois 2004, 426).

8. In a study of Mafia operations in the Sicilian city of Gela, Becucci (2011) showed that the arrival of criminal organizations transformed local life, expanding institutional mistrust and patron-client relations, and promoting acceptance of violence as a tool for conflict resolution.

TABLE 1 Dynamics of crime in Tatarstan

YEAR	REGISTERED CRIMES	MURDERS	CRIMES COMMITTED BY AN ORGANIZED GROUP	CRIMES COMMITTED WITH THE USE OF FIREARMS
1987	25,534	—	—	—
1988	28,093	—	—	—
1994	61,907	662	—	269
1995	59,417	651	—	239
1996	52,817	589	—	167
1997	49,322	587	—	225
1998	52,963	613	—	211
1999	72,161	690	502	187
2000	70,238	645	991	173
2001	71,266	653	954	124
2002	70,238	589	1,062	106
2003	58,866	605	873	102
2004	63,529	548	758	88
2005	92,232	502	832	40
2006	105,105	426	716	28
2007	81,251	345	1,245	21
2008	81,183	327	1,957	18
2009	70,623	293	999	24
2010	58,769	274	290	13
2011	55,318	280	640	16

Source: Tartarstan MVD statistics in Nafikov (2012, 356).
Note: — indicates no data available.

Gruppirovshchiki sensed that they could come under attack at any moment, and being part of a gang might be of little immediate help. Many had stories about having been assaulted by drunks on the streets or in cafes and restaurants. Fights could result from minor altercations but, as Risat recounted, the consequences could be deadly:

> During the last such fight, I was hit on the head with the back of an axe. A friend and I were sitting in an open-air cafe, eating kebabs and drinking. My friend made a comment about the quality of the kebab, and an argument broke out. Then these blockheads run out with axes and clubs. To cut a long story short, we got beaten into a pulp, and my friend spent a month in hospital. But we were avenged. That same day, in the evening, the cafe was torn apart and burned to the ground, while the blockheads were dealt with, and I never saw them again.

Many stories involved violent altercations on the road, during various festivals and in the context of weekend "relaxation" where gruppirovshchiki would suddenly come under attack from drunks. Just like nongang youths, they could find themselves in the wrong place in the wrong time. Zhenia recalled:

> When I was a *smotriashchii* I constantly had to attend *strelki* as I needed to see what the young ones were capable of. One time, we nearly got butchered. The little ones had got themselves into trouble again, but it was a simple matter, and we were in the right, so my age group and I decided that only the little ones would go to the *strelka*, plus me to make sure things went smoothly. So there we are, five of us in the appointed place, no one else around. Then several cars and a minivan drive up fast. Some grown-up men with guns run out, grab us, and throw us in the minivan without saying a word. We'd already pissed ourselves with fear, but I managed to ask, after being hit several times, what manner of bespredel it was to start a war, and such a serious one at that, over some brats' minor misdemeanors. And then this comedy plot emerges—it turns out they had scheduled a *strelka* with some other lads in the same time and place, but the others were either late or they'd sensed something was amiss. So they apologized to us and drove us back.

Several accounts involved the sisters of gang members being victims of sexual harassment or rape. Vlad told us about his friend's sister:

> A sister of my pal went with her friend to a birthday at someone's apartment where they only knew the host. I told them, "Don't go," but they didn't listen and went anyway. And during the night they come running back, all in tears, with torn clothes, one with her fly on the trousers torn. They wanted to rape them. My pal collected us all, called all the lads who lived nearby, and we all went to that apartment. The girls rang the bell, the door opened, and we went in straight away—wham, a blow on one's mug, then on the second, then on the third. We beat them all to a pulp, took the food from their fridge, took their vodka, broke their plates, tore their curtains. We got our revenge alright.

In another case, the girlfriends of Trofim and another gang member were subjected to sexual harassment when they holidayed outside Kazan:

> Two of our girlfriends rented a house at a holiday resort, not far from the village where we had our dacha. Once one of them runs up to us

> with a black eye and tells us that some drunken guy came over and wanted to meet them. He brought vodka with him. They sat there drinking vodka, then this guy started to harass them, wanted to rape them, then broke a window and gave one girl a black eye. The girls started to shout that they have friends who will stand up for them. And he says: "Let them come here at nine this evening. If they do not come, we'll rape you, and if they do, we'll rape them." We gathered together, about thirty people, went to the resort and stood there waiting. We see some shmuck looks out from one of the cottages. When he saw how many people came he pissed himself. He started shouting that he is from the street [i.e., a gang member]. We started talking to him and he finally admitted that he is not from the street and just knows a district prosecutor from Kazan very well. Just as we were about the start beating him, he shouted that OMON [the commando unit of the police] had arrived. We hit him a couple of times and ran away. Later on one of our lads said that they beat him several years before that because he tried to have a go at them while drunk.

In another case a gang member was bullied while serving in the army. Grisha explained:

> Our smotriashchii told us about a case when the elders went outside Kazan for a *razborka*. The reason was this: one of our lads was serving in the army nearby, but he had big troubles with the older *dedy* [conscripts]. You know how they test the youngsters in the army—they'll tell you to wash their socks or clean the latrine with a toothbrush. If you refuse, they will kick you a couple of times, and normally that's it, meaning that you've passed the test. But our lad was seriously harassed, and each time he was beaten severely. He called our smotriashchii, told him everything, and asked that they come and help. The elders, who were the most gym trained, got into the car and went there. They started talking to the *dedy*, one of whom was beaten up to serve as an example. He had to go to the military hospital afterward, and the others were warned: "If you don't leave our lad alone, we will come again and beat you all to pulp." After that our guy had no more problems, and he finished his service without any troubles.

When a person's safety can only be ensured through some form of patronage, it is no wonder that the gangs retain their popularity among young people. This does not just apply to the world of the gangs. This gang's patronage over its member serving in the army has parallels with that of another organization, the Kremlin-organized youth movement Nashi. In its recruitment drive, Nashi promised that its members would be "curated" by the organization during their army conscription. Their regiment would know they are under Nashi patronage and that older members from the nearby area would come to a youngster's defense if he got into trouble from hazing.[9]

The whole Weltanschauung of gruppirovshchiki is molded by their belief in the efficacy and ubiquity of violence, both in the street milieu and at the state level. Risat said:

> Violence can help you achieve what you want—this is how the world is, and it is not for us to change it. Everything in our world is built on violence. There is compulsion everywhere, and don't you think that this only concerns the lads. Let's say, when laws are passed in our country and everybody protests, people shriek and shout that this is not what we want, do those in power listen? They don't give a damn, and this is violence, violence on behalf of the state.

Fighting Fire with Fire

Gang members live in a violent world, which they help to create but which is larger than their own system of private violent regulation. In this world both they and members of their social networks, their "nearest and dearest," are also vulnerable. The need to establish themselves and their gangs as sources of local power creates a constant possibility of violent confrontations and wars. The ability to use one's violent resource, project willingness to use force, or avoid a confrontation through competent verbal performance makes life safer, but it cannot remove the threat.

The world of nonstate violence is a world without one dominant power. It is a world where mutually accepted political authority is absent and where, to use the words of Hobbes, people exist "without a common power to keep them in quiet" (Hobbes 1996 [1651], 83). Hobbes's description of what happens in prestate tribal societies corresponds very well to the realities of gang life: "Every man looketh that his companion should value him, at the same rate he sets upon himself: and upon all signs of contempt, or undervaluing, naturally endeavours, as far as he dares (which amongst them that have no common power to keep them in quiet, is far enough to make them destroy each other)

9. Personal communication from Dmitrii Gromov on his research on Nashi.

to extort a greater value from his contemners, by damage; and from others, by the example" (83).

According to the Hobbesian thesis, in a world without sovereign authority, one's status—and ultimately one's life—depends on one's reputation for violence.

In a situation of multiple and overlapping power regimes and networks people are constantly confronted by the possibility of private violence. In Russia, the process of internal pacification, the removal of violence from everyday life, which, according to Elias (1978, 77), was central to the development of peaceful civil society in the West, is far from complete. There is a whole field of nonstate violence, creating powerful currents, penetrating social relations, and charging interactions on and off the streets. People are involved in ad hoc and segmented systems of personal violence that involve various agents, including state agents acting in a private capacity, professional criminals, and individuals who resort to violence in a situational rather than systematic fashion. Although gang members navigate this world with relative ease, they also remain highly vulnerable. Violence can never be effectively contained or ritualized; it always overflows (Girard 2005). The gang may be seen by its members as an organization that can effectively protect them from violence, but in practice they are merely fighting fire with fire and gambling that they're not the ones who'll get burned.

9

GANG CULTURE AND THE WIDER RUSSIAN SOCIETY

Since the end of the Soviet Union, the street lads and bandits have acquired a prominent place in Russia's public discourse and popular culture. Depending on the section of Russian society, they and their groups represent either social evil, an embodiment of violence and greed and rejection of civilized norms and conventions, or a social utopia, a world of brotherly bonds and natural fairness.

The figure of the lad, whether viewed as a street hooligan or as a member of a criminal organization, is either an object of ridicule and hatred—often with derogatory class connotations—or the epitome of self-reliant dominant masculinity. Whether people love the lads or hate them, the influence of gang culture on post-Soviet Russian society has been profound. Their language is understood and used by diverse groups of the population, while references to their poniatiia are commonly employed to describe public life in Russia and the behavior of the country's power elite.

In this chapter I address the cultural influence of the gang in contemporary Russian society, and how the vocabulary born in the networks that exist in the shadow of the state has come to reflect the social ruptures created by the collapse of socialism, and to express some of the fundamental features of the society that has since emerged.

Dissemination of Street and Criminal Cultures

Before market reforms, the influence of illicit social organizations—the gang and the vory community—on wider public life beyond the world of the streets and delinquency zones of Soviet Union was relatively limited. In unofficial popular culture it mainly took the form of songs about the romantic lives of criminal outlaws and the bitter fortunes of those who ended up behind bars. These songs were sung by workers and members of the intelligentsia alike at birthdays and weddings, around kitchen tables, or during tourist expeditions, or they were requested by diners from restaurant bands. The popularity of these songs can be traced to the mid-1950s, when former prisoners started being released en masse from the Gulag (Dobson 2009), and they are popular to the present day.[1]

After the start of the transition from socialism, the language of street lads and bandits, and of their cultural relatives, the vory, began to dominate mass communication. It entered the lexicon of television presenters and public figures and has remained part of the everyday Russian vocabulary, including terms such as *patsan* (street lad), *lokh* (inept non-streetwise individual), *bespredel* (lawlessness), *razvod* and *kidalovo* (deception), *obratka* and *otvetka* (return fight), and specific references to *poniatiia* (the code), such as *patsan skazal, patsan sdelal* (what the lad says, the lad does) and *otvechat' za bazar* (answer for one's words). The street and criminal cultures supply ready-made linguistic formulae and systems of classification that people from a wide variety of social backgrounds use in order to describe what a "real man" should be. In a study of constructions of masculinity among Russian men conducted by Marina Yusupova (forthcoming), some of the interviewees, who had never been members of criminal gangs or seen the inside of a prison, used criminal distinctions such as *avtoritetnyi patsan* (authoritative lad, *avtoritet*), *baklan* (nongang young man), and *pidaras* (pederast), a pariah in the criminal system, to describe their conceptions of proper and improper manhood. The bandit and prison versions of poniatiia are widely known and often seen as one code. In a national survey conducted by the Levada Center in 2013, 38 percent of respondents said that they had a general understanding of poniatiia, 5 percent knew them well, and 3 percent tried to follow them in their lives (Levada Center 2013).

The wide cultural dissemination of illicit codes can in part be explained by the ubiquity of street culture in Russia and by the large number of people who have experienced incarceration. The traditionally high rates of incarceration in Russia have made prison culture readily available, particularly in the peripheral areas

1. Today, the radio station Chanson, which transmits prison songs, has a rating of 10% of the Russian radio audience (Solopov 2013).

where ex-prisoners were allowed to settle in Soviet times—beyond 101 kilometers from main population centers and where the street youth culture absorbed the language of criminal society like a sponge.

According to some estimates, in the Soviet Union every fourth man had first-hand experience of detention and incarceration (Abramkin 2007). Although in comparison with the Soviet period, the post-Soviet Russian prison population has declined, the country still has the third-largest prison population in the world.[2] Some authors believe that because of the high-incarceration regime, prison culture has directly affected the culture and behavior of broad sections of the Soviet and post-Soviet population, far beyond the world of the streets. According to Rustem Khanipov (2008), the influence of prison culture stretches from folklore and slang to the direct influence of prison status systems (division into the prison elite, ordinary inmates, and abject outcasts) on the larger society, with ordinary Russians following the criminal code and criminal classifications in their daily lives. Valerii Abramkin (2007) has argued that the male prison culture resonates with popular conceptions of justice because it embodies the norms of archaic societies that are organized around the values of brotherhood and fairness and with respected elders acting as sources of traditional authority. In the 1990s, when state law and order collapsed, the poniatiia became the only extant common law system that created a semblance of moral order.

While the importance of street and prison cultures for Russian society cannot be overestimated, it is unlikely that the social orders of particularistic societies that operate in the shadow of the state can be mechanistically extended to a complex modern society. Rather, the prominent place of gang and prison poniatiia in the Russian system of cultural communication reflects the nature of social struggles in Russia during the course of market transformation and the continuing presence of patrimonial relations as it has emerged from these struggles.

The Lads' Logic in Public Life

Following the collapse of the Soviet Union, Russian society was profoundly transformed as it became an arena for battles for recognition, wealth, and power. While some individuals energetically fought to divide the country's assets, others, whose lives had been settled and orderly, were suddenly exposed to the omnipresence of violence and the need to fight for survival. New struggles brought to life

2. Incarceration rates in the USSR were 780 per 100,000 of national population in 1936; 1,500 in 1941; 2,700 in 1953; and 847 in 1986. In the Russian Federation in 2013 they were at 475 per 100,000, with a total prison population of about 680,000 (Luneev 2006; Walmsley 2013).

new heroes—the lads and the bandits, with their own systems of violent regulation. They also paved the way for the rise to power of representatives of other militant cultures—the army, secret services, and law enforcement—who became the core of Putin's ruling elite (Kryshtanovskaya and White 2003). They brought with them their cultural systems based on a warrior's outlook and a dualistic vision of society as divided into us and them, Russia and the West, good guys and bad guys, loyal citizens and traitors.

While representatives of these militant cultures were on the rise, the fortunes of the intelligentsia were moving in the other direction. In postsocialist Russia, where reforms favored the new moneyed class, members of the former Soviet intelligentsia lost their status along with their material prosperity.[3] With this decline, the values of refinement, restraint, politeness, and rejection of crass materialism that had long been part of the ethos of Russian intelligentsia—and were promoted from the 1930s as *kulturnost'* (culturedness) by the Communist leadership as part of the country's modernization drive—were also becoming a thing of the past. In this respect, we can say that in recent years Russia has undergone a *decivilizing* process, the opposite of Elias's (1978) civilizing process in which violence was progressively taken out of social life in European states.[4] This is when the language and classifications produced in archaic, premodern, patrimonial, militant social systems started to permeate the wider Russian cultural sphere.

As Beumers and Lipovetsky (2009, 37) argue, in the popular culture of the 1990s, violence became routinized and perceived as an ordinary part of the present. It was also glamorized, as "the habit for violence was presented as a characteristic of the elite, as a major condition for social success." The dismantling of the established social and cultural hierarchies and the resurgence of private violence in the course of the frantic redivision of assets going on across Russia helps to explain the saturation of popular literature, theater, television, and film with images and narratives of violence. Known as *chernukha*, this tendency to portray social life in a dark, negative way became characteristic of Russian popular culture from the late 1980s. Although *chernukha* initially exposed violence, cynicism, and greed as abject human qualities, in the 1990s it began to celebrate them. Beumers and Lipovetsky, while pointing out that celebration of violence is a feature of postmodern societies generally, also quoted Eliot Borenstein (2008, 17–19), who noted that in the Russian society of the 1990s, "in a world in which

---

3. On the changing status of the intelligentsia, see, e.g., Patico (2008).

4. Elias (1978) acknowledged that the civilizing process can halt or regress. On the concept of "decivilizing process," see, e.g., Mennell (1990).

the private has been made public for the first time, and in which the publicly owned has been privatized, the rhetoric of neo-chernukha is, if anything, that of overexposure: let us see once again what horrifies us every day. . . . Chernukha functioned discursively as an unhealthy habit widely enjoyed even as it was derided."

As Beumers and Lipovetsky (2009) show, at this time the rituals and rhetoric of popular violence rose from the depths and began to dominate social, economic, and cultural communication. Poniatiia, the language of popular violence, reflected the social chaos and the new raging battles for resources and recognition.

Since the 2000s, however, with the stabilization of the political regime under Putin, the language of informal violent groups and networks, including their poniatiia, has ceased to be the language of social crisis and has instead become the language that best seems to capture the extant rules of social and political life. There is a sense in Russia that there is a parallel system of rules whose principles are never entirely formulated yet are clearly understood by wide sections of the population and used by those in positions of authority, whether these are officials or criminals.

Commentators began to refer to poniatiia when describing the actual system of governance operating in Russia (as opposed to the one based on written law). Poniatiia were now used to describe corrupt, illegal practices that put force above the rule of law and parochial connections and favors above formal justice. Representatives of the liberal intelligentsia often accuse the ruling elite, and Putin personally, of "living by poniatiia." Thus, references to poniatiia were made in relation to the transfer of ownership of the Yukos oil group to the state-owned Rosneft company in what was considered by Putin's critics, and subsequently confirmed by international courts, to be a gross violation of legality.[5] Putin is often accused of using street and criminal slang—for example, when he promised to drown Chechen terrorists "in the can" (*mochit' v sortire*) or "smash in the mugs" (*otovarit' dubinoi po golove*) of those who organize public protests.

The figure of the street lad has also become an emblem of all that is antithetical to the ideals of civilized life. The lad symbolizes the primitive and brutal forms of social behavior of those brought up in the street jungle—explosive violence, obsessive desire for retaliation for perceived slights, respect for might, and ruthless exploitation of the weak.[6] When commenting on the lack of civility in public

---

5. Both the Permanent Court of Arbitration in The Hague and the European Court of Human Rights in Strasbourg found in favor of Yukos shareholders in July 2014.

6. This is in no way new. As Joan Neuberger (2010, 229) showed, in late imperial Russia and in the Soviet Union, public anxieties about civilization and barbarity were projected onto the figure of the hooligan, the historical predecessor of a lad.

life and the reliance on primitive force, people often refer to the lads' rules. As the Moscow journalist and historian Nikolai Svanidze noted in an interview on the Ekho Moskvy radio station (Larina 2012), the ruling elite behave according to the lads' code and show no willingness to accommodate any political opposition: "Politeness, propriety, mild manners, readiness to compromise or to have a discussion are equated with weakness in our country. These are not lad qualities."

The lads and their rules of behavior are invoked when commentators talk about the primacy of group obligations over universal norms. Here weakness cannot be shown, and retaliation for an affront should be swift and certain. This is how Alexei Venediktov (2013), the chief editor of the Ekho Moskvy radio station, explained the criminal prosecution of the Russian opposition politician Alexei Navalny, who had previously promised to put Putin in prison: "'Alright,' the boss probably thought, 'you said that I would be in prison under your rule, and now you'll be in prison under mine.' This is called *obratka* [revenge] lad style."

In oppositional commentary, Russia's behavior in the international arena is often compared to the behavior of a gang and Putin himself to a street lad. Putin's own references to his early youth spent on the streets of Leningrad play well into these representations. He told the journalists interviewing him for his first biography, "I was a hooligan, not a [Young] Pioneer. . . . I really was a bad boy" (Putin 2000, 18). Putin's photos and television clips frequently portray him striking a heroic pose, playing with wild animals, or crossing a river on a horse, proudly displaying his muscular torso. He flies a fighter jet, descends into the ocean in a military submarine, or dives to lift ancient amphorae from the bottom of the Black Sea. He appears fascinated with the idea of the hero, with the world of manliness, virility, and dominance, so unlike the drab bureaucratic world of the geriatric Soviet rulers or the drunken shambles of Boris Yeltsin's later years.

Many commentators, such as the political journalist Stanislav Belkovskii, have explained Putin's annexation of Crimea in 2014 as "lads' logic" (*patsanskaia logika*). In Belkovskii's (2014) opinion, Putin's response to what he saw as the West's attempts to draw Ukraine into its orbit needed a demonstration of force by Russia: "How could he choose not to teach a lesson to these arrogant people, the Western elites, who think that they are entitled to do whatever they want, while Russia and many others, whom they consider second-class nations, can do nothing? That is how it used to be, but not anymore. Because he is a lad." Commenting on the consequences of the Crimean annexation and Russian support for separatists in South-East Ukraine, another journalist, Leonid Radzikhovsky (2014), suggested that "Putin's main miscalculation is, of course, his inability to foresee the reaction of the West. He was sure that the West was composed of weaklings and cowards, greedy, feeble and pathetic, of worthless people who would cringe and crawl away into their holes at the first sign of pressure. In short, he saw them as weak, helpless botanists whose only response to the appearance of a real lad would be to wipe their glasses, apologize, and beg for mercy."

The affinity between the lads' rules and the unwritten rules of state power is perhaps best demonstrated by the admiration the Kazan lads themselves expressed toward Putin in our interviews (something unthinkable for the vory, who profess complete rejection of the state and all its agents). Putin was praised for his tough demeanor and readiness to use force when necessary. In Il'nar's opinion: "Putin, although he is from the KGB, is a 'correct person' [meaning a person following the code]." Il'sur explained: "I like Putin because I like his harsh policies for improving Russia's image. The incident with the beating of the ambassador's children in Poland and the reprisals is just classic *obratka.* Putin has shown that he's not going to take any crap from anyone. That sort of guy gets respect, both on the street level and in international relations."

In the instance cited by Il'sur, two Polish diplomats and a journalist were attacked in Moscow in presumed retaliation for the mugging of three young people from Russian diplomats' families in a Warsaw park. The Moscow attacks, whose perpetrators were widely believed to be associated with Putin's youth movement, Nashi, occurred directly after Putin called the Polish incident an "unfriendly act" in relation to Russia.

This praise for Putin is a good example of the convergence between the official and unofficial Russia. No longer do the criminal classes feel that they are in total opposition to the state. For their part, public figures similarly believe that making gestures and expressions deriving from the worlds of the street and the *zona* may give them additional legitimacy.

A Criminal Utopia

Although for members of the intelligentsia the lads, the bandits, and their culture are equated with a slide into primitive brutality, for many ordinary Russians the moral order of the gang retains a certain romantic attraction. As already mentioned, the gang sees its own order as superior to the amoral, egotistical, and undisciplined relations of the outside world. This view of the gang as a *Gemeinschaft* and its members as embodiments of tough masculinity (as well as the legacy of popular tropes of outlaws who stand against the oppressive system) resonates with wide sections of the population and finds its expression in the popularity of prison songs, movies, and other cultural products that glorify the Russian vory and bandits. Similarly to the medieval European tradition in which bandits came to be seen by ordinary folk as fighters against injustice (Hobsbawm 1985), Russian criminal outlaws have been widely perceived as keeping the flame of truth and justice alight, even in the confines of prison.

"Heroic" masculinity is also always in demand, and the recent success of the sitcom *Fizruk* (PE teacher), seen in spring 2014 by every third Russian between the ages of fourteen and forty-four (Broadcasting 2014), testifies to the continuing mass fascination with the figure of the bandit warrior of the 1990s. The hero of the sitcom is an ex-bandit who has fallen on hard times. The 1990s are now a distant memory, and in the present day, his violent skills are no longer required. With the aid of a false diploma he obtains a teaching job in a Moscow school. Mocked at first as a kind of Neanderthal, he gradually comes to earn the respect of students and teachers for his directness, courage, virility, and adventurousness, all the masculine qualities that he has in abundance and other male heroes in the sitcom, who are presented as caricatures of manhood, are lacking.

A particularly enthusiastic response to the gang and its culture can be found among people who are marginalized and excluded from supportive networks and economic opportunities. In my study of street homelessness in Moscow in the 1990s, I found that some of the street young men dreamed of joining the vory or bandit gangs—and made some practical steps toward doing so by building their criminal reputations and sending money and food to the *zona*. They were attracted to these groups not so much by the prospect of the income to be derived from criminal activities (although this was also important) but by the chance to join a close society where they could really belong, find protection and care, and where relations would be, they thought, equal and fair (Stephenson 2008). As seventeen-year-old Mikhail in my 1998 Moscow focus group said:

> MIKHAIL: Make a *vor* Russian president, and the Russians will be well looked after! Prices will drop immediately; stealing will drop 80 percent; and everybody will have enough. The only criminals left will be petty tricksters who envy others' wealth. There will be no police either.
>
> S.S. (AUTHOR): Who would maintain order?
>
> MIKHAIL: You and me, ourselves. The vory will look after order. Vory share all the money to the last ruble. They have a brotherhood.

Yet the views of the marginalized residents of the streets were not far from the idealizations of the gang by members of the establishment. Salagaev, Shashkin, and Konnov (2006) even found that some representatives of Tatarstan law enforcement bodies favorably compared the gang mores with those in their own institutions: "In many expert judgments, we found nostalgic feelings about the sense of collectivism that was typical for Soviet law enforcement agencies. Individualization and the lack of spirit of 'professional corporation' in the police were compared to friendly and even family-like relationships in the gang."

The long-running and highly rated television series *Glukhar'*, and its follow-up, *Karpov*, actually portrayed a police station run like a classic gang, with its own obshchak, provision of kryshy to businessmen, and a patrimonial social structure in which tough but fair avtoritet-like senior officers treated their subordinates almost as family members whose best interests they had at heart. Although the station's nominal purpose was to protect law and order, in practice the characters did not treat "law" as a relevant concept to their activity; instead they followed informal rules and their own understanding of justice, effectively taking the law into their own hands. Arsenii Khitrov suggests that the message of the series is that informal rules are morally superior to the soulless cruelty of the law and that corruption is merely another form of favor between fellow human beings (quoted in Romanenko 2013).

Poniatiia and Patrimonial Networks

The street and criminal poniatiia have come to express some important features of Russian society as a whole and not just of the worlds that seem antithetical to mainstream society. When people use the language of poniatiia when describing social reality unrelated to life in the underworld (when they talk about the system of employment or political government, for example), this indicates that social life in all these spheres is seen as organized according to similar principles. In his analysis of prison culture and its influence on Russian society, Anton Oleinik (2001, 2003) has suggested that many of the features of life in prison (lack of a clear border between the spheres of public and private, lack of interpersonal trust beyond a small circle of associates, distrust in public authority) are congruent with the institutional conditions in wider Russian society. This, he suggested, creates conditions for wide dissemination of the prison culture. I would extend this argument to say that poniatiia, whether originating in prison or in other social spaces where alternative modes of social regulation exist (such as the streets), also provide a perfect vocabulary to describe the continuing prevalence of premodern, patrimonial relations that coexist with modern bureaucratic authority in Russian life (see, e.g., Kryshtanovskaya and White 2011; Urban 2012; Ledeneva 2013).

Relations based on patrimonial favors and dependencies can be found in many spheres of life that are far from the worlds of the street and prison. One example can be found in the social practices of the contemporary art community in Moscow, whose members are united in networks that cut across hierarchical positions, and where the better-established artists, critics, and curators in Moscow help their less-fortunate colleagues (often people with few resources, coming from provincial areas) with work or housing. In return, the latter often provide low-cost or even free services and end up in precarious, insecure employment (Chekhonadskikh 2012). Analyzing flexibility and precariousness in the Russian service sector, Clement (2007, 94) pointed out that industrial relations tend to be regulated by informal rules and agreements, in which the rights and responsibilities of workers are not contractually fixed and the bosses see themselves as benevolent patrons rather than contract-bound employers.

Poniatiia, a word originating in the criminal culture, is now a term used to signify informal rules and conventions that have become a substitute for modern law. The phrase "to work according to poniatiia," used in relation to organizational practices across the Russian economy, commonly means sharing one's illegal income with superiors and keeping quiet about various corrupt practices. It can also be used to refer to the state of affairs in which members of powerful clans support one another, providing access to resources and shielding their affairs from independent investigation or legal enquiry. Political leaders may respect their obligations to the members of their inner circle while acting in a volatile, unpredictable "bad guy" manner with the rest of the world, just like the bandits' leaders and the lads on the streets. Within Russia, people seen as outsiders to the system are denied rights, while a lack of respect shown to a member of the in-group demands immediate retribution. (As Putin said in a television interview in 2000, "Those who hurt us won't live three days.")

In this system the figure of the ruler also acquires neopatrimonial characteristics. It has been argued that Putin's regime is increasingly drifting toward "plebiscitarian patrimonialism, in which the Russian leadership claims the right to rule the state as if the state were its personal property, as long as the results of this arbitrary rule are electorally ratified by the people" (Hanson 2011, 36).

The parallels between the bandit gang and its poniatiia and the larger Russian society are many. In a satirical piece, the political scientist Vladimir Pastukhov (2012) suggested that in Russia, in addition to the written constitution there is also an unwritten version based on poniatiia. Unlike the legal document, the unwritten constitution is followed to the letter by the Russian authorities, and its principles are well understood and respected by the citizenry. Here is an extract from his text:

> The Poniatiia Constitution
> ***Article 1.***
> The strong may do anything. All power in Russia belongs to the strong; the power of the strong cannot be limited by anything other than strength.
>
> ***Article 2.***
> The law exists for the weak. The weak are obliged to obey the laws written by the strong. The strong are not obliged to obey the laws they write for the weak. [. . .]
>
> ***Article 6.***
> The strong cannot be called to account for crimes they have committed, except where they have trespassed on the rights of someone stronger. [. . .]
>
> ***Article 8.***
> The weak have no right to protection from the strong. The weak are strong in relation to those weaker than themselves. An attempt by the weak to defend against the strong is a crime.
>
> ***Article 9.***
> Property belongs to the strong. [. . .]
>
> ***Article 10.***
> True citizenship belongs to the strong. The strong are born to strong parents or become strong by relation or acquaintance or by having their strength acknowledged by other strong persons.
>
> ***Article 11.***
> Conflicts between the strong are resolved according to poniatiia. [. . .]
>
> ***Article 13.***
> The strong are ruled by the strongest. The strongest is not elected or appointed but promotes himself. Elections are necessary to make the predetermined result seem believable. (Pastukhov 2012)

Most of the key features of gang order that I have described in this book are present in Pastukhov's description of the unwritten law of Russian state: the radical distinction between those who have all the power and rights and the defenseless "commoners"; the unbreakable connection between power and money; the social recognition that is granted only to the strongmen; conflict resolution between the strongmen on the basis of poniatiia; the patrimonial privilege of the leader. From the streets to the corridors of power, we find the same basic structures in social life and political authority.

A New Lingua Franca

The vocabulary of the gang, a patrimonial organization par excellence, has acquired such prominence in Russian public discourse and culture because it reflects the state of Russian society, with the weakness of modern legal and rational order and the preponderance of personalized, networked social forms.

The bandits' code that organizes the gang's social reproduction—poniattia—has become the language of the Russian transition to capitalism. As previously stable structures of Soviet society crumbled and various enterprising networks fought with each other for resources, the mental orientations of militant tribal gangs, encapsulated in the gang code, acquired a prominent place in the sphere of public communication. The dominant groups that formed acquisitive clans developed warrior outlooks and quasi-tribal loyalties, something that the language of poniatiia could express very well. At the same time, the dispossessed saw the prison and criminal cultures as embodying the values of equality and fairness and as providing collective welfare absent elsewhere in society.

The gang's own code is eroding, but the bandits' cultural influence in wider Russian society shows no sign of diminishing. In a Russia still very far from the ideal of a modern society based on the rule of law, the code provides a vocabulary for describing the rule of might, the clan-like relations that thrive at all levels of the social hierarchy, and the brutal masculinity that is still celebrated in mass culture and political behavior.

Conclusion

OUT OF THE SHADOWS?

Having surveyed the evolution of Russian gangs, what can we now say about the gangs themselves and the wider Russian society?

The gangs, warrior alliances of young males, mainly survive in modern society on the edges of the disciplinary power of school, work, and the penal system. They are multifaceted, patrimonial social forms where adolescents learn to be men through camaraderie and violence, and where they explore delinquent thrills and develop various pecuniary projects. In certain historical periods, however, when the structures of state and economy become weakened and destabilized, they can evolve and grow into powerful vehicles of social organization and economic accumulation. This is what happened in the late Soviet Union when a vast shadow economy appeared in the country. Members of the youth street gangs moved in to take advantage of the rise of shadow entrepreneurs and to participate in the division of the spoils. This social reorganization "from below" led to an explosion of violence, to territorial gang wars, and eventually to the emergence of durable neighborhood gangs. These developments took place against the background of growing social differentiation in the Soviet Union and the increasing disappointment of young people with their prospects in the socialist system; for some gang warriors the world of their street brotherhood and the new economic opportunities it now offered began to present an attractive alternative to the boredom of factory work.

In the 1990s the Soviet Union and its systems of employment and enterprise-based welfare collapsed, reducing the opportunities for young people to move into legitimate work or making the prospect of doing so unattractive, given the low pay and insecurity of such employment. At the same time, the gang could be easily mobilized to become a launching pad into a "better" life through organized violence and illicit business schemes. Alternative spaces outside the sphere of state control, with their own localized systems of violent regulation that had previously existed in the margins, now stretched to include the whole of the society. With the systemic destabilization of social life and profound corruption of the police and state bureaucracy, the gang managed to capture control over businesses, acquire significant influence in the community, and penetrate state institutions, with some groups turning into autonomous ruling regimes in their areas.

From the 2000s, with the modernization of the economy and the strengthening of the state, the space that the gangs could occupy contracted. They lost much of their territorial power, but entrepreneurial gangs did not disappear altogether. Instead they adapted and found niches in the multiple interstices between formal and informal, mainstream and shadow economic spheres. Depending on the degree of their inclusion in social networks, the gang members could either resign themselves to criminality or be in a position to exploit every possible opportunity to make a living. The "double helix" model of gang members' transitions to adulthood reflects the persistent features of Russian society, in which formal and informal, legal and criminal forms are closely intertwined.

The long aftermath of the violence unleashed with the collapse of the state socialist system in Russia in the 1990s, with its brutalizing effect on public life and culture, and the persistence of self-serving clans subsuming the modern state and civil society, continues. Expectations that the explosion of organized private violence after the collapse of the Soviet Union would be redeemed by history, as competing violent agents eventually paved the way for the triumph of a law-based state, have proved to be overly optimistic. There does not seem to be a straight path of evolution from a society ruled by primitive violence to one with rational and legal state forms, and we see that clan-like horizontal networks that are bound by personal obligations and material dependencies, and that suppress dissent and retaliate violently against perceived challenges, extend all the way from the world of the streets to the corridors of state power. State enforcers often operate in tandem with leaders of criminal gangs, while violent predatory groups remain firmly entrenched in many Russian regions, particularly in poorer areas that have been left behind by economic development elsewhere and by Russia's integration into the global market.

The gangs remain an integral part of Russian society, and seeing them like this requires a different lens from the one normally used when we look at such organizations. It is common to see the gang as a collection of socially excluded and damaged individuals experiencing some profound deficits (in income, education, social connections, aspirations, positive role models, etc.) and left to survive in the shadow of modern institutions through crime and violence. But if we move our sociological gaze from exclusion to incorporation, we can see that individual gang members are included in various ways both in their groups and in the larger society. They can simultaneously be dangerous outsiders, members of self-serving closed societies, and a part of "us." The way they are treated and the chances of incorporation offered to them can influence whether they move further in one direction or the other.

What does the future hold for the Russian gang? Street life—which previously united generations of young men living in socially and ethnically mixed Soviet neighborhoods—will of course continue, but it will increasingly be relegated to the social and spatial periphery. From being organizations with a relatively broad constituency and reasonably well integrated into wider society, street gangs in these deprived areas will most likely become the domain of excluded young men, uniting low-class and ethnic minority groups who live on the wrong side of the law with little chance of reentering mainstream society. As in other Western and developing societies, the gangs will provide these youths with identity, protection, transgressive pleasures, and sources of illegal income, although involvement in global illegal drug markets—an almost inescapable destiny of youth living in the spaces of exclusion in postindustrialized societies—will most certainly mean that more disruptive and volatile violence will enter the picture and significantly destabilize the community.

In more prosperous urban areas (such as Moscow and Kazan) we are likely to see a variety of coexisting street groups, including street peer groups, territorial elites, and entrepreneurial gangs, all of which will remain a part of the local social fabric. Some organizations, such as street peer groups and territorial elites, will probably have relatively short lives; other groups, including the remnants of those gruppirovki that have existed in the community since at least the end of the 1980s, will find new entrepreneurial niches to exploit. So far, the drug economy has played a relatively small role in these groups' reproduction, although evidence suggests that gang involvement in the drug business is increasing. As long as gang members' engagement in the drug trade remains limited, and as long as members retain their access to legitimate opportunity structures, individual gang members will continue to be able to leave the gang as they grow older or to use the gang as a source of social capital to pursue careers in a variety of areas, where legality and illegality are tightly interwoven.

Far from being some socially isolated and pernicious entity, a collection of parasites emerging out of nowhere to feed on the social body, street gangs have long been part of Russian society. They emerged from neighborhood networks, and their members' tribal attachments have coexisted with much wider social memberships. But whether the future lads will be able to graduate from their youthful associations and become incorporated into the institutions of modern society or whether they will be permanently confined to life in its deeper shadows will depend on factors that are beyond the control of the street youths themselves and that are determined by much wider national and even global processes.

Appendix

DEVELOPMENT OF TATARSTAN GANGS: THREE EXAMPLES

Zhilka

Zhilka emerged in Kazan at the beginning of the 1980s. Its leader, Khaidar Zakirov (Khaider), was born in 1962. The area in which he grew up, Zhilploshchadka, was one of the poorest in the city, populated by recent migrants from rural areas who lived in overcrowded, run-down communal apartments and barracks. Much of Zakirov's childhood and youth took place in the streets. When he was fourteen he was attacked in the courtyard of his building by two drunken hooligans. Zakirov killed one of them. As a minor, under Russian law he received a suspended sentence, and he soon became the informal leader of his street. In 1984 he was convicted of organizing a massive arranged combat against rival gangs at Lake Lebiazhie in which five hundred lads took part. For that he received a six-year sentence in a penal colony. On his release in 1990, Zakirov found a different Russia. The members of his gang had moved into racketeering of street kiosks and outdoor markets. Zakirov, however, had more far-reaching ambitions.

At the beginning of the 1990s, Zakirov organized audacious operations in large-scale theft of produce from the local chemical company Orgsintez. Zhilka started to steal polyethylene powder from rail carriages stationed near the Orgsintez plant and then sell it back to the plant, using connections with friends and relatives who worked at Orgsintez and corrupt officials. These operations allowed his gang to rise and expand quickly. Zakirov was thought to be the first gangster in Tatarstan who forced the management of a large company (in this case Orgsintez) to pay tribute to the gang. Other large companies fell in line. According to the Russian investigative journalist Andrei Konstantinov, company managers would agree to pay right after their first conversation with Zakirov. Nobody reported what was said, but after a conversation with him they left deadly pale. As a result of these "agreements," the bandits started getting around 20 percent of all the companies' profits. By 1993 Zhilka's obshchak held tens of millions of dollars (Konstantinov 2012, 350).

Zakirov created an alliance of eighteen local streets, each with its own leader, and started expanding into other areas of Kazan. He had an ambition to create a single common obshchak into which all the gangs would pay. Although he had many allies, there were gangs that did not agree with this plan, and, after several attempts on his life, he was finally killed in 1996. One of the reasons for the conflict was Zakirov's unwillingness to own a business—the direction in which other gangs were actively moving. When one gangster, Boriskovo avtoritet Lenar Rechapov (Uzkii), offered Zakirov a business partnership, Zakirov replied that he followed a code that did not allow gruppirovshchiki to trade or personally engage in business. This would turn them into *barygi* (traders), an inferior category according to the criminal code. Zakirov told Uzkii that he would now demand money from him as from a *baryga* (Safarov 2012, 106).

Zakirov's death in 1996 at the hands of the rival Sevastopol'skie gang did not put an end to Zhilka's power. Over the course of the 1990s, the leaders of Zhilka established protection over two Kazan banks, a helicopter plant, and a glass-making factory in the neighboring Mari El Republic. The gruppirovka also protected the pharmaceutical company Tatkhimfarmpreparaty, the insurance company Ingosstrakh-Volga, and the building materials company Stroiplast, while its street-level enforcers controlled a casino in the Arena night club and a street market in Kazan. It also had business interests in the Avtovaz automobile plant in Tolyatti (Beliaev and Sheptitskii 2012, 227). Zhilka continues its existence to this day, but it has been significantly weakened by both internal warfare and external challengers, and by a criminal trial that ended in 2010. Its ground-level structures, the youth gangs, still exist and are progressively moving into the drug trade, which was not allowed under Zakirov (263).

Khadi Taktash

The Khadi Taktash gruppirovka has also had a long history, beginning in 1980 as a local street gang. Its leader, Radik Galiakberov (Radzha), was born in 1966. He started his career as an ordinary street lad and then served a spell in a penal colony for minors for hooliganism. Sometime after this, Radzha and his close circle of friends sought to associate themselves with the criminal underworld.

Radzha wanted to join the vory v zakone but was not accepted because of having served in the Soviet Army (prohibited for vory). His close associate, Radik Khusnutdinov (Rakosha), was crowned as a vor v zakone as late as 1996 but was killed soon afterward (Safarov 2012, 117–118). In the early 1990s, conflict developed between two groups of Khadi Taktash members, the older ones, who wanted the gang to live according to the old vory v zakone tradition (which prohibited the accumulation of personal wealth), and the younger ones, who wanted to do "business" unencumbered by the vory's strict code. The vory demanded that the younger members of the gruppirovka share their profits from racketeering. Galiakberov, being on the side of the vory, organized the killing of several criminal avtoritety from the opposing younger faction. Fearing reprisals, he escaped to Moscow together with several associates, and for a while he visited Kazan only occasionally. In 1994 he returned and became the undisputed leader of Khadi Taktash in Kazan. The group "protected" significant segments of the prostitution business and racketeered shops, restaurants, banks, and two cemeteries. They also established control over the spa complex Zdorovie ("Health") and turned it into a brothel. Khadi Taktash actively participated in the drug trade, including heroin and cocaine. Although Khadi Taktash was seriously weakened by its trial in 2002, at which Galiakberov received a life sentence in prison, its youth structures have remained in place in Kazan (Konstantinov 2012, 358).

29th Kompleks

The 29th Kompleks was based in Naberezhnye Chelny. As is common with gangs, its name derives from the housing development in the city where most of the initial members lived.

The 29th Kompleks started its business operations in the late 1980s and early 1990s by muscling into the system of sales of spare parts for KAMAZ trucks. It then moved on to more substantial financial control of KAMAZ. The gang's leadership (Adygan Saliakhov, Yuri Eremenko, and Aleksander Vlasov) created companies that traded in KAMAZ vehicles, earning a percentage from every sale. The gang also controlled the company's soccer club (likewise called KAMAZ).

Like many other Tatarstan gangs, it expanded its operations into Moscow, at first "helping" local companies to collect unpaid debts. Eventually, it came to control many commercial companies in the Russian capital and in other areas. It set up kryshy for alcohol-producing companies in Tatarstan, the Udmurt Republic, and Kirov Oblast and was involved in the distribution of vodka, which was produced in companies under its control and unreported to the tax authorities, to affiliated shops and restaurants. In Moscow Oblast it "protected" meat-producing farms and processing companies and a soy food processing factory. The gang also set kryshy for large food markets and hotel chains in various cities. It ran protection rackets on several stretches of the motorway linking Samara and Ufa, where it received tribute from the owners of kiosks, cafes, gas stations, and other companies that did their business by the roadside. The gang controlled a mineral water producing facility in Nikolaev (Ukraine) and offshore companies in Cyprus. It took part in a gang alliance running a protection racket in the Sevastopol'skaia Hotel in Moscow and established various fictitious companies for the purpose of money laundering. In many of the companies that the gang protected, it established control over the finances. The gang often moved from taxing the profits of a company to establishing ownership or part-ownership through bribing corrupt state officials and fraud. For nominal sums, it acquired the shares of state companies that were being privatized. In order to appropriate the Elabuga meat processing plant, for example, the gang created a company with founding capital of 2,000 rubles (around $70). Through various machinations, it eventually acquired 85.25 percent of the plant, with the enterprise's assets reaching a value of 500 million rubles in 2000 (Nafikov 2012). In a series of criminal trials that started in 2004 and ended in 2013 the majority of the avtoritety of 29th Kompleks received lengthy prison sentences.

Key to Interviewees

GANG INTERVIEWEES, KAZAN, JUNE–SEPTEMBER 2005

Aidar, 29, Russian, higher education, businessman
Ansar, 21, Tatar, university student (finance)
Anvar, 17, Tatar, secondary education, unemployed
Arkadii, 25, Russian, university student (management), part-time worker in the family business
Banan, 23, Tatar, higher education, odd jobs
Bogdan, 23, Russian, secondary education, unemployed
David, 29, Russian, doctor and businessman
Farit, 20, Tatar, university student (physics), owner of several stalls at the market
Garik, 24, Tatar, university student (engineering)
Grisha, 23, Russian, university student (agriculture), part-time factory worker
Il'nar, 35, Tatar, secondary vocational education, casual laborer
Il'sur, 26, Tatar, higher education, worker in private security company
Ispug, 26, Tatar, higher education, lawyer
Kolia, 23, Russian, secondary vocational education, loader
Koshmar, 23, Tatar, higher education, musician
Kirill, 25, Russian, secondary education, car mechanic
Maksim, 21, Russian, secondary vocational education, driver in a construction company
Nafik, 27, Tatar, secondary vocational education, engineer
Nemets, 25, Tatar, higher education, worker in an oil company
Pavel, 18, Russian, university student (teaching college), odd jobs
Petia, 23, Russian, secondary vocational education, ex-gang member, factory worker
Potap, 23, Russian, incomplete secondary education, unemployed
Radik, 18, Tatar, university student (taxation)
Risat, 24, Tatar, ex-gang member, higher education, lawyer
Seva, 22, Russian, secondary education, unemployed
Tadjik, 19, Tatar, university student
Trofim, 21, Russian, university student (technology), engineer in a computer company
Tsigan, 24, Tatar, higher education, part-owner of a construction company
Tuigun, 20, Tatar, university student (aviation)
Viktor, 17, Russian, vocational school student
Vlad, 20, Russian, secondary vocational education, self-employed (construction)
Zhenia, 24, Russian, secondary vocational education, food shop owner

EXPERT INTERVIEWEES, KAZAN, JUNE–SEPTEMBER 2005

A. Head of investigation department of a Kazan police precinct

B. Investigator, Tatarstan Republican Prosecution Service

D. Deputy head of the Group for Prevention of Crime among Minors in a Kazan police precinct

E. Investigator in a Kazan police precinct

F. Former school psychologist, Kazan

K. Head of the Group for Prevention of Crime among Minors in a Kazan police precinct

M. Deputy head of Investigations in a Kazan police precinct

MK. School psychologist, Kazan

MT. Investigator in a Kazan police precinct

N. Investigator in a Kazan police precinct

O. Schoolteacher, Kazan

MOSCOW FOCUS GROUPS 2006 (CITED PARTICIPANTS)

Alexei, 16
Andrei, 15
Boris, 16
Dmitrii, 17
Ivan, 16
Konstantin, 17
Marat, 15
Mikhail, 17
Vadim, 13

CITED KAZAN INTERVIEWEES 2011

Airat, 17, local resident
Alik, 17, local resident
K. Owner of an office supplies company
L. Owner of a pharmaceutical company
Nikita, 42, former gang member
Nikolai, 18, local resident
R. Taxi driver
S. Taxi driver

Methodological Note

The fieldwork for this book took place in Kazan and Moscow. The study in Kazan was conducted in 2005. It involved thirty-two semistructured interviews with members of various gangs across the city. The interviewees were males between seventeen and thirty-five, reflecting the male character of street gangs, whose rules explicitly prohibit female membership. They were of both Russian and Tatar ethnicity. The interviews were tape-recorded and transcribed. Interviews were also conducted with former gang members, local young people who were not members of gangs, teachers and school psychologists, and representatives of the police (*militia*) and the Prokuratura (State Prosecution Service). All of the interviewees gave informed consent. Gang members were assured that neither they nor their gangs would be identified in the transcripts and research outputs. (All gang members' names have been changed.) The lack of focus on specific named gangs helped overcome a potential pitfall of gang research—that of glamorizing gang activities and building the gangs' "brands" (Klein 1971; Aldridge, Medina-Ariza, and Ralphs 2008). As trust was a crucial issue for the interviews, we did not ask our interviewees direct questions about the business activities of their gangs and their own criminal pursuits. Nevertheless, many volunteered such information and were especially open when it came to describing group violent practices.

Access to interviewees—gang members—was achieved by building on initial contacts with local residents, friends, neighbors, relatives, and former schoolmates of the researchers. The fact that the principal field investigator in our Kazan project, Rustem Safin, also lived at the research site where gangs were endemic meant that that there were some shared understandings of the local context, as well mutual acquaintances and friends. Obviously, interviewing gang members can be fraught with danger, and here the researcher's local "reputation" was an invaluable asset, a form of social capital that would otherwise be difficult to build. My Kazan colleagues also asked their university students, some of whom were current or former gang members, to help with getting access to gang interviewees.

In the interviews, gang members talked about their groups repeatedly as normal members of the community who fight against *bespredel* (lawlessness). These narratives may have been partly influenced by the desire of the interviewees to present themselves and their groups in a positive light. Whether the gang members themselves wholeheartedly believed in this legitimizing discourse is hard to say. They also downplayed the "criminal" side of their business. Some of the elements of their reports may have questionable veracity. What is important, however, is that these constructions were echoed by many of the local residents and even agents of state power. The gangs were perceived not merely as a source of violence and danger (although this discourse was also present in the interviews) but also as a "necessary evil," an agent of social regulation in a situation in which the state was weak, inefficient, and corrupt. In other words, irrespective of the actual veracity of these legitimizing narratives, their very existence is indicative of the ways in which the role and functions of the gangs are constructed by both their members and by members of the wider society (see also Ries 2002). In 2011 I returned to Kazan and conducted additional interviews with former gang members, businessmen, taxi drivers, and local residents.

Because one of the key foci of my research was on the social roots of criminal gangs, and in particular the imperatives of street culture that influence many of the dispositions of gang members, I decided to expand the research to a study of territorial groups that are not involved in organized criminality. This part of the study took place in Moscow from June to September 2006. Together with Rustem Maksudov, I conducted twenty-three in-depth interviews with members of street peer groups from a variety of peripheral areas of Moscow. The participants were between twelve and seventeen. The interviews took place in young people's homes and on the streets. Access to interviewees was achieved using the snowballing technique. We also conducted six focus groups with members of territorial groups, all of which took place in a school for juvenile delinquents in the South-Eastern Administrative Okrug of Moscow. The school is an "educational institution of a closed type." It belongs to the Moscow Department of Education. Its students are referred to it by courts for minor offences (mainly hooliganism and theft) as an alternative to criminal punishment. Each focus group consisted of six to eight people. All of the interviews and focus groups were tape-recorded and transcribed. All interviewees gave their informed consent to be interviewed.

We encountered many practical and ethical issues in the course of our research. The expediency of conducting focus groups in an institution, for example, needed to be counterbalanced with the unavoidable issues around trust. We sought to resolve this by first conducting participant observation in the school and establishing preliminary contact with most of the focus group participants. Focus groups themselves proved to be a very good method for accessing collective representations of street life and norms of violent conduct. Often, after initial hesitation, young people gave each other implicit permission to talk about topics that would otherwise be morally proscribed and avoided. The practices of violence were recounted with particular animation. Some of the stories of the young people's street pursuits, and the accounts of their strict subordination to codes of honor, may have had problematic veracity; however, we were mainly interested in understanding the meanings of different practices for young people (see also Graue, Walsh, and Ceglowski 1998, 120). In my analysis I have given greater credence to what was said when the young people were reliving their street experiences than to some of their other accounts such as their personal histories of law breaking.

Glossary

Throughout the book I have adopted the convention of using Russian terms in italics with English explanations in parenthesis where they first occur. For words that are used frequently I dispense with italics after the first use. In addition, I have chosen to use the English translations: "lad" (in Russian: *patsan*, a colloquial term used generally for a young man or boy and, more specifically, a young gang member or a member of a street organization) and "street" (in Russian: *ulitsa*, here meaning street group).

Russian	Description/Context
avtoritet/avtoritety	"authority"—member(s) of the leadership of a gang
bandit/bandity	"bandit"—adult member(s) of a gang
baryga/barygi	trader(s)
bespredel	lawlessness, chaos, anarchy, unregulated violence
bespredelshchik	person who uses violence indiscriminately
blat	informal exchange
botanik	"botanist"—a young person who is not streetwise
bratva	"brotherhood"— gang members
brigada	"brigade"—the basic unit of a gang (see also semeika)
byk, byki	"bull(s)," gang members who do violent work
chukhan, chushpan	young man who is not streetwise (not a gang member)
deliuga/deliugi	criminal operation(s), hustle or scam
dvor	courtyard
dvorovye kompanii	courtyard groups
fartsovka	black market trading in goods often bought from foreigners
firma/firmy	"firm(s)," gang(s)
gopnik/gopniki	thug, hooligan, derogatory name for working-class youth(s)—often used as a synonym for gang member(s)
gruppirovka/gruppirovki	large gang(s)
gruppirovshchik/gruppirovshchiki	member(s) of a gruppirovka
gruzit'	to persuade (literally "to weigh down")
khrushchevka/khrushchevki	low-cost apartment block(s) introduced during the Khrushchev era in the late 1950s and early 1960s
kidalovo	deception
komers/komersy	businessman

Komsomol	Soviet youth organization
kontora/kontory	gang(s)
krysha/kryshy	"roof(s)"—private protection
kryshevanie	protection operation
liuber/liubery	member(s) of the Liubertsy youth subculture in the 1980s
lokh/lokhi	prison or gang term used to describe civilian(s) or "commoner(s)" who can be harassed and victimized
mazhor	young person from a well-off family
militia	term used for "police" in the Soviet Union and Russia up to 2011
motanie	gang lifestyle
motalka/motalki	gang
neformal/neformaly	member of a noncriminal youth subculture
obshchak/obshchaki	common fund/treasury held by a criminal group
organizovannaia prestupnaia gruppa (OPG)	organized criminal group
organizivannoe prestupnoe soobshchestvo (OPS)	organized criminal community, alliance of organized criminal groups
otmorozok/otmorozki	"thawed-out"—a hooligan, a person who violates the normative limits on violence
otvetka (or *obratka)*	return (or revenge) fight
patsan/patsany	"lad" —used generally for a young man or boy and, more specifically, a young gang member or a member of a street organization
poniatie/poniatiia	(mutual) "understanding(s)"—rule(s) of conduct in criminal communities, now commonly used to describe informal conventions or rules.
professional'no-tekhnicheskoe uchilishche (PTU)	vocational school
Prokuratura	State Prosecution Service
razborka	showdown between gangs
razvod	extortion/deception
semeika/semeiki	"family," in prison a group sharing one cell or barrack, but also the basic unit of a gang (see also brigada)
shchemit'	"to oppress"—a term used to describe protection operations and extortion
silovye struktury	the coercive agencies of the state (e.g., the police, military, security services, customs)
silovik/siloviki	"enforcers," member(s) of the silovye struktury
skhodniak	gang meeting

sladkii	"sweet one," a repeat victim of extortion
smotriashchii/smotriashchie	"overseer(s)" supervising a unit within the gang or the whole gang
smotriashchii za obshchakom	overseer of a common fund
strelka/strelki or *strela/strely*	meeting(s) arranged to resolve disputes
terpila	"sufferer," someone who has accepted their victimization
tochka/tochki	small business overseen by a gang
tsekhovik/tsekhoviki	Soviet-era managers of state companies who engaged in off-the-books production and distribution
tselevik	"purposeful one," a young man who tries to develop contacts with criminals in order to join their groups
ulitsa	"street"—a street gang
vor/vory (or *vor v zakone / vory v zakone)*	"thief" or "thief-in-law," a member of Russia's professional criminal society
zagruzka	conversational dominance based on the gangs' code
zikher	transgression (i.e., an act in contravention of the code)
zona	"the zone"—collective name for Soviet/Russian prisons and labor camps

References

Abadinsky, Howard. 1994. *Organized Crime.* 4th ed. Chicago: Nelson-Hall.

Abramkin, V. 2007. "Bratstvo kak strategiia." *Smysl* 11:105–7.

Adamson, Christopher. 2000. "Defensive Localism in White and Black: A Comparative History of European-American and Africo-American Gangs." *Ethnic and Racial Studies* 23 (2): 272–98.

Ageeva, L.V. 1991. *Kazanskii fenomen: mif i real'nost'.* Kazan: Tatarskoe knizhnoe izdatel'stvo.

Akbarov, N. G. 1999. *Sostoianie i tendentsii prestupnosti nesovershennoletnikh. Regional'nye problemy bor'by i profilaktiki.* Kazan: Izdatel'stvo Kazanskogo universiteta.

Aksakov, S. T. 1955. *Sobranie sochinenii.* Vol. 2. Moscow: Gosudarstvennoe izdatel'stvo khudozhestvennoi literatury.

Aldridge, Judith, Juanjo Medina-Ariza, and Robert Ralphs. 2008. "Dangers and Problems of Doing 'Gang' Research in the UK." In *Street Gangs, Migration and Ethnicity,* ed. F. v. Gemert, D. Peterson, and I.-L. Lien, 31–46. Cullompton, UK: Willan.

Anderson, Elijah. 1990. *Streetwise: Race, Class, and Change in an Urban Community.* Chicago: University of Chicago Press.

——. 1999. *Code of the Street: Decency, Violence, and the Moral Life of the Inner City.* New York: Norton.

Antipin, Vladimir. 2011. "Beshenye eritrotsity." *Russkii reporter* (January 19).

Antipin, Vladimir, Victor Diatlikovich, and Maxim Gladkii. 2010. "Likhie devianostye vozvrashchaiutsia: grozit li Rossii novaia volna banditizma i kto s nei budet borotsia." *Russkii reporter* (October 7).

Anzhirov, Igor' Viktorovich. 2010. "Strukturnye osobennosti i spetsifika deiatel'nosti etnicheskikh prestupnykh soobshchestv v sovremennoi Rossii." *Obshchestvo: politika, ekonomika, pravo* 2:7–13.

Arendt, Hannah. 1972. "On Violence." In *Crises of the Republic: Lying in Politics, Civil Disobedience, On Violence, Thoughts on Politics and Revolution.* New York: Harcourt Brace Jovanovich.

Arias, Enrique Desmond. 2006a. *Drugs and Democracy in Rio de Janeiro: Trafficking, Social Networks, and Public Security.* Chapel Hill: University of North Carolina Press.

——. 2006b. "Trouble en Route: Drug Trafficking and Clientelism in Rio de Janeiro Shantytowns." *Qualitative Sociology* 29 (4): 427–45.

Arias, Enrique Desmond, and Daniel M. Goldstein. 2010. *Violent Democracies in Latin America.* Durham: Duke University Press.

Arlacchi, Pino. 1983. *Mafia, Peasants and Great Estates: Society in Traditional Calabria.* Cambridge: Cambridge University Press.

——. 1986. *Mafia Business: The Mafia Ethic and the Spirit of Capitalism.* London: Verso.

——. 1988. "Some Observations on Illegal Markets." In *The New European Criminology,* ed. V. Ruggerio, Nigel South, and Ian Taylor, 203–15. London: Routledge.

Baal', E. G. 1990. "Problemy kriminologicheskogo izucheniia neformalnykh grupp, ob'edinenii, dvizhenii." In *Kriminologi o neformalnykh molodezhnykh ob'edineniiakh,* ed. I. I. Karpets, 130–43. Moscow: Iuridicheskaia literatura.

——. 1991. "V konflikte s zakonom." In *Po nepisannym zakonam ulitsy*, ed. K. Igoshev and G. Min'kovskii, 35–40. Moscow: Iuridicheskaia literatura.

Baldaev, D. S., and A. Plutser-Sarno. 2003. *Russian Criminal Tattoo Encyclopaedia*. Göttingen, DE: Steidl-Fuel.

Ball, Alan M. 1994. *And Now My Soul Is Hardened: Abandoned Children in Soviet Russia, 1918–1930*. Berkeley: University of California Press.

Barker, Gary. 2005. *Dying to Be Men: Youth, Masculinity and Social Exclusion*. London: Routledge.

Batchelor, Susan. 2009. "Girls, Gangs and Violence: Assessing the Evidence." *Probation Journal* 56 (4): 399–414.

Bayart, Jean-François. 1999. "'The 'Social Capital' of the Felonious State or the Ruses of Political Intelligence." In *The Criminalization of the State in Africa*, ed. J.-F. Bayart, S. Ellis, and B. Hibou, 32–48. Oxford: J. Currey.

——. 2009. *The State in Africa: The Politics of the Belly*. 2nd ed. Cambridge: Polity.

Bayart, Jean-François, Stephen Ellis, and Beatrice Hibou. 1999. "Introduction." In *The Criminalization of the State in Africa*, ed. J.-F. Bayart, S. Ellis, and B. Hibou, xiii–xviii. Oxford: J. Currey.

Becucci, Stefano. 2011. "Criminal Infiltration and Social Mobilisation against the Mafia. Gela: A City between Tradition and Modernity." *Global Crime* 12 (1): 1–18.

Belanovsky, Sergei. 1990. "Subkultura liuberov." *Personal Website of Sergei Belanovsky*. http://sbelan.ru/node/47796, accessed July 30, 2013.

——. 2009. "'Zhdan" i 'kommunary' (konets 1980-kh godov)". In *Molodezhnye ulichnye gruppirovki: vvedenie v problematiku*, ed. D.V. Gromov, 124–31. Moscow: IEA RAN.

Beliaev, Maksim, and Andrei Sheptitskii. 2012. *Banditskaia Kazan*. Vol. 1. Kazan: Tatpoligraf.

Belkovskii, Stanislav. 2014. "Putin—respekt i uvazhukha." *Colta.ru* (March 24). http://www.colta.ru/articles/society/2576, accessed May 1 2014.

Bell, Catherine. 1992. *Ritual Theory, Ritual Practice*. New York: Oxford University Press.

Bernshtam, T. A. 1988. *Molodezh v obriadovoi zhisni russkoi obshchiny XIX–nachala XX veka: polovozrastnoi aspekt traditsionnoi kultury*. Leningrad: Nauka.

Beumers, Birgit, and Mark Lipovetsky. 2009. *Performing Violence: Literary and Theatrical Experiments of New Russian Drama*. Bristol, UK: Intellect.

Biznesonline. 2010. "V spisok samykh bogatykh rossiian popali bratia Khairulliny, Radik Shaimiev i Al'bert Shigabutdinov." *Business-gazeta* (February 20). http://www.business-gazeta.ru/text/20672/, accessed March 1, 2011.

——. 2012. "Takie gruppirovki byli v kazhdom dvore . . ." *Business-gazeta* (June 21). http://www.business-gazeta.ru/article/61546/, accessed July 21, 2012.

Bliakher, Leonid. 2012. "Regionalnye barony." *Otechestvennye zapiski* 48 (3). http://magazines.russ.ru/oz/2012/3/b49.html, accessed May 1, 2014.

Blok, Anton. 1974. *The Mafia of a Sicilian Village, 1860–1960: A Study of Violent Peasant Entrepreneurs*. Oxford: Blackwell.

Borenstein, Eliot. 2008. *Overkill: Sex and Violence in Contemporary Russian Popular Culture*. Ithaca: Cornell University Press.

Bourdieu, Pierre. 1977. "Symbolic Power." In *Identity and Structure: Issues in the Sociology of Education*, ed. D. Gleeson, 112–19. Driffield, UK: Nafferton.

——. 1984. *Distinction: A Social Critique of the Judgement of Taste*. Cambridge: Harvard University Press.

Bourdieu, Pierre, and Loïc Wacquant. 1992. *An Invitation to Reflexive Sociology*. Chicago: University of Chicago Press.

Bourgois, Philippe I. 1995. *In Search of Respect: Selling Crack in El Barrio*. Cambridge: Cambridge University Press.

——. 2004. "The Continuum of Violence in War and Peace: Post-Cold War Lessons from El Salvador." In *Violence in War and Peace: An Anthology*, ed. N. Scheper-Hughes and P. I. Bourgois, 425–33. Malden, MA: Blackwell.

Breslavsky, Anatoliy. 2009. "Youth and 'the Movement'—Social Life in a Rural District of Buryatia." *Inner Asia* 11 (1): 83–95.

Broadcasting. 2014. "Teleserial *Fizruk* prodlen na vtoroi sezon" (May 6). http://www.broadcasting.ru/newstext.php?news_id = 99920, accessed May 18, 2014.

Brotherton, David, and Luis Barrios. 2004. *The Almighty Latin King and Queen Nation: Street Politics and the Transformation of a New York City Gang.* New York: Columbia University Press.

Bushuev, Aleksei. 2009. *Razvitie politicheskogo soznaniia molodezhy Respubliki Tatarstan v 1985–2004 godakh. Istoriko-sotsiologicheskii aspekt.* Kazan: Kazanskii Kreml'.

Caldwell, Melissa L. 2004. *Not by Bread Alone: Social Support in the New Russia.* Berkeley: University of California Press.

Campbell, Anne. 1991. *The Girls in the Gang.* 2nd ed. Cambridge, MA: B. Blackwell.

Canetti, Elias. 1973. *Crowds and Power:* Harmondsworth, UK: Penguin.

Castells, Manuel. 2001. *The Internet Galaxy: Reflections on Internet, Business, and Society.* Oxford: Oxford University Press.

Catanzaro, Raimondo. 1992. *Men of Respect: A Social History of the Sicilian Mafia.* New York: Free Press.

Cederstrom, Carl, and Peter Fleming. 2012. *Dead Man Working.* Winchester, UK: Zero Books.

Chalidze, Valerii I. 1977. *Criminal Russia: Essays on Crime in the Soviet Union.* New York: Random House.

Chekhonadskikh, Maria. 2012. "Trudnosti perevoda: prekaritet v teorii i na praktike." *Khudozhestvennyi zhurnal* 79–80. http://xz.gif.ru/numbers/79–80/chekhonadskih, accessed May 1, 2013.

Cheloukhine, Serguei. 2008. "The Roots of Russian Organized Crime: From Old-Fashioned Professionals to the Organized Criminal Groups of Today." *Crime, Law and Social Change* 50:353–74.

Cheloukhine, Serguei, and M. R. Haberfeld. 2011. *Russian Organized Corruption Networks and Their International Trajectories.* New York: Springer.

Chernysh, M. 2003. "Social Mobility Patterns and Life Strategies of Young People in Contemporary Russia." In *From Pacesetters to Dropouts: Post-Soviet Youth in Comparative Perspective,* ed. T. R. Horowitz, B. Kotik-Friedgut, and S. Hoffman, 27–41. Lanham, MD: University Press of America.

Chesney-Lind, Meda, and John M. Hagedorn. 1999. *Female Gangs in America: Essays on Girls, Gangs and Gender.* Chicago: Lake View Press.

Clarke, Simon. 1999. "Poverty in Russia." *Problems of Economic Transition* 42 (5): 5–55.

——. 2002. *Making Ends Meet in Contemporary Russia: Secondary Employment, Subsidiary Agriculture and Social Networks.* Cheltenham, UK: Edward Elgar.

Clausewitz, Carl von. 2005 [1873]. *On War*, trans. J. J. Graham. London: Routledge.

Clement, Carine. 2007. "Fleksibilnost' po-rossiiski: ocherk o novykh formakh truda i podchineniia v sphere uslug." *Sotsioligicheskii zhurnal* 4:74–96.

Cloward, Richard Andrew, and Lloyd Edgar Ohlin. 1961. *Delinquency and Opportunity: A Theory of Delinquent Gangs.* London: Routledge & Kegan Paul.

Cohen, Albert Kircidel. 1955. *Delinquent Boys: The Culture of the Gang.* Glencoe, IL: Free Press.

Cohen, Stanley. 1972. *Folk Devils and Moral Panics: The Creation of the Mods and Rockers.* London: MacGibbon & Kee.

Collins, Randall. 1988. "The Durkheimian Tradition in Conflict Sociology." In *Durkheimian Sociology: Cultural Studies,* ed. J. Alexander, 107–28. Cambridge: Cambridge University Press.

——. 2004. *Interaction Ritual Chains.* Princeton Studies in Cultural Sociology. Princeton: Princeton University Press.

——. 2008. *Violence: A Micro-Sociological Theory.* Princeton: Princeton University Press.

——. 2011. "Patrimonial Alliances and Failures of State Penetration." *Annals of the American Academy of Political and Social Science* 636 (1): 16–31.

Connell, Raewyn. 2005. *Masculinities.* 2nd ed. Cambridge: Polity.

Connell, Raewyn, and James Messerschmidt. 2005. "Hegemonic Masculinity: Rethinking the Concept." *Gender and Society* 19 (6): 829–59.

Connell, Robert. 1987. *Gender and Power: Society, the Person, and Sexual Politics.* Cambridge: Polity.

Connor, Walter D. 1972. *Deviance in Soviet Society: Crime, Delinquency, and Alcoholism.* New York: Columbia University Press.

Conquergood, Dwight. 1994. "Homeboys and Hoods: Gang Communication and Cultural Space." In *Group Communication in Context: Studies of Natural Groups,* ed. L. R. Frey, 23–55. Hillsdale, NJ: L. Erlbaum.

Cremin, Colin. 2011. *Capitalism's New Clothes: Enterprise, Ethics and Enjoyment in Times of Crisis.* London: Pluto.

Decker, Scott H., and Barrik Van Winkle. 1996. *Life in the Gang: Family, Friends, and Violence.* Cambridge: Cambridge University Press.

Deleuze, Gilles, and Felix Guattari. 1983. *Anti-Oedipus: Capitalism and Schizophrenia.* London: Continuum.

——. 2004. *A Thousand Plateaus: Capitalism and Schizophrenia.* London: Continuum.

Delphi. 2011. "Rossiia i strany Baltii—tikhaia perezagruzka otnoshenii" (July 4). http://ru.delfi.lt/opinions/comments/rossiya-i-strany-baltii-tihaya-perezagruzka-otnoshenij.d?id = 47253995, accessed July 15, 2011.

Densley, James A. 2013. *How Gangs Work: An Ethnography of Youth Violence.* New York: Palgrave Macmillan.

Dobson, Miriam. 2009. *Khrushchev's Cold Summer: Gulag Returnees, Crime, and the Fate of Reform after Stalin.* Ithaca: Cornell University Press.

Dolgova, A. 2003. *Prestupnost', ee organizovannost' i kriminal'noe obshchestvo.* Moscow: Moskovskaia kriminologicheskaia assotsiatsiia.

——. 2004. *Prestupnost' v Rossii nachala 21 veka i reagirovanie na nee.* Moscow: Moskovskaia kriminologicheskaia assotsiatsiia.

Downes, David M. 1966. *The Delinquent Solution: A Study in Subcultural Theory.* London: Routledge & Kegan Paul.

Du Gay, Paul. 1996. *Consumption and Identity at Work.* London: Sage.

Dubovitskii, Natan. 2009. *Okolonolia.* Moscow: Media-gruppa "Zhivi."

Durkheim, Emile. 1915. *The Elementary Forms of the Religious Life: A Study in Religious Sociology,* trans. J. W. Swain. London: George Allen & Unwin.

——. 1933 [1893]. *The Division of Labor in Society,* trans. G. Simmon. Glencoe, IL: Free Press.

——. 1938. *The Rules of Sociological Method*, trans. G. Simmon. New York: Free Press.

Eisenstadt, S. N. 1956. "Ritualized Personal Relations: Blood Brotherhood, Compadre, Etc.: Some Comparative Hypotheses and Suggestions." *Man* 96:90–95.

Elias, Norbert. 1978. *The Civilizing Process.* New York: Urizen Books.

Ermakov, V. D. 1990. "Dosug, uchoba i protivopravnoe povedenie." In *Kriminologi o neformalnykh molodezhnykh ob'edineniiakh,* ed. I. I. Karpets, 238–47. Moscow: Iuridicheskaia literatura.

Eruslanov, Oleg. 2014. "Fin podoshel Prokurature po vsem stat'iam." *Kommersant* (January 8). http://www.kommersant.ru/doc/2380687, accessed January 20, 2014.

Esbensen, Finn-Aage, Dana Peterson, Terrance J. Terrance, and Adrienne Freng. 2009. "Similarities and Differences in Risk Factors for Violent Offending and Gang Membership." *Australian and New Zealand Journal of Criminology* 3:310–35.

Fagan, Jeffrey. 1989. "The Social Organization of Drug Use and Drug Dealing among Urban Gangs." *Criminology* 27: 633–69.

Farrington, David P. 2000. "Explaining and Preventing Crime: The Globalization of Knowledge." *Criminology* 38:1–24.

Favarel-Garrigues, Gilles, and Anne Le Huérou. 2004. "State and the Multilateralization of Policing in Post-Soviet Russia." *Policing and Society* 14 (1): 13–30.

Fedorenko, Maksim, and Sergei Sleptsov. 2010. "Kushchevskii sindrom Rossii: prestupnye gruppirovki sroslis' s militsiei i diktuiut pravila zhisni." *Agumenty i fakty* (December 1). http://www.aif.ru/incidents/22112, accessed December 2, 2010.

Ferrell, Jeff, and Clinton Sanders. 1995. *Cultural Criminology.* Boston: Northeastern University Press.

Filin, Anton. 2012. "V Ul'ianovske deistvuiet 16 prestupnykh gruppirovok." *mosaica.ru* (August 1). http://mosaica.ru/actual/2012/08/01/257, accessed July 20, 2013.

Filippov, F. P. 1989. *Ot pokoleniia k pokoleniiu. sotsial'naia podvizhnost'.* Moscow: Mysl'.

Finckenauer, James O., and Y. A. Voronin. 2001. *The Threat of Russian Organized Crime.* Washington, DC: US Department of Justice.

Fürst, Juliane. 2008. "Between Salvation and Liquidation: Homeless and Vagrant Children and the Reconstruction of Soviet Society." *Slavonic and East European Review* 86 (2): 232–58.

——. 2010. *Stalin's Last Generation: Soviet Post-War Youth and the Emergence of Mature Socialism.* Oxford: Oxford University Press.

Gainullin, Anton. 2013. "Gopniki v Kazani: kak sebia vesti s nimi." *Pro Kazan.ru.* http://live.prokazan.ru/live/view/135, accessed July 29, 2013.

Galeotti, Mark. 2000. "The Russian Mafiya: Economic Penetration at Home and Abroad." In *Economic Crime in Russia,* ed. A. V. Ledeneva and M. Kurkchiyan, 31–42. The Hague: Kluwer Law International.

——. 2006. "The Criminalisation of Russian State Security." *Global Crime* 7 (3–4): 471–86.

——. 2008. "The World of the Lower Depths: Crime and Punishment in Russian History." *Global Crime* 9 (1): 84–107.

——. 2012. "Transnational Aspects of Russian Organized Crime." Russia and Eurasia Programme meeting summary. *Chatham House* (July 17). http://www.chathamhouse.org/sites/files/chathamhouse/public/Research/Russia%20and%20Eurasia/170712summary.pdf, accessed June 18, 2013.

Gallant, Thomas W. 1999. "Brigandage, Piracy, Capitalism and State Formation." In *States and Illegal Practices,* ed. J. M. Heyman. Oxford: Berg.

Gambetta, Diego. 1993. *The Sicilian Mafia: The Business of Private Protection.* Cambridge: Harvard University Press.

——. 2009. *Codes of the Underworld: How Criminals Communicate.* Princeton: Princeton University Press.

Garfinkel, Harold. 1967. *Studies in Ethnomethodology.* Englewood Cliffs, NJ: Prentice-Hall.

Garland, David. 1985. *Punishment and Welfare: A History of Penal Strategies.* Aldershot, UK: Gower.

Garot, Robert. 2010. *Who You Claim: Performing Gang Identity in School and on the Streets.* New York: New York University Press.

Gataullin, A. F., and R. R. Maksudov. 2002. "Transformatsiia form organizatsii podrostkov: materialy issledovaniia, provedennogo v 1992–1993 godakh Sotsiologicheskoi laboratoriei Kazanskogo Gosudarstvennogo universiteta." *Vestnik Vosstanovitel'noi Iustitsii* 4: 17–26.

Geraci, Robert P. 2001. *Window on the East: National and Imperial Identities in Late Tsarist Russia.* Ithaca: Cornell University Press.

Gerber, Theodore P., and Sarah E. Mendelson. 2008. "Public Experiences of Police Violence and Corruption in Contemporary Russia: A Case of Predatory Policing." *Law and Society Review* 42 (1): 1–43.

Gilinsky, Yakov. 2006. "Crime in Contemporary Russia." *European Journal of Criminology* 3 (3): 259–92.

——. 2007. "Women in Organized Crime in Russia." In *Women and the Mafia: Female Roles in Organized Crime Structures,* ed. G. Fiandaca, 225–34. New York: Springer.

Girard, René. 2005. *Violence and the Sacred.* London: Continuum.

Glazov, Yuri. 1976. "'Thieves' in the USSR—a Social Phenomenon." *Survey* 22:141–56.

Goffman, Erving. 1953. "Communication Conduct in an Island Community." PhD diss., University of Chicago.

——. 1967. Where the Action Is. In *Interaction Ritual,* ed. E. Goffman. 149–270. Harmondsworth, UK: Penguin.

Goldman, Wendy Z. 1993. *Women, the State and the Revolution: Soviet Family Policy and Social Life, 1917–1933.* Cambridge: Cambridge University Press.

Goldstein, Paul. 1985. The Drugs/Violence Nexus: A Tripartite Conceptual Framework. *Journal of Drug Issues* 39:143–74.

Golovin, V. V., and M. L. Lurie. 2005. "Boi na mostu, ili s kem voiuiut podrostki." In *Mir i voina: kulturnye konteksty sotsialnoi agressii,* ed. I. O. Ermachenko and L. P. Repina, 127–34. Moscow: IVI RAN.

——. 2008. "Ideologicheskie i territorialnye soobshchestva molodezhi: megapolis, provintsialnii gorod, selo." *Etnograficheskoe obozrenie* 1:56–70.

Gorsuch, Anne E. 2000. *Youth in Revolutionary Russia: Enthusiasts, Bohemians, and Delinquents* Bloomington: Indiana University Press.

Graue, M. Elizabeth, Daniel J. Walsh, and Deborah Ceglowski. 1998. *Studying Children in Context: Theories, Methods, and Ethics.* Thousand Oaks, CA: Sage.

Gromov, D. V. 2006. "Liuberetskie ulichnye molodezhnye kompanii 1980-kh godov: subkul'tura na pereput'e istorii." *Etnograficheskoe obozrenie* 4: 23–38.

——. 2009. "Podrostkovo-molodezhnye ulichnye gruppirovki kak ob'ekt etnograficheskogo issledovaniia." In *Molodezhnye ulichnye gruppirovki: vvedenie v problematiku,* ed. D.V. Gromov, 8–72. Moscow: IEA RAN.

Gromov, D. V., and S. A. Stephenson. 2008. "Patsanskie pravila: normirovanie povedeniia v ulichnykh gruppirovkakh." In *Molodye moskvichi: krosskulturnoe issledovanie,* ed. M. I. Martynova and N. M. Lebedeva, 427–56. Moscow: RUDN.

Grossman, Gregory. 1977. "The 'Second Economy' of the USSR." *Problems of Communism* 26 (5): 25–40.

Gurov, A. 1990. *Professionalnaia prestupnost'.* Moscow: Iuridicheskaia literatura.

Haavio-Mannila, Elina. 1958. *Kylätappelut: Sosiologinen Tutkimus Suomen Kylätappeluinstituutiosta* [with a summary in English entitled "Village Fights"]. Helsinki: Porvoo.

Hagedorn, John M. 2007. "Gangs, Institutions, Race, and Space: The Chicago School Revisited." In *Gangs in the Global City: Alternatives to Traditional Criminology,* ed. J. M. Hagedorn, 13–33. Urbana: University of Illinois Press.

——. 2008. *A World of Gangs: Armed Young Men and Gangsta Culture.* Minneapolis: University of Minnesota Press.

Hagedorn, John M., and Perry Macon. 1988. *People and Folks: Gangs, Crime, and the Underclass in a Rustbelt City.* Chicago: Lake View Press.

Hall, Steve, Simon Winlow, and Craig Ancrum. 2008. *Criminal Identities and Consumer Culture: Crime, Exclusion and the New Culture of Narcissism.* Cullompton, UK: Willan.

Hallsworth, Simon. 2005. *Street Crime.* Crime and Society Series. Cullompton, UK: Willan.

——. 2011. "Gangland Britain? Realities, Fantasies and Industry." In *Youth in Crisis? 'Gangs', Territoriality and Violence,* ed. B. Golston, 183–97. London: Routledge.

——. 2013. *The Gang and Beyond: Interpreting Violent Street Worlds.* Basingstoke, UK: Palgrave MacMillan.

Hallsworth, Simon, and John Lea. 2011. "Reconstructing Leviathan: Emerging Contours of the Security State." *Theoretical Criminology* 15 (2): 141–57.

Hallsworth, Simon, and Daniel Silverstone. 2009. "'That's Life, Innit': A British Perspective on Gun Crime and Social Order." *Criminology and Criminal Justice* 9 (3): 359–77.

Hallsworth, Simon, and Tara Young. 2005. "On Gangs and Guns: A Critique and a Warning." *ChildRight* 220:14–16.

Handelman, Stephen. 1994. *Comrade Criminal: The Theft of the Second Russian Revolution.* London: Michael Joseph.

Hanson, Philip. 2014. "Reiderstvo: Asset-Grabbing in Russia." *Chatham House* (March 1). www.chathamhouse.org/publications/papers/view/198133, accessed May 15, 2014.

Hanson, Stephen E. 2011. "Plebiscitarian Patrimonialism in Putin's Russia: Legitimating Authoritarianism in a Postideological Era." *Annals of the American Academy of Political and Social Science* 636 (1): 32–48.

Harding, Simon. 2014. *The Street Casino: Survival in Violent Street Gangs.* Bristol, UK: Policy Press.

Hayward, Keith J. 2004. *City Limits: Crime, Consumer Culture and the Urban Experience.* London: GlassHouse.

Hebdige, Dick. 1988. *Hiding in the Light: On Images and Things.* London: Comedia.

Hess, Henner. 1998. *Mafia and Mafiosi: Origin, Power and Myth.* London: C. Hurst.

Hobbes, Thomas. 1996 [1651]. *Leviathan.* The World's Classics. Oxford: Oxford University Press.

Hobbs, Dick. 2013. *Lush Life: Constructing Organized Crime in the UK.* Oxford: Oxford University Press.

Hobsbawm, Eric. 1985. *Bandits.* 2nd ed. Harmondsworth, UK: Penguin.

Holquist, Peter. 1997. "Information Is the Alpha and Omega of Our Work: Bolshevik Surveillance in Its Pan-European Context." *Journal of Modern History* 69:415–450.

——. 2000. "What's So Revolutionary about the Russian Revolution? State Practices and the New-Style Politics, 1914–1921." In *Russian Modernity: Politics, Knowledge, Practices,* ed. D.L. Hoffmann and Y. Kotsonis, 87–111. Basingstoke, UK: Macmillan.

Holzlehner, Tobias. 2007. "'The Harder the Rain, the Tighter the Roof': Evolution of Organized Crime Networks in the Russian Far East." *Sibirica* 6 (2): 51–86.

Humphrey, Caroline. 1999. "Russian Protection Rackets and the Appropriation of Law and Order." In *States and Illegal Practices,* ed. J.M. Heyman, 199–232. Oxford: Berg.

——. 2002. *The Unmaking of Soviet Life: Everyday Economies after Socialism.* Culture and Society after Socialism. Ithaca: Cornell University Press.

Isangulov, Il'dar. 2006. *U Poslednei cherty: dokumenty i fakty o deiatel'nosti mafii v Respublike Bashkortostan.* Moscow: Gainullin.

Iskhakov, D. M. 1998. "Sovremennyi natsionalizm tatar." *Panorama-forum, Kazan State University.* http://www.kcn.ru/tat_ru/politics/pan/index.php?tbut=13&sod=2, accessed July 16, 2011.

Iurieva, Irina, and Olga Iliukhina. 2007. "Delezh asfal'ta." *Ogoniok* 6. http://www.ogoniok.com/4982/, accessed July 16, 2013.

Jacobs, Bruce A. 2000. *Robbing Drug Dealers: Violence beyond the Law.* New Lines in Criminology. New York: Aldine de Gruyter.

Jarcho, Victor N. 1972. "Byla li u drevnikh grekov sovest'? K izobrazheniiu cheloveka v atticheskoi tragedii." In *Antichnost' i sovremennost'. K 80-letiiu F. A. Petrovskogo,* 251–63. Moscow: Nauka.

Jenkins, Richard. 2002. *Pierre Bourdieu.* London: Routledge.

Jimerson, Jason B., and Matthew K. Oware. 2006. "Telling the Code of the Street." *Journal of Contemporary Ethnography* 35 (1): 24–50.

Kabanov, S. F. 1928. *Bor'ba s ugolovnoi prestupnost'iu v derevne.* Moscow: Izdatel'stvo NKVD RSFSR.

Kanev, Sergei. 2012. "Barbi, Gromov i Shoigu." *Novaia gazeta* (June 15). http://www.novayagazeta.ru/inquests/53090.html, accessed June 20, 2012.

——. 2014. "Mezhdu 'kryshei' i podpol'iem." *Novaia gazeta.* March 24.

Kara-Murza, S. G. 2013. *Anomiia v Rossii: prichiny i posledstviia.* Moscow: Nauchnyi ekspert.

Karbainov, N. I. 2009. "'Ei, khunkhuz, kuda idiosh? Zdes' bratva, i ty umriosh!': 'Ulichnye voiny' v Ulan-Ude." In *Molodezhnye ulichnye gruppirovki: vvedenie v problematiku,* ed. D.V. Gromov. Moscow: IEA RAN.

Karyshev, Valerii. 1998. *Zapiski "banditskogo advokata": zakulisnaia zhizn' bratvy glazami "zashchitnika mafii."* Moscow: EKSMO.

——. 2005. *Russkaia mafiia, 1988–2005: kriminal'naia khronika novoi Rossii.* Moscow: EKSMO.

Kashelkin, A. 1990a. "Mezhregionalny kriminologicheskii analiz podrostkovo-molodezhnykh gruppirovok s antiobshchestvennoi napravlennost'iu." In *Sotsiologicheskie aspekty gosudarstvenno-pravovoi raboty v usloviiakh perestroiki.* Kazan: Kazan State University.

——. 1990b. "Nasilie kak forma antiobshchestvennogo povedeniia molodezhnykh gruppirovok." In *Kriminologi o neformalnykh molodezhnykh ob'edineniiakh,* ed. I.I. Karpets, 232–38. Moscow: Iuridicheskaia literatura.

Katz, Jack. 1988. *Seductions of Crime: Moral and Sensual Attractions in Doing Evil.* New York: Basic Books.

Kelly, Catriona. 2007. *Children's World: Growing Up in Russia, 1890–1991.* New Haven: Yale University Press.

Khanipov, R.A. 2008. "Ukorenennost' tiuremnykh i kriminalnykh praktik v kul'ture sovremennogo rossiiskogo obshchestva." *Mir Rossii* 3: 132–48.

Kharkhordin, Oleg. 1999. *The Collective and the Individual in Russia: A Study of Practices.* Berkeley: University of California Press.

Kintrea, Keith, Jon Bannister, and Jon Pickering. 2011. "'It's Just an Area—Everybody Represents It': Exploring Young People's Territorial Behaviour in British Cities." In *Youth in Crisis? 'Gangs', Territoriality and Violence,* ed. B. Goldson, 55–71. London: Routledge.

Klein, Malcolm Ward. 1971. *Street Gangs and Street Workers.* Englewood Cliffs, NJ: Prentice-Hall.

Koehler, Jan. 1999. "The School of the Street: Organising Diversity and Training Polytaxis in a (Post-) Soviet Periphery." *Anthropology of East Europe Review* 17 (2): 39–52.

Konstantinov, Andrei. 2004. *Banditskii Peterburg: Dokumental'nye ocherki.* Vol. 1. St. Petersburg: Neva.

——. 2012. *Banditskaia Rossiia.* Moscow: Astrel'.

Kontos, Louis, David Brotherton, and Luis Barrios. 2003. *Gangs and Society: Alternative Perspectives.* New York: Columbia University Press.

Kosterina, I. V. 2008. "Konstrukty i praktiki maskulinnosti v provintsial'nom gorode: gabitus 'normalnykh patsanov.'" *Zhurnal sotsiologii i sotsial'noi antropologii* 11 (4): 122–40.

Kostiuchenko, Elena. 2010. "Nam zdes' zhit'." Part 3. *Novaia gazeta* (December 8). http://www.novayagazeta.ru/data/2010/138/18.html, accessed March 3, 2011.

Kotkin, Stephen. 1995. *Magnetic Mountain: Stalinism as a Civilization.* Berkeley: University of California Press.

Kozlov, A. S. 1998. *"Kozel na sakse": i tak vsiu zhizn'.* Moscow: Vagrius.

Kozlov, V. A. 1999. *Massovye besporiadki v SSSR pri Khrushcheve i Brezhneve.* Novosibirsk: Sibirskii khronograf.

Kryshtanovskaya, Olga, and Stephen White. 2003. "Putin's Militocracy." *Post-Soviet Affairs* 19 (4): 289–306.

——. 2011. "The Formation of Russia's Network Directorate." In *Russia as a Network State: What Works in Russia When State Institutions Do Not?,* ed. V. Kononenko and A. Moshes, 19–38. Basingstoke, UK: Palgrave Macmillan; Helsinki: Ulkopoliittinen Instituutti.

Kuleshov, Ye.V. 2001. "Representatsiia maskulinnosti v sovremennoi podrostkovoi subkul'ture (na materiale polevykh issledovanii v g.Tikhvine)." In *Mifologiia i povsednevnost': gendernyi podkhod v antropologicheskikh distsiplinakh,* ed. K.A. Bogdanov and A. A. Panchenko, 260–71. St. Petersburg: Aleteiia.

Lacan, Jacques. 1998. *On Feminine Sexuality: The Limits of Love and Knowledge.* New York; London: Norton.

Lane, David. 1985. *Soviet Economy and Society.* Oxford: Blackwell.

LaPierre, Brian. 2006. "Private Matters or Public Crimes: The Emergence of Domestic Hooliganism in the Soviet Union, 1939–1966." In *Borders of Socialism: Private Spheres of Soviet Russia,* ed. L. H. Siegelbaum, 191–207. New York: Palgrave Macmillan.

——. 2012. *Hooligans in Khrushchev's Russia: Defining, Policing, and Producing Deviance during the Thaw.* Madison: University of Wisconsin Press.

Larina, Kseniia. 2012. "Personal'no Vash." *Echo Moskvy* (June 8). http://www.echo.msk.ru/programs/personalno/896770-echo/, accessed July 10, 2012.

Lauger, Timothy R. 2012. *Real Gangstas: Legitimacy, Reputation, and Violence in the Intergang Environment.* New Brunswick, NJ: Rutgers University Press.

Lea, John. 2001. *Crime and Modernity: Continuities in Left Realist Criminology.* London: Sage.

Ledeneva, Alena V. 1998. *Russia's Economy of Favours: Blat, Networking, and Informal Exchange.* Cambridge: Cambridge University Press.

——. 2013. *Can Russia Modernise? Sistema, Power Networks and Informal Governance.* Cambridge: Cambridge University Press.

Leeson, Peter T. 2009. *The Invisible Hook: The Hidden Economics of Pirates.* Princeton: Princeton University Press.

Lenta.ru. 2010. "Gubernator Kubani priznal sushchestvovanie band vo vsekh raionakh kraiia" (November 21). http://lenta.ru/news/2010/11/24/bands/, accessed January 1, 2013.

Levada Center. 2006. "Rossiia dlia russkikh . . . ?" (August 25). http://www.levada.ru/press/2006082500.html, accessed December 24, 2010.

——. 2013. "Rossiiane o tiur'me i ee etike." July 6. http://www.levada.ru/08-07-2013/rossiyane-o-tyurme-i-ee-etike, accessed January 2, 2014.

Levi, Michael. 1987. *Regulating Fraud: White-Collar Crime and the Criminal Process.* London: Tavistock.

Levinson, Alexei. 2005. "Vsia vasha natsiia takaia." *Neprikosnovennyi zapas* 1. http://magazines.russ.ru/nz/2005/1/lev7.html, accessed May 10, 2010.

——. 2006. "Rossiia v kol'tse." *Neprikosnovennyi zapas* 3. http://magazines.russ.ru/nz/2006/47/le10.html, accessed May 7, 2010.

——. 2009. "Proshloe—ne navsegda." *Neprikosnovennyi zapas* 2. http://magazines.russ.ru/nz/2009/2/le.html, accessed May 10, 2010.

Likhachev, D.S. 1935. "Cherty pervobytnogo primitvizma vorovskoi rechi." In *Iazyk i myshlenie*, Proceedings of the USSR Academy of Sciences. Vol. 3, 47–100. Moscow-Leningrad: Institut iazyka i myshleniia imeni N. Ia. Marra.

Lubimtseva, Maria. 2012. "Dusha cheloveka bol'she chem den'gi, bol'she, chem zheludok." *slon.ru* (October 3). http://slon.ru/calendar/event/835291/, accessed July 12, 2013.

Luneev, V. 2006. "Prestuplenie i nakazanie v Rossii." *Demoskop Weekly* 239–40. http://demoscope.ru/weekly/2006/0239/tema07.php, accessed February 10, 2014.

Lyman, Michael D., and Gary W. Potter. 2004. *Organized Crime*. 3rd ed. Upper Saddle River, NJ: Pearson Prentice-Hall.

MacDonald, Robert, and Jane Marsh. 2005. *Disconnected Youth? Growing Up in Britain's Poor Neighbourhoods.* Basingstoke, UK: Palgrave Macmillan.

Martin, Roderick. 1977. *The Sociology of Power.* London: Routledge & Kegan Paul.

Matich, Olga. 2006. "Mobster Gravestones in 1990s Russia." *Global Crime* 7 (1): 79–104.

McAlister, Siobhán, Phil Scraton, and Deena Haydon. 2011. "Place, Territory and Young People's Identity in the 'New' Northern Ireland." In *Youth in Crisis? 'Gangs', Territoriality and Violence,* ed. B. Goldson, 89–109. London: Routledge.

McAuley, Mary. 2009. *Children in Custody: Anglo-Russian Perspectives.* London: Bloomsbury.

McCann, Leo. 2005. *Economic Development in Tatarstan: Global Markets and a Russian Region.* London: RoutledgeCurzon.

McDonald, Brian. 2000. *Elephant Boys: Tales of London and Los Angeles Underworlds.* Edinburgh: Mainstream.

McGrellis, Sheena. 2005. "Pure and Bitter Spaces: Gender, Identity and Territory in Northern Irish Youth Transitions." *Gender and Education* 17 (5): 515–29.

McIlwaine, Cathy, and Caroline O. N. Moser. 2006. "Living in Fear: How the Urban Poor Perceive Violence, Fear and Insecurity." In *Fractured Cities: Social Exclusion, Urban Violence and Contested Spaces in Latin America,* ed. K. Koonings and D. Kruijt, 111–37. London: Zed.

Mennell, Steven. 1990. "Decivilising Processess: Theoretical Significance and Some Lines of Research." *International Sociology* 5(2): 205–23.

Merton, Robert K. 1957. *Social Theory and Social Structure.* New York: Free Press.

Messerschmidt, James W. 1993. *Masculinities and Crime: Critique and Reconceptualization of Theory.* Lanham, MD: Rowman & Littlefield.

——. 2000. *Nine Lives: Adolescent Masculinities, the Body, and Violence.* Boulder, CO: Westview Press.

Miller, Jody. 2000. *One of the Guys: Girls, Gangs, and Gender.* New York: Oxford University Press.

Miller, Walter. 1958. "Lower Class Culture as a Generating Milieu of Gang Delinquency." *Journal of Social Issues* 14:5–19.

——. 1982. *Crime by Youth Gangs and Youth Groups in the United States.* Washington, DC: Department of Justice.

Modestov, Nikolai. 2001. *Moskva banditskaia: dokumental'naia khronika kriminal'nogo bespredela 80–90-kh godov XX veka.* Moscow: Tsentrpoligraf.

Moore, Joan W. 1991. *Going Down to the Barrio: Homeboys and Homegirls in Change.* Philadelphia: Temple University Press.

Morozov, Igor Aleksandrovich, and Irina Semionovna Sleptsova. 2004. *Krug igry: prazdnik i igra v zhisni severorusskogo krest'ianina (XIX–XX vv.).* Moscow: INDRIK.

Mukhariamova, L. M., I. B. Morenko, L. N. Salakhatdinova, and R. G. Petrova. 2004. "Yazyk obucheniia v shkole kak factor dostupnosti vysshego obrazovaniia (na primere Respubliki Tatarstan)." In *Dostupnost' vysshego obrazovaniia v Rossii,* ed. S.V. Shishkin, 64–68. Moscow: Nezavisimyi Institut Sotsialnoi Politiki.

Murtazin, Irek. 2007. *Mintimir Shaimiev: poslednii President Tatarstana.* Vol. 1. Cheboksary, Chuvash Republic: Cheboksarskaia tipografiia No. 1.

——. 2013. "Khorosho otmylsia." *Novaia gazeta.* September 27.

Muzychenko, Vladimir. 2010. "Ekho 'Kazanskogo fenomena': molodezhnye gruppirovki 20 let spustia." *Kazanskie Vedomosti.* February 5.

Nafikov, Ildus Saidovich. 2012. *Tenevaia ekonomika i organizovannaia prestupnost' v usloviiakh krupnogo goroda.* Kazan: Poznanie.

Nasyrov, Albert. 2008. "Kazanskie gruppirovki." *Kommersant.* March 17.

Nazpary, Joma. 2002. *Post-Soviet Chaos: Violence and Dispossession in Kazakhstan.* London: Pluto Press.

Neuberger, Joan. 1993. *Hooliganism: Crime, Culture, and Power in St. Petersburg, 1900–1914.* Berkeley: University of California Press.

newsru.com. 2012. "V Moskve zaderzhan predpolagaemyi gangster OPS 'Zhilka'" (February 9). http://www.newsru.com/crime/09feb2012/zhilkakillerarst.html, accessed October 12, 2013.

Nicolson, Adam. 2014. *The Mighty Dead: Why Homer Matters.* Kindle ed. London: HarperCollins.

Nightingale, Carl Husemoller. 1993. *On the Edge: A History of Poor Black Children and Their American Dreams.* New York: Basic Books.

OCCRP (Organized Crime and Corruption Project). 2011. "Individuals Involved in the Tax Fraud against Hermitage and the Torture and Death of Sergei Magnitsky." https://www.reportingproject.net/proxy/jdownloads/Tormex%20Users%20A%20Proxy%20World/doc_tormex_users_06.pdf, accessed May 10, 2014.

Olate, Rena, Christopher Salas-Wright, and Michael G. Vaughn. 2012. "Predictors of Violence and Delinquency among High Risk Youth and Youth Gang Members in San Salvador, El Salvador." *International Social Work* 55 (3): 383–401.

Oleinik, Anton N. 2001. "'Zhisn' po poniatiiam': institutsionalnyi analiz povsednevnoi zhisni 'prostogo sovetskogo cheloveka.'" *Polis* 2:40–51.

——. 2003. *Organized Crime, Prison, and Post-Soviet Societies.* Aldershot, UK: Ashgate.

Omel'chenko, Elena L. 1996. "Young Women in Provincial Gang Culture: A Case Study of Ul'ianovsk." In *Gender, Generation and Identity in Contemporary Russia,* ed. H. Pilkington. London: Routledge.

——. 2006. "Smert' molodezhnoi kultury i rozhdenie stilia 'molodezhnyi.'" *Otechestvennye zapiski* 30 (3): 167–79.

Osipian, Ararat L. 2012. "Predatory Raiding in Russia: Institutions and Property Rights after the Crisis." *Journal of Economic Issues* 46 (2): 1–11.

Ovchinskii, V. S. 1990. "Gastrolnye poezdki antiobshestvennykh gruppirovok podrostkov i molodezhi—novyi fenomen." In *Kriminologi o neformalnykh molodezhnykh ob'edineniiakh,* ed. I. I. Karpets, 192–96. Moscow: Iuridicheskaia literatura.

Padilla, Felix M. 1992. *The Gang as an American Enterprise.* New Brunswick, NJ: Rutgers University Press.

Pallot, Judith, Laura Piacentini, and Dominique Moran. 2012. *Gender, Geography, and Punishment: The Experience of Women in Carceral Russia.* Oxford: Oxford University Press.

Paoli, Letizia. 2003. *Mafia Brotherhoods: Organized Crime, Italian Style.* Oxford: Oxford University Press.

——. 2004. "Mafia and Illegal Markets—Exception and Normality." In *Organised Crime in Europe: Concepts, Patterns and Control Policies in the European Union and Beyond,* ed. C. Fijnaut and L. Paoli, 263–302. Dordrecht, NLD: Springer.

Pastukhov, Vladimir. 2012. "Poniatiinaia Konstitutsiia." *polit.ru* (April 11). http://polit.ru/article/2012/04/11/constitution/, accessed May 12, 2013.

Patico, Jennifer. 2008. *Consumption and Social Change in a Post-Soviet Middle Class.* Stanford: Stanford University Press.

Petrusewicz, Marta. 1996. *Latifundium: Moral Economy and Material Life in a European Periphery.* Ann Arbor: University of Michigan Press.

Piacentini, Laura. 2004. *Surviving Russian Prisons: Punishment, Economy and Politics in Transition.* Cullompton, UK: Willan.

Pilkington, Hilary. 1994. *Russia's Youth and Its Culture: A Nation's Constructors and Constructed.* London: Routledge.

——. 2002. *Looking West? Cultural Globalization and Russian Youth Cultures.* University Park: Pennsylvania State University Press.

Pitts, John. 2008. *Reluctant Gangsters: The Changing Shape of Youth Crime.* Cullompton, UK: Willan.

Plaksii, S. I. 1990. "Chego bol'she—pliusov ili minusov u molodezhnykh neformalnykh ob'edinenii." In *Kriminologi o neformalnykh molodezhnykh ob'edineniiakh,* ed. I. I. Isakov, 84–90. Moscow: Iuridicheskaia literatura.

Ploux, François. 2007. "La violence des jeunes dans les campagnes du Sud-Ouest au XIXème siècle: ethos agonistique et masculinité." *Revue d'histoire de l'enfance irrégulière* 9. http://rhei.revues.org/2072, accessed May 12, 2014.

Ponomareva, Elli Iakovlevna. 2014. "Sotsial'noe prostranstvo kucha: teorii i praktiki neformal'noi konfliktologii erevanskikh kvartalov." Master's thesis, European University at St. Petersburg.

Postnova, Vera. 2006. "Shestnadtsat' chelovek na skamie podsudimykh.'" *Nezavisimaia gazeta* (September 18). http://www.ng.ru/ngregions/2006–09–18/22_kazan.html, accessed September 28, 2010.

Presdee, Mike. 2000. *Cultural Criminology and the Carnival of Crime.* London: Routledge.

ProKazan.ru. 2012. "Nazvany samye opasnye raiony Kazani, v kotorykh mozhno narvatsia na gopnikov" (May 5). http://m.prokazan.ru/newsv2/59326.html, accessed May 10, 2013.

Prozumentov, L. M., and A. V. Sheksler. 1990. "Tipologiia prestupnykh grupp nesovershennoletnikh." In *Kriminologi o neformalnykh molodezhnykh ob'edineniiakh,* ed. I. I. Karpets, 196–231. Moscow: Iuridicheskaia literatura.

Prusenkova, Nadezhda. 2013. "Delo Domnikova: oproshen vitse-gubernator Lipetskoi oblasti Sergei Dorovskii." *Novaia gazeta* (November 6). http://www.novayagazeta.ru/news/148597.html, accessed January 1, 2014.

Putin, Vladimir Vladimirovich. 2000. *First Person: An Astonishingly Frank Self-Portrait by Russia's President Vladimir Putin.* London: Hutchinson.

Radzikhovsky, Leonid. 2014. "Itogi goda." *Online TV* (December 26). http://www.onlinetv.ru/video/2054/?autostart=1, accessed December 27, 2014.

Raleigh, Donald J. 2006. *Russia's Sputnik Generation: Soviet Baby Boomers Talk about Their Lives.* Bloomington: Indiana University Press.

Rawlinson, Patricia. 2010. *From Fear to Fraternity: A Russian Tale of Crime, Economy and Modernity.* London: Pluto.

Razinkin, V. 1995. *Vory v zakone i prestupnye klany.* Moscow: Kriminologicheskaia Assotsiatsiia.

Remington, Thomas F. 2011. *The Politics of Inequality in Russia.* Cambridge: Cambridge University Press.

RFE/RL. 2005. "Kazan: History of a City." *Radio Free Europe* (May 5). http://www.rferl.org/featuresarticle/2005/06/6f668e1d-53f3–4d85–8cb6–9603a8204128.html, accessed May 10, 2011.

Ries, Nancy. 2002. "'Honest Bandits' and 'Warped People': Russian Narratives about Money, Corruption, and Moral Decay." In *Ethnography in Unstable Places: Everyday Lives in Contexts of Dramatic Political Change,* ed. C. J. Greenhouse, E. Mertz, and K. B. Warren, 276–315. Durham: Duke University Press.

Rodgers, Dennis. 2006. "The State as a Gang: Conceptualizing the Governmentality of Violence in Contemporary Nicaragua." *Critique of Anthropology* 26 (3): 315–30.

——. 2009. "Living in the Shadow of Death: Gangs, Violence and Social Order in Urban Nicaragua, 1996–2002." In *Youth Violence in Latin America,* ed. D. Rodgers and G. A. Jones, 25–44. New York: Palgrave Macmillan.

Romanenko, Kseniia. 2013. "Molodye uchenye: Arsenii Khitrov." *theoryandpractice.ru* (November 14). http://theoryandpractice.ru/posts/8031-molodye-uchenye-khitrov, accessed July 25, 2014.

Rousseau, Jean-Jacques. 1993 [1754]. *The Social Contract; and Discourses,* trans. G. D. H. Cole, revised and augmented J. H. Brumfitt and John C. Hall, ed. and updated P. D. Jimack. London: Dent.

Ruggiero, Vincenzo. 1996. *Organized and Corporate Crime in Europe: Offers That Can't Be Refused.* Aldershot, UK: Dartmouth.

Safarov, Asgat Akhmetovich. 2012. *Zakat Kazanskogo fenomena: istoriia likvidatsii organisovannykh prestupnykh formirovanii Tatarstana.* Kazan: Tatarskoe knizhnoe izdatel'stvo.

Salagaev, Alexander. 1999. "Podrostkovo-molodezhnoe territorial'noe soobshchestvo delinkventnoi napravlennosti kak ob'ekt teoreticheskogo issledovaniia." PhD diss., St. Petersburg State University.

——. 2001. "Evolution of Delinquent Gangs in Russia." In *The Eurogang Paradox: Street Gangs and Youth Groups in the US and Europe,* ed. M. W. Klein, H. Yu Kerner, C. L. Maxson, and E. Weitekamp, 195–202. Dordrecht, NL: Kluwer Academic Publishers.

——. 2005. "Issledovaniia podrostkovo-molodezhnykh delinkventnykh soobshchestv (gruppirovok) v Rossii i v byvshem SSSR." In *Deviantnoe povedenie v sovremennoi Rossii v fokuse sotsiologii,* ed. A. Salagaev and M. Pozdniakova, 184–95. Moscow: Institut Sotsiologii RAN.

Salagaev, Alexander, and Alexander Shashkin. 2002. "Nasilie v molodezhnykh gruppirovkakh kak sposob konstruirovaniia maskulinnosti." *Zhurnal sotsiologii i sotsial'noi antropologii* 1 (5): 151–60.

——. 2005a. "After-Effects of the Transition: Youth Criminal Careers in Russia." In *Youth—Similarities, Differences, Inequalities.* Reports of the Karelian Institute, ed. V. Puuronen, J. Soilevuo-Grønnerød, and J. Herranen, 154–72. Joensuu, FI: University of Joensuu.

——. 2005b. "Violence and Victimization on the Street: Power Struggle and Masculine Hierarchies in Russia." In *Violence in Youth Microcultures,* ed. T. Hoikkala and L. Suurpaa, 14–47. Helsinki: Finnish Youth Research Network.

Salagaev, Alexander, Alexander Shashkin, and Aleksei Konnov. 2006. "One Hand Washes Another: Informal Ties between Organized Criminal Groups and Law-Enforcement Agencies in Russia." *Journal of Power Institutions in Post-Soviet Societies* 4–5. http://pipss.revues.org/449, accessed May 1, 2013.

Sánchez-Jankowski, Martín. 1991. *Islands in the Street: Gangs and American Urban Society.* Berkeley: University of California Press.

Sandberg, Sveinung. 2008. "Street Capital: Ethnicity and Violence on the Streets of Oslo." *Theoretical Criminology* 12 (2): 153–71.

Sauvadet, Thomas. 2005. "Causes et conséquences de la recherche de capital guerrier chez les jeunes de la Cité." *Déviance et Société* 29 (2): 113–26.

——. 2006. *Le capital guerrier: Concurrence et solidarité entre jeunes de Cité.* Paris: Armand Colin.

Schelling, Thomas. 1971. "What Is the Business of Organized Crime?" *Journal of Public Law* 20: 71–84.

Scheper-Hughes, Nancy. 1992. *Death without Weeping: The Violence of Everyday Life in Brazil.* Berkeley: University of California Press.

Scheper-Hughes, Nancy, and Philippe I. Bourgois. 2004. *Violence in War and Peace: An Anthology.* Malden, MA: Blackwell.

Schneider, Jane, and Peter T. Schneider. 1976. *Culture and Political Economy in Western Sicily*. New York: Academic Press.

Scott, Gregory S. 2004. "Jabbing Blow, Pitching Rocks, and Stacking Paper: How Drug-Selling Street Gangs Organize the Reentry of Male Ex-Convicts into the Community." In *From Crime to Employment: Critical Issues in Crime Reduction for Corrections,* ed. J.L. Krienert and M.S. Fleisher, 106–40. Lanham, MD: AltaMira Press.

Scott, James C. 1998. *Seeing Like a State: How Certain Schemes to Improve the Human Condition Have Failed.* New Haven: Yale University Press.

Serio, Joseph D., and Vyacheslav Razinkin. 1995. "Thieves Professing the Code: The Traditional Role of Vory v Zakone in Russia's Criminal World and Adaptations to New Social Reality." *Low Intensity Conflict and Law Enforcement* 4 (1): 72–88.

Shaliapin, F. I. 1926. *Stranitsy iz moei zhisni.* Leningrad: Priboi.

Shanin, Theodor. 1986. *The Roots of Otherness: Russia's Turn of Century.* Vol. 1, *Russia as a "Developing Society."* New Haven: Yale University Press.

Shashkin, Alexander. 2009. "Ulitsa: svoi i chuzhie." In *Molodezhnye ulichnye gruppirovki: vvedenie v problematiku,* ed. D.V. Gromov, 149–84. Moscow: IEA RAN.

Shaw, Clifford Robe, and Henry Donald Mackay. 1942. *Juvenile Delinquency and Urban Areas.* Chicago: University of Chicago Press.

Shchepanskaia, T. B. 2001. "Zony nasiliia (po materialam russkoi sel'skoi i sovremennykh subkulturnykh traditsii)." In *Antropologiia nasiliia,* ed. V.V. Bocharov and V.A. Tishkov, 115–77. St. Petersburg: Nauka.

Shearing, C.D. 1992. "The Relation between Public and Private Policing." In *Modern Policing.* Chicago: University of Chicago Press.

Shelley, Louise. 2006. "The Drug Trade in Contemporary Russia." *China and Eurasia Forum Quarterly* 4 (1): 15–20.

Sheptitskii, Andrei. 2009. "Vorovskoi Tatarstan." *Vremia i den'gi* (July 8). http://www.aferizm.ru/criminal/ops/st_k_kazan_vori.htm, accessed May 10, 2012.

Shevchenko, Olga. 2009. *Crisis and the Everyday in Postsocialist Moscow.* Bloomington: Indiana University Press.

Shevelev, Mikhail. 2010. "General-maior militsii Vladimir Ovchinskii—o patriotakh i liberalakh." *Radio Svoboda* (December 29). www.svobodanews.ru/content/article/2262376.html, accessed May 10, 2013.

Shlapentokh, Vladimir. 1996. "Early Feudalism—the Best Parallel for Contemporary Russia." *Europe-Asia Studies* 48 (3): 393–411.

Shtele, Natalia. 2012. "V Tatarstan vozvrashchaetsia epokha gruppirovok i razborok?" *Argumenty i Fakty* (January 16). http://www.kazan.aif.ru/incidents/details/83843, accessed May 16, 2013.

Shubkin, V. N. 1965. "Molodezh vstupaet v zhisn'." *Voprosy filosofii* 5:57–70.

Sibiriakov, S. L. 1990. "Ulichnye gruppirovki molodezhi v g. Volgograde." In *Kriminologi o neformalnykh molodezhnykh ob'edineniiakh*, 168–76. Moscow: Iuridicheskaia literatura.

Sidorenko-Stephenson, Svetlana. 2000. "Prostitution and Young People in Russia." In *Youth Prostitution in the New Europe: A Growth in Sex Work*, ed. D. Barrett, E. Barrett, and N. Mullenge, 108–26. Lyme Regis, UK: Russell House Publishing.

Siegel, Dina. 2012. "Vory v Zakone: Russian Organized Crime." In *Traditional Organized Crime in the Modern World: Responses to Socioeconomic Change*, ed. D. Siegel and H. G. v. d. Bunt, 37–48. New York: Springer.

Smol'nikov, P. 1989. "Razgovor s liderom kazanskoi molodezhnoi gruppirovki." *Zdorov'ie* (May 8). http://lechebnik.info/513/22.htm, accessed May 10, 2013.

Sokolov, Vsevolod. 2004. "From Guns to Briefcases: The Evolution of Russian Organized Crime." *World Policy Journal* 21 (1): 68–74.

Solopov, Maksim. 2013. "Pri zone i zhivem." *gazeta.ru* (July 9). http://www.gazeta.ru/social/2013/07/08/5417477.shtml, accessed July 9, 2013.

Spencer, Jonathan. 2008. Foreword to *Global Vigilantes*, ed. D. Pratten and A. Sen, x–xii. New York: Columbia University Press.

Spergel, I. 1984. "Violent Gangs in Chicago: In Search of Social Policy." *Social Service Review* 58:199–206.

Stenson, Kevin. 2005. "Sovereignty, Biopolitics and the Local Government of Crime in Britain." *Theoretical Criminology* 9 (3): 265–87.

Stephenson, Svetlana. 2001. "Street Children in Moscow: Using and Creating Social Capital." *Sociological Review* 49 (4): 530–47.

——. 2006. *Crossing the Line: Vagrancy, Homelessness and Social Displacement in Russia.* Aldershot, UK: Ashgate.

——. 2008. "Searching for Home: Street Youth and Organized Crime in Russia." In *Globalizing the Streets: Cross-Cultural Perspectives on Youth, Social Control, and Empowerment*, ed. D. Brotherton and M. Flynn, 78–92. New York: Columbia University Press.

——. 2012. "The Violent Practices of Youth Territorial Groups in Moscow." *Europe-Asia Studies* 64 (1): 69–90.

Sullivan, Mercer L. 1989. *"Getting Paid": Youth Crime and Work in the Inner City.* Ithaca: Cornell University Press.

Suttles, Gerald Dale. 1968. *The Social Order of the Slum: Ethnicity and Territory in the Inner City.* Chicago: University of Chicago Press.

Sykes, Gresham, and David Matza.1957. "Techniques of Neutralization: A Theory of Delinquency." *American Sociological Review* 22:664–70.

Tabeev, E. F. 2007. *Tatarstan—eto Rossiia.* Moscow: Institut Sotsial'no-politicheskikh Issledovanii RAN.

Taylor, Brian D. 2011. *State Building in Putin's Russia: Policing and Coercion after Communism.* Cambridge: Cambridge University Press.

Taylor, Carl S. 1990. *Dangerous Society.* East Lansing: Michigan State University Press.

Thrasher, Frederic Milton. 1963 [1927]. *The Gang: A Study of 1,313 Gangs in Chicago.* Chicago: University of Chicago Press.

Tilly, Charles. 1974a. Foreword to *The Mafia of a Sicilian Village, 1860–1960: A Study of Violent Peasant Entrepreneurs* by Anton Block, xiii–xvi. Oxford: Blackwell.

——. 1974b. "Rural Collective Action in Modern Europe." CRSO Working Paper no. 96 (April), University of Michigan, Ann Arbor.

Tönnies, Ferdinand. 1963 [1887]. *Community and Society.* New York: Harper and Row.

Tsipursky, G. V. 2009. "'Obshchestva,' 'shtaby,' 'kluby': molodezhnoe gorodskoe khuligantsvo v ottepel'nye gody Sovetskoi Rossii." In *Molodezhnye ulichnye gruppirovki: vvedenie v problematiku*, ed. D.V. Gromov, 73–93. Moscow: IEA RAN.

Udovenko, Yuri. 2008. *Zazerkal'e: avtoritet zakonov ili zakon "avtoritetov."* Naberezhnye Chelny, Republic of Tatarstan.

UNDP (United Nations Development Programme). 1998. "Poverty in Transition." New York: UNDP Regional Bureau for Europe and the CIS.

Urban, Michael E. 2012. *Cultures of Power in Post-Communist Russia: An Analysis of Elite Political Discourse.* Cambridge: Cambridge University Press.

Vardanian, Anastasia. 2010. "V Orle uchastnikam banditskoi gruppirovki na vsekh dali 97 let t'ur'my." *Komsomolskaia pravda* (December 17). http://www.kp.ru/online/news/797508, accessed May 6, 2014.

Varese, Federico. 2001. *The Russian Mafia: Private Protection in a New Market Economy.* Oxford: Oxford University Press.

——. 2011. *Mafias on the Move: How Organized Crime Conquers New Territories.* Princeton: Princeton University Press.

——. 2012. "How Mafias Take Advantage of Globalization: The Russian Mafia in Italy." *British Journal of Criminology* 52:235–53.

——. 2013. "The Structure and the Content of Criminal Connections: The Russian Mafia in Italy." *European Sociological Review* 29 (5): 899–909.

——. 2014. "Protection and Extortion." In *The Oxford Handbook of Organized Crime*, ed. L. Paoli. Oxford: Oxford University Press, 343–58.

VCSOC (Vladivostok Center for Research on Organized Crime, Far Eastern State University). 2004. "Dal'nii Vostok: khronika organizovannoi prestupnosti (obzor pressy 1997–August 2003 g.g.)." http://www.debri-dv.com/article/2125, accessed May 5, 2013.

Venediktov, Alexei. 2013. "Razvorot." *Ekho Moskvy* (July 18). http://www.echo.msk.ru/programs/razvorot/1117562-echo, accessed August 20, 2013.

Venkatesh, Sudhir Alladi. 1997. "The Social Organization of Street Gang Activity in an Urban Ghetto." *American Journal of Sociology* 103 (1): 82–111.

——. 2000. *American Project: The Rise and Fall of a Modern Ghetto.* Cambridge: Harvard University Press.

——. 2006. *Off the Books: The Underground Economy of the Urban Poor.* Cambridge: Harvard University Press.

Verdery, Katherine. 1996. *What Was Socialism and What Comes Next?* Princeton: Princeton University Press.

Vigil, James Diego. 1988. *Barrio Gangs: Street Life and Identity in Southern California.* Austin: University of Texas Press.

Vikulova, Aleksandra. 2014. "'Mordve' dali 100 let." *Kommersant* (January 16). http://www.kommersant.ru/doc/2384650, accessed March 5, 2014.

Volkov, Vadim. 2000. "Organized Violence, Market Building, and State Formation." In *Economic Crime in Russia*, ed. A. V. Ledeneva and M. Kurkchiyan, 43–61. The Hague: Kluwer Law International.

——. 2002. *Violent Entrepreneurs: The Use of Force in the Making of Russian Capitalism.* Ithaca: Cornell University Press.

——. 2012. *Silovoe predprinimatel'stvo. XXIi vek. Ekonomiko-sotsiologicheskii analiz.* St. Petersburg: European University at St. Petersburg.

Wacquant, Loïc. 2006. "Three Pernicious Premises in the Study of the American Ghetto." In *Gangs in the Global City: Alternatives to Traditional Criminology*, ed. J.M. Hagedorn, 34–53. Urbana: University of Illinois Press.

Walker, Charles. 2009. "From 'Inheritance' to Individualization: Disembedding Working-Class Youth Transitions in Post-Soviet Russia." *Journal of Youth Studies* 12 (5): 531–45.

Walmsley, Roy. 2013. "World Prison Population List." 10th ed. *International Centre for Prison Studies.* http://www.prisonstudies.org/sites/prisonstudies.org/files/resources/downloads/wppl_10.pdf, accessed February 10, 2014.

Weber, Max. 1978 [1922]. *Economy and Society: An Outline of Interpretive Sociology.* Berkeley: University of California Press.

Whyte, William Foote. 1993. *Street Corner Society: The Social Structure of an Italian Slum.* 4th ed. Chicago: University of Chicago Press.

Wieder, D. Lawrence. 1974. *Language and Social Reality: The Case of Telling the Convict Code.* The Hague: Mouton.

Williams, Christopher, V.I. Chuprov, and I.U. Zubok. 2003. *Youth, Risk, and Russian Modernity.* Burlington, VT: Ashgate.

Willis, Paul E. 1977. *Learning to Labour: How Working Class Kids Get Working Class Jobs.* Farnborough, UK: Saxon House.

Wilson, Eric. 2009. "Deconstructing the Shadows." In *Government of the Shadows: Parapolitics and Criminal Sovereignty*, ed. E. Wilson, 13–55. New York: Pluto Press.

Winton, Alisa. 2005. "Youth, Gang and Violence: Analysing the Social and Spatial Mobility of Young People in Guatemala City." *Children's Geography* 3 (2): 167–84.

Wolfgang, Marvin E., and Franco Ferracuti. 1967. *The Subculture of Violence.* London: Tavistock.

Wright, Alan. 2006. *Organised Crime.* Cullompton, UK: Willan.

Wrong, Dennis Hume. 1994. *The Problem of Order: What Unites and Divides Society.* Cambridge: Harvard University Press, 1995.

Yablonsky, Lewis. 1962. *The Violent Gang.* New York: MacMillan.

Yagodkin, V. N. 1981. "How Child Labour Was Eradicated in the USSR: Integrating School and Society." Population and Labour Policies Working Paper. Geneva: International Labour Organisation.

Yakovlev, V. 1987. "Kontora liuberov." *Ogoniok* 5:21–22.

Young, Jock. 1999. *The Exclusive Society: Social Exclusion, Crime and Difference in Late Modernity*. London: SAGE.

——. 2007. *The Vertigo of Late Modernity*. London: SAGE.

Young, Tara. 2009. "Girls and Gangs: 'Shemale' Gangsters in the UK?" *Youth Justice* 9 (3): 224–38.

Yusupova, Marina. Forthcoming. "Masculinity, Criminality, and Russian Men." *Sextures.*

Zabrianskii, G. I. 1990. "Mekhanizm formirovaniia antisotsialnykh podrostkovykh i iunosheskikh grupp." In *Kriminilogi o neformalnykh molodezhnykh ob'edineniiakh*, ed. I.I. Karpets, 46–55. Moscow: Iuridicheskaia literatura.

Zagrebneva, Oksana. 2011. "V Kazani chlen OPG vymogal s biznesmena 30 mln rublei za 'kryshevanie.'" *Kazan-Times* (August 22). http://kazan-times.ru/stories/863, accessed July 12, 2013.

Zakharova, E. Iu. 2010. "Tbilisskaia ulitsa kak sreda muzhskoi sotsializatsii." *Laboratorium: Zhurnal sotsialnykh issledovanii* 1:182–204.

Index

29th Kompleks (gang), 59, 77, 80, 86n2, 241–42; leader of, 79, 95; organization of, 97–98
56th Kvartal (gang), 53, 59, 86n2, 216

Abramkin, Valerii, 225
adulthood, transitions to, 136, 163, 236; criminal, 136–37; professional, 138–40; working-class, 137–38
age, of gang members, 24, 55–56, 99
age-based cohorts, in gangs, 12, 20, 30, 99, 100, 105. *See also* older gang members; younger gang members
Ageeva, L. V., 23, 24, 27, 28, 30, 32, 33–34
Aidarovskie OPG, 82
Aksakov, S. T., 22
Anderson, Elijah, 170–71, 172, 205
anomie (normlessness), 44
Antipov, Sergei, 25–27
Arendt, Hannah, 71
Arlacchi, Pino, 66, 129, 154n2
autonomous ruling regimes, 21, 59, 63
avtoritety (gang leaders), 30, 100, 105; law enforcement agencies and, 78, 158–59; pursuit of legitimacy by, 80, 81–83, 96; as ritual specialists, 96, 100, 108; and younger gang members, growing tensions between, 119–20, 123–24

Banda Tagirianova, 77
bandit gangs *(banditskie gruppirovki)*, 12; capitalist transition of 1990s and, 4; in Moscow, 36, 61; in Tatarstan, 11, 56–59. *See also* entrepreneurial gangs
bandity (bandits), use of term, 48, 247
Baranov, Vladimir, 78
Barrios, Luis, 17, 128n1
Bashkartostan, 84
Bayart, Jean-François, 52, 68, 74
Belanovsky, Sergei, 36, 38, 40, 41
Bell, Catherine, 196
bespredel (lawlessness), 224, 247; dissolution of Soviet Union and, 44–45, 48–51, 56–57, 63; extreme violence as, gang code on, 177, 178–79; gangs as fighters against, 114, 154–55, 245–46

Beumers, Birgit, 226, 227
black market, Soviet-era, and gangs, 4, 24, 27–28, 29–30, 37, 41
blat (informal exchange), 27, 247
Blok, Anton, 66, 154n2
bodybuilding, gang members and, 38, 39
Borenstein, Eliot, 226
Boriskovo gang, 47, 60, 240
botanists (non-streetwise young men), 194–96
Bourdieu, Pierre, 190, 191, 194, 205n6
Bourgois, Philippe I., 148, 201, 205, 217
Brazil: neoliberal transformation in, 68; violence in, 217
Breslavsky, Anatoliy, 62, 168, 200
brigada (basic gang unit), 105, 110–12
Britain, gangs in: antisocial behavior orders (ASBOs) targeting, 162; estrangement from social institutions, 128; evolution of, 25
brotherhood ethos, gangs and, 114–16, 125–26, 134–36, 138
Brotherton, David, ix, 128n1
Bulatov, Boris, 79
Buriatiia, gangs in, 62, 168, 200
business(es): appropriation/raiding of, 85, 87n3; extortion and protection of, 46, 68–74, 239–40. *See also* protection operations
business, gang, 65, 81–83, 86–90; changes in late 1990s, 86–90; operation of, 117
business corporations: gangs compared to, 93, 116, 117–19, 125, 126; gangs members' penetration of, 81–83, 85
businessmen: cooperation with gangs, 77; extortion by state authorities, 69, 74; relations with gangs, 68–69, 73; victimization by gangs, 57–58, 65

Campbell, Ann, 28, 106
Canetti, Elias, 202
capitalist transition, in Russia: gangs during, 2, 3–4, 46–47, 65–68, 119, 145–46, 187, 225–26, 236; historically unique nature of, 67–68; social crisis during, 3, 48–50, 63–64

career strategies, of gang members, 140–43
Castells, Manuel, 118
Catanzaro, Raimondo, 66, 154n2, 157
Central Asia, migrants from: animosity toward, 144; and drug trade, 88, 144
Chainiki gang, 30
Chalidze, Valerii I., 106n1, 182, 183
charitable activities, gangs and, 79, 80, 145
Cheliabinsk, gangs in, 167
Cheloukhine, Serguei, 25, 88
chernukha (narratives of violence), 226–27
Chicago school, social disorganization theory of, 127
Chuvash Republic, gangs in, 167
civil war, events of 1990s compared to, 64
Clausewitz, Carl von, 190
clothes, of gang members, 27, 168, 202; prohibition on selling, 173–74, 175
Cloward, Richard Andrew, 127, 149
code of conduct: ethnographic approach to, 170–71; ethnomethodological approach to, 171–72; in organized fights, 22, 24; of street peer groups, 38; of *vory v zakone,* 179–80, 182–83, 185–86. *See also poniatiia* (gang code of conduct)
Code of the Streets (Anderson), 170–71
Cohen, Albert Kircidel, 7n3
Cohen, Stanley, 40
Collins, Randall, 5, 6, 7n4, 8, 17, 18, 94, 112, 178, 190
Connell, Raewyn, 18, 194n4
Connell, Robert, 6n2
Conquergood, Dwight, 93
consumerism, and gang membership, 24, 146n5
corruption, 27, 77, 151, 157, 231, 236
crime: committed by outsiders, territorial gangs' response to, 144, 154–55. *See also* organized crime
culture, Russian: gangs and, 3, 223–25, 227–31; violence and, 226–27

dance halls, 24, 30, 32, 37
Dan'shin, Sergei, 26
deceit, use by gangs, 209–12
Decker, Scott H., 128
Deleuze, Gilles, 63, 94, 117
democracy, in gang organization, 152, 174, 176, 178
Densley, James A., 93, 128
Dobson, Miriam, 180, 224
Dolgova, A., 32n5, 59, 80, 83, 156
domestic violence, 217
domination: gangs and struggle for, 2, 31, 51, 63, 73–74; nonphysical strategies of, 200–202; younger gang members and strategies of, 74–75
Domnikov, Igor', 77
Dom Obuvi (gang), 46
"double helix" model, of gangs' social membership, 13, 102, 140–43, 149, 236
Downes, David, 143
drug addicts, gang views on, 109, 154, 175
drug trade: gangs and, 88–89, 103, 164, 237, 240, 241; migrants and, 88, 144; prohibition on, gang code and, 89, 174, 175, 188
Durkheim, Emile, 44, 108, 112, 115, 118
dvorovye kompanii. See street peer groups

egalitarianism, gangs and, 105, 115
Ekaterinburg, gangs in, 168
Elias, Norbert, 222, 226
entrepreneurial gangs, 12, 20; adaptation after 2000s, 167, 236; black market activities and, 27–28; evolution of youth street groups into, 8, 25–27, 35–36, 93; preconditions for emergence of, 41–43, 52–53; in rural areas, 55, 62. *See also* bandit gangs *(banditskie gruppirovki)*
entrepreneurialism, criminal behavior seen as, 52, 117, 145–46
Eremenko, Yuri (Erema), 80, 241
Ermakov, V. D., 42
ethnic background, of gang members, 56
ethnic gangs, and heroin trade, 88
ex-convicts: as gang leaders, 25, 36, 37, 47, 61; return to gang, 122–23
expulsion, from gang, 108–9, 121–22
extortion: of bus and taxi companies, 87; of businesses, 239–40; gang code used to legitimize, 70–71; gang members as victims of, 213–14; interrogation preceding, 201–2; by police, 69, 74, 87, 162; privatization of state enterprises and, 46; progression in gang operations from, 68; young victims of, 29, 75–76, 196–200. *See also* protection operations

family backgrounds, of gang members, 129–30, 132, 136–39
Far East, Russian: development of gangs in, 36–37, 61–62; gang protection in, 156; *vory v zakone* in, informal justice by, 152–53
fartsovka (black market trading), 24, 41, 247
Ferracuti, Franco, 7n3
feudalism, transition from, postsocialist transformation compared to, 63, 67

fights: at dance halls, 37; territorial, 18, 19–20, 22, 24, 30–32
Finogenov, Andrei, 167
Fizruk (sitcom), 230
focus groups, use of, 246
friendships: among gang members, 110–12, 114, 138; as motivation for gang membership, 131–32, 134–35
Fürst, Juliane, 19

Galeotti, Mark, 25, 56, 73, 84, 99, 117, 149, 152, 167, 182
Galiakberov, Radik (Radzha), 79, 95, 207, 240–41
Gambetta, Diego, 66, 69, 128
gaming arcades, gangs and, 83, 88, 117
gang(s): appeal of, 5; as business organizations, 93, 116; definition of, 2, 6; evolution of, 7–8; in modern society, 235; as patrimonial organizations, 93–94, 106; in times of crisis, 5, 7, 9, 235; as tribal alliances/warrior brotherhoods, 2, 5–7, 178–79; typology of, 17–21
gang(s), Russian: in 1990s vs. 2000s, 169; basic unit of *(brigada)*, 105, 110–12; capitalist transition of 1990s and, 2, 3–4, 46–47, 65–68, 119, 145–46, 187, 225–26, 236; changing composition of, 54–56; cultural influence of, 3, 223–25, 227–31; economic activities of, 65, 81–83, 86–90, 117; egalitarian structures of, 105, 115; entrenchment of, 125–26, 236–38; as flexible networked organizations, 97–99, 116–17; future of, 237; inadequate research on, 10–11; international operations of, 60, 98–99; origins of, 4, 29, 34, 37; parallels with larger society, 231–33; and popular justice, 153–57, 245–46; romanticized image of, 34, 134, 229–31; shadow economy and, 8, 24–25, 27, 29–30, 37; social dislocation and membership in, 49–50, 51; and social order, 153–57; in Soviet era, 8–9, 16, 35–40; unique characteristics of, 148; *vory v zakone* and, 4, 37–38. *See also specific gangs*
gang members: age of, 24, 55–56, 99; age-based cohorts of, 12, 20, 30, 99, 100, 105; aspirations of, 140, 142, 145, 150; brotherhood ethos of, 114–16, 125–26, 134–36, 138; criminal transitions of, 136–37; diversity of, 149–50; "double helix" model of social membership of, 13, 102, 140–43, 149, 236; educational background of, 55, 129, 131–32; as entrepreneurs, 145–46; ethnic backgrounds of, 56; family backgrounds of, 129–30, 132, 136–39; growing tensions among, 119–25, 126; incorporation into communities, 9, 13, 26, 28, 78–83, 127, 128, 129, 140–43, 146–50, 153, 169, 185, 187, 236–38; interviews with, 245; leaving gang, 99, 108–9, 121–22; legitimizing discourse of, 28, 245–56; letters by, 33–35; meet-ups of, 99, 107–8; mobilization of, 112–14; multiple career strategies of, 140–43, 149; nationalism of, 144; older, 100, 122–23; on outsiders, 72, 75, 194–96; private life of, right to, 177; promotion of, 103–4, 117; prosecution of, 85–86, 161–62; punishment of, 108–9, 121–22; qualities of, 76, 94, 95, 190; reasons for joining gang, 51–52, 54, 55, 131–35, 136, 140–41, 143, 149, 150, 168–69; recruitment of, 54, 101–2, 124, 132, 136; registration by police, 160–61; self-perception of activities of, 27–28, 34, 37, 145–46, 149, 154; sense of moral superiority of, 114–15, 154; social background of, 54–56, 128–31; social networks of, 9, 110–12, 146–48, 177; and sports, 5, 31, 36, 38, 39, 54, 102, 131–32, 188; status of, 103; transitions to adulthood, 136–40, 163, 236; as victims of extortion, 213–14; *vory v zakone* and, relationship with, 183, 184, 211; *vory v zakone* distinguished from, 141, 142, 146, 147, 157, 185, 186–87. *See also* lads; leaders; younger gang members
Garland, David, 163
Gataullin, A. A., 24, 26, 28, 30, 55
Gemeinschaft, concept of, 116
Gilinsky, Yakov, 84, 106n3
Girard, René, 91, 222
Goffman, Erving, 18, 194
gopniki: use of term, 11, 48, 51; walking style of, 193–94
Govorukhin, Sviatoslav, 82
graffiti, 5
Griaz' gang, 60, 78
Grinin, Oleg (Grinia), 216
Gromov, Dmitrii, 12, 40, 64
Grossman, Gregory, 24
group fights, arranged, 19–20, 22, 24
Gruppirovka Fina, 167
gruppirovki, 47; emergence of, 51–53. *See also* bandit gangs *(banditskie gruppirovki)*
Guattari, Felix, 63, 94, 117

Gulag culture, 180, 224
Gusev, Nikolai, 79
Gus'-Khrustalnyi, gang regime in, 166

Haberfeld, M. R., 88
Hallsworth, Simon, ix, 17, 19, 116, 117n6, 162, 163, 201
Harding, Simon, 7n4, 205n6
Hebdige, Dick, 9
heroin trade, 88, 89
Hobbesian state of nature: gang life compared to, 221–22; Russian society of 1990s compared to, 44, 67
Hobbs, Dick, 7, 17, 25
Hobsbawm, Eric, 6, 230
Hollywood movies, Russian gangs imitating, 95, 211–12
homeless children: in Moscow of 1990s, 49–50, 230; in postrevolutionary Russia, 19
hooliganism, 10
housing patterns, and youth street gangs, 12
Humphrey, Caroline, 45, 63n3, 70

individualism: penetration in Russian society, 52; of Western gang members, 146n5
initiation rituals, absence in Russian gangs, 101, 102
insignia, gang, 27, 30
intelligentsia, in postsocialist Russia, 226
Israilov, Aidar, 82
Italian Mafia: changes in social composition of, 129; and drug trade, 89; and everyday violence, 217n8; and informal justice, 154n2; initiation rituals in, 102; lower-ranking members in, 103; Russian gangs compared to, 66, 147, 148, 157, 169; structure of, 105
Izmailovskaia gruppirovka, 61

Jarcho, Viktor, 179
justice. *See* popular justice

Karyshev, Valerii, 60, 185
Kaspiiskie gang, 87
Katz, Jack, 18, 134, 190, 192, 193, 201, 205
Kazakhstan, 50
Kazan: development of organized crime in, 46–47; educational and employment opportunities in 2000s, 128, 149; entrenchment of street gangs in, 125; escalation of violence in, 31–32, 56–58; evolution of street organizations in, 23–31; gang businesses in, 87–88; gangs in, 16, 33, 34, 35–36, 51–59, 164–65, 239–42; geographic expansion of gangs of, 32–33, 59–60, 241–42; industrialization and urbanization of, 22–23; letters by gang members in, 33–35; organized fights in, 22, 25; population and history of, 21–23; protection operations in, 57–58, 70, 72; research and fieldwork in, 11–12, 245–46; social incorporation of gang members in, 13, 26; territory divided among gangs in, 58–59; traditional forms of youth violence in, 22; xenophobia in, 144
Khadi Taktash gang, 29–30, 240–41; cemetery branch of, 83; collaboration with police, 79; gang wars and, 57, 207; leader of, 95; organization of, 98
Khanipov, Rustem, 225
Khantimirov, Zavdad (Dzhavda), 24, 25, 26, 32
Kharkhordin, Oleg, 152
Khitrov, Arsenii, 231
Khusnutdinov, Radik (Rakosha), 241
Kirienko, Valerii, 60
Kladbishchenskie gang, 83, 98
Klein, Malcolm Ward, 17, 245
Konnov, Aleksei, 77–78, 84, 147, 158, 230
Konstantinov, Andrei, 72, 82, 240, 241
Kosterina, Irina, 48n1, 168, 201
kryshy (roofs), 65; in 2000s, 84; business, 68–74; choice of, importance of, 73; personal, 75–76. *See also* protection operations
Kushchevskaia village, gang regime in, 165–66

Lacan, Jacques, 105
lads *(patsany)*: categories and definitions, 47–48, 224; cultural references to, 3, 224, 227–28; meaning of term, 180, 248. *See also* gang members
language, gang, 247–49; mainstream penetration of, 3, 224, 231–34; Putin's use of, 227
LaPierre, Brian, 10, 41
Latin America: gangs in, 21, 154n2; neoliberal transformation in, 67–68
law enforcement bodies, Russian: approaches to street organizations, 159–64; collusion with gangs, 77–80. *See also* police
lawlessness: and role of gangs, 155. *See also* *bespredel*
leaders, gang, 36, 61, 105; assassinations of, 95; assimilation into legitimate business and political structures, 65, 78, 80, 81–83, 90, 96; ex-convicts as, 25, 36, 37, 47, 61; first generation of, 92; networked structures

and, 97–99; police contacts with, and crime control, 158–59; political careers of, 78, 80, 82–83, 85, 96; prosecution of, 85–86; qualities of, 76, 94, 95; rise to power, 94, 104; and street gang members, 96–97, 98; theatrics employed by, 95–96; and younger gang members, growing tensions between, 119–20, 123–24. *See also* *avtoritety*
Ledeneva, Alena, 27, 45, 84, 148, 231
Lenin, Vladimir, 23
Likhachev, Dmitrii, 179n4
Lipovetsky, Mark, 226, 227
liubery groups, 38–40, 52, 61, 64; assimilation into wider society, 82; evolution into entrepreneurial gangs, 62–63
Lobachevskii, Nikolai, 141
lokhi (non-gang civilians), 224, 248; gang members' attitude toward, 72, 75, 194–96
Lukin, Valerii, 163

Macon, Perry, 17, 93
mafia: evolution of gangs into, 8, 20. *See also* autonomous ruling regimes; Italian Mafia
Magnitsky, Sergei, 84–85
Maksudov, Rustem, 24, 26, 28, 30, 55, 246
Mansur (Liubertsy sportsman), 62–63
Manty group, 28
Markelov, Victor, 85
masculinity, social construction of: gang members and, 224, 229–30; street peer groups and, 18; warrior figure and, 6
Matza, David, 34
mazhory (privileged young men), 248; attacks on, 38, 75
McCann, Leo, 146
media, portrayal of gangs in, 33–35, 230–31
medieval warrior elites, Russian gangs compared to, 63, 229–30
Medvedev, Dmitry, 165
meet-ups, gang, 99, 107–8
membership: in street organizations, 24. *See also* gang members
Merton, Robert K., 44, 127, 149
Messerschmidt, James W., 6n2, 18
mobilization, of gang members, 112–14
moral rules. *See* code of conduct
Moran, Dominique, 180
Mordovia Republic, gangs in, 167
Moscow: arranged combats in outskirts of, 20; entrepreneurial gangs in, 36, 61; homeless children in, 49–50, 230; interviews with members of street peer groups in, 246; Kazan gangs in, 32–33, 59, 60, 88, 241–42; liubery groups in, 38–40, 62–63; youth subcultural groups in, 49
murders: in 1990s, 4, 57, 58; contract killing, 95, 103; of gang members, 95, 114; gang wars and, 207, 209

Naberezhnye Chelny, gangs in, 29, 54, 55, 77, 79, 97, 241–42
Nafikov, Il'dus, 47, 55, 56, 80, 97, 98
Nashi (youth movement), 82, 221, 229
nationalism, of gang members, 144
Navalny, Alexei, 228
neformaly (subculture groups), 248; gang members' prejudice against, 38, 39, 144
neoliberal reform, 67–68; and ideological orientation of youth, 52; predatory relations associated with, 67
Neuberger, Joan, 10, 19, 227n
newspapers, gang members' letters to, 33–35
Nicaragua, neighborhood networks in, 52
night clubs, fights in, 203–4
nomenclature, gang: in post-Soviet era, 47–48; in Soviet era, 30
nonstreet youth: gang members' attitudes toward, 194–96, 204; victimization of, 29, 74–75, 196–200
Novosibirsk, gangs in, 166–67
Novotatarksaia Sloboda (gang), 28, 32

obshchak (common fund), of gang, 12, 27, 28, 93, 248; and business operations, 117; collection of funds for, 29, 33, 36, 71; model for, 37; requirement to pay into, 176; *smotriashchii* for, 100; use of, 98, 100–101
Ohlin, Lloyd Edgar, 127, 149
older gang members, 100, 122–23. *See also* *avtoritety;* leaders; *smotriashchie*
Oleinik, Anton N., 37, 152n1, 180, 183, 231
Omel'chenko, Elena, 11, 61, 106, 107
Orekhovskaia gruppirovka, 61
Orel, gangs in, 167
organized crime, Russian: in 2000s, 84–86; ad hoc structure of operations in, 117; economic interest and, 51–53; evolution of, 7–8, 50, 60–61; institutionalization of, 59, 151; origins of, 4–5, 43, 46–47. *See also* gang(s), Russian
organized criminal communities (OPS), 11, 47
organized criminal groups (OPG), 47, 161
otvetka (revenge attack), 204, 206, 207, 224
Ovchinskii, Vladimir, 33, 82

Pallot, Judith, 180
Paoli, Letizia, 21, 59, 70, 89, 102, 103, 105, 119, 147

parking lots, street gangs and business of, 78, 86–87, 168
Pastukhov, Vladimir, 232
patrimonial alliances: gangs as, 93–94, 106; premodern, 5, 6n1; ubiquity in modern Russia, 231–32, 236
patrimonial power, 94
patsany. *See* gang members; lads
perestroika: racketeering during, 46. *See also* Soviet Union, dissolution of
Perm, organized crime in, 66, 72
Pervaki gang: gang wars and, 20, 57; membership in, 99; origins of, 29; recruitment by, 54
Piacentini, Laura, 180
pidziuki (kids), in gang structure, 100
Pilkington, Hilary, 11, 12, 17n1, 30, 39, 41
Podatev, Vladimir (Pudel'), 37, 83
police: collaboration with *liubery*, 39, 40; collusion with gangs, 4, 27, 28, 77–80, 84, 87, 89, 166, 167, 236; contact with gang leadership, and crime control, 158–59; crackdown on gangs, 159–63; distrust of, 155, 156; drug trade and, 89; extortion by, 69, 74, 87, 162; gang members' encounters with, 215–16; personal contacts with, gang members and, 147–48, 153, 183; protection by, in 2000s, 84
politics: gang members in, 78, 80, 82–83, 85, 96, 142; gang members' views on, 145
poniatiia (rules of conduct in criminal communities), 170, 248; appeal to, and prevention of violence, 209–11; drug trade and consumption prohibited by, 89, 174, 175, 188; evolution of, 187; ex-convicts as gang leaders and, 36; and extortion/protection operations, 70–71, 72, 76; flexible nature of, 172, 173, 185; fundamental principles of, 12, 173–77; gang as patrimonial society and, 93; gang members' pride in, 114; learning of, 172–73; mainstream references to, 3, 9, 224, 225, 227, 231–34; origins of, 179–82; as quasi-tribal moral system, 178–79; state policies compared to, 228–29; trade prohibited by, 117, 173, 175, 187–88, 240; on violence, 103, 178–79, 198, 203; vs. *vory* code, 182–83, 185–86
popular culture: gangs in, 230–31; violence in, 226–27
popular justice: gangs and, 153–57, 245–46; historical tradition in Russia, 152–53
prison(s): gang members' attitudes toward, 184; informal social control in, 152; and Russian culture, 180, 224–25. *See also* ex-convicts; *vory v zakone*
prison code, of *vory v zakone*, 179–80, 182–83, 185–86
prison culture, influence on mainstream society, 224–25, 231
prisoners, in gang wars, 208, 209
privatization of state enterprises: extortion accompanying, 46; gang leaders profiting from, 81, 227, 242
promotion, of gang members, 103–4, 117
prosecution, of gang members, 85–86, 161–62
prostitution: Kazan gangs and, 88, 241; migrants and, 144; organized networks of, protection in, 49
protection: criminal communities and sense of, 49–50; gang membership and, 132, 133, 217–21, 222; violence as, 212–13
protection operations: of businesses, 68–74; capitalist transition and, 46, 66–68; corporate financial operations and, 81; demand for, 73, 155–56; entrepreneurial gangs and, 27; escalation in violence and, 57–58; gang code and, 70–71, 72, 76; gangs and, 4, 65, 68–76; personal, 75–76; predatory nature of, 70–71; security companies and, 84, 86; *vory v zakone* and, 25
punishment, of gang members, 108–9, 121–22
Putin, Vladimir: gang culture and, 227, 228–29, 232; patrimonial role of, 232; system of informal governance under, 84, 91

Radzhovskie gang, 98
Radzikhovsky, Leonid, 228–29
Rawlinson, Patricia, 84, 169
razborka (showdown between gangs), 57, 58n2, 102, 220, 248
Razinkin, V., 180
razvod (extortion), 70, 71, 75, 76, 224, 248
Rechapov, Lenar (Uzkii), 240
recruitment, of gang members, 54, 101–2, 132; difficulties in, 124
registration, of gang members, preventative power of, 160–61
reputation, violence and, 203–6
Ries, Nancy, 156, 246
rituals: arranged fights as, 12, 18, 20, 22; *avtoritety* and, 96, 100, 108; corporate, 117–18; gang, 36, 80, 100, 107–9, 125, 134
Rodgers, Dennis, 21, 52, 126n8, 154n2, 164
Rousseau, Jean-Jacques, 63
Ruggiero, Vincenzo, ix, 81
rule of law, absence of: and gangs' role, 155. *See also bespredel*

rural areas: entrepreneurial gangs in, 55, 62; territorial gangs in, 7, 19
Russian dream, gang members and, 145–46

Safarov, Asgat, 23, 29, 30, 31, 32, 41, 46, 47, 57, 58n2, 59, 78, 79, 82, 83, 85–86, 88, 95, 114, 124, 125, 153, 160, 207, 217, 240, 241
Safin, Rustem, 11, 245
Saint Petersburg, gangs in, 59, 60, 72
Salagaev, Alexander, 10, 11, 76, 77–78, 79, 84, 147, 158, 230
Saliakhov, Adygan (Alik), 79, 95, 241
Sánchez-Jankowski, Martin, 17, 54, 93, 130n3, 146n5
Sauvadet, Thomas, 201
Schelling, Thomas, 70, 87
Scheper-Hughes, Nancy, 217
schools: extortion at, 29, 76; gang members in, 143; vocational, in 1970s, 42
Scott, James C., 10
security companies: gang members in, 83, 97; vs. gang protection business, 84, 86
semeika (family), 248; of gang members, 105, 110; of prison inmates, 26. *See also brigada*
Sevastopol'skie gang, 59, 85, 240
shadow economy, Soviet: contraction at end of 1990s, 86; and gang evolution, 8, 24–25, 27, 29–30, 37, 235; and working-class youth, 42, 43. *See also* black market
Shagvaliev, Renat (Skippy), 29
Shaimiev, Mintimir, 46, 74, 85–86
Shaliapin, F. I., 22, 25
Shashkin, Alexander, 11, 76, 77–78, 79, 84, 147, 158, 197, 230
Shashurin, Sergei, 82
Shchekochikhin, Yurii, 16
Shelley, Louise, 88
Siegel, Dina, 25, 186
skinheads, vs. gangs, 156, 177
Skriabin, Sergei, 26
smotriashchie (supervisors), gang, 105; assimilation in community, 167; police contact with, and crime control, 158–59; role of, 97, 100, 102, 108, 120, 219
social networks, of gang members, 146–48; "double helix" model of, 13, 102, 140–43, 149, 236
social order, gangs and, 153–57
socioeconomic differentiation, increase in: among gang members, 119–20, 126; in Soviet Union of 1970s-80s, 41, 43
Sokolov, Vsevolod, 25
solidarity, gang, 112–13, 125–26; decaying of, 123–25
Solntsevskaia gruppirovka, 61, 98–99, 107, 167
songs, prison, popularity of, 224
Soviet Union: communal courts in, 152; gang nomenclature in, 30; hooliganism in, 10; reluctance to admit existence of gangs in, 31, 33, 40–41; shadow economy in, and gang evolution, 8, 24–25, 27, 29–30; territorial fights in, 19–20; *vory v zakone* in, 186; working-class youth in, reduced opportunities for, 41–42; youth gangs in, 8–9, 16, 35–40
Soviet Union, dissolution of: and appeal of gang membership, 235–36; *bespredel* (lawlessness) associated with, 44–45, 48–51, 63–64
Spencer, Jonathan, 152
sports, gang members and, 5, 31, 36, 38, 39, 54, 102, 131–32, 188
sportsmen, as gang leaders, 36, 62
stariki (elders), in gang structure, 100
starshie (seniors), in gang structure, 100
state, Russian, and criminal networks, 8, 147–48, 231–33
state authorities, Russian: cooperation with gangs, 77–80, 84–85, 147–48, 236; predation by, 69, 74; public's distrust of, 155, 156
state companies: cooperation with gangs, 77; privatization of, 46, 81, 227, 242
street organizations: evolution of, 20–21, 23–27, 38–39; working-class youth and, 6–7, 54–55. *See also* street peer groups; territorial elites/gangs; youth street associations
street peer groups *(dvorovye kompanii)*, 9–10, 17–18; code of conduct of, 38; evolution of, 20–21, 23–27, 38–39; in post-Soviet era, 50; transition to gangs from, 101, 131–32, 148; transition to market economy and, 46–47
streets *(ulitsy)*, 47, 249
strelki (meetings to resolve conflicts), 58, 102, 215–16, 219
subculture groups. *See neformaly*
sub-Saharan Africa, neoliberal transformation in, 67, 68
supera (superiors), in gang structure, 100
supervisors, gang. *See smotriashchie*
Surkov, Vladislav, 151
Suttles, Gerald Dale, 18
Svanidze, Nikolai, 228
Sykes, Gresham, 34

Tabeev, E. F., 74, 156
Tagirianov, Eduard, 77, 80

Tambov gang, 167
Tatarstan, 22; crackdown on gangs in, 85–86, 160; crime levels in, 124, 218*t*; development of organized crime in 1990s, 46–47; educational and employment opportunities in 2000s, 128, 149; entrenchment of street gangs in, 125; gang penetration of businesses in, 81–82; gangs in, 239–42; geographic expansion of gangs of, 32–33, 59–60; informal networks in, 146; law enforcement bodies in, collusion with gangs, 77–80; violent street groups in, 11, 16, 56–59. *See also* Kazan
tattoos: gang members and, 143; *vory v zakone* and, 183
taxi drivers: extortion of, 87; relations with gangs, 155, 157
Taylor, Brian, 84
television, gang culture on, 230–31
Teplokontrol' district, Kazan, 23–24; street gangs from, 24, 25–27
territorial demarcation, gangs and, 30
territorial elites/gangs, 18–20; and arranged combats, 19–20; in Kazan, 24; in rural areas, 7, 19; structure of, 99–102; transformation into entrepreneurial gangs, 25–27, 60–61; transformation of street peer groups into, 24, 35, 38–39
Thrasher, Frederic, 2, 23
Tiap-Liap gang, 25–27, 52; collaboration with police, 79; origins of, 24, 53; trial of, 11, 27–28, 32, 78; violence unleashed by, 31–32
Tilly, Charles, 7, 71, 72, 169
Timofeev, Sergei (Silvestr), 61
Tkachev, Aleksander, 165
Tolstoy, Leo, 23
Tönnies, Ferdinand, 116
trade, prohibition against, gang code and, 117, 173, 175, 187–88, 240
trafficking, gangs and, 88
Transneft' corporation, 166
treasury, gang. *See obshchak*
tribal life, gang as form of, 2, 178–79
Tsapki gang, 165–66
Tsapok, Aleksander, 165
Tsapok, Nikolai, 165
tsarist Russia, popular justice in, 152
tsekhoviki, 24
Tsipursky, Gleb, 180

Ul'ianovsk, gangs in, 61, 168
ulitsy (streets), 47, 249
United States: code of the streets in, 170–71; entrepreneurial gangs in, 146n5; evolution of gangs in, 25; gang members' estrangement in, 128; gangs and informal justice in, 154n2; history of street gangs in, 28; restraining orders used in, 162; Russian gang members' attitudes toward, 144
university education: among gang members, 55, 129, 131–32; decreased opportunities for, 42
urbanization, and youth street gangs, 12, 23, 43
urban periphery: arranged combats in, 20; *liubery* subculture in, 38–40; territorial elites/gangs in, 19
Utiaganov, Zafar, 85

Van Winkle, Barrik, 128
Varese, Federico, 66, 72, 98, 107
Vasin, Evgenii (Dzhem), 153
Venediktov, Alexei, 228
village(s): entrepreneurial gangs in, 55, 62; popular justice in, 152; territorial gangs in, 7, 19
village fights, 19, 20
violence: affective meaning of, 192; appeal to gang code and avoidance of, 209–11; against businessmen, 58; code of the streets and, 170–71; vs. conversational practices, 200–202, 205, 209, 214–15; drug trade and, 237; entrepreneurial gangs and, 20; escalation of, 31–32, 35, 56–58; everyday, 9, 217–22, 236; gang code on, 103, 177, 178–79, 198, 203; learning of, 190–93; limits to, organized fights and, 22, 24; mastery of, gangs and, 4; by police, 162; in popular culture, 226–27; as protection, 212–13; and reputation, 203–6; ritualization of, 12, 18, 20, 196–200; state and nonstate, 1; strategies of, 189–90; territorial elites and, 18, 19, 24; threats of, and conflict resolution, 212–15; younger gang members and, 102, 103
Vladivostok, gangs in, 37, 61–62
vocational schools, in 1970s, 42
Volkov, Vadim, 4, 46, 56, 59, 67, 84, 151, 172n2, 182, 186
Volochaevskie gang, 98
vory v zakone (professional criminals), 25, 137, 182; code of conduct of, 179–80, 182–83; decline in prestige of, 184, 186–87; gang members distinguished from, 141, 142, 146, 147, 157, 185, 186–87; and gangs, origins of, 4, 37–38, 47; influence in 1990s,

183–84; informal justice by, 152–53; recent changes in society of, 186; relationship with gang members, 183, 184, 211; romantic idealization of, 230; in Tatarstan, 47

walking style, of gang members, 193–94
warrior brotherhood, gang as, 2, 5–7, 179
warrior figure: and masculinity, social construction of, 6; of Russian gang member, 190; and violence, 203–4
wars, gang, 31, 56–57, 206–9
weapons: gang code on, 175; in gang wars, 207, 209, 211; increased use of, gang evolution and, 27, 32, 33, 35, 57; in territorial fights, rules on use of, 19, 20, 24
weapons trade, gangs and, 88
Weber, Max, 5, 6n1, 84, 105n2, 115, 178
Whyte, William Foote, 25
Wieder, D. Lawrence, 171, 173
Willis, Paul, 143, 194
Wolfgang, Marvin E., 7n3
women: in gangs, 106–7; sexual exploitation by employers, 50; sexual exploitation by gang members, 33; subordinate position of, gang code on, 176
working-class youth: and mass staged combats, 19; and shadow economy, 42, 43; Soviet, reduced opportunities for, 41–42, 43; and street gangs, 6–7, 54–55
Wrong, Dennis, 44

Yablonsky, Lewis, 25, 103
Yakemenko, Vassilii, 82
younger gang members, 100; complaints about lack of opportunities, 120–21; growing tensions with leaders, 119–20, 123–24; police approach to, 160–61; roles of, 102–3; strategies of domination, 74–75, 196–200
youth street associations: evolution of, 7–8, 25–27, 35–36, 50, 63, 93; gang leaders' ties to, 96–97; and origins of Russian organized crime, 4–5, 47, 60–61; shadow economy and, 25, 27; state policies toward, 163–64; as traditional social form, 5–6, 16–17; urbanization and, 12, 23. *See also* street peer groups *(dvorovye kompanii)*
Yusupov, Radik (Drakon), 85
Yusupova, Marina, 224

Zabrianskii, Gennadii, 41
Zakharovich, Mikhail, 26
Zakirov, Khaidar (Khaider), 96, 153, 239–40
Zavadskii, Leonid, 62
Zhilka gang, 47, 78, 239–40; and contract killing, 95; leader of, 96; penetration into community, 153; in Saint Petersburg, 60; trial of, 153
zikher (violation of gang code), 249; rules regarding, 109, 177; use in extortion, 71, 197, 211